Marvin A. Sweeney

Form and Intertextuality in Prophetic and Apocalyptic Literature

WIPF & STOCK · Eugene, Oregon

Marvin A. Sweeney, born 1953; 1983 Ph.D., Claremont; Professor of Hebrew Bible at the Claremont School of Theology and Professor of Religion at the Claremont Graduate University Claremont, California (USA).

Wipf and Stock Publishers
199 W 8th Ave, Suite 3
Eugene, OR 97401

Form and Intertextuality in Prophetic and Apocalyptic Literature
By Sweeney, Marvin A.
Copyright©2005 Mohr Siebeck
ISBN 13: 978-1-60899-418-2
Publication date 2/15/2010
Previously published by Mohr Siebeck, 2005

This edition reprinted 2010 by Wipf and Stock through special arrangement with Mohr Siebeck Gmbh & Co. KG.

Preface

This volume presents a selection of my essays on the study of the prophetic literature of the Hebrew Bible and related apocalyptic and proto-apocalyptic texts. As the title of the volume indicates, they reflect fundamental concerns with the continued development of form- and literary-critical exegetical methodology as well as the burgeoning interest in intertextuality in biblical scholarship. Many of these essays have been published elsewhere over the course of some seventeen years, but a number of the essays in this volume appear in print for the first time.

I would like to express my deep appreciation to two friends and colleagues who have been instrumental in instigating the publication of this volume and seeing it through the press. Professor Dr. Hermann Spieckermann, Editor of the Forschungen zum Alten Testament series, initially invited me to contribute this volume to the series, and he has provided a number of welcome suggestions during the course of our collaboration on this and other projects. Dr. Henning Ziebritzki, Lektor in Theologie for Mohr Siebeck Publishers, has provided invaluable support and assistance in the preparation of this volume for publication. Conversation with both of these gentlemen has ranged over a variety of issues in relation to the publication of this volume and other areas of interest. Thanks are due to Ms. Tanja Mix for her careful work on this volume.

I would also like to thank Brill Academic Publishers, Continuum Publishing Company, the William B. Eerdmans Publishing Company, the Institute for Antiquity and Christianity, Peeters Publishers, *Shofar: An Interdisciplinary Journal for Jewish Studies*, the Society of Biblical Literature, and the Walter de Gruyter Publishing Company, for permission to republish essays in this volume.

I am indebted to my student assistant, Danny Zelaya, whose keen eye saved me from many embarrassing and confusing errors. Any errors that remain are my own responsibility.

I am especially indebted to my wife, Muna, and our daughter, Leah, who make all things possible with their love and support, and who constantly remind me what is most important in life.

I regret to say that my father, Jack H. Sweeney of Decatur, Illinois, passed away on November 3, 2004, during the final editing of this volume for publication. My father was the sixteenth of seventeen children born to my grandfather, Walter Issac Sweeney, a West Virginia coal miner, and to my grandmother, Callie

Beth Stanley Sweeney, a descendant of the Mataponi Indians. Because I have already dedicated my first book (*Isaiah 1–4 and the Post-Exilic Understanding of the Isaianic Tradition* [BZAW 171; Berlin and New York: Walter de Gruyter, 1988]) to my father and the memory of my mother, I would like to honor the paternal side of my family by dedicating this volume of nineteen essays to my grandparents and to their seventeen children.

San Dimas, California
March 2005 / Adar Sheni 5765

Marvin A. Sweeney

N.B. In keeping with some streams of Jewish tradition, the terms YHWH, G-d, L-rd, etc., are employed to express the sanctity of the Divine Name.

*Dedicated to the Memory of
my Grandparents*

Walter Issac Sweeney, z"l
Callie Beth Stanley Sweeney, z"l

And to their Children

Samuel Sweeney, z"l
Sylvia Cunningham, z"l
Harry Sweeney, z"l
Bess Hight, z"l
Mae Farley
Maude Turner, z"l
Joe Sweeney, z"l
Mary Sweeney, z"l
Ruby Sweeney, z"l
(died in infancy)
Dock J. Sweeney, z"l
(killed in action near Remagen, World War II)
Mamie "Tootsie" Smith
Leonard Sweeney, z"l
Lakie Smith
June Atkinson
Audrey Miles
Jack H. Sweeney, z"l
Norman D. Sweeney

Contents

Preface V
Abbreviations XI

Introduction 1

Part 1: Isaiah 11

1. The Book of Isaiah as Prophetic Torah 13
2. On Multiple Settings in the Book of Isaiah 28
3. On *ûmĕśôś* in Isaiah 8:6 36
4. Prophetic Exegesis in Isaiah 65–66 46

Part 2: Jeremiah 63

5. The Masoretic and Septuagint Versions of the Book of Jeremiah in
   Synchronic and Diachronic Perspective 65
6. The Truth in True and False Prophecy 78
7. Structure and Redaction in Jeremiah 2–6 94
8. Jeremiah 30–31 and King Josiah's Program
   of National Restoration and Religious Reform 109

Part 3: Ezekiel 123

9. Ezekiel: Zadokite Priest and Visionary Prophet of the Exile ... 125
10. The Destruction of Jerusalem as Purification in Ezekiel 8–11 ... 144
11. The Assertion of Divine Power in Ezekiel 33:21–39:29 156

Part 4: The Book of the Twelve Prophets 173

12. Sequence and Interpretation in the Book of the Twelve 175
13. The Place and Function of Joel in the Book of the Twelve 189
14. Micah's Debate with Isaiah 210
15. Zechariah's Debate with Isaiah 222

Part 5: Apocalyptic and Proto-Apocalyptic Texts 237

16. The Priesthood and the Proto-Apocalyptic Reading of Prophetic and Pentateuchal Texts 239
17. The End of Eschatology in Daniel? Theological and Socio-Political Ramifications of the Changing Contexts of Interpretation 248
18. Davidic Typology in the Forty Year War Between the Sons of Light and the Sons of Darkness 262
19. Pardes Revisited Once Again: A Reassessment of the Rabbinic Legend concerning the Four Who Entered Pardes 269

Source Index 283
Author Index 291

Abbreviations

AB	Anchor Bible
ABD	*Anchor Bible Dictionary*
AGAJU	Arbeiten zur Geschichte des antiken Judentums und des Urchristentums
AnBib	Analecta Biblica
AO	*Acta Orientalia*
AOAT	Alter Orient und Altes Testament
AOS	American Oriental Series
ATANT	Abhandlungen zur Theologie des Alten und Neuen Testaments
ATD	Das Alte Testament Deutsch
BDB	Brown, Driver, Briggs, *A Hebrew and English Lexicon of The Old Testament* (Oxford: Clarendon, 1974)
BEATAJ	Beiträge zur Erforschung des Alten Testaments und des Antiken Judentums
BETL	Bibliotheca Ephemeridum Theologicarum Lovaniensium
BHS	*Biblia Hebraica Stuttgartensia*
BibInt	Biblical Interpretation Series
BibSem	The Biblical Seminar
BibThS	Biblisch-Theologische Studien
BJS	Biblical and Judaic Studies
BKAT	Biblischer Kommentar Altes Testament
BN	*Biblische Notizen*
BWANT	Beiträge zur Wissenschaft vom Alten und Neuen Testament
BZ	*Biblische Zeitschrift*
BZAW	Beihefte zur Zeitschrift für die Alttestamentliche Wissenschaft
CAT	Commentaire de l'ancien Testament
CBQ	*The Catholic Biblical Quarterly*
CBQMS	Catholic Biblical Quarterly Monograph Series
CBET	Contributions to Biblical Exegesis and Theology
ContCom	Continental Commentaries
CR:BS	*Currents in Research: Biblical Studies*
CTM	Calwer Theologische Monographien
DJD	Discoveries in the Judaean Desert
EB	Études bibliques
EvT	*Evangelische Theologie*

FAT	Forschungen zum Alten Testament
Fest.	Festschrift
FOTL	Forms of the Old Testament Literature
HAR	*Hebrew Annual Review*
HAT	Handbuch zum Alten Testament
HKAT	Handkommentar zum Alten Testament
HSM	Harvard Semitic Monographs
HSS	Harvard Semitic Studies
HTR	*Harvard Theological Review*
HUCA	*Hebrew Union College Annual*
IBT	Interpreting Biblical Texts
ICC	International Critical Commentary
IDB	*The Interpreter's Dictionary of the Bible*
IDB[S]	*The Interpreter's Dictionary of the Bible Supplementary Volume*
Int	Interpretation
JBL	*Journal of Biblical Literature*
JNES	*Journal of Near Eastern Studies*
JQR	*Jewish Quarterly Review*
JR	*Journal of Religion*
JSOT	*Journal for the Study of the Old Testament*
JSOTSup	Journal for the Study of the Old Testament Supplement Series
JSPSup	Journal for the Study of the Pseudepigrapha Supplements
JSS	*Journal of Semitic Studies*
KAT	Kommentar zum Alten Testament
KHAT	Kurzer Hand-Commentar zum Alten Testament
LXX	Septuagint
MGWJ	*Monatsschrift für Geschichte und Wissenschafts des Judentums*
MT	Masoretic Text
NCeB	New Century Bible
OBO	Orbis Biblicus et Orientalis
OBT	Overtures to Biblical Theology
OPIAC	Occasional Papers of the Institute for Antiquity and Christianity
OTG	Old Testament Guides
OTL	Old Testament Library
OTS	*Oudtestamentische Studiën*
RB	*Revue biblique*
SAC	Studies in Antiquity and Christianity
SB	Sources bibliques
SBB	Stuttgarter biblische Beiträge
SBLDS	Society of Biblical Literature Dissertation Series

SBLSym	Society of Biblical Literature Symposium Series
SBS	Stuttgarter Bibelstudien
SBT	Studies in Biblical Theology
SJ	Studia Judaica
SJLA	Studies in Judaism in Late Antiquity
SPB	Studia Post-biblica
SSN	Studia semitica neerlandica
ST	*Studia Theologica*
TDNT	*Theological Dictionary of the New Testament*
TSAJ	Texts and Studies in Ancient Judaism
TSK	*Theologische Studien und Kritiken*
UUÅ	Uppsala universitets årsskrift
VT	*Vetus Testamentum*
VTSup	Vetus Testamentum Supplements
WMANT	Wissenschaftliche Monographien zum Alten und Neuen Testament
ZAW	*Zeitschrift für die alttestamentliche Wissenschaft*
ZRGG	*Zeitschrift für Religions- und Geistesgeschichte*

Introduction

The study of prophetic literature over the past century has changed markedly since the 1892 publication of Bernhard Duhm's ground-breaking commentary on the book of Isaiah.[1] Working under the influence of the prevailing concerns with source-critical analysis and literary-historical reconstruction, Duhm revolutionized the study of the book of Isaiah and prophetic literature in general with his identification of Proto-, Deutero-, and Trito-Isaiah within the present form of the book. Although earlier scholarship on the book of Isaiah had long posited the work of the eighth century prophet,[2] Isaiah ben Amoz, in chapters 1–39, and the work of an anonymous exilic period prophet beginning in Isaiah 40, Duhm's commentary finally signaled the acceptance and legitimacy of efforts to reconstruct the purported "original" forms of Isaiah's prophetic oracles as well as those of later anonymous prophets and writers whose work appeared elsewhere in the book.

Subsequent scholarship showed similar concerns in the study of all the prophetic books. Duhm himself followed up his work on Isaiah with a 1901 commentary on the book of Jeremiah that concentrated on identifying and analyzing three distinct groups of materials, including the true prophecy of the prophet Jeremiah largely in Jeremiah 1–25; 30–31, Baruch's life history of the prophet in Jeremiah 26–29; 32–45, and later supplements to the book in Jeremiah 46–51; 52 and elsewhere.[3] Mowinckel's monograph on Jeremiah refined Duhm's work by identifying key sources, including source A, the words of the prophet in Jeremiah 1–25; source B, the biographical prose purportedly written by Baruch ben Neriah in Jeremiah 19–20; 26; 28–29; and 36–44; source C, the sermonic prose material, much like the sermonic prose of Deuteronomy, that appears throughout the book;

---

[1] Bernhard Duhm, *Das Buch Jesaia* (HKAT 3/1; Göttingen: Vandenhoeck & Ruprecht, 1892). For surveys of the study of prophetic literature, see Marvin A. Sweeney, *The Prophetic Literature* (IBT; Nashville: Abingdon, forthcoming); Joseph Blenkinsopp, *A History of Prophecy in Israel* (Louisville: Westminster John Knox, 1996); David L. Petersen, *The Prophetic Literature: An Introduction* (Louisville: Westminster John Knox, 2002).

[2] See Marvin A. Sweeney, "On the Road to Duhm: Isaiah in Nineteenth Century Critical Scholarship," *As Those Who are Taught: The Reception of Isaiah from the LXX to the SBL* (ed. C. Mathews McGinnis and P. Tull; SBLSym; Atlanta: Society of Biblical Literature, forthcoming).

[3] Bernhard Duhm, *Das Buch Jeremia* (KHAT 11; Tübingen and Leipzig: Mohr Siebeck, 1901).

and source D, the late supplementary material in Jeremiah 30–31; 46–51; 52; and elsewhere.[4] Gustav Hölscher's 1924 monograph on Ezekiel likewise applied source-critical tools combined with his all too common view of the fundamental incompatibility of prophetic and priestly identity to argue that only about one-seventh of the book represented the authentic poetic oracles of the ecstatic prophet.[5] Otherwise, the book had been heavily edited by later redactors who presented Ezekiel as a priestly ritualist and legalist to serve as a model for the later Jewish community. Such a contention of course represents the anti-Semitic stereotypes prevalent among many scholars of the time, but it also points to the concern to identify the authentic oracles of the prophet that were embedded in the work of the later redactors of the prophetic books. A host of studies pursued similar concerns among the individual books of the Twelve Prophets.[6]

Of course, these early studies produced rather fragmented readings of the prophetic literature as scholars focused almost exclusively on the individual prophetic oracles in an attempt to sift the later writings of the prophets' redactors for the gems of authentic prophetic sayings. In these early studies, materials identified as the work of later redactors tended to be pushed aside as irrelevant and even distorting as redactors were seen as figures that did not fully understand the authentic work of the prophets and even modified or misrepresented their work in order to present the prophets in relation to later conceptualizations and needs. But through the course of the twentieth century, scholars began to recognize the need to pay close attention to the tradents and redactors of earlier traditions. Von Rad's study of the J-stratum of the Pentateuch and Noth's study of the Deuteronomistic History demonstrated that later compilers and editors must also be recognized as a creative authors and theologians even when they shaped and reworked the earlier works of "original authors."[7] Such work had its impact on the study of prophetic literature as well as scholars began to reexamine the redactional compositions found within the prophetic books and to take them quite seriously as theological literature.

Ultimately, this work led to the recognition of the defining role that redaction plays in the presentation of prophetic literature. The prophetic books were the products of later redaction, insofar as the books' editors selected, reworked,

---

[4] Sigmund Mowinckel, *Zur Komposition des Buches Jeremia* (Kristiana: Jacob Dybwad, 1914).

[5] Gustav Hölscher, *Hezekiel, der Dichter und das Buch. Eine literarkritische Untersuchung* (BZAW 39; Giessen: Töpelmann, 1924).

[6] See, e. g., the commentaries that nevertheless treated the Book of the Twelve as individual books collected into their present context, Karl Marti, *Das Dodekapropheton* (KHAT 13; Tübingen: Mohr Siebeck, 1904); A. Van Hoonacker, *Les Douze Petits Prophètes* (Paris: Gabalda, 1908).

[7] Gerhard von Rad, "The Form-Critical Problem of the Hexateuch," *The Problem of the Hexateuch and other Essays* (London: SCM, 1966) 1–78; Martin Noth, *The Deuteronomistic History* (JSOTSup 15; Sheffield: JSOT Press, 1981).

arranged, and supplemented the authentic oracles of the prophets in an effort to present a portrayal of the prophet that would articulate a coherent historical and theological understanding of the significance of the prophet's life, work, and conceptualization of G-d, the people of Israel/Judah, and the major events of the prophet's time.[8] Von Rad's celebrated *Old Testament Theology* played no small role in alerting scholars to the need to consider the reading of past tradition by the both the prophets and their tradents.[9] Studies on Isaiah by Barth, Vermeylen, and Clements pointed to the influence of the so-called Assyrian or Josianic redactions in Isaiah;[10] studies on Jeremiah by Thiel, Nicholson, H. Weippert, and others, pointed to the influence of Deuteronomic theology in the shaping of the book;[11] Zimmerli's commentary on Ezekiel uncovered a tradition-historical process by which both the prophet and his tradents engaged in the reading and interpretation of past tradition to produce the present form of the book;[12] Wolff's commentaries on various of the Twelve Prophets likewise points to the interrelationship between tradition-history, redaction, and inner-biblical exegesis in the formation of prophetic books.[13] Such understandings of the redaction of the prophetic books resulted in the recognition that the redactors were indeed the major theologians of the Bible who shaped the presentation of the prophets into the present forms of the prophetic books.

The renewed focus on the redaction-critical study of the prophetic literature in latter half of the twentieth century naturally raises a much broader set of literary-critical concerns. If indeed the final forms of the prophetic books – and perhaps the earlier stages of prophetic composition that might stand behind the present form of the books – are the product of redaction, the first question must focus on the role played by the final form or shape of the book itself in the book's interpre-

---

[8] For discussion of the place of redaction-criticism within modern critical exegesis, see Rolf Knierim, "Criticism of Literary Features, Form, Tradition, and Redaction," *The Hebrew Bible and its Modern Interpreters* (ed. D. A. Knight and G. M. Tucker; Chico: Scholars Press, 1985) 123–65.

[9] Gerhard von Rad, *Old Testament Theology* (2 vols.; New York: Harper and Row, 1962–65).

[10] Hermann Barth, *Die Jesaja-Worte in der Josiazeit* (WMANT 48; Neukirchen-Vluyn: Neukirchener, 1977); Ronald E. Clements, *Isaiah 1–39* (NCeB; London: Marshall, Morgan, and Scott; Grand Rapids: Eeerdmans, 1980); J. Vermeylen, *Du Prophète d'Isaïe à l'apocalyptique* (2 vols.; EB; Paris: Gabalda, 1977–78).

[11] Winfred Thiel, *Die deuteronomistische Redaktion von Jeremia 1–25* (WMANT 41; Neukirchen-Vluyn: Neukirchener, 1973); idem, *Die deuteronomistische Redaktion von Jeremia 26–45* (WMANT 52; Neukirchen-Vluyn: Neukirchener, 1981); E. W. Nicholson, *Preaching to the Exiles: A Study of the Prose Tradition of the Book of Jeremiah* (New York: Schocken, 1970); Helga Weippert, *Die Prosareden des Jeremiabuches* (BZAW 132; Berlin and New York: Walter de Gruyter, 1973).

[12] Walther Zimmerli, *Ezekiel* (Hermeneia; 2 vols.; Philadelphia: Fortress, 1979–83).

[13] Hans W. Wolff, *Hosea* (Hermeneia; Philadelphia: Fortress, 1974); idem, *Joel and Amos* (Hermeneia; Philadelphia: Fortress, 1977); idem, *Obadiah and Jonah* (ContCom; Minneapolis: Augsburg, 1986); idem, *Micah* (ContCom; Minneapolis: Augsburg, 1990); idem, *Haggai* (ContCom; Minneapolis: Augsburg, 1988).

tation, viz., how do we interpret synchronic literary form, both of the prophetic books as a whole and of the literary components that comprise those books?[14] The question of the unity of the book of Isaiah plays an important role in this debate particularly since acceptance of Duhm's tripartite reading has become so widespread.[15] How did Isaiah come to form a single book that included the work of three or more historically distinct prophets and their redactors? Early interpreters, such as Elliger and Mowinckel had already begun to raise the question of the interdependence of Isaiah's major components,[16] but later scholars such as Becker, Clements, Steck, Melugin, Conrad, Williamson, the present writer, and others began to pursue the question of the formation of the book of Isaiah with great intensity.[17] Lundbom, Holladay, Carroll, and Seitz wrote influential studies and commentaries on Jeremiah that probed the role of redaction in producing the final form of the book,[18] and studies by Tov, Stipp, Goldman, and Stuhlman have taken account in the advances in the both the textual and the literary study of the LXX version of Jeremiah to point to the importance of considering the final forms of both the Masoretic and Septuagint versions of the book.[19] Greenberg's "holistic" approach to Ezekiel, Levenson's reconsideration of Ezekiel's traditio-historical dimensions, and Darr's literary-theological commentary have

---

[14] Marvin A. Sweeney, "Formation and Form in Prophetic Literature," *Old Testament Interpretation: Past, Present, and Future. Essays in Honor of Gene M. Tucker* (ed. J. L. Mays et al; Nashville: Abingdon, 1995) 113–26.

[15] Marvin A. Sweeney, "The Book of Isaiah in Recent Research," *CR:BS* 1 (1993) 141–62.

[16] Karl Elliger, *Deuterojesaja in seinem Verhältnis zu Tritojesaja* (BWANT 4/11; Stuttgart: W. Kohlhammer, 1933); Sigmund Mowinckel, "Die Komposition des Jesajabuches," *AO* 11 (1933) 267–92.

[17] J. Becker, *Isaias – Der Prophet und Sein Buch* (SBS 30; Stuttgart: Katholisches Bibelwerk, 1968); Ronald E. Clements, "The Unity of the Book of Isaiah," *Int* 36 (1982) 117–29; Odil Hannes Steck, *Bereitete Heimkehr. Jesaja 35 als redaktionelle Brücke zwischen dem Ersten und dem Zweiten Jesaja* (SBS 121; Stuttgart: Katholisches Bibelwerk, 1985); Roy F. Melugin, *The Formation of Isaiah 40–55* (BZAW 141; Berlin and New York: Walter de Gruyter, 1976); Edgar W. Conrad, *Reading Isaiah* (OBT 27; Philadelphia: Fortress, 1991); H. G. M. Williamson, *The Book Called Isaiah: Deutero-Isaiah's Role in Composition and Redaction* (Oxford: Clarendon, 1994); Marvin A. Sweeney, *Isaiah 1–4 and the Post-Exilic Understanding of the Isaianic Tradition* (BZAW 171; Berlin and New York: Walter de Gruyter, 1988).

[18] Jack R. Lundbom, *Jeremiah: A Study in Ancient Hebrew Rhetoric* (SBLDS 18; Missoula: Scholars Press, 1975); William L. Holladay, Jr., *Jeremiah* (Hermeneia; 2 vols.; Philadelphia: Fortress, 1986–89); Robert R. Carroll, *Jeremiah: A Commentary* (OTL; Philadelphia: Westminster, 1986); Christopher R. Seitz, *Theology in Conflict: Reactions to the Exile in the Book of Jeremiah* (BZAW 176; Berlin and New York: Walter de Gruyter, 1989).

[19] Emanuel Tov, "Some Aspects of the Textual and Literary History of the Book of Jeremiah," *Le Livre de Jérémie* (ed., J. Lust; BETL 54; Leuven: Peeters and Leuven University Press, 1981) 145–67; Yohanan Goldman, *Prophétie et royauté au retour de l'exil* (OBO 118; Freiburg: Universitätsverlag; Göttingen: Vandenhoeck & Ruprecht, 1992); Hermann-Josef Stipp, *Das masoretische und alexandrinische Sondergut des Jeremiabuches* (OBO 136; Freiburg: Universitätsverlag; Göttingen: Vandenhoeck & Ruprecht, 1994); Louis Stuhlman, *Order Amid Chaos: Jeremiah as Symbolic Tapestry* BibSem 57; Sheffield: Sheffield Academic Press, 1998).

played important roles in pointing scholarly attention to final form, structure, and theological perspective of Ezekiel as a whole.[20] The redaction-critical study of Nogalski, Jones' analysis of the textual versions, and the present writer's commentary likewise raise the questions of the formation and form of the Book of the Twelve.[21]

The second question pertains to the role of intertextuality, particularly the role played by the reading and interpretation – or reinterpretation – of earlier texts and traditions within the prophetic literature. Again, von Rad's *Old Testament Theology* plays an important role in stimulating consideration of the prophet's and tradent's interaction with earlier tradition, e. g., Isaiah and the Davidic tradition, Jeremiah and the Mosaic or Levitical tradition, and Ezekiel and the Zadokite tradition.[22] Clements, Vermeylen, Melugin, and Kratz pay special attention to the role of inner biblical exegesis in the book of Isaiah as later redactors read the earlier oracles of the prophet and interpreted them in relation to later times and concerns.[23] Other works examine Second Isaiah's reading of biblical tradition outside of Isaiah, such as Anderson's and Kiesow's studies of Second Isaiah's use of the Exodus tradition, and the general intertextual studies of Second Isaiah by Willey (a.k.a., Tull) and Sommer.[24] Noteworthy intertextual work on Jeremiah appears in the monograph by Wendel,[25] and Zimmerli's work on Ezekiel has been noted above.[26] Willi-Plein examines inner-biblical readings by Hosea, Amos, and Micah; Wolff and Bergler emphasize Joel's intertextual readings; and a string of studies by Mason, Larkin, Tai, and others take up intertextual refer-

---

[20] Moshe Greenberg, *Ezekiel 1–20* (AB 22; Garden City: Doubleday, 1983); idem, *Ezekiel 21–37* (AB 22A; New York: Doubleday, 1997); Jon D. Levenson, *Theology of the Program of Restoration of Ezekiel 40–48* (HSM 10; Missoula: Scholars Press, 1976); Katheryn Pfisterer Darr, "Ezekiel," *The New Interpreter's Bible* (ed., L. E. Keck et al; Nashville: Abingdon, 2001) 6:1073–1607.

[21] James D. Nogalski, *Literary Precursors to the Book of the Twelve* (BZAW 217; Berlin and New York: Walter de Gruyter, 1993); idem, *Redactional Processes in the Book of the Twelve* (BZAW 218; Berlin and New York: Walter de Gruyter, 1993); Barry Alan Jones, *The Formation of the Book of the Twelve: A Study in Text and Canon* (SBLDS 149; Atlanta: Scholars Press, 1995); Marvin A. Sweeney, *The Twelve Prophets* (Berit Olam; 2 vols.; Collegeville: Liturgical, 2000).

[22] See note 9 above.

[23] Clements, *Isaiah 1–39;* Vermeylen, *Du prophète*; Melugin, *The Formation of Isaiah 40–55*; Reinhard Gregor Kratz, *Kyros im Deuterojesaja-Buch* (FAT 1; Tübingen: Mohr Siebeck 1991).

[24] Bernhard W. Anderson, "Exodus Typology in Second Isaiah," *Israel's Prophetic Heritage* (ed. B. W. Anderson and W. Harrelson; London: SCM, 1962) 177–95; Klaus Kiesow, *Exodustexte im Jesajabuch* (OBO 24; Freiburg: Universitätsverlag; Göttingen: Vandenhoeck & Ruprecht, 1979); Patricia Tull Willey, *Remember the Former Things: The Recollection of Previous Texts in Second Isaiah* (SBLDS 161; Atlanta: Scholars Press, 1997); Benjamin D. Sommer, *A Prophet Reads Scripture: Allusion in Isaiah 40–66* (Stanford: Stanford University Press, 1998).

[25] Ute Wendel, *Jesaja und Jeremia* (BibThS 25; Neukirchen-Vluyn: Neukirchener, 1995).

[26] See note 12 above.

ences in Zechariah.²⁷ Indeed, more general studies of prophetic conflict note that prophets frequently disagree, and they are not afraid to cite or name each other when they do so.²⁸ We have become accustomed to think of prophets so named as false prophets, but in fact Jeremiah's confrontation with Hananiah, a prophet whose message reflects the Isaian tradition, suggests that they included prophets that tradition might regard as true. Indeed, such prophetic conflict or dialog appears between books, as Steck's or Bosshard-Nepustil's studies on the parallels between Isaiah and the Book of the Twelve might suggest.²⁹ Past scholars were taught to think of inner-biblical exegesis as the mark of late composition or even apocalyptic concerns, but the fact of the matter is that intertextuality, including inner-biblical exegesis, pervades the entire prophetic corpus and frequently serves as an indicator of the engagement, debate, and disagreement that so frequently took place between the prophets and their tradents.

Finally, a word must be said about apocalyptic and proto-apocalyptic literature. Based on its use of mythological and heavenly themes and motifs and the reading of the book of Revelation in Christianity as a pointer to the second coming of Jesus, apocalyptic literature purportedly focuses on the world beyond.³⁰ To a large extent this is true, insofar as it employs heavenly images and mythological patterns to make its points. But this must not blind us to the historical and social impact that such literature was meant to serve. The book of Daniel employs heavenly visions and readings of the portents to point to the anticipated victory of the Hasmoneans and their supporters against the Seleucid monarch Antiochus IV. The War Scroll from Qumran employs similar means to call for the victory of the Sons of Light, Jews who held to the covenant, over the Sons of Darkness, the wicked of the world led by the Roman army. Rabbi Akiva's martyrdom, suffered at the hands of the Romans in the aftermath of the failed Bar Kochba revolt, was read as an indication that Jews of future genera-

---

[27] Ina Willi-Plein, *Vorformen der Schriftexegese innerhalb des Alten Testaments* (BZAW 123; Berlin and New York: Walter de Gruyter, 1971); Wolff, *Joel and Amos*; Siegfried Bergler, *Joel als Schrift interpret* (BEATAJ 16; Frankfurt am Main: Peter Lang, 1988); Rex Mason, "The Use of Earlier Material in Zechariah 9–14: A Study in Inner Biblical Exegesis," *Bringing out the Treasure: Inner Biblical Allusion in Zechariah 9–14* (ed., M. J. Boda and M. H. Floyd; JSOTSup 370; London: Continuum, 2003) 1–208; Katrina J. A. Larkin, *The Eschatology of Second Zechariah. A Study in the Formation of a Mantological Wisdom Anthology* (CBET 6; Kampen: Kok Pharos, 1994); Nicholas Ho Fai Tai, *Prophetie als Schriftauslegung. Traditions- und kompositionsgeschichtliche Studien* (CTM 17; Stuttgart: Calwer, 1996).

[28] E.g., James A. Sanders, "The Hermeneutics of True and False Prophecy," *Canon and Authority* (ed., G. W. Coats and B. O. Long; Philadelphia: Fortress, 1977) 21–41; James L. Crenshaw, *Prophetic Conflict* (BZAW 124; Berlin and New York: Walter de Gruyter, 1971).

[29] Odil Hannes Steck, *The Prophetic Books and their Theological Witness* (St. Louis: Chalice, 2000); Erich Bosshard-Nepustil, *Rezeptionen von Jesaja 1–39 im Zwölfprophetenbuch* (OBO 154; Freiburg: Universitätsverlag; Göttingen: Vandenhoeck & Ruprecht, 1997).

[30] See the discussion of apocalyptic in John J. Collins, *Daniel, with an Introduction to Apocalyptic Literature* (FOTL 20; Grand Rapids: Eerdmans, 1984) 2–24, esp. 4, where his definition of apocalyptic indicates its supernatural, otherworldly, and eschatological dimensions.

tions should emulate his qualities *in this world in order to sanctify* it so that they too could enter Pardes or appear before the heavenly throne. Issues of literary form and intertextual relationships play important roles in apocalyptic literature, but ultimately, apocalyptic literature employs its heavenly images to address the needs of this world. In contrast to Hanson's reading of proto-apocalyptic literature as the work of visionary groups, Cook demonstrates that it is the work of priestly circles who employed the images and concepts of the heavenly realm made manifest in the Temple to articulate their understandings of the times in which they lived.[31]

It is in relation to this growing interest in the study of the formal characteristics of the prophetic literature and its intertextual relationships that the present writer's essays have appeared over the course of nearly two decades. This volume does not include a complete set of essays, but it presents a representative sample of key studies – most previously published, but some unpublished – on each of the major prophetic books and selected apocalyptic and related works from the Bible, Qumran, and Rabbinic literature. Each study, in some manner or another, takes up the fundamental questions of formal literary analysis and intertextual study in an effort to apply these methodological standpoints to the interpretation of the literature at hand.

The first section deals with the book of Isaiah, which has stood at the center of debate concerning the implications of reading a work written by multiple writers as a single, coherent work of literature. "The Book of Isaiah as Prophetic Torah," originally published in *New Visions of Isaiah* (ed. R. F. Melugin and M. A. Sweeney; JSOTSup 214; Sheffield: Sheffield Academic Press, 1996) 50–67, examines the implications of reading the final form of the book of Isaiah as an example of prophetic Torah or instruction. "On Multiple Settings in the Book of Isaiah," originally published in *Society of Biblical Literature 1993 Seminar Papers* (ed. E. H. Lovering, Jr.; Atlanta: Scholars Press, 1993) 267–73, examines the impact of reading Isaiah as a single work on the interpretation of the royal oracles in the various diachronic segments of the book. "On *ûměśôś* in Isaiah 8:6," originally published in *Among the Prophets: Language, Image and Structure in the Prophetic Writings* (ed. P. R. Davies and D. J. A. Clines; JSOTSup 144; Sheffield: Sheffield Academic Press, 1993) 42–54, examines the reading of the enigmatic imagery of Isa 8:6 in the textual versions of the book of Isaiah and in Isa 66:10–14. "Prophetic Exegesis in Isaiah 65–66," originally published in *Writing and Reading the Scroll of Isaiah: Studies of an Interpretative Tradition* (ed. C. C. Broyles and C. A. Evans; VTSup 70/1–2; Leiden: Brill, 1997) 1:455–74, likewise focuses on the interpretation of earlier Isaian tradition within the so-called Trito-Isaiah.

---

[31] See Paul Hanson, *The Dawn of Apocalyptic* (Philadelphia: Fortress, 1975); Stephen L. Cook, *Prophecy and Apocalypticism: The Postexilic Social Setting* (OBT; Minneapolis: Fortress, 1995).

The second section takes up the book of Jeremiah, which brings the study of the Septuagint version of the book to the question of its formation as well as its interaction with the Isaian tradition. "The Masoretic and Septuagint Versions of the Book of Jeremiah in Synchronic and Diachronic Perspective," previously unpublished, examines the distinctive literary forms of both the Masoretic and Septuagint versions of Jeremiah with an eye to discerning their distinctive perspectives and socio-historical settings. "The Truth in True and False Prophecy," originally published in *Truth: Interdisciplinary Dialogues in a Pluralistic Age* (ed. C. Helmer and K. De Troyer; Studies in Philosophical Theology 22; Leuven: Peeters and Leuven University Press, 2003) 9–26, examines the reading of the Isaian tradition in the book of Jeremiah with an interest in elucidating the question of true and false prophecy in the Bible. "Structure and Redaction in Jeremiah 2–6," originally published in *Troubling Jeremiah* (ed. A. R. Diamond, K. O'Connor, and L. Stuhlman; JSOTSup 260; Sheffield: Sheffield Academic Press, 1999) 200–16, examines the final literary form of Jeremiah 2–6 in an effort to reconstruct an earlier form of this text and the hermeneutical perspectives that led to the rereading of an oracle concerned with the downfall of the northern kingdom of Israel to one concerned with Judah. "Jeremiah 30–31 and King Josiah's Program of National Restoration and Religious Reform," originally published in *Zeitschrift für die Alttestamentliche Wissenschaft* 108 (1996) 569–83, engages in a similar study of a text concerned with the restoration of both Israel and Judah.

The third section takes up the book of Ezekiel, which entails recognition of the prophet's identity as a Zadokite priest in relation to the literary and theological interpretation of the book and its components. "Ezekiel: Zadokite Priest and Visionary Prophet of the Exile," originally published in the *Occasional Papers of the Institute for Antiquity and Christianity* (Number 41; Claremont: Institute for Antiquity and Christianity, 2001) and in an earlier version in the *Society of Biblical Literature 2000 Seminar Papers* (Atlanta: Society of Biblical Literature, 2000) 728–51, focuses on the implications of Ezekiel's Zadokite identity in interpreting the literary structure and theological perspectives of the book. "The Destruction of Jerusalem as Purification in Ezekiel 8–11," previously unpublished, examines Ezekiel's use of the Yom Kippur scapegoat tradition from Leviticus 16 as a means to interpret the significance of the destruction of Jerusalem. "The Assertion of Divine Power in Ezekiel 33:21–39:29," previously unpublished, examines the literary form, priestly ideology, and intertextual relationships of Ezekiel 33:21–33:29 in an effort to demonstrate its rhetorical character as an argumentative text that asserts divine power in answer to questions raised by the destruction of Jerusalem and the Temple.

The fourth section takes up the Book of The Twelve Prophets, which only recently has been recognized by modern scholars as a coherent book rather than only a collection of Twelve Minor Prophets. "Sequence and Interpretation in the Book of the Twelve," previously published in *Reading and Hearing the Book of the Twelve* (ed. J. D. Nogalski and M. A. Sweeney; SBLSym 15; Atlanta: Society of Biblical Literature, 2000) 49–64, examines the different orders of books in the Masoretic and Septuagint versions of the Book of the Twelve in an effort to identify their distinctive hermeneutical perspectives. "The Place and Function of Joel in the Book of the Twelve," originally published in *Thematic Threads in the Book of the Twelve* (ed. P. L. Redditt and A. Schart; BZAW 325; Berlin and New York: Walter de Gruyter, 2003) 133–54 and in an earlier version in *Society of Biblical Literature 1999 Seminar Papers* (Atlanta: Society of Biblical Literature, 1999) 570–95, examines the literary form and intertextual relationships of the book of Joel in an effort to discern its overall concerns and place within the MT and LXX sequences of the Book of the Twelve. "Micah's Debate with Isaiah," originally published in *Journal for the Study of the Old Testament* 93 (2001) 111–24, presents a slightly revised comparative examination of the so-called "swords into plowshares" oracle in Isaiah 2:2–4 and Micah 4:1–5 in an effort to discern the distinctive reading of this oracle in each prophetic book. "Zechariah's Debate with Isaiah," originally published in *The Changing Face of Form Criticism for the Twenty-First Century* (ed. M. A. Sweeney and E. Ben Zvi; Grand Rapids and Cambridge: William Eerdmans, 2003) 335–50, examines the literary form of the book of Zechariah and its intertextual relations with the book of Isaiah in order to elucidate its very distinctive presentation of the prophet Zechariah.

The fifth section takes up Proto-Apocalyptic and Apocalyptic Literature, which is so frequently read as in relation to otherworldly concerns but in fact very pointed addresses the concerns of the human world. "The Priesthood and the Proto-Apocalyptic Reading of Prophetic and Pentateuchal Texts," originally published in *Knowing the End from the Beginning: The Prophetic, the Apocalyptic, and their Relationships* (ed. L. L. Grabbe and R. D. Haak; JSPSup 46; London: Continuum, 2003) 167–78, examines the importance of recognizing Zadokite priestly perspective in the intertextual reading of earlier biblical tradition in the so-called proto-apocalyptic works of Joel; Ezekiel 38–39; and Zechariah. "The End of Eschatology in Daniel? Theological and Socio-Political Ramifications of the Changing Contexts of Interpretation," originally published in *Biblical Interpretation* 9 (2001) 123–40, examines the literary form, priestly character, and mythological imagery of the book of Daniel in an effort to read the entire book as a critique of Antiochus IV. "Davidic Typology in the Forty Year War between the Sons of Darkness and the Sons of Light," originally published in shortened form in the *Proceedings of the Tenth World Congress of Jewish Studies. Division A: The Bible and its World* (ed. D. Assaf; Jerusalem: World Union of Jewish Studies, 1990) 213–20, examines the portrayal of the war between the Sons of Light and the Sons of Darkness in relation to the career of King David as portrayed in biblical literature. "Pardes Revisited Once Again," originally published in *Shofar: An Interdisciplinary Journal for Jewish*

Studies 22/4 (Summer 2004) 43–56, examines the intertextual references in the well-known Talmudic legend concerning the four who entered Pardes in an effort to identify the overall concerns of the narrative.

Altogether, the papers presented in this volume point to a fundamental interest in a close, methodologically-controlled reading of the prophetic books and the apocalyptic literature. It is the present writer's hope that readers will find in them a stimulus for their own continuing engagement in this theologically creative and profoundly important literature.

Part 1: Isaiah

1. The Book of Isaiah as Prophetic Torah

I

Perhaps one of the best known passages in the entire Hebrew Bible is the magisterial vision in Isa 2:2–4 of the nations streaming to Zion in the latter days to receive YHWH's Torah:

> It shall come to pass in the latter days that the mountain of the house of the L-rd shall be established as the highest of the mountains, and shall be raised above the hills; and all the nations shall flow to it, and many peoples shall come, and say, 'Come, let us go up to the mountain of the L-rd, to the house of the G-d of Jacob; that he may teach us his ways and that we may walk in his paths.' For out of Zion shall go forth the law (*tôrâ*) and the word of the L-rd from Jerusalem. He shall judge between the nations, and shall decide for many peoples' and they shall beat their swords into ploughshares and their spears into pruning hooks; nation shall not lift up sword against nation, neither shall they learn war any more (adapted from RSV).

This passage is generally understood as the prophet's vision of eschatological peace and coexistence among the nations of the world and thereby constitutes a vision of new world order in which YHWH's sovereignty is recognized by all the earth.[1] Furthermore, it is not simply a vision for the nations; Israel, or "the house of Jacob" as it is called in this context, is invited in v. 5 to join the nations on Zion to walk in the light of YHWH, "O house of Jacob, come, let us walk in the light of the L-rd" (RSV). One of the key terms in this passage is the Hebrew word *tôrâ*, here translated as "law." Scholars generally recognize that this translation is incorrect, in that it is heavily influenced by the Greek term *nomos*, "law."[2] The polemical intent in such a translation is clear in that *nomos* is employed throughout the New Testament as the Greek equivalent of *tôrâ* in order to contrast the caricatured, rigid and unbending Mosaic "law" of the Old Testament with the proclamation of G-d's love and grace in the form of the new gospel. The Hebrew word *tôrâ* is more properly translated as "instruction,"[3] as indicated by its derivation from the *hiphil* form of the root *yrh*, which means "to guide" or "to instruct."

---

[1] See Hans Wildberger, *Jesaja 1–12* (BKAT 10/1; Neukirchen-Vluyn: Neukirchener Verlag, 1972) 88–90.
[2] *TDNT* 4:1058–85.
[3] *TDNT* 4:1046.

It is on this basis that exegetes generally interpret Isa 2:2–4 as a vision that depicts G-d's "instruction" of the nations from Zion in the eschatological age.[4] Although the word *tôrâ* elsewhere in the Hebrew Bible is employed as a technical term to refer to the Pentateuch or Five Books of Moses, scholars generally presuppose that the prophetic context, which in Christian theology is diametrically opposed to the legal context of the Pentateuch, establishes the meaning of *tôrâ* as "instruction," which has nothing to do with Mosaic Torah. This mundane understanding of the word *tôrâ* is reinforced by the appearance of the verb *yrh* in Isa 2:3, "that he may teach us (*wĕyōrēnû*) his ways that we may walk in his paths." Although a legal sense is suggested in v. 4 by the portrayal of YHWH's judging the cases of the nations ("He shall judge [*wĕšāpaṭ*] between the nations, and shall decide [*wĕhôkîaḥ*] for many peoples," there is no suggestion that the term *tôrâ* here refers in any way to Mosaic legislation.

The placement of Isa 2:2–4 in the context of Isaiah 1–39, often labeled First Isaiah because of its presentation of the words and actions of the eighth-century prophet Isaiah ben Amoz, likewise reinforces this understanding. Because Isaiah lived and spoke during the eighth century, it is unlikely that he would have been aware of Mosaic Torah, which did come to prominence in Judah until the fifth-century reforms of Ezra. The fact that Isa 2:2–4 may have been composed by a much later author writing during the time of the exile[5] is rarely taken into account. Nevertheless, the sixth-century context for the writing of this passage and the use of *tôrâ* in Deutero-Isaiah precludes reference to Mosaic Torah. Not only does Ezra appear a century after this time, but the prophetic context for the writing of this passage and the works of Deutero-Isaiah continues to play a role in the interpretation of the term *tôrâ*.

Recent shifts in the paradigm for reading the book of Isaiah may begin to change this understanding of *tôrâ* in Isa 2:2–4. The past paradigm of historically-based critical scholarship led scholars to read Isaiah 1–39; 40–55; and 56–66 as separate literary works, based on the conclusion that each of these segments reflected the writings of prophets from the eighth, sixth, and fifth centuries respectively. But more recent scholarship has employed a literary and redactional paradigm to read the book of Isaiah as a literary whole, while at the same time recognizing that it includes material that was composed by various writers over the course of some four hundred years or more.[6] This leads to the conclusion that the book of Isaiah achieved its full and final form at some point during the fifth

---

[4] Wildberger, *Jesaja 1–12* 88–90.

[5] See Marvin A. Sweeney, *Isaiah 1–4 and the Post-Exilic Understanding of the Isaianic Tradition* (BZAW 171; Berlin and New York: Walter de Gruyter, 1988) 134–84.

[6] Rolf Rendtorff, "The Book of Isaiah: A Complex Unity. Synchronic and Diachronic Reading," *Society of Biblical Literature 1993 Seminar Papers* (ed. E. H. Lovering Jr.; Atlanta: Scholars Press, 1993) 8–20; Marvin A. Sweeney, "The Book of Isaiah in Recent Research," *CR:BS* 1 (1993) 141–62.

century B.C.E., in conjunction with the reform program of Ezra and Nehemiah.[7] This conclusion is supported by the observation that Ezra's return to Jerusalem and program of religious reform is presented in part as a fulfillment of prophecy in the book of Isaiah.[8]

This obviously has implications for the understanding of *tôrâ* in Isa 2:2–4 and elsewhere in the book of Isaiah. Although it is unlikely that the eighth-century prophet Isaiah, or even any of the other Isaianic writers prior to the time of Ezra, employed the term *tôrâ* in reference to Mosaic Torah, it is likely and even probable that Ezra understood the term in reference to his own reform program that was based explicitly upon Mosaic Torah. Certainly, the invitation to the house of Jacob to come to Zion to learn YHWH's Torah would support his understanding of the teachings of Mosaic Torah. On the other hand, the inclusion of the nations in this scenario would seem to contradict Ezra's program which called upon Jewish men to send away their gentile wives and children (Ezra 10). Given the fifth-century context for the composition of the final form of Isaiah, one may legitimately ask whether the book of Isaiah supports Ezra's reforms, and if so, how the vision of the teaching of Torah at Zion would relate to that reform.

II

In order to understand the meaning of the term *tôrâ* in the context of the book of Isaiah as a whole, it is first necessary to establish the literary form and setting of the book. A full discussion of this issue is not possible within the limits of the present context, but the reader may turn to the introduction of my recent commentary on Isaiah 1–39 which takes up this issue in detail.[9] The following is a summary of that discussion.

As indicated by the superscription of the book in Isa 1:1, the book of Isaiah constitutes "the vision of Isaiah ben Amoz which he saw concerning Judah and Jerusalem in the days of Uzziah, Jotham, Ahaz, (and) Hezekiah, kings of Judah." The book is formulated as a prophetic exhortation to Judah and Jerusalem to adhere to YHWH's covenant. This is evident in that parenetic or exhortational material in Isaiah 1 and 55 that calls upon the people to accept YHWH's terms appears at key points in the structure of the book. The placement of this exhortational material in relation to the instructional material that constitutes the balance of the book defines the overall generic character of the book of Isaiah as a prophetic exhortation. In its present form, the exhortational material interacts with the instructional material so that the appeal to adhere to YHWH's covenant

---

[7] Sweeney, *Isaiah 1–4*; idem, *Isaiah 1–39, with an Introduction to Prophetic Literature* (FOTL 16; Grand Rapids and Cambridge: Eerdmans, 1996).

[8] Klaus Koch, "Ezra and the Origins of Judaism," *JSS* 19 (1974) 173–97.

[9] Sweeney, *Isaiah 1–39* ad loc.

in Isaiah 1 and 55 is supported by the instructional material that demonstrates how the people have failed to do so in the past and how adherence will befit them in the future.

The structure of the book comprises two basic parts that are identified by various features of the text. The first part, in Isaiah 1–33, focuses on YHWH's projected plans for worldwide sovereignty at Zion in that these chapters are designed to project judgment against Jerusalem, Judah, Israel and the nations, followed by restoration once the judgment is complete. The second part, in Isaiah 34–66, focuses on the realization of YHWH's plans for worldwide sovereignty at Zion in that these chapters presuppose that the judgment (or at least the initial stage of judgment at the hands of Assyria and Babylonia) is over and that the period of restoration is about to begin with the return of the people to Jerusalem.

This structural division is supported by several other factors. The first is the transitional function of Isaiah 36–39 within the structure of the book as a whole. Past scholars have generally concluded that these chapters form the conclusion to the First Isaiah material in Isaiah 1–39, insofar as these chapters portray the statements and activities of Isaiah ben Amoz during the Assyrian siege of Jerusalem in 701 B.C.E.[10] But more recent studies demonstrate that Isaiah 36–39 does not close the material devoted to First Isaiah; instead, it introduces the material that appears beginning in Isaiah 40.[11] Thus, Isa 36:6–7 presents Isaiah's prediction of the Babylonian exile which is presupposed throughout the rest of the book. Likewise, Isaiah 36–39 presents a portrayal of Hezekiah in a time of crisis that is designed deliberately to idealize Hezekiah and to contrast his faithfulness in YHWH's promises of security for Jerusalem and the House of David with Ahaz' faithless rejection of the same promises in a similar time of crisis as portrayed in Isa 6:1–9:6.[12] The presentation of Ahaz's response to YHWH's promises through the prophet Isaiah demonstrates the behavior and attitudes that lead to the judgment outlined in the prophet's vocation account in Isaiah 6 and that are elaborated upon throughout Isaiah 1–33. The presentation of Hezekiah's response to YHWH's promises delivered through the prophet Isaiah demonstrates the behavior and outlook that lead to the restoration announced in the renewed prophetic commission in Isa 40:1–11 and that are elaborated upon throughout the balance of the book. By means of this contrast, the portrayal of

---

[10] E. g., Otto Eissfeldt, *The Old Testament: An Introduction* (trans. P. R. Ackroyd: Oxford: Blackwell, 1995) 304.

[11] Peter R. Ackroyd, "Isaiah 36–39: Structure and Function," *Von Kanaan bis Kerala* (Fest. J. M. P. van der Ploeg; AOAT 211; ed. J. R. Ellis et al.; Neukirchen-Vluyn: Neukirchener Verlag, 1982) 3–21; Christopher R. Seitz, "The Divine Council: Temporal Transition and New Prophecy in the Book of Isaiah," *JBL* 109 (1990) 229–47; idem, *Zion's Final Destiny: The Development of the Book of Isaiah – A Reassessment of Isaiah 36–39* (Minneapolis: Fortress, 1991).

[12] Sweeney, *Isaiah 1–4* 12–17.

Hezekiah defines the model of faithful behavior expected of those who are to be included in YHWH's covenant.

The transitional function of Isaiah 34–35 likewise plays a constitutive role in establishing the structure of the book. Scholars frequently note that these chapters were composed much later than the material in First Isaiah, and many maintain that both chapters, especially Isaiah 35, were written either by Deutero-Isaiah or the prophet's immediate followers.[13] Regardless of the circumstances of their composition, both chapters play a transitional role in that they reflect upon the themes of judgment from Isaiah 1–33 and simultaneously point forward to the new possibility of salvation and restoration articulated in the second half of the book. In this regard, Isaiah 34–35 constitute an introduction to Isaiah 34–66 that is parallel to Isaiah 1 and its introductory role in relation to Isaiah 1–33.[14] Both passages begin with a call to attention directed to the world at large to witness respectively YHWH's punishment against Israel in Isaiah 1 and YHWH's punishment against the nations in Isaiah 34. The call to witness Israel's punishment in Isaiah 1 corresponds to the concern with the punishment and purification of Jerusalem, Judah and Israel evident throughout Isaiah 1–33, and the call to witness the nations' punishment in Isaiah 34 corresponds to the concern to establish YHWH's world-wide sovereignty over all the nations evident in Isaiah 34–66. Likewise, Isaiah 35 portrays the return of the exiled Jews through the wilderness to Zion, which takes up the concern for the anticipated return to Zion announced in Isa 11:11–16 and 27:12–13 and the imminent return to Zion announced in 40:1–11 and 62:10–12.[15]

Other factors also establish the two-part structure of the book of Isaiah. Isaiah 1–33 anticipates the punishment and subsequent restoration of Jerusalem, Judah and Israel; Isaiah 34–66 presupposes that this punishment is completed and that the restoration is now taking place. Isaiah 1–33 anticipates the downfall of Jerusalem's enemies, identified as Assyria (Isa 10:5–34; 14:24–27) and Babylon (Isa 13:1–14:23); Isaiah 34–66 presupposes the downfall of YHWH's major enemies, identified as Edom (Isaiah 34; 63:1–6) and Babylon (Isaiah 46–47). Isaiah 1–33 anticipates the reign of the righteous Davidic monarch which will inaugurate an era of peace (Isa 9:1–6; 11:1–16; 32:1–20); Isaiah 34–66 presupposes the continuing role of the Davidic covenant for Israel (Isa 55:3), but portrays the rule

---

[13] Wildberger, *Jesaja 28–39* (BKAT 10/3; Neukirchen-Vluyn: Neukirchener Verlag, 1982) 1330–41, 1355–59; R. E. Clements, *Isaiah 1–39* (NCeB; London: Marshall, Morgan, and Scott; Grand Rapids: Eerdmans, 1980) 271–77.

[14] William H. Brownlee, *The Meaning of the Qumran Scroll for the Bible* (New York: Oxford University Press, 1964); Craig A. Evans, "On the Unity and Parallel Structure of the Book of Isaiah," *VT* 38 (1988) 129–47.

[15] Cf. Odil Hannes Steck, *Bereitete Heimkehr. Jesaja 35 als redaktionelle Brücke zwischen dem Ersten und dem Zweiten Jesaja* (SBS 121; Stuttgart: Katholische Bibelwerk, 1985).

of Cyrus as the initial manifestation of YHWH's righteous rule in Zion (Isaiah 44:24–28; 45:1–7; 60–62; 65–66).[16]

Each half of the book displays its own distinct structure which posits interplay between the exhortational and the instructional material. The structure of each is determined in part by the interrelationships between the textual blocks that constitute the structural subunits of the two halves.

Isaiah 1–33 begins with the introductory parenesis in Isaiah 1 that constitutes the prologue for the entire book of Isaiah as well as the introduction for the first half of the book.[17] It is identified by the superscription in Isa 1:1 and it portrays YHWH's intention to purify and redeem Jerusalem. The instructional material in Isaiah 2–33 constitutes the balance of the first half of the book. It is identified by the superscription in Isa 2:1 and it announces the projected "Day of YHWH" as indicated by the frequent references to the "day" in the first half of the book. Essentially, the "Day of YHWH" identifies YHWH's plans to establish worldwide sovereignty by punishing and thereby purifying Jerusalem, Israel and the nations in preparation for divine rule. Four major sub-units comprise this portion of the book. Isaiah 2–4 constitutes a prophetic announcement concerning the preparation of Zion for its role as the center for YHWH's world rule; it thereby serves as a key text in identifying the overall concern of the first half of the book. Isaiah 5–12 constitutes prophetic instruction concerning the significance of Assyrian judgment against Israel in that it projects the restoration of righteous Davidic rule over Israel. Isaiah 13–27 constitutes a prophetic announcement concerning the preparation of the nations for YHWH's world rule from Zion. Isaiah 28–33 constitutes prophetic instruction concerning YHWH's plans to establish the royal savior in Jerusalem.

Isaiah 34–66 takes up the realization of YHWH's plans for worldwide sovereignty at Zion. This half of the book begins with prophetic instruction concerning the realization of YHWH's worldwide sovereignty at Zion in Isaiah 34–54. This textual block comprises three major sub-units defined by their respective generic characters and concerns. Isaiah 34–35 constitutes prophetic instruction concerning YHWH's power to return the redeemed exiles to Zion. Isaiah 36–39 constitutes royal narratives concerning YHWH's deliverance of Jerusalem and Hezekiah that portray YHWH's covenant. Isaiah 40–54 constitutes prophetic instruction that presents a series of arguments designed to prove that YHWH is maintaining the covenant and restoring Zion. The second half of Isaiah 34–66 appears in Isaiah 55–66 which constitutes a prophetic exhortation to adhere to YHWH's covenant. The exhortation proper appears in Isaiah 55, which defines

---

[16] Cf. Reinhold Gregor Kratz, *Kyros im Deuterojesajabuch. Redaktionsgeschichtliche Untersuchungen zu Entstehung und Theologie von Jes 40–55* (FAT 1; Tübingen: Mohr Siebeck, 1991).

[17] Georg Fohrer, "Jesaja 1 als Zusammenfassung der Verkündigung Jesajas," *ZAW* 74 (1962) 251–68.

the generic character of the whole. The substantiation that supports the exhortation appears in Isaiah 56–66 in the form of prophetic instruction concerning the character of the reconstituted covenant community in Zion. These chapters include prophetic instruction concerning the proper observance of the covenant in Isaiah 56–59; a prophetic announcement of salvation for the reconstituted covenant community in Isaiah 60–62; and prophetic instruction concerning the process of selection for the reconstituted covenant community in Isaiah 63–66.

Overall, the final form of the book of Isaiah presents an argument or exhortation to adhere to YHWH's covenant and thereby to be numbered among the righteous who will survive YHWH's judgment against the wicked in preparation for the establishment of the new creation in which YHWH's rule from Jerusalem will be manifested throughout the world (see esp. Isaiah 65–66). Altogether, the final form of the book of Isaiah is designed to support the reforms of Ezra in the late fifth century B.C.E. Several arguments support this contention.

First, the universal perspective of the book of Isaiah includes nations that comprised the Persian Empire during the fifth century B.C.E. All of the nations listed in the oracles against the nations in Isaiah 13–23, including Babylon, Assyria, Philistia, Moab, Aram and Israel, Ethiopia and Egypt, Midbar Yam (the Tigris-Euphrates delta region), Dumah, Arabia, Jerusalem and Tyre were all incorporated into the Persian empire. Greece is notably absent, which precludes a later date in the Hellenistic period. Persia is likewise not listed as one of the nations subjected to YHWH's judgment, but Isa 21:2 identifies Elam and the Medes as the parties responsible for Babylon's downfall, and Isa 44:24–45:7 identifies Cyrus, the Persian monarch, as YHWH's anointed king and Temple builder. In addition, the importance of the downfall of Babylon in the book of Isaiah reflects Cyrus's subjugation of the city. This suggests that YHWH's worldwide rule is identified with the rule of the Persian empire.

Second, the final form of the book of Isaiah presupposes that the Temple has already been rebuilt (see Isaiah 56; 60–62), but the full manifestation of YHWH's rule has not yet occurred (see Isaiah 65–66). This corresponds to the situation of the late-fifth century B.C.E. when Nehemiah and then Ezra returned to Jerusalem to begin their work. Nehemiah took measures to restore support for the Temple and to repopulate the city of Jerusalem (Nehemiah 3–7; 11–13). Ezra's reform measures were designed to establish the Torah or Five Books of Moses as the basic guidelines to establish Jewish identity and life centered at the Temple in Jerusalem (Nehemiah 8–10; Ezra 7–10). Insofar as the book of Isaiah is designed to reestablish ideal Jewish life in Zion based on Torah (cf. Isa 2:2–4), it shares the same goal as Ezra's reform.

Third, the final form of the book of Isaiah presupposes a distinction between the righteous and the wicked, and calls upon its readers (or hearers) to identify with the righteous and thereby to avoid the final judgment against the wicked (see Isaiah 1:27–28; 65–66). Such a perspective corresponds to the program of

Ezra who attempted to define a righteous Jewish community during the course of his reforms. Many see the book of Isaiah in opposition to Ezra's reforms in that Isa 56:1–8 and 66:8–24 make it quite clear that the righteous include eunuchs and foreigners.[18] Ezra, on the other hand, required that Jewish men send away their gentile wives and children, and therefore could not have envisioned the righteous community portrayed in Isaiah. But this view overlooks several important points. The book of Isaiah does not address the issue of intermarriage; it addresses the issue of proper observance of the covenant. The eunuch or foreigner who observes the covenant is acceptable in the Temple. There is no indication that Ezra's reforms exclude the foreigner who adopts the covenant of Judaism; that is, who converts to Judaism. In this regard, the Ezra traditions indicate only that foreign wives and children were banished, not foreign husbands, but no consideration is given to the possibility that such husbands adopted Judaism or that their children were raised as Jews. If foreign wives of Jewish men raised their children as pagans, so Jewish wives of foreign men would raise their children as Jews. Hence, there was no need to expel foreign husbands as they present little threat of apostasy.

Finally, the book of Isaiah and Ezra's reforms share various other points in common. Both employ the term *ḥārēd*, "one who trembles," to describe those who adhere to YHWH's covenant (Isa 66:2, 5; Ezra 9:4; 10:3); both polemicize against those who fail to observe the covenant; both emphasize observance of the Sabbath as the cornerstone of the covenant (Isa 56:1–8; 58:13–14; Neh 9:14; 10:31; 13:15–22); both emphasize YHWH's Torah; both support the centrality of the Temple; and neither precludes the participation of foreigners or eunuchs who convert to Judaism. Altogether, the book of Isaiah is a book that may well support Ezra's reforms. In this respect, it is no accident that Ezra's reform program is presented as fulfillment of prophecy in Isaiah.[19] Thus, Ezra refers to the people as the "holy seed" (Ezra 9:2; cf. Isa 6:13) and a "remnant" (Ezra 9:8; cf. Isa 4:2; 10:20; 37:31–32), and Ezra's return to Jerusalem is presented as a second Exodus in keeping with the new Exodus proclaimed in the book of Isaiah.[20] In this regard, the liturgical form of passages such as Isaiah 12 and 35 would suggest that the book of Isaiah might have been read as part of the liturgy of the Temple.[21] Certainly Ezra's reading of the Torah to the people during Sukkot in Nehemiah 8–10 constitutes a liturgical occasion. Sukkot stresses the themes of the ingathering of the grape and wine harvest together with the theme of forty years of wilderness wandering. These themes appear frequently throughout

---

[18] E.g., Claus Westermann, *Isaiah 40–66: A Commentary* (OTL; trans. D. M. G. Stalker; Philadelphia: Westminster, 1969) 312–15.

[19] Koch, "Ezra and the Origins of Judaism."

[20] Koch, "Ezra and the Origins of Judaism"; J. G. McConville, "Ezra-Nehemiah and the Fulfillment of Prophecy," *VT* 36 (1986) 205–24.

[21] J. H. Eaton, "The Isaiah Tradition," *Israel's Prophetic Tradition* (Fest. P. R. Ackroyd; ed. R. Coggins et al.; Cambridge: Cambridge University Press, 1982) 58–76.

the book of Isaiah (e.g., Isaiah 11:11–16; 12; 27:12–13; 35:8–10; 40:1–11; 62:10–12), which would facilitate the people's understanding of the Exodus theme of the Torah by pointing out that the experience of exile at the hands of Assyria and Babylon and restoration at the hands of YHWH would constitute a second Exodus and restoration during the Persian period.

III

The term *tôrâ* appears twelve times in the book of Isaiah: 1:10; 2:3; 5:24; 8:16, 20; 24:5; 30:9; 42:4, 21, 24; and 51:4, 7. These texts stem from several different historical settings in relation to the composition of the book of Isaiah, and therefore represent different understandings of the meaning of the term *tôrâ*.[22] In order to establish the meaning of the term in the book of Isaiah, each occurrence of the term must first be examined in relation to its immediate literary and historical context. Afterwards, the usage of the term *tôrâ* must be examined in relation to the overall literary context of the book of Isaiah as a whole. Such study will facilitate understanding of both the hermeneutics employed in the composition and development of the book of Isaiah and the meaning of the term *tôrâ* in the final form of the text.

The term *tôrâ* in Isa 1:10 appears in the larger context of Isa 1:10–17, which demands that the people heed "the teaching of our G-d" (*tôrat 'lhynw*). This text constitutes a prophetic instruction concerning the proper role of sacrifices. It dates to the latter part of the eighth century B.C.E., during the period of Hezekiah's reforms prior to his revolt against Sennacherib in 705–01 B.C.E. It apparently represents Isaiah's criticisms against Hezekiah's reform measures by which he cleansed the Temple of foreign or pagan influence and established purified YHWHistic sacrifice as a means to reestablish the Temple as the religious center of the Davidic kingdom. In this scenario, the purified Temple stands as a powerful symbol of Judean independence from Assyrian rule. Isaiah's criticisms are directed against Hezekiah's program and his clear plans for revolt against the Assyrians. He employs standard stereotypical terminology for the criticism of the monarchy that emphasizes the need to do justice and to protect the widow and the orphan. Such language and imagery is typically employed to characterize just rule and proper royal policy in the ancient Near East.[23] The use of the term, *tôrat 'lhynw*, "the teaching of our G-d," here parallel to *dĕbar yhwh*, "the word of YHWH," signifies the normal priestly instruction concerning proper ritual procedure in the Temple in Jerusalem. The prophet employs the term in a satiri-

---

[22] Joseph Jensen, *The Use of tôrâ in Isaiah: His Debate with the Wisdom Tradition* (CBQMS 3; Washington: Catholic Biblical Association of America, 1973).

[23] F. C. Fensham, "Widow, Orphan, and the Poor in Ancient Near Eastern Legal and Wisdom Literature," *JNES* 21 (1962) 129–39.

cal manner to demonstrate his point that "the Torah of YHWH" in this instance does not pertain to correct sacrificial procedure, but to the underlying purpose that the sacrifice serves. In his view, Hezekiah's Temple reform and plans to revolt against Assyria will only bring the nation to ruin.

The term *tôrâ* in Isa 2:3 appears in the context of Isa 2:2–4, which portrays the nations streaming to Zion to learn the "teaching" (*tôrâ*) of YHWH that will settle their disputes. This text stems from the sixth-century redaction of the book of Isaiah which portrays the Persian conquest of Babylon, the return of exiled Jews to Jerusalem, and the restoration of the Jerusalem Temple as manifestations of YHWH's world-wide rule. The nations are portrayed as subject to YHWH's rule which inaugurates an era of world peace. The term *tôrâ*, again parallel to *děbar yhwh*, "the word of YHWH," apparently refers to YHWH's instruction on the proper way to conduct international relations. It appears in the context of the legal resolution of disputes between the nations, in which YHWH is portrayed as the typical ancient Near Eastern monarch who employs his "Torah" as a means to settle disagreements among his subjects. In this sense, Torah signifies a means to bring about worldwide order.

The term *tôrâ* in Isa 5:24 appears in the context of Isa 5:8–24, which enumerates instances of the people's rejection of "the teaching of YHWH Ṣeba'ot." Isaiah 5:24 constitutes a concluding summary of the crimes detailed throughout the passage. It presents Isaiah's rationale for the fall of the northern kingdom of Israel to Assyria in 724–21 B.C.E. The expression *tôrat yhwh ṣěbā'ōt*, "the teaching of YHWH of Hosts," parallel to *'imrat qědôš yiśrā'ēl*, "the word of the Holy One of Israel," apparently refers to the norms of social conduct, especially those that pertain to property rights, that are presupposed throughout Isa 5:8–24. Apparently, the prophet points to the abuse and violation of these norms as the cause of YHWH's decision to bring the Assyrians to punish the northern kingdom (cf. Isa 5:25–30).

The occurrences of *tôrâ* in Isa 8:16 and 8:20 appear in the context of the prophet's command to seal or bind up "the testimony" (*tě'ûdâ*) and the "teaching" (*tôrâ*) in Isa 8:16–9:6. It apparently refers to the prophet's efforts to put away his teachings until a more propitious time at which they might be understood or realized. The historical context of this passage relates to the Syro-Ephraimitic War of 735–32 B.C.E. in which the Assyrian empire first invaded Israel to protect Judah from a combined Israelite-Aramean assault that was designed to overthrow the Davidic dynasty and to bring Judah into an anti-Assyrian coalition. Isaiah 8:16–9:6 expresses Isaiah's view that the Assyrian innovation represents an opportunity for the house of David to reestablish its rule over the former northern kingdom, but King Ahaz's refusal to act on this premise forced the prophet to give up his efforts. The term *tôrâ* appears in parallel with *tě'ûdâ*, "testimony," which apparently refers to the document written by the prophet in Isa 8:1–4 to name his child symbolically in reference to the anticipated fall of the Syro-Ephraimitic coalition to Assyria. In this instance, *tôrâ* simply refers to the prophet's teachings on this matter insofar as he states that the "Torah" and "Testimony" are to be bound up and sealed among his "teachings" (*limmudāy*, "my teachings").

The occurrence of the plural *tôrōt* in Isa 24:5 appears in the larger context of Isaiah 24–27, which outlines a scenario for the establishment of YHWH's rule over the nations following a period of worldwide upheaval. This text stems from the sixth-century redaction of the book of Isaiah, and portrays the world-wide disruption occasioned by the fall of Babylon to Persia as a manifestation of the establishment of YHWH's sovereignty on earth. The term *tôrōt* is employed in parallel to *ḥōq*, "statute," and refers to the violation of the "laws" or "norms" that constitute the "eternal covenant" (*bĕrît ʿôlām*) by which the earth's "inhabitants" dwell on the land. This appears to be a reference to the laws that govern the structure of creation rather than to any given body of divine teachings. The term *tôrâ (tôrōt)* then refers to a cosmic principle of order in the world.

The occurrence of the term *tôrat yhwh*, "the instruction of YHWH," in Isa 30:9 appears in the context of Isaiah 30, which expresses the prophet's dissatisfaction with the people for sending an embassy to Egypt to conclude an alliance against Assyria. The passage dates to the latter part of the eighth century B.C.E., and it was apparently written by Isaiah in conjunction with his polemic against King Hezekiah's efforts to secure support for his planned revolt against the Assyrian empire. The prophet characterizes the people as rebellious in v. 9, and he states that "they are not willing to hear the Torah of YHWH." As in Isaiah 8:16–9:6, Isa 30:8 indicates the prophet's intention to record his words for a later time. In this instance, the term *tôrat yhwh* apparently refers to the prophet's words, which express the teachings of YHWH concerning Hezekiah's projected alliance with Egypt.

The occurrence of *tôrâ* in Isa 42:4 appears in the context of Isa 42:1–4, the first of the so-called "Servant Songs" in the writings of Second Isaiah. The text is part of the writings of Second Isaiah, which date to the middle of the sixth century B.C.E. In its present context, it is a part of a larger textual subunit in Isa 41:1–42:13 which contends that YHWH is the master of human events. This supports the overall purpose of Second Isaiah to demonstrate that YHWH maintains the covenant with Israel and that YHWH is restoring Zion. The text presents "his teaching" (*tôrātō*); that is, the teaching of the Servant, in relation to the "justice" (*mišpāṭ*) that the Servant will establish among the nations of the earth (Isa 42:1). Insofar as Second Isaiah contends that YHWH is both creator and ruler of the world, *tôrâ* and *mišpāṭ* apparently refer to the principles by which order will be established among the nations of the earth.

The occurrences of the term *tôrâ* in Isa 42:21, 24 appear in the context of the larger textual sub-unit Isaiah 42:14–44:23, which argues that YHWH is the redeemer of Israel. Again, this passage forms a part of the writings of the Second

Isaiah from the sixth century B.C.E. As part of the author's attempt to argue that YHWH is the redeemer of Israel, the text maintains in Isa 42:21 that YHWH attempted to "magnify Torah and make (it) glorious" (*yagdîl tôrâ wĕya'dîr*), but that Israel was not willing to accept this teaching, as Isa 42:24 states, "and they were not willing to walk in his ways, and they did not listen to his Torah (*bĕtôrātô*)." The immediate context gives no clues as to the specific meaning of *tôrâ* other than to identify it as the "teaching" of YHWH that was initially rejected by the Servant Israel (cf. Isa 42:19), thereby bringing YHWH's punishment upon itself. Despite this rejection, the context makes it clear that YHWH is now prepared to redeem the blind and deaf Servant Israel as an example to the nations of YHWH's power.

Finally, the occurrences of the term *tôrâ* in Isa 51:4, 7 appear in the larger context of Isaiah 49–54, which contends that YHWH is restoring Zion. Again, this passage is a part of the writings of the sixth-century prophet Second Isaiah. In both cases, the term is employed in a context which calls upon the people of Israel and the nations to listen to YHWH so that they may understand the significance of the restoration of Zion as an act of YHWH. Isaiah 51:4 employs the reference to the *tôrâ* that will go forth from YHWH in parallel to YHWH's "justice" (*mišpāṭ*) that will serve as "a light for the peoples" (*lĕ'ôr 'ammîm*), and Isa 51:7 refers to YHWH's Torah (lit., "my Torah," *tôrātî*) which is in the heart of the people. Again, the context identifies *tôrâ* as a term that refers to the principles of order and justice among the nations of the earth.

IV

When one considers the meaning of the term *tôrâ* in relation to the final form and setting of the book of Isaiah, it becomes apparent that the broader literary context plays a determinative role in defining the interpretation of the term. This is not to say that the immediate literary context no longer serves as an important criterion for establishing the meaning of *tôrâ*. Rather, the broader literary context acts together with the immediate context to incorporate the individual occurrences of the term into an overall conception of *tôrâ* in the book of Isaiah. In this regard, the meaning of *tôrâ* in Isaiah must be considered in relation to the meaning of the other occurrences of the term. Although it is debatable whether the individual authors of Isaiah intended such a comprehensive view of *tôrâ* when they wrote the passages in which the term occurs, the meaning of *tôrâ* takes on a hermeneutical life of its own when it is considered in relation to its full literary and interpretative context in the final form of the book of Isaiah.[24]

---

[24] Gerald T. Sheppard, "The Book of Isaiah: Competing Structures according to a Late Modern Description of Its Shape and Scope," *Society of Biblical Literature 1992 Seminar Papers* (ed. E. H. Lovering Jr.; Atlanta: Scholars Press, 1992) 549–82.

When the individual occurrences of *tôrâ* are considered in relation to the other instances of the term in Isaiah, several common features begin to emerge that provide criteria for establishing a comprehensive understanding of the meaning of *tôrâ* in the book of Isaiah. First, although *tôrâ* is clearly understood as the teaching of the prophet in Isa 8:16, 20, it is very clearly identified in several instances as the "Torah of our G-d" (*tôrat 'lhynw*), Isa 1:10); "the Torah of YHWH of Hosts" (*tôrat yhwh ṣĕbā'ôt*, Isa 5:24); the "Torah of YHWH" (*tôrat yhwh*, Isa 30:9); "my (i.e., YHWH's) Torah" (*tôrātî*, 51:7); and "his (i.e., YHWH's) Torah (*bĕtôrātô*, Isa 42:24). Likewise, Torah proceeds from YHWH (Isa 2:3; 51:4), and it is identified as the "word of YHWH" (*dĕbar yhwh*, Isa 1:10; 2:3) or the "saying of the Holy One of Israel ('*imrat qĕdôš yiśrā'ēl*, Isa 5:24). Second, several occurrences of the term make it clear that *tôrâ* is to be written down and stored away for the future when it will be understood by later generations. Thus, the prophet commands, "Bind up the testimony, seal the Torah among my teachings" in Isa 8:16 (cf. Isa 8:20), and "now, go write it (Torah) before them upon a tablet, and upon a book inscribe it" in Isa 30:8. Third, it is equated with YHWH's "justice" (*mišpāṭ*) in Isa 42:4 and 51:4 or YHWH's "righteousness" (*ṣedeq*) in Isa 42:21 and 51:7, in which capacity it serves as a means to establish the norms of proper conduct among nations (Isa 2:4; 42:4) and within Israel itself (Isa 2:5; 5:24; 42:24; 51:7). Finally, it refers to a principle of cosmic order which stands at the foundation of the structure of creation (Isa 24:5).

The sum total of these occurrences identifies *tôrâ* as the teaching of YHWH, expressed by the prophet, which stands as the norm for proper conduct by both Israel and the nations, and which stands as the norm for order in the created world. It is likewise identified as something that is not properly understood in the time of the prophet, but the full significance of which will be apparent at a future time in which YHWH's worldwide sovereignty is recognized. As such, *tôrâ* signifies YHWH's revelation to both Israel and the world at large.

In this regard, the symbolism of the revelation of YHWH's Torah to the nations and Jacob at Zion in Isa 2:2–4, 5 becomes especially important in that it establishes an analogy of the revelation of Torah to Israel (and to the nations, represented by Egypt and the Pharaoh) in the Sinai pericope of the Pentateuch (Exodus 19–Numbers 10). Just as Mount Sinai serves as the locus of revelation to Israel in the Mosaic traditions, so Zion serves as the locus of revelation to Israel and the nations in the book of Isaiah.[25] The revelation of Torah at Mount Sinai provides guidance or instruction in the norms of proper behavior for the people of Israel. Likewise, the revelation of Torah at Mount Zion provides guidance or instruction in the norms of proper behavior for the nations as well as for the people of Israel.

---

[25] Cf. Jon D. Levenson, *Sinai and Zion: An Entry into the Jewish Bible* (New York: Winston [Seabury], 1985).

The significance of this observation for understanding the book of Isaiah in relation to Mosaic Torah is reinforced by the prominent role played by the motif of the return of the exiles to Zion in the book of Isaiah. Scholars have long noted that Second Isaiah portrays the return of the Babylonian exiles to Zion as a second or a renewed Exodus analogous to that of the Mosaic period.[26] Thus, Isa 40:1–11 portrays the highway through the wilderness that will bring the exiles to Zion in analogy to the "way of the wilderness" and the "King's Highway" that brought the Mosaic generation through the wilderness to the promised land. Isaiah 43:14–21 identifies YHWH as the One who makes a path in the sea and subdues horse and chariot in analogy to the splitting of the sea and the defeat of the Egyptian chariotry in the exodus from Egypt (Exodus 14–15). Isaiah 48:20–21 portrays YHWH's making water flow from the rock in the desert in analogy to the water produced by Moses when he struck the rock in the wilderness (Exod 17:1–7; Num 20:2–13). Finally, Isa 51:10–11 makes it very clear that the goal of the guidance through the wilderness is to bring Israel back to Zion, just as Exod 15:13–18 identified the goal of Israel's journey through the sea and the wilderness as YHWH's mountain and sanctuary. In this regard, the witness of the nations plays an important role in establishing YHWH's reputation just as the witness of the nations plays a similar role in Second Isaiah.

This concern with the return of Israel to Zion as an analogy to the Exodus and Wilderness tradition is not limited only to the writings of Second Isaiah; it permeates the rest of the book of Isaiah as well. Isaiah 4:2–6 portrays the sanctuary at Zion covered by a cloud by day and flaming fire by night in analogy to the pillar of smoke and flame that guided Israel through the wilderness and eventually settled upon the tabernacle which symbolizes the Temple (Exod 13:21–22; cf. 40:34–38). The motif of YHWH's closing the eyes and ears of the people so that they do not understand and repent in Isaiah 6 calls to mind the hardening of Pharaoh's heart so that he does not thwart YHWH's demonstration of power in the Exodus (Exod 7:1–5; 14:8), and Isaiah's unclean lips (Isa 6:5) recall the uncircumcised lips of Moses (Exod 6:12, 30). Isaiah 10:24–26 and 11:11–16 portray YHWH's rod of punishment against Assyria in analogy to the rod of Moses that punished Egypt at the Exodus (Exodus 7–11; 14), and the result is the return of the exiles to Zion along the highway (cf. Isa 27:12–13; 35:1–10; 62:10–12).

---

[26] Bernhard W. Anderson, "Exodus Typology in Second Isaiah," *Israel's Prophetic Heritage* (Fest. J. Muilenburg; ed. B. W. Anderson and W. Harrelson; New York: Harper and Row, 1962) 177–95; idem, "Exodus and Covenant in Second Isaiah and Prophetic Tradition," *Magnalia Dei/The Mighty Acts of G-d* (Fest. G. E. Wright; ed. F. M. Cross Jr. et al.; Garden City: Doubleday, 1976) 339–60; K. Kiesow, *Exodustexte im Jesajabuch* (OBO 24; Freiburg: Editions Universitaires; Göttingen: Vandenhoeck & Ruprecht, 1979).

Very clearly, the understanding of *tôrâ* in the final form of the book of Isaiah is presented in relation to a new Exodus instigated by YHWH to return the exiled Jews to Zion and to establish YHWH's worldwide sovereignty.

V

In sum, the book of Isaiah as a whole portrays the revelation of YHWH's Torah to the nations and Israel in analogy to the revelation of Torah to Israel and the nations in the Mosaic tradition. This has obvious implications for understanding the role of the book of Isaiah in relation to the reform and restoration program of Ezra and Nehemiah, based upon Mosaic Torah. Whereas the Mosaic tradition portrays this revelation as a means to establish Israel in its own land, the Isaiah tradition portrays the revelation as a means to demonstrate YHWH's worldwide sovereignty and to reestablish Israel in Zion. Likewise, the Mosaic revelation of Torah establishes the norms of life for the people of Israel insofar as it conveys the laws that govern both community life and sacred worship. But the book of Isaiah also focuses on Israel's relationship to the nations of the world insofar as it establishes Israel's role in Zion, the center for YHWH's world sovereignty where the nations come to recognize YHWH's rule. In short, Mosaic Torah defines Israel's internal relationship within its own community; the book of Isaiah defines Israel's relations among the nations. Both define Israel as a holy community. Both therefore serve the ends of Ezra's reforms, insofar as the goal of the program was to reestablish Israel as a holy community in Jerusalem.

2. On Multiple Settings in the Book of Isaiah

I

One of the primary achievements of the Isaiah seminar is the recognition of both the synchronic and diachronic character of the book of Isaiah.[1] Although Isaiah contains blocks of material that were composed, at least in part, in relation to distinct socio-historical settings, the present form of Isaiah constitutes a discreet literary entity in and of itself, rather than a collection of two, three, or more originally independent prophetic compositions. Scholars have come to recognize that although some of these components have a demonstrable compositional history, they can no longer be treated entirely in isolation from the literary context of the book as a whole. Indeed, some scholars have correctly questioned whether blocks such as chapters 1–39 or 56–66 ever existed as independent prophetic compositions.[2]

This recognition has important implications for the recognition of Isaiah in that it calls into question the standard historical-critical model for writing commentaries on separate parts of Isaiah, such as Isaiah 1–39; 40–55; 56–66; or even 40–66, as if they were separate books. Although the original composition of the individual texts in the book ranges at least from the eighth through the fifth centuries B.C.E.,[3] the emergence of a sixty-six chapter book of Isaiah presents a new literary context that will necessarily affect the interpretation of all of its constituent subunits. Whether the constituent texts are composed relatively early or relatively late in the book's compositional history, the full literary form of the book will define the framework in which all the constituent sub-units function as well as the overall interpretational context to which they contribute and which, in turn, will influence their interpretation. Commentators must therefore account for individual texts from the book *both* in relation to the compositional settings

---

[1] See Rolf Rendtorff, "The Book of Isaiah: A Complex Unity. Synchronic and Diachronic Reading," *Society of Biblical Literature 1991 Seminar Papers* (ed. E. H. Lovering Jr.; Atlanta: Scholars Press, 1991) 8–20.

[2] Rolf Rendtorff, "Zur Komposition des Buches Jesajas," *VT* 34 (1984) 295–320; Christopher R. Seitz, "Isaiah 1–66: Making Sense of the Whole," *Reading and Preaching the Book of Isaiah* (ed. C. R. Seitz; Philadelphia: Fortress, 1988) 105–26.

[3] Marvin A. Sweeney, *Isaiah 1–4 and the Post-Exilic Understanding of the Isaianic Tradition* (BZAW 171; Berlin and New York: Walter de Gruyter, 1988).

in which they were produced *and* in relation to the later literary contexts or settings in which these texts appear.

This brief paper will therefore attempt to examine the role that such multiple settings play in the interpretation of the book of Isaiah. It will first examine recent developments in the conceptualization of setting and its relationship to the interpretation of biblical texts. It will then examine the royal psalm of thanksgiving in Isa 9:1–6 in relation to its compositional setting and the subsequent literary settings in which it functions. Isaiah 9:1–6 serves as an example of the impact of multiple settings on the interpretation of texts in Isaiah in that it plays a major role in defining the overall perspectives and expectations of the book throughout the history of its composition and its interpretation is, in turn, influenced by the literary settings in which it appears.

II

Form-critical methodology presupposes an integral relationship between literature and human life so that any discussion of the interpretation of biblical texts must address the question of setting, including both *Sitz im Leben*, the social contexts in which genres function, and situation, the specific circumstances in which texts function. It is not always possible to reconstruct the original compositional setting of a text, but every text is composed in relation to a specific set of social and historical circumstances that play a major role in defining its overall outlook, modes of expression, and concerns. Although the compositional setting of the text does not necessarily determine the meaning of a text after the time of its composition, its form and initial intention is determined in large measure by its author and the setting which the author composes the text.

The concept of *Sitz im Leben* has undergone some development in the history of form-critical discussion. In his analysis of the literary history of the concept of *Sitz im Leben*, Martin Buss demonstrates that Hermann Gunkel's conceptualization of *Sitz im Leben* synthesized two major elements: "a concern with genres and a historical focus on originating circumstances."[4] This conceptualization combines a concern with literature, whether oral or written, and the socio-historical circumstances in which it is written and which play a major role in defining its literary form and intention. The interrelationship between literature and its socio-historical setting, whether that of the author or that of its readers, must play a primary role in the interpretation of literature. But Buss points out that Gunkel made an invalid distinction between the authentic "oral" or "life" situations in which a text is composed and its artificial "written" stages.[5] This distinction is

---

[4] Martin J. Buss, "The Idea of *Sitz im Leben* – History and Critique," *ZAW* 90 (1978) 157–70, see esp. p. 157.

[5] Buss, "The Idea of *Sitz im Leben*," 157–60.

undoubtedly rooted in nineteenth century Romanticist conceptions of the purity and spontaneity of the primitive religious spirit as opposed to the mechanical pedanticism of scribes who did not comprehend the spiritual impulses of the oral literature. Gunkel's emphasis on the "original" circumstances of a text's composition therefore placed undue emphasis on defining the interpretation of a text in relation to the author's setting and intentions, but he overlooked the setting in which a text is received as a significant element of its interpretation.

More recent methodological discussion of the sociology of language has developed Gunkel's ideas by placing greater emphasis on the interrelationship between texts and the socio-historical settings that generate them.[6] Thus, Steck emphasizes a literary-sociological conception of setting in which literary genres must be defined in relation to both the literary context in which they appear and the socio-cultural conditions and circumstances that produce them.[7] Richter defines three types of settings that define texts, including institutions, the style of the epoch, and literature itself.[8] This last point is particularly important in that it emphasizes the formative role of literature, or the *Sitz in der Literatur*,[9] alongside the more customary *Sitz im Leben* in the composition of texts. In other words, literature itself provides a component of the setting in which literature is created.

Literature also plays a role in defining social reality, and this role must be examined in order to understand fully the interaction between literature and human life. In reference to myth, for example, Rolf Knierim points out that myth creates reality ritually in that myth is inseparably related to this ritual setting.[10] Likewise, the studies of oral literature by Parry and Lord demonstrate that each performance of oral literature is a unique social event in that each performance creates a new literary text that is heard for the first time by the audience on hand.[11] In both cases, the performance of ritual or oral literature plays a constitutive role in the creation of social reality in that the performances reinforce social identity by reiterating the world views, mores, social practices, history, and other facts that define the culture.

Both of these examples focus on the performance of oral literature, but written literature can play a similar role in defining social reality. The liturgical reading

---

[6] Buss, "The Idea of *Sitz im Leben*," 165–70; see esp. Rolf P. Knierim, "Old Testament Form Criticism Reconsidered," *Int* 27 (1973) 435–68.

[7] Odil H. Steck, *Exegese des Alten Testaments. Leitfaden der Methodik* (12th edition; Neukirchen-Vluyn: Neukirchener, 1989) 114–19.

[8] Wolfgang Richter, *Exegese als Literaturwissenschaft. Entwurf einer alttestamentlichen Literatur Theorie und Methodologie* (Göttingen: Vandenhoeck & Ruprecht, 1971) 145–48.

[9] Richter, *Exegese als Literaturwissenschaft* 148.

[10] Knierim, "Old Testament Form Criticism Reconsidered," 438; cf. Mircea Eliade, *The Myth of the Eternal Return, or, Cosmos and History* (Bollingen Series 46; Princeton: Princeton University Press, 1954).

[11] A. B. Lord, *The Singer of Tales* (New York: Atheneum, 1974).

of Torah, for example, regularly reinforces the social and religious identity of Jewish communities. In the case of Ezra's reading of the Torah upon his return to Jerusalem in the late fifth century, the implementation of the written Torah's stipulations and the authority granted to those stipulations by the history of YHWH's interaction with Israel as presented in the Torah together play a constitutive role in defining the reality of the post-exilic Jewish community. Likewise, Koch demonstrates that Ezra's return to Jerusalem is presented in part as a fulfillment of prophecy in the book of Isaiah, in that Ezra's return is presented as the "second Exodus" announced by Second Isaiah that was designed to reestablish the "holy seed" in Jerusalem (Ezra 9:2; cf. Isa 6:13).[12]

Insofar as the postexilic Jewish community provided an important social context for the composition of biblical texts, one may note that the interaction of literature and human life results in the creation of both texts and social reality. As canonical critics note, the continued interaction of literature and social reality prompts the creation of more texts, and this in turn results in the reinforcement of existing social realities or the creation of new ones.[13] Literature and human life interact to create and to sustain each other.

III

The interaction between socio-historical and literary setting is particularly important in relation to the book of Isaiah with its long and complex literary history that extends through for centuries or more. The book clearly underwent various redactions during this period in which both socio-historical and literary factors were relevant in the composition of its various editions. My commentary on Isaiah 1–39 argues that the book underwent four major stages of composition.[14] Lack of space precludes a full defense of the details of this model, but it will suffice to demonstrate the principle that the interpretation of a text will be influenced by its setting. The first stage comprises an undefined body of 8th century oracles from Isaiah ben Amoz that appear throughout chapters 1–10; 14–23; and 28–31. The second stages comprises a 7th century Josianic edition of Isaiah in chapters 5–23; 28–33; and 36–37 that was designed to announce and justify King Josiah's program of national restoration. The third stage comprises a late-6th century edition of Isaiah in chapters 2–55; 60–62 that points to the return of Jews

---

[12] Klaus Koch, "Ezra and the Origins of Judaism," *JSS* 19 (1974) 173–97.

[13] James A. Sanders, "Adaptable for Life: The Nature and Function of Canon," *Magnalia Dei – the Mighty Acts of G-d: Essays on the Bible and Archaeology in Memory of G. Ernest Wright* (ed. F. M. Cross Jr., et al.; Garden City: Doubleday, 1976) 531–60; idem, "Hermeneutics in True and False Prophecy," *Canon and Authority: Essays in Old Testament Religion and Theology* (ed. G. W. Coats and B. O. Long; Philadelphia: Fortress, 1977) 21–41.

[14] Marvin A. Sweeney, *Isaiah 1–39, with an Introduction to Prophetic Literature* (FOTL 16; Grand Rapids and Cambridge: Eerdmans, 1996).

to Jerusalem and the rule of Cyrus as a manifestation of YHWH's sovereignty over the world. Finally, the fourth stage comprises a late-fifth century edition of the entire book of Isaiah that looks forward to the manifestation of YHWH's world sovereignty following the cleaning of Jerusalem and the world from evil. In light of this compositional history, the interpreter must ask not only about the social setting of the composition of texts within the book, but also about the role that earlier texts play in defining the social realities that result in the composition of later editions and texts within the book. Furthermore, the interpreter must ask whether or how these later literary contexts influence texts that were composed at an earlier time.

Isaiah 9:1–6 plays a particularly important role in the book of Isaiah throughout all the stages of its composition. It is constituted as a royal psalm of thanksgiving[15] that announces the reign of a monarch who will lead the people out of a period of darkness and oppression in order to establish a kingdom of peace, justice, and righteousness guaranteed by YHWH. When considered apart from its literary context, Isaiah 9:1–6 provides no clue as to the identity of the monarch or the historical circumstances of his reign; it only maintains that he will establish "the throne of David" (v. 6) as the basis for his ideal reign. But when it is considered in relation to the literary contexts of the four editions of Isaiah outlined above, Isaiah 9:1–6 provides prophetic justification for specific political and religious policies that relate to the socio-historical settings of each edition of the book. The interpretation of Isaiah 9:1–6 is thereby determined in part by the conceptual outlook and the literary and socio-historical setting of each edition of the book in which it appears.

In the case of the eighth-century oracles of Isaiah ben Amoz, there is no clear evidence that enables scholars to determine the specific literary form of an eighth-century book of Isaiah. Nevertheless, the immediate literary context in Isaiah 8:1–9:6 makes it clear that Isaiah 9:1–6 must be read in relation to the prophet's statements concerning the Syro-Ephramitic War and the consequences of Tiglath-Pileser's defeat of the northern kingdom of Israel in 734–732 B.C.E. when the Galilee and Trans-Jordan regions were stripped from Israel and incorporated as provinces of the Assyrian empire.[16] Isaiah 8:1–9:6 and especially 8:16–9:6, is constituted as a prophetic disputation that asks the addressees to choose between two positions outlined in v. 23. The first will disparage the loss of the lands of Zebulun and Naphtali and lead to the pessimistic outlook for the land described in vv. 21–22. But the second position will recognize the value of

---

[15] On the generic identification of this psalm, see Hermann Barth, *Jesaja-Worte in der Josiazeit. Israel und Assur als Thema einer produktiven Neuinterpretation der Jesajaüberlieferung* (WMANT 48; Neukirchen-Vluyn: Neukirchener, 1977) 148–51.

[16] For the following understanding of the eighth century context of Isaiah 8:1–9:6, see Marvin A. Sweeney, "A Philological and Form-Critical Reevaluation of Isaiah 8:1–9:6," *HAR* 14 (1994) 215–31.

the Assyrian incorporation of these territories as provinces in that it provides the opportunity for the Davidic monarch to reassert Davidic rule over the northern kingdom of Israel. In this setting, Isaiah 9:1–6 is directed to King Ahaz, and it urges him to seize the opportunity presented by the Assyrian victory to reunite the tribes of Israel.[17]

When read in relation to the 7th-century Josianic edition of Isaiah, Isaiah 9:1–6 plays a somewhat similar legitimizing role, albeit in very different literary and socio-historical conditions. Within the literary context of Isaiah 5–12,[18] the passage stands in between an unflattering portrayal in Isaiah 7 of King Ahaz's lack of trust in YHWH's promises of security for Jerusalem and the monarchy as expressed in the Davidic covenant tradition (see esp. Isa 7:9b) and the presentation of the ideal Davidic monarch who will rule following the collapse of the Assyrian king. Both Isaiah 7 and 11 appear to be the products of the Josianic redaction,[19] and it is noteworthy that Isaiah 11 portrays the major elements of Josiah's program, including a child's rule of peace (vv. 5–9) in Zion; the return of the exiles from Assyria, Egypt, and elsewhere (vv. 11–12, 15–16); the reunification of Israel and Judah (v. 13) and their domination of lands that formerly constituted the Davidic empire (v. 14).[20] In this regard, Isaiah 9:1–6 must also be understood as a reference to and legitimization of the coming reign of Josiah, and it would likely play a role in motivating the composition of the Josianic texts that prepare the reader for the reign of the righteous Davidic monarch, including Isaiah 7; 11; and 32.

When read in relation to the late-sixth century edition of the book of Isaiah in chapters 2–55; 60–62,[21] Isaiah 9:1–6 again provides legitimization for a specific view of royal power, but in very different political and socio-historical circumstances. The late-sixth century sees the rise of the Persian empire of Cyrus the Great and the return of Jews from Babylonian exile so that they might

---

[17] On Isaiah's attitude toward Ahaz and potential Davidic control of the north during the Syro-Ephraimitic War, see Stuart A. Irvine, *Isaiah, Ahaz, and the Syro-Ephraimitic Crisis* (SBLDS 123; Atlanta: Scholars Press, 1990) 133–77, 215–33.

[18] For a study of Isaiah 5:1–10:4 as a product of the Josianic redaction of Isaiah, Conrad E. L'Hereux, "The Redactional History of Isaiah 5.1–10.4," *In the Shelter of Elyon: Essays on Ancient Palestinian Life and Literature in Honor of G. W. Ahstrōm* (ed. W. B. Barrick and J. R. Spencer; JSOTSup 31; Sheffield: JSOT Press, 1984) 99–119.

[19] See the relevant sections of my *Isaiah 1–39* for full argumentation.

[20] For full discussion of the Josianic character of Isaiah 11, see my study, "Jesse's New Shoot in Isaiah 11: A Josianic Reading of the Prophet Isaiah," *A Gift of G-d in Due Season: Essays on Scripture and Community in Honor of James A. Sanders* (ed. R. D. Weis and D. M. Carr; JSOTSup 225; Sheffield: Sheffield Academic Press, 1996) 103–18.

[21] For this definition of the sixth-century edition of Isaiah, see the model of the "Great Book of Isaiah" (*Grossjesajabuch*) postulated by Odil H. Steck, "Trito-Jesaja im Jesajabuch," *The Book of Isaiah/Le Livre d'Isaïe* (ed. J. Vermeylen; BETL 81; Leuven: Peeters and Leuven University Press, 1989) 361–406, esp. 373–9; idem, *Bereitete Heimkehr.Jesaja 35 als redaktionelle Brücke zwischen dem Ersten und dem Zweiten Jesaja* (SBS 121; Stuttgart: Katholisches Bibelwerk, 1985) 45– 79.

rebuild Jerusalem and the temple. These events are presupposed throughout the sixth-century edition of the book in which no Davidic monarch is evident in chapters 40–55; 60–62. Rather Cyrus is explicitly named as YHWH's messiah and temple builder (Isa 44:28; 45:1) and the Davidic promise is applied not to a specific Davidic scion, but to the people of Israel at large (Isa 55:3). In this context, YHWH's plans for the world are identified with and manifested in the establishment of the Persian empire[22] so that the restoration of Zion will point to YHWH as the actual world sovereign, recognized by Israel and the nations (cf. Isaiah 2:2–4; 60–62) who authorizes Cyrus to act. Isaiah 9:1–6 (cf. Isaiah 11; 32) announces righteous Davidic rule, but it lacks reference to a specific Davidic figure. It thereby justifies YHWH's sovereignty exercised through Cyrus as a legitimate expression of the Davidic promise of peaceful and righteous rule from Zion.

Finally, the late-fifth century edition of Isaiah anticipates the manifestation of YHWH's world rule from Zion in Isaiah 66, but it presupposes that Jerusalem must first be cleansed of evil (see Isaiah 1; 2–4; 65–66).[23] When read in relation to the political upheaval that wracked the Persian empire from the late-sixth through the fifth centuries, the final form of the book of Isaiah presents such conflict as the necessary prelude that prepares the world for the manifestation of YHWH's rule of righteousness and peace. Isaiah 9:1–6 therefore points to ultimate goal of peaceful and just kingship in the book, but the absence of reference to a specific king enables it to be read in relation to the announcements of YHWH's sovereignty in Isaiah 66 and similar texts from earlier editions of the book (e. g., Isaiah 2:2–4; 32; 60–62). In this regard, Isaiah 9:1–6 justifies a future vision of YHWH's rule, which again portrayed as the ultimate fulfillment of the Davidic promise.

IV

In conclusion, the above discussion of the function of Isaiah 9:1–6 in the various literary and socio-historical settings of the successive editions of the book of Isaiah demonstrates the constitutive role that setting plays in the interpretation of this text. Because it anticipates the peaceful reign of a righteous Davidic monarch, Isaiah 9:1–6 aids in defining the literary character and in justifying the conceptual outlook of the various editions of the book. But it does so in part because it contains no reference to a specific monarch. This enables the passage to be understood in relation to the very different religio-political agendas and conceptual outlooks that characterize the successive editions of Isaiah in rela-

---

[22] Cf. Reinhold Gregor Kratz, *Kyros im Deuterojesaja-Buch* (FAT 1; Tübingen: Mohr Siebeck, 1991) 175–91.

[23] See Sweeney, *Isaiah 1–4* 96–99, esp. 99 n. 224.

tion to their respective socio-historical settings. This discussion thereby points to the adaptability of this text to various settings. It further demonstrates that the emergence of the final form of the book of Isaiah is due in part to the dynamic character of the prophetic word in that later readers and authors of the book of Isaiah were able to see its applicability to their own socio-historical settings and religio-political agendas.[24] In short, these later readers and authors believed that Isaiah ben Amoz addressed their own situations, and they produced successive editions of the book that presented the fulfillment of Isaiah's oracles in their own times.

---

[24] Cf. Christopher R. Seitz, *Zion's Final Destiny: The Development of the Book of Isaiah. A Reassessment of Isaiah 36–39* (Minneapolis: Fortress, 1991) esp. 39–45, who points to the fulfillment of Isaiah's positive portrayal of Zion's future as a basis for the continued growth of the book of Isaiah.

3. On ûměśôś in Isaiah 8:6

I

The appearance of the Hebrew term *ûměśôś* in in Isa 8:6 has long constituted a difficult exegetical crux. In its present form, the term is a combination of a conjunctive *waw* with the construct form of the *mem*-preformative noun *māśôś*, which means "exultation" or "rejoicing." Unfortunately, a noun makes little sense in the present context in that the following clause, *'et-rĕṣîn ûben-rĕmalyāhû*, "Rezin and the son of Remaliah," begins with the direct object particle *'et-*, which normally requires an antecedent verb. The fact that *māśôś* appears in its construct form only complicates the issues, since a genitive noun does not appear after *ûměśôś*. Consequently, a verbal form parallel to *ma'as hā'ām hazzeh*, "this people has rejected," would best fit this passage. Because of the problems posed by the verse in its present form, *ûměśôś* is frequently understood as a verbal noun and *'et-* as the preposition "with" so that the verse literary means "and rejoicing with Rezin and the son of Remaliah."[1] But this rendering is awkward and continues to provoke attempts to explain or emend the unusual form of the verse.

On the other hand, prior attempts to resolve the problem by explaining the grammatical form of *ûměśôś* as a verbal noun or by emending the passage have hardly proved satisfactory. After surveying these attempts and the readings of the ancient versions, this paper will propose a new solution to the problem based on the results of recent research concerning the emergence of the final form o the book of Isaiah in the late fifth century. It argues that Isa 8:6 originally contained the reading *ûměśôś 'et-*, on the basis of the interpretation of the passage presupposed in Isa 66:10–14, which employs similar vocabulary and themes to describe the rejoicing of Jerusalem and the inflowing glory of the nations following the defeat of YHWH's enemies.

---

[1] Cf. Stuart Irvine, *Isaiah, Ahaz, and the Syro-Ephraimitic Crisis* (SBLDS 123; Atlanta: Scholars Press, 1990) 185.

II

An attempt to interpret *ûmĕśôś* as a verbal noun appears as early as the late thirteenth/early fourteenth century in the commentary of R. David Kimḥi. Commenting on the phrase *ûmĕśôś ʾet-rĕṣîn*, he says that "they (i. e., many in Judah and Jeusalem) will be exulting and rejoicing with them (i. e., Rezin and ben Remaliah) if they will be ruling in Jerusalem."[2] He further states that *mĕśôś* is in the construct state with *ʾet-*, but he does not explain how *ʾet-* is to be understood. Kimḥi was followed by W. Gesenius, who argues that *mĕśôś* is a verbal noun used poetically as a finite verb.[3] Gesenius claims that the verb *śûś* stands here with the accusative as in Isa 35:1. He further says that *mĕśôś* is in the construct state because of the following preposition and cites *kĕśimḥat baqqāṣîr* in Isa 9:2 as a supporting example.[4] But this interpretation must be rejected. Although the verb *śûś* is commonly followed by the preposition *ʿal* (Deut 28:63; 30:9; Isa 62:5; Jer 32:41; Zeph 3:17; Ps 119:162) or *bĕ* (Isa 61:10; 65:19; Pss 19:6; 35:9; 40:17; 68:4; 70:5; 119:14; Job 39:21), it never appears with the direct object preposition *ʾēt*. The only other example of a construct form followed by a direct object pronoun appears in Jer 33:22, *mĕśārĕtê ʾōtî*, "those who minister to me," but this reading is problematic and frequently is emended.[5]

Gesenius' Hebrew Grammar attempts a different approach by identifying this phrase as an example of the use of the construct state before the preposition *ʾēt*, "with,"[6] but such a construction does not appear elsewhere in the Hebrew Bible. Barthélemy et al attempt to revive this understanding by pointing to the use of the same root with the preposition *ʾēt*, "with," in Isa 66:10.[7] Unfortunately, the phrase reads, *śîśû ʾittāh māśôś*, "exult with her (in) exultation." This indicates the use of the preposition following the verbal form, but it also indicates that a nominal construction would be unusual. Furthermore, the use of the direct object preposition *ʾēt* in parallel statements in Isa 8:6a and twice in Isa 8:7a suggests that *ʾēt* should not be understood as "with" in Isa 8:6b, but as the direct object marker.

---

[2] For a critical edition of this text, see L. Finkelstein, *The Commentary of David Kimḥi on Isaiah* (Columbia University Oriental Series 19; New York: Columbia University, 1926) 55.

[3] Wilhelm Gesenius, *Philologisch-kritischer und historiker Commentar über den Jesaia* (Leipzig: F. C. W. Vogel, 1820–21) 1/1:322.

[4] Gesenius, *Jesaia* 1/1:333.

[5] Cf. BHS note; Wilhelm Rudolph, *Jeremia* (HAT 12; Tübingen: Mohr Siebeck, 1968) 218; William L. Holladay, Jr., *Jeremiah 2* (Minneapolis: Fortress, 1989) 227.

[6] W. Gesenius, E. Kautzsch, and A. E. Cowley, *Gesenius' Hebrew Grammar* Oxford: Clarendon, 1983) sec. 130a.

[7] D. Barthélemy et al, *Critique textuelle de l'ancien Testament. II. Isaïe, Jérémie, Lamentations* (Freiburg: Universitätsverlag; Göttingen: Vandenhoeck & Ruprecht, 1986) 50.

The most commonly accepted solution to this problem is to emend the texts from *ûmĕśôś* to *ûmāsôs*.[8] This proposal was originally made by Hitzig, who notes the difficulties pertaining to the phrase *ûmĕśôś ʾet* and argues that a scribal misreading of *śin* for *samek* resulted in the change of *ûmĕśôś* to *ûmĕsôs*, "and dissolving."[9] This emendation presupposes the appearance of the term *kinsôs* in Isa 10:18 and combines a conjunctive *waw* with the infinitive absolute of the verb *mss*, "to dissolve, melt." Hitzig argues that the accusative *ʾet* appears in place of the expected *mippĕnê*, "because of," and cites the use of *ʿrṣ* in Job 31:34 as an example of this implicit use of an accusative construction. In the present context, the phrase is interpreted as a reference to the people's "dissolving" or "melting" in fear before Rezin and the son of Remaliah as in the RSV translation, "Because this people have refused the waters of Shiloaḥ that flow gently and melt in fear before Rezin and the son of Remaliah."

Bredenkamp likewise emends *ûmĕśôś* to *ûmĕsôs*, but maintains that the infinitive absolute form functions in an adverbial sense (e. g., "gently) that modifies "the waters that flow slowly (and gently)."[10] He argues that *ʾet* means "*coram, praesente*," indicating that "this people rejected the waters ... in the face of (i. e., because of) Rezin and ben Remaliah." Giesebrecht follows Bredenkamp's infinitive absolute rendering but retains the consonantal text as *ûmāsôs* (i. e., "the waters that flow slowly and exultantly").[11] He consequently deletes the last four words of v. 6b as a gloss. Finally, Duhm combines the solutions of Hitzig and Bredenkamp by emending *ûmĕśôś* to the perfect verbal form *māsas* and arguing that *ʾet* entered the text in place of the original *min* as a result of the scribal error that produced *ûmĕśôś*.[12]

But the emendation of *ûmĕśôś* to various forms of *mss* also presents problems.[13] Chief among them is that it does not properly account for the following *ʾet*. The verb *māsôs* in the sense of "despair" commonly requires the cause of despair to be introduced by *millipnê* (Ps 97:5), *mippĕnê* (Josh 5:1; Mic 1:4; Ps

---

[8] Otto Procksch, *Jesaja I* (KAT 9; Leipzig: A. Deichert, 1930) 131, 133; Hans Wildberger, *Jesaja 1–12* (BKAT 10/1; Neukirchen-Vluyn: Neukirchener, 1972) 321; Ronald E. Clements, *Isaiah 1–39* (NCeB; London: Marshall, Morgan and Scott; Grand Rapids: Eerdmans, 1980) 96; Otto Kaiser, *Isaiah 1–12: A Commentary* (OTL; Philadelphia: Westminster, 1983) 183.

[9] Ferdinand Hitzig, *Der Prophet Jesaja* (Heidelberg: C. F. Winter, 1833) 98–9.

[10] C. J. Bredenkamp, *Der Prophet Jesaia* (Erlangen: A. Deichert, 1887) 49.

[11] F. Giesebrecht, "Die Immanuelweissagung," *TSK* 61 (1888) 217–64, esp. 225–9.

[12] Bernhard Duhm, *Das Buch Jesaia* (Göttingen: Vandenhoeck & Ruprecht, 1914) 57. Cf. Karl Marti, *Das Buch Jesaja* (KHAT 10; Tübingen: Mohr Siebeck, 1900) 84. Cf. J. Lindblom, *A Study of the Immanuel Section Isaiah: Isa. vii, 1–ix, 6* (Lund: Gleerup, 1958) 44, who emends *ûmĕśôś* to *ûmĕsôs* and renders *ʾēt* as the preposition "with," so that the passage refers to "this people," which "dissolves together with Rezin and the son of Remaliah." Although Lindblom's suggestion accounts for *ʾēt*, the emendation of *ûmĕśôś* to *ûmĕsôs* presents problems in that textual evidence for the emendation is entirely lacking. For an analysis of the textual versions, see below.

[13] K. Fullerton, "The Interpretation of Isaiah 8, 5–10," *JBL* 43 (1924) 253–89, esp. 265–7.

68:3) or *min* (Isa 34:3). Attempts to emend *'et-* to *mippĕnê* or *millipnê*,[14] *min*,[15] or *miśś'ēt*[16] lack a firm textual basis and must be rejected. Likewise, Hitzig's and Bredenkamp's attempts to render *'et-* in this sense are somewhat forced. Furthermore, the suggestion that *ûmāsôs* can be understood in an adverbial sense parallel to *lĕ'aṭ* and that the clause *'et-rĕṣîn ûben-rĕmalyāhû* is a gloss[17] is also unsatisfactory for a number of reasons. These include the grammatical difficulties of reading the infinitive *ûmāsôs* in an adverbial sense and the unlikely hypothesis that the glossator would have equated the waters of Shiloaḥ with Rezin and the son of Remaliah.[18] Likewise, Fullerton's suggestion to reject all of v. 6b as a gloss does not satisfactorily account for the supposed glossator's choice of the peculiar form *ûmĕśôś* or even the emended *ûmāsôs*.[19]

Finally, Schroeder's attempt to claim that *ûmĕśôś* is a gloss on *rĕṣîn* merely avoids the issue and results in a statement that condemns the people for rejecting Rezin and the son of Remaliah,[20] which makes little sense in view of Isaiah's condemnation of these rulers (Isa 7:1–9; cf. 17:1–6). Likewise, Klein's explanation that the grammatical difficulties of this verse represent Isaiah's poetic license sidesteps the problem, despite his attractive interpretation of the verse in relation to v. 7 and his cogent observations about the parallel of *mā'as 'ēt* and *ûmĕśôś 'ēt*.[21]

III

Any attempt to resolve the problems posed by Isa 8:6 must take account of the ancient textual versions of this passage. A survey of these texts indicates that there is no support for an emendation of *ûmĕśôś* to *ûmāsôs* or any other expression based on the root *mss*. Nor is there evidence for the deletion of v. 6b as a gloss. It does indicate, however, that each version employs a verbal form in place of *ûmĕśôś*. The fact that each verb is based on the Hebrew root *śwś/śyś* and that the verbal forms vary among the translations suggests that each version presupposes the reading *ûmĕśôś* and attempts to render it in a verbal sense.

---

[14] Marti, *Jesaja* 84.
[15] Duhm, *Jesaia* 57.
[16] Karl Budde, "Jesaja 8,6b," *ZAW* 44 (1926) 65–67; Wildberger, *Jesaja 1–12* 321.
[17] Giesebrecht, "Die Immanuelweissagung," 227–9; cf. BHS note; Procksch, *Jesaja I* 131, 133; Clements, *Isaiah 1–39* 96.
[18] Fullerton, "Isaiah 8, 5–10," 267–8.
[19] Fullerton, "Isaiah 8, 5–10," 269–70.
[20] O. Schroeder, "*ûmĕśoś* eine Glosse zu raṣon," *ZAW* 32 (1912) 301–2.
[21] H. Klein, "Freude an Rezin," *VT* 30 (1980) 229–34.

The text of 1QIsaᵃ reads Isa 8:6 as *yʿn kyʾ mʾs hʿm hzh ʾt my hšwlḥ hhwlkym lʾwṭ wmśwś ʾt rṣyn wʾt bn (rm)l(y)h*,²² "Because this people has rejected the waters of the one who sends (i. e., YHWH) which run gently and causes Rezin and the son of Remaliah to rejoice." The original editors of this manuscript read *wmśwś*,²³ a *hiphil* masculine singular participle based on the verb root *śwś*, "to exult, rejoice," combined with a conjunctive *waw*.²⁴ The use of the *hiphil* form of this verb accords well with the following *ʾēt*. In the present context, it refers to the people's rejection of the waters of Shiloaḥ (or in accordance with 1QIsaᵃ, *haššōlēaḥ*, "the one who sends," i. e., YHWH) as the cause for Rezin's and the son of Remaliah's rejoicing. Nevertheless, this reading does not appear to reflect the "original" text of Isa 8:6 but the Qumran scribe's attempt to interpret the passage. The introduction of the extra direct object particle *wʾt* before *bn (rm)l(y)h* (cf. MT: *ûben rĕmalyāhû*) suggests the scribe's attempt to support the verbal rendering of an original *wmśwś* as *wmśyś*. That the scribe was willing to take liberties with this text is evident from the rendering of *ʾēt mê haššilōaḥ*, "the waters of Shiloaḥ," as *ʾt my hšwlḥ*, "the waters of the one who sends." This is a reference to YHWH who elsewhere in Isaiah is portrayed as the one who sends "a word" against Jacob (Isa 9:7) and sends Assyria against Israel (Isa 10:6).

Targum Jonathan reads *ḥĕlap degaṣ ʿamāʾ hadēn bĕmalkûtāʾ dĕbêt dawîd dimdabĕrāʾ lĕhôn bināḥ kĕmê šilôḥāʾ dĕnagĕdîn bināḥ wĕʾitrĕʿîʾû birṣîn ûbar rĕmalyâ*,²⁵ "Because this people loathed the kingdom of the house of David which led them gently like the kingdom of the house of David which led them gently like the waters of Shiloaḥ which flow gently and preferred Rezin and the son of Remaliah." Again, the choice of the verb *wĕʾitrĕʿîʾû*, "and they preferred," demonstrates that *ûmĕśôś* stands behind this text. The Aramaic verb *rʿy* means, "to desire, take delight in." In its present *ithpeal* perfect form, it means "and they delighted in" or "and they chose," which demonstrates the translator's attempt to render the disputed expression as a verbal form in reference to the people's preference of Rezin and the son of Remaliah over the Davidic dynasty.

The LXX reads *dia to mē boulesthai ton laon touton to hudōr tou silōam to poreuomenon hēsuchei alla boulesthai echein ton Raassōn kai ton huion*

---

²² For a photographic edition of this text, see John C. Trevor, *Scrolls from Qumran Cave I: The Great Isaiah Scroll; The Order of the Community; The Pesher to Habakkuk* (Jerusalem: The Albright Institute of Archaeological Research and the Shrine of the Book, 1972) 28–9.

²³ Millar Burrows, John C. Trevor, William H. Brownlee, *The Dead Sea Scrolls of St. Mark's Monastery. I.The Isaiah Manuscript and the Habakkuk Commentary* (New Haven: American Schools of Oriental Research, 1950) pl. vii.

²⁴ This is indicated by the sharply angled hook shape of the letter in question, similar to the *yod*'s of *my*, *hhwlkym*, and *rṣyn* from the same line in the manuscript. Like these *yod*'s, the letter is much shorter than the *waw* that appears at the beginning of the word as well as those of *hšwlḥ*, *hhwlkym*, *lʾwṭ*, and *wʾt* (cf. Barthélemy et al, *Critique textuelle de l'ancien Testament II* 49.

²⁵ For a critical edition of this text, see Alexander Sperber, *The Bible in Aramaic. III. The Latter Prophets according to Targum Jonathan* (Leiden: Brill, 1962) 16.

Romeliou basilea eph' humōn,[26] "Because this people did not want the water of Siloam which goes gently but wanted to have Rezin and the son of Remaliah as king over you." The use of the expression *boulesthai echein ... basilea eph' humōn*, "wanted to have ... as king over you," corresponds to a verbal understanding of *ûmĕśôś*, but the translator's understanding of the conjugation is ambiguous. It could be *hiphil* in that the people's choice of Rezin and the son of Remaliah as their rulers would certainly cause Rezin and the son of Remaliah to rejoice. After all, their attack against Judah during the Syro-Ephraimitic War was designed to gain them control of the Davidic throne insofar as it was an attempt to remove the ruling Davidic monarch and replace him with a certain be Tabeel (Isa 7:1–6). On the other hand, the Greek expression may reflect an understanding of *ûmĕśôś* as "delight in" or "choose" as represented by Targum Jonathan. Unfortunately, the use of the infinitive *boulesthai* gives no indication of the conjugation of the verbs in the Hebrew *Vorlage*, but the use of *mē boulesthai/ boulesthai*, "did not want/wanted," indicates the translator's attempt to associate *mā'as* and *ûmĕśôś* as parallel verbal forms that were related by assonance. The appearance of *eph' humōn*, "over you," merely reflects the translator's attempt to harmonize the third-person pronouns referring to the people in the Hebrew text of vv. 6–8 with the second-person pronoun applied to Emmanuel at the end of v. 8.

The Vulgate reads *pro eo quod abiecit populus iste aquas Siloae quae vadunt cum silentio et adsumpsit magis Rasin et filium Romeliae*,[27] "in view of the fact that this people left the waters of Shiloah which run silently and stood by Resin and the son of Remaliah instead." Like LXX, the use of *adsumpsit magis*, "stood by ... instead," indicates the translator's attempt to render a verbal expression based on *ûmĕśôś*, but it gives no clue as to how the translator would have conceived the conjugation of this expression.

Finally, the Peshitta reads *'l d'šlyw 'm' my' dšlwḥ' drdyn bšly' wḥdyw brṣn wbbr rwmly'*,[28] "Because this people rejected the waters of Shiloaḥ which run securely and have rejoiced in Rezin and the sons of Remaliah." The use of *wḥdyw* indicates an attempt to render the disputed expression as a verbal statement, but the use of the *peal* perfect form of the verb instead of the *aphal* participle indicates that the translator had *ûmĕśôś* in the *Vorlage*.

---

[26] For a critical edition of this text, see Joseph Ziegler, editor, *Septuaginta: Vetus Testamentum Graecum Auctoritate Academiae Litterarum Gottingensis Editum. XIV. Isaias* (Göttingen: Vandenhoeck & Ruprecht, 1967) 150.

[27] For a critical edition of this text, see R. Weber, editor, *Biblia Sacrum iuxta Vulgatum Versionem* (Stuttgart: Württembergische Bibelanstalt, 1975) 1104.

[28] For a critical edition of this text, see S. P. Brock, *The Old Testament in Syriac according to the Peshitta Version. Part III/1. Isaiah* (Leiden: Brill, 1987) 14.

IV

The preceding survey of scholarship on Isa 8:6 and the ancient textual versions establish two basic points. First, the presence of *ûmĕśôś* in this verse presents difficult grammatical and syntactical problems that prior attempts to explain the form or to emend it have failed to resolve. Second, the ancient textual versions uniformly presuppose the term *ûmĕśôś*, but render it as a verbal expression based on the root *śwś/śyś* from which *ûmĕśôś* is derived. Obviously, these points indicate the need to present a new solution for the problem of the appearance of *ûmĕśôś* in Isa 8:6. Furthermore, they demonstrate that any proposed solution must explain the presence of *ûmĕśôś* in the present form of the verse.

The versions point to a potential solution by positing a *hiphil* form of the verb *śwś/śyś*. This is especially clear in 1QIsa^a, which reads *ûmĕśîś*, and Targum Jonathan and Peshitta which employ readings that would be rendered in Hebrew by the *waw*-consecutive *hiphil* imperfect *wayyāśîśû* (cf. LXX and Vulgate). Nevertheless, although each of these readings offers certain advantages, neither is entirely satisfactory.

The reading *ûmĕśôś* takes *hāʿām hazzeh*, "this people," from the beginning of the verse as its subject and provides a parallel based on assonance for the initial verb *mʾs*, "reject." It also forms an appropriate antecedent for the following direct object particle and provides a syntactical parallel with v. 7, which employs the participial form *māʿăleh*, "raises up," as the antecedent for two object clauses introduced by *ʾēt*. But the participial form of *ûmĕśîś* presents a problem in that it is an unlikely syntactical parallel for the perfect verb *māʾas*, which introduces the verse. Rather, the participle form of *ûmĕśîś* in 1QIsa^a appears to be derived from the following *māʿăleh* in v. 7 and the preceding *hahōlĕkîm* in v. 6a.

The readings *wĕʾitrĕʿîʾû* in Targum Jonathan and *wḥdyw* in the Peshitta both appear to presuppose the *waw*-consecutive *hiphil* imperfect plural form *wayyāśîśû*, although the verb does not appear to be in the *Vorlage* of either version. Such a form would provide an appropriate antecedent for the direct object particle in v. 6b, but the change in number conflicts with the singular formation of the verb *māʾas* in v. 6a and its grammatically singular subject *hāʿām*. The problem v. 6a could be solved by positing the singular form *wayyāśîś* for Isa 8:6, but the form *yāśîś* appears elsewhere in the Hebrew Bible only in the *qal* conjugation (Deut 28:63; Isa 62:5; Zeph 3:17; Ps 19:6; Job 39:21). The 3ms imperfect *hiphil* form of *śwś/śyś* is identical to the 3ms imperfect *qal* form, but the *hiphil* form of the verb is attested only in Rabbinic and Qumran Hebrew, and there only occasionally.[29] Consequently, *wayyāśîś* would be the only *hiphil* form of

---

[29] M. Jastrow, *A Dictionary of the Targumim, the Talmud Babli and Yerushalmi, and the Midrashic Literature* (Brooklyn: P. Shalom, 1967) 1542–3.

the verb in the entire Hebrew Bible. Although such a solution is not impossible, the absence of other *hiphil* forms of *śwś/śyś* undermines its credibility.

This means that there is no secure alternative to the reading *ûmĕśôś* in Isa 8:6. But a solution to the problem may appear in relation to recent research concerning the emergence of the final form of the book of Isaiah, especially insofar as many texts in Trito-Isaiah appear to develop themes and readings that are present in First or Second Isaiah.[30] Isaiah 66:10–14 is particularly significant in this regard in that it contains several important lexical and thematic associations with Isa 8:6–8. Isaiah 66:10–11 calls for rejoicing with the restored Jerusalem, here portrayed as a mother with suckling infants at her breast. Verses 12–14 convey YHWH's promise to extend the "glory of the nations" (*kĕbôd gôyim*; cf. *wĕʾet-kol-kĕbôdô* in Isa 8:7) over her "like a river of peace and like an overflowing stream" (*kĕnāhār šālôm ûkĕnahal šōṭēp*; cf. Isa 8:8 on *šāṭap*). It would appear that the author of Isa 66:10–14 intended to present this text as the ultimate fulfillment of YHWH's pledge to inundate the people with the "river" (*nāhār*) of the kings of Assyria "and all his glory" (*wĕʾet-kol-kĕbôdô*) in Isa 8:6–8.

Not only does Isa 66:10–14 present a thematic and lexical correspondence to Isa 8:6–8, it also has a bearing on the reading *ûmĕśôś* in Isa 8:6. Isaiah 66:10bα reads *śîśû ʾittāh māśôś*, "rejoice with her (in) exultation." This reading is especially significant for understanding *ûmĕśôś* in Isa 8:6. Not only does Isa 66:10b contain the noun *māśôś*, but it also includes the phrase *śîśû ʾittāh*, "rejoice with her." This phrase represents the only text in the Hebrew Bible in which the verb *śwś/śyś* takes *ʾēt*, "with," indicating an indirect object. The reading is all the more remarkable in that the preceding phrase in v. 10a *śimḥû yĕrûšālayim wĕgîlû bāh*, "rejoice with Jerusalem and celebrate with her," likewise contains the only instance in the Hebrew Bible in which the *qal* form of the verb *śmḥ* is

---

[30] H. Odeberg, *Trito-Isaiah (Isaiah 56–66): A Literary and Linguistic Analysis* (UUÅ, Theologi 1; Uppsala: Alqvist & Wiksell, 1931) 62–74, 94; Rémi Lack, *La symbolique du livre d'Isaïe. Essay sur l'image littéraire comme element de structuration* (AnBib 59; Rome: Biblical Institute Press, 1973); Brevard S. Childs, *Introduction to the Old Testament as Scripture* (Philadelphia: Fortress, 1979); W. Brueggemann, "Unity and Dynamic in the Isaiah Tradition," *JSOT* 29 (1984) 89–107; Rolf Rendtorff, "Zur Komposition des Jesajabuches," *VT* 34 (1984) 295–320; idem, "Jesaja 6 im Rahmen der Komposition des Jesajabuches," *The Book of Isaiah/Le Livre d'Isaïe* (ed. J. Vermeylen; BETL 81; Leuven: Leuven University Press and Peeters, 1989) 73–82; W. A. M. Beuken, "Isa 56.9–57.13 – An Example of the Isaianic Legacy of Trito-Isaiah," *Tradition and Reinterpretation in Jewish and Early Christian Literature: Essays in Honor of Jürgen C. H. Lebram* (ed. J. W. Van Henten et al.; Leiden: Brill, 1986) 48–64; idem, "Servant and Herald of Good Tidings: Isaiah 61 as an Interpretation of Isaiah 40–55," in J. Vermeylen, ed., *The Book of Isaiah* 411–42; Marvin A. Sweeney, *Isaiah 1–4 and the Post-Exilic Understanding of the Isaianic Tradition* (BZAW 171; Walter de Gruyter, 1988); J. Vermeylen, "L'unité du livre d'Isaïe," in J. Vermeylen, ed., *The Book of Isaiah* 11–53; Odil Hannes Steck, "Trito-Jesaja im Jesajabuch," in J. Vermeylen, ed., *The Book of Isaiah* 361–406; cf. R. E. Clements, "The Unity of the Book of Isaiah," *Int* 36 (1980) 117–29; idem, "Beyond Tradition History: Deutero-Isaianic Development of First Isaiah's Themes," *JSOT* 31 (1985) 95–113.

followed by *'ēt*. Inasmuch as Isa 66:10–14 appears to be derived from Isa 8:6–8, this indicates that the author of Isa 66:10–14 read *ûměśôś* in Isa 8:6.

The reading may appear awkward, but it must stand. The reason for its awkward nature becomes clear, however, when it is considered in relation to the sexual imagery that stands behind both Isa 66:10–14 and Isa 8:6–8. Isaiah 66:7–9 presents the imagery of Zion's giving birth to children prior to the commands to rejoice with Jerusalem in Isa 66:10–14. Isaiah 8:6–8, on the other hand, ends with a reference to the Assyrian king's "stretching out his wings" (*wěhāyâ muṭṭôt kěnāpāyw*, "and the extending of his wings"), thereby filling the land of Emmanuel (i. e., Judah) with the overflowing waters of the great and mighty river mentioned in vv. 7–8. The spreading of wings or skirts frequently serves as an idiomatic reference to marriage or sexual relations (Ezek 16:8; Ruth 3:9; cf. Deut 23:1; 27:20), as does the imagery of flowing waters (Song 4:15; Prov 5:15–20; 9:13–18). Although the sexual imagery is not explicit until v. 8, it is clear that in rejecting the waters of Shiloaḥ, Judah opens itself to another lover, or rapist as the case may be, in the form of the Assyrian king.[31] Certainly, this associates Isa 8:5–8 with Isa 8:1–4, where Isaiah reports his sexual relations with the prophetess that resulted in the birth of Maher-Shalal-Hash-Baz.[32] In this respect, the awkward nature of the reading *ûměśôś 'ēt* in Isa 8:6 becomes significant. Although *māśôś* usually refers to general rejoicing, its appearance in the context of Jerusalem's giving birth in Isa 66:10 and the rejoicing of the bride-

---

[31] Scholars frequently argue that "this people" in v. 6a refers to the northern kingdom of Israel in that they rejected the Davidic dynasty by following Rezin and Pekah (e. g., L. C. Rignell, "Das Orakel 'Maher-salal Has-bas,'" *ST* 10 [1957] 40–52, 41–2). But there are several reasons for maintaining that "this people" refers to Judah: 1) the northern kingdom had rejected the house of David long before their decision to follow Rezin and Pekah; 2) the reference to Emmanuel in v. 8 indicates that Judah is threatened in this passage; and 3) the "waters of Shiloaḥ" are frequently taken as a reference to the Davidic dynasty (so Kimḥi and Targum Jonathan) or as a symbol of YHWH's guarantee of security to Jerusalem. Note that Isa 7:3 locates Isaiah's encounter with Ahaz at "the end of the conduit of the upper pool on the highway to the Fuller's Field" (RSV). Inasmuch as Ahaz appears to be inspecting his water system in anticipation of a siege by Israel and Aram, Isaiah's reference to the people's rejection of "the waters of Shiloaḥ" suggests their lack of confidence in the city's defenses. The fact that Ahaz eventually summoned Assyrian assistance in the Syro-Ephraimitic War (2 Kgs 16:7–9) indicates that he likewise lacked confidence in the city's ability to resist a siege. Insofar as the Syro-Ephraimitic coalition would be concerned to augment their forces by bringing Judah into its camp against the Assyrians, their attack would be designed to remove Ahaz and convince the Judean population to join the coalition rather than to destroy the country. Isaiah 8:6 suggests that such a strategy was working. Cf. Irvine, *Isaiah, Ahaz, and the Syro-Ephraimitic Crisis* 189–91, who relates the imagery of "the waters of Shiloaḥ" to the role that the Giḥon spring plays in guaranteeing the security of the Davidic dynasty.

[32] It also has implications for understanding *qešer*, "conspiracy," in Isa 8:12 and the general concern with the people's need to fear YHWH in Isa 8:11–15. The root of *qešer* literally means "to bind, join," which may suggest a further sexual *double entendre* insofar as the people had rejected YHWH's promises of security in favor of an alliance with the Syro-Ephraimitic coalition.

groom over his bride in Isa 62:5 indicates that the term can be used in reference to marriage. Like the general imagery of water in Isa 8:6–7, the lexical meaning of *māśôś* in v. 6 is non-specific, but the awkward nature of the reading disrupts the syntax of vv. 6–7 and calls attention to itself. Inasmuch as the term *māśôś* and the imagery of waters suggests the possibility of sexual connotations, the term conveys a *double entendre* that is only realized in v. 8 when the extended skirts of the Assyrian monarch fill the land. In this respect, the awkward phrasing of *ûměśôś 'et-rěṣîn ûben-rěmalyāhû* is a deliberate attempt to prepare the unsuspecting reader for the sexual metaphor of v. 8.

Just as the book of Isaiah as a whole sees the Assyrian invasions and later the Babylonian captivity as divine punishment that precede the restoration of the people, so also the associated sexual and river imagery of Isa 8:6–7 and 66:10–14 present parallel but contrasting descriptions of the circumstances that led to the punishment and the results of the restoration. In conclusion, it should be noted that inasmuch as Isa 66:10–14 appears as part of the climax of the book of Isaiah, it corresponds to the imagery at the beginning of the book (Isa 2:2–4) of the nations "flowing" (*wěnāhărû*, Isa 2:2) to Zion to receive YHWH's Torah. By basing the description of rejoicing in Isa 66:10–14 on the language and imagery of Isa 8:6–8, the author of Isa 66:10–14 presents evidence that *ûměśôś* appears in the text of Isa 8:6 in the time of Trito-Isaiah, generally ascribed to the fifth century, and establishes a major link in the overall structure of the final form of the book.[33]

---

[33] This is a slightly revised version of a paper read at the Southeastern Regional Meeting of the Society of Biblical Literature, Atlanta, March 15–17, 1991. I would like to thank the Yad Hanadiv/Barecha Foundation which provided the funds for my 1989–90 sabbatical at the Hebrew University of Jerusalem where the research for this paper was completed.

4. Prophetic Exegesis in Isaiah 65–66

I

The role of Isaiah 1 as Introduction to the book of Isaiah has long been recognized by scholars. Georg Fohrer's seminal study of the chapter makes this clear in that he points to the means by which Isaiah 1 encapsulates the essential message of the book, whether it is conceived as Isaiah 1–39 or as Isaiah 1–66, including both the judgment to be leveled against Jerusalem and Judah by YHWH and the ultimate redemption of Jerusalem and Judah once the punishment is completed.[1] Scholars have also noted the lexical correspondence between Isaiah 1 and Isaiah 65–66, indicating that Isaiah 65–66 takes up a great deal of the vocabulary of Isaiah 1, and thereby forms a literary envelope that ties the entire book together.[2] Nevertheless, no full study of Isaiah 65–66 has been undertaken that demonstrates the role of these chapters as the conclusion to the book of Isaiah. Although scholars have treated these chapters in relation to Isaiah 1 and to Deutero- or Trito-Isaiah, relatively little attention has been given to examining the message of these chapters in relation to the material in First Isaiah that would establish their role in relation to the book as a whole.[3]

---

[1] Georg Fohrer, "Jesaja 1 als Zusammenfassung der Verkündigung Jesajas," *ZAW* 74 (1962) 251–68.

[2] See Leon J. Liebreich, "The Compilation of the Book of Isaiah," *JQR* 46 (1955–56) 259–77; Rémi Lack, *La symbolique du livre d'Isaïe* (AnBib 59; Rome: Pontifical Biblical Institute, 1973) 139–42; Marvin A. Sweeney, *Isaiah 1–4 and the Post-Exilic Understanding of the Isaianic Tradition* (BZAW 171; Berlin and New York: Walter de Gruyter, 1988) 21–4; idem, *Isaiah 1–39, with an Introduction to Prophetic Literature* (FOTL 16; Grand Rapids and Cambridge: Eerdmans, 1996) ad loc.

[3] See Anthony J. Tomasino, "Isaiah 1.1–2.4 and 63–66, and the Composition of the Book of Isaiah," *JSOT* 53 (1993) 81–98, who argues that Isaiah 63–66 have been patterned on Isaiah 1, and J. Vermeylen, *Du prophète d'Isaïe à l'apocalyptique* (EB; Paris: Gabalda, 1977–78) 2:504–11, who argues that all of Isaiah 56–66 builds upon Isaiah 1. For the relations of Isaiah 56–66 to Deutero- and Trito-Isaiah, see the citations below. Also see David Carr, "Reaching for Unity in Isaiah," *JSOT* 57 (1993) 61–80, esp. 72–75, who raises questions as to whether Isaiah 1 and 65–66 can serve as introduction and conclusion respectively to the book of Isaiah, based primarily on differences in the rhetorical aims of each pericope. See now David Carr, "Reading Isaiah from Beginning (Isaiah 1) to End (Isaiah 56–66): Multiple Modern Possibilities," in *New Visions of Isaiah* (ed. R. F. Melugin and M. A. Sweeney; JSOTSup 214; Sheffield: JSOT Press, 1996) 188–218, where he develops this perspective further. He argues that Isaiah 1 predicts judgment in an effort to urge the audience to repent, whereas Isaiah 65–66 presupposes that the judgment already fixed. But his analysis misses the rhetorical point of positing such certain

This question is especially important not only in relation to the debate concerning the literary form of the book of Isaiah as a whole, but in relation to the debate concerning scribal prophecy within the book of Isaiah as well. Scholars have consistently pointed to the dependence of Trito-Isaiah on Deutero-Isaiah. Mowinckel, Elliger, and Bonnard, among others, have argued that Trito-Isaiah is the product of Deutero-Isaiah's disciple(s) who elaborated upon the message of the master.[4] Jones, Ackroyd, and Rendtorff point to the influence of Trito-Isaiah in presenting the material concerning First Isaiah,[5] and Vermeylen and Beuken point to Trito-Isaiah's role as an interpreter of both First or Second Isaiah.[6] The citation of Isa 11:6–9 in Isa 65:25 has long been recognized by scholars,[7] although most consider it to be a later gloss, and the influence of Isa 8:6–8 on Isa 66:10–14 has recently been identified by the present writer.[8] Most recently, Lau points to the character of Trito-Isaiah as scribal prophecy, insofar as Isaiah 56–66 presents its theological message by reference to earlier biblical texts, both within the book of Isaiah and in other biblical writings.[9] According to Lau, Isaiah 65–66 cite a variety of Isaianic texts from Isaiah 1; 11; 49; 54; 60–62, etc., as part of a larger effort in Trito Isaiah to define the task and whereabouts the "Servant" of YHWH. According to Lau, such exegetical work stems from circles of Deuteronomistically influenced Levites and priests, and points to the origins of later midrashic exegesis. Nevertheless, because he views Isaiah 65–66

---

judgment that has not yet been realized. By defining the qualities of the righteous as "one who trembles" at YHWH's word, etc. (66:2) and by reiterating the word of YHWH as expressed in Isaiah 1 and elsewhere in the book, Isaiah 65–66 calls upon those who stand in judgment to join those who tremble at the word of YHWH. Judgment is decreed for the wicked, but the audience still has the choice counted among the wicked or the righteous.

[4] Sigmund Mowinckel, "Die Komposition des deuterojesajanischen Buches," *ZAW* 49 (1931) 87–112, 242–60; Karl Elliger, *Deuterojesaja in seinem Verhältnis zum Tritojesaja* (BWANT 63; Stuttgart: W. Kohlhammer, 1933); P.-E. Bonnard, *Le Second Isaïe, son disciple et leurs éditeurs* (EB; Paris: Gabalda, 1972).

[5] Douglas Jones, "The Traditio of the Oracles of Isaiah of Jerusalem," *ZAW* 67 (1955) 226–46; Peter Ackroyd, "Isaiah I–XII: Presentation of a Prophet," *VTSup* 29 (1978) 16–48; Rolf Rendtorff, "Zur Komposition des Buches Jesajas," *VT* 34 (1984) 295–320.

[6] Vermeylen, *Du prophète*; W. A. M. Beuken, "Isaiah, chapters lxv–lxvi: Trito-Isaiah and the Closure of the Book of Isaiah," *Congress Volume: Leuven 1989* (VTSup 43; Leiden: Brill, 1991) 204–21.

[7] Odil H. Steck, "'... ein kleiner Knabe kann sie leiten.' Beobachtungen zum Tierfrieden in Jesaja 11, 6–8 und 65, 25," *Alttestamentlicher Glaube und Biblische Theologie* (Fest. H. D. Preuss; ed. J. Hausmann and H.-J. Zobel; Stuttgart: W. Kohlhammer, 1992) 104–13; J. T. A. G. M. van Ruiten, "The Intertextual Relationship between Isaiah 65:25 and Isaiah 11:6–9," *The Scriptures and the Scrolls* (Fest. A. S. Van der Woude; ed. F. García Martínez et al.; VTSup 49; Leiden: Brill, 1992) 31–42.

[8] M. A. Sweeney, "On *ûmĕśôś* in Isaiah 8.6," *Among the Prophets: Language, Image, and Structure in the Prophetic Writings* (ed. P. R. Davies and D. J. A. Clines; JSOTSup 144; Sheffield: JSOT Press, 1993) 42–54.

[9] Wolfgang Lau, *Schriftgelehrte Prophetie in Jes 56–66. Eine Untersuchung zu den literarischen Bezügen in den letzten elf Kapitaln des Jesajabuches* (BZAW 225; Berlin and New York: Walter de Gruyter, 1994).

as a conglomeration of originally smaller textual units, he does not take up the question of the role of these chapters as the conclusion to the book of Isaiah.

Clearly, Isaiah 65–66 cite and interpret earlier texts in the book of Isaiah, including not only material from chapter 1 but from throughout the entire book as well. Furthermore, these chapters not only conclude the book of Isaiah, but present a scenario for YHWH's creation of a "new heaven and new earth" in which the wicked will be destroyed and the nations will bring the exiled people of Israel and Judah back to Jerusalem as part of a world-wide revelation of YHWH's sovereignty. Insofar as this revisits the themes of the first part of the book, such as Isaiah 1 which points to destruction for the wicked and restoration for the righteous, and Isaiah 2–4 which combines a portrayal of the nations' pilgrimage to Zion following its purification from evil with an invitation to Jacob/Israel to return, it points to the role of Isaiah 65–66 as the conclusion of the book of Isaiah. Consequently, the balance of this paper examines the literary character of Isaiah 65–66, including its structure, its place in the book of Isaiah, its citation of earlier Isaianic texts, and its literary integrity, in an effort to define this role.

II

Isaiah 65–66 is demarcated by its consistent formulation as the prophet's report of YHWH's speeches concerning the fate of the righteous and the wicked. This demarcation is evident from the appearance of prophetic messenger speech formulas and other YHWH speech formulas that appear throughout the chapters and the first-person singular formulation of the speeches which clearly refer to YHWH. This stands in contrast to the preceding lament in Isa 63:7–64:12 in which the psalmist is the speaker who appeals for YHWH to act against the wicked. These chapters appear at the conclusion of the book of Isaiah as part of the larger block of material in Isaiah 55–66 that exhorts the book's addressees to join the restored covenant community centered at Zion.[10] They form part of the textual sub-unit in Isaiah 63–66 which presents YHWH's approach against Edom as the Divine Warrior who destroys the wicked (63:1–6) and the people's lament in which they appeal for mercy (63:7–64:12). Isaiah 65–66 follow immediately upon the lament, and constitute the report of YHWH's response to the lament, in which YHWH reiterates the decision to provide salvation for the righteous (who become part of the covenant community at Zion) and death for the wicked who refuse YHWH's offer.[11] By outlining the future for those who

---

[10] For a full discussion of the overarching structure of this material within the book of Isaiah, see Sweeney, *Isaiah 1–4* 87–99.

[11] For discussion of the role of Isaiah 65–66 as a response to the lament in Isa 63:7–64:12, see Charles C. Torrey, *The Second Isaiah: A New Interpretation* (New York: Scribner's, 1928) 466–7; Bonnard, *Le Second Isaïe* 462–3; O. H. Steck, "Tritojesaja im Jesajabuch," in *The Book*

accept or reject the invitation to become a part of the covenant community in Zion, Isaiah 65–66 play a major role in defining the goals and agenda of the book of Isaiah and thereby constitutes a fitting conclusion.

The structure of Isaiah 65–66 is determined by a combination of thematic and formal features, including the identifications of the addressees of each textual sub-unit and the various YHWH speech formulas that define each subunit. Overall, three major sub-units constitute Isaiah 65–66, including 65:1–7, 65:8–25, and 66:1–24.[12] The units work together to state the basic problem of the refusal by some to seek YHWH (65:1–7) and to address both the wicked (65:8–25) and the righteous (66:1–24) concerning their contrasting fates for refusing or accepting YHWH's invitation to join the covenant community centered around Zion.

The first major sub-unit of the passage is Isa 65:1–7. These verses are demarcated by their formulation as the prophet's report of a speech by YHWH. This is evident from the YHWH speech formula, *ʾāmar yhwh*, "says YHWH," which appears in v. 7, and the first person singular formulation of the verb forms and pronouns that indicate the speaker. The speech is not addressed to any specific party, but employs third person objective address forms to describe the refusal by the wicked to call upon YHWH. Two second person masculine plural suffix pronouns appear in v. 7aα, *ʿăwōnōtêkem waʿăwōnōt ʾăbôtêkem yaḥdāyw*, "(and I will requite ...) your sins and the sins of your fathers together," but the rest of v. 7 employs third person masculine plural forms to designate the "sinners," which is consistent with vv. 1–7 as a whole. The shift to second person plural address forms in this instance may be a gloss influenced by the proximity of second person masculine plural address forms for the wicked in Isa 65:8–25, especially in vv. 11–15.[13] The text breaks down into two basic components based upon the prophetic judgment speech pattern.

Verses 1–5 comprise the report of YHWH's statement concerning the Deity's readiness to be sought by those who were not seeking, including statements concerning YHWH's attempts to offer aid to the people and the people's refusal to acknowledge YHWH. Consequently, vv. 1–5 function as the indictment of the people for wrongdoing. Verses 6–7 constitute a second component, initially identified by the exclamatory statement, "Behold! It is written before Me,"

---

of Isaiah – Le Livre d'Isaïe (ed. J. Vermeylen; BETL 81; Leuven: Leuven University Press and Peeters, 1989) 400–1, n. 119, reprinted in *Studien zu Tritojesaja* (BZAW 203; Berlin and New York: Walter de Gruyter, 1991) 3–45, esp. 40–1, n. 119; idem, "Beobachtungen zur Anlage von Jes 65–66," *Studien zu Tritojesaja* 217–28, esp. 221–25, originally published in *BN* 38–39 (1987) 103–16; Brooks Schramm, *The Opponents of Third Isaiah: Reconstructing the Cultic History of the Restoration* (JSOTSup 193; Sheffield: JSOT Press, 1995) 154–6.

[12] Contra Steck, "Beobachtungen zur Anlage von Jes 65–66," 224–5.

[13] According to BHS, both the LXX and the Peshitta substitute third-person masculine plural forms consistent with the immediate literary context. 1QIsa[a], however, retains the second-person masculine plural formulation.

which conveys YHWH's intentions not to remain silent in the face of rejection by the people, but to require their evil deeds. Verses 6–7 thereby constitute the announcement of punishment in the overall prophetic judgment speech pattern. Nevertheless, the introductory statement in vv. 1–2, in which YHWH states, "I was ready to be sought by those who did not ask," etc., indicates that the passage is designed not only to announce judgment against the wicked, but to appeal to the audience to accept YHWH's offer and not to be included among the wicked.

The second major sub-unit is Isa 65:8–25. This section is demarcated by two different features. The first are the various YHWH speech formulas, including the messenger speech formulas in vv. 8, *kōh ʾāmar yhwh*, "thus says YHWH," and 13, *lākēn kōh ʾāmar ʾădōnāy yhwh*, "therefore, thus says my L-rd, YHWH," and the concluding YHWH speech formula, *ʾāmar yhwh*, "says YHWH," in v. 25. The second is the formulation of the passage as a first person singular speech by YHWH which addresses the wicked, that is, "those who abandon YHWH," (v. 11), with second person masculine plural verbal and pronoun forms. The speeches by YHWH also discuss the righteous, but they employ third person objective language, indicating that the righteous are described to the wicked who are directly addressed.

Isaiah 65:8–25 falls into two basic components, each of which is introduced by a version of the prophetic messenger speech formula. Verses 8–12 articulate the principle that not all of the people will be destroyed, and this modifies the perspective of vv. 1–7 that make no distinction within the people. Rather, vv. 8–12 maintain that YHWH will preserve a portion of the people to act as the "seed" from Jacob, who will "possess My mountain" from Judah (v. 9). This principle is articulated on the basis of an analogy with the harvest of grapes: just as the cluster of new grapes (*hattîrôš bāʾeškōl*) is not destroyed as there might be some value that will come from it, so YHWH will not destroy the people entirely so that the "seed" for a new beginning might emerge.[14] Verses 8–10 are formulated in objective address language to describe the principle, whereas vv. 11–12 are formulated in second person masculine plural address language directed to "those who abandon YHWH" (v. 11) in order to inform them that they have been designated for the sword because of their evil deeds.

The second component of Isa 65:8–25, vv. 13–25, is likewise introduced by a version of the prophetic messenger speech form, *lākēn kōh ʾāmar ʾădōnāy yhwh*, "therefore, thus says my L-rd, YHWH." The introductory *lākēn*, "therefore," indicates that this unit follows upon vv. 8–12 by defining the practical consequences of the principle articulated in these verses, that is, vv. 13–25

---

[14] The term *tîrôš* generally refers to "new wine," and thus to wine that is not fully aged. Here it seems to refer to the grapes from which the wine will be made. The passage seems to suggest that the *tîrôš* is not entirely suitable for consumption, but proper processing will make it so. See J. F. Ross, "Wine," *IDB* 4:849–52. On the term *tîrôš*, see BDB 440.

describe the punishment for the wicked and the benefits of the righteous. The YHWH speech reported in vv. 13–15a employs second person masculine plural verbal and pronoun forms to address the wicked directly and to describe their upcoming suffering in contrast to the experience of the righteous. Verses 15b–25 employ third person objective forms to describe the restoration and benefits of the righteous in great detail. Especially noteworthy are references at the end of the passage which tie it into the larger framework of Isaiah 65–66. Verses 23b identifies the righteous as "the seed blessed by YHWH," thereby tying this unit into vv. 8–12, in which YHWH states that a seed from Jacob will be preserved as a possible blessing. Verses 24a states that "before they (i. e., the righteous) call, I will answer," which contrasts with the situation described in vv. 1–7 where YHWH stood ready but the people did not call.

The third major sub-unit is Isa 66:1–24. Again, this sub-unit is demarcated both by its thematic and formal features. The first is the prophetic messenger formula in Isa 66:1, *kōh ʾāmar yhwh*, "Thus says YHWH," which introduces the sub-unit and identifies the following material as a speech by YHWH. The second is the call to attention formula in Isa 66:5, *šimĕʿû dĕbar-yhwh haḥărēdîm ʾel dĕbārô*, "Hear the word of YHWH, you who tremble at his word," which again introduces the following material and identifies it as a speech by YHWH. Other formulas that identify this material as a report of YHWH's speeches included the oracular formulas of vv. 2, 17, and 22, *nĕʾum yhwh*, "oracle of YHWH"; the subordinate messenger formula of v. 12, *kî kōh ʾāmar yhwh*, "for thus says YHWH"; the YHWH speech formulas of vv. 20, 21, and 23, *ʾāmar yhwh*, "says YHWH"; and modified forms of the YHWH speech formula in v. 9, *yōʾmar yhwh*, "says YHWH," and *ʾāmar ʾlhyk*, "says your G-d." The speeches by YHWH are all formulated in characteristic first person singular form, but they differ from the preceding material in Isaiah 65 in that the second person masculine plural address forms are no longer directed to the wicked but to the righteous. When the speeches shift to third person objective language, they now describe the wicked and not the righteous as in Isaiah 65. The passage falls into two major parts. Isaiah 66:1–4 is introduced by its own prophetic messenger speech formula in v. 1. The addressee of the speech is unclear: the second person masculine address form in Isa 66:1b, "what is this house that you would build (*tibnû*) for me?" is somewhat ambiguous in that the context provides no clue as to whether the question is addressed to the righteous or the wicked. It simply addresses those who would build the Temple for YHWH. Nevertheless, the reference to "the one who trembles (*wĕḥārēd*) at My word," in v. 2b indicates that this pericope is to be read in relation to Isa 66:5–24, which is addressed to "those who tremble (*haḥărēdîm*) at His word." Overall, the passage reports YHWH's statement that the humble or those who tremble at YHWH's word will be restored and the wicked will be punished. Verses 1–2 describe YHWH's intentions to look to the humble, and vv. 3–4 employ third person objective language to describe YHWH's intention to punish the evil. The concluding statements in v. 4, "because I called and no one answered, I spoke and they did not hear," recall YHWH's waiting to be called by the people in Isa 65:1–7. Likewise, the reference in v. 4b, "and they did evil in My eyes and that in which I did not delight they chose," recalls the similar statement in Isa 65:12 addressed to the wicked.

The second major component of Isa 66:1–24 is vv. 5–24. As noted above, this pericope is introduced by the call to attention which calls the audience to hear the report of the following speech by YHWH. Again, the speeches are formulated in first person singular form, and they employ second person masculine forms to address the righteous. The text includes two basic components, each of which begins with a statement by the prophet that introduces the speeches by YHWH. Verses 1–14 report YHWH's announcements concerning the birth of a new world order centered at Zion. Verses 5–6 announce the upcoming shame of the wicked and vv. 7–14 employ the imagery of childbirth to announce the creation of the new world order and call for the rejoicing of the righteous. The second basic component in vv. 15–24 begins with the introductory connective *kî*, "for," which ties this text to vv. 5–14. It begins with the prophet's statements concerning the coming of YHWH in vv. 15–16, and continues with a report of a series of YHWH's speeches in vv. 17–24, including individual speeches identified by their respective oracular or speech formulas in vv. 17, 18–20, 21, 22, and 23. Within these speeches, vv. 17–20 employ third person objective language to describe the punishment of the wicked, and vv. 21–24 employ second person masculine forms to address the righteous. Verse 22 ties the passage into the overall framework of Isaiah 65–66. It refers to the continuing "seed" that will stand before YHWH (cf. 65:9); and it refers to the continuing "name" of the righteous (cf. 65:15).

The structure of Isaiah 65–66 may be represented as follows:

Report of YHWH's Response to the Community: YHWH will Act to Requite the Evil and to Reward the Righteous in a New Creation Centered at Zion	65:1–66:24
I. Report of YHWH's announcement that YHWH will requite evil (prophetic judgment speech pattern)	65:1–7
A. YHWH was ready, but people did not call (grounds for punishment)	65:1–5
B. YHWH will requite evil (announcement of Punishment)	65:6–7
II. Report of YHWH's address to the wicked: the seed of Jacob will be restored in new creation on Zion, but the wicked will be punished	65:8–25
A. statement of principle that not all will be destroyed, only the wicked	65:8–12
1. concerning preservation of seed from Jacob	65:8–10
2. concerning slaughter of wicked	65:11–12

B. announcement of punishment for the wicked and restoration of the righteous	65:13–25
1. concerning punishment of the wicked	65:13–15a
2. concerning restoration of the righteous	65:15b–25
III. Report of YHWH's address to the righteous: announcement of restoration	66:1–24
A. statement that the humble who tremble at YHWH's word will be restored and the wicked punished	66:1–4
1. concerning restoration of the humble who tremble at YHWH's word	66:1–2
2. concerning punishment of the wicked	66:3–4
B. announcement of restoration in the new creation at Zion	66:5–24
1. concerning the birth of the new world at Zion	66:5–14
a. humiliation of the wicked	66:5–6
b. the birth of the new world at Zion	66:7–14
2. concerning YHWH's coming to create the new world at Zion	66:15–24

Altogether, the structure of Isaiah 65–66 demonstrates that its purpose is to announce the creation of a new world order centered at Zion, to define the character of those who will be a part of the new world order, and to exhort the audience to join in the new creation. After stating the principle that YHWH will come to punish the wicked in Isa 65:1–7, it addresses both the wicked in Isa 65:8–25 and the righteous in Isa 66:1–24 in an effort to convince the audience to become part of the "see" from Jacob that will "possess" YHWH's holy mountain (65:9).

III

In order to clarify the function of Isaiah 65–66 as the conclusion to the book of Isaiah as a whole, it is necessary to examine its references to other texts and motifs from throughout the book. As noted above, scholars have already identified an interrelationship between Isaiah 65–66 and various texts in Proto- Deutero- and Trito-Isaiah. The following discussion extends these observations to include Isaiah 2–4; 6; 11; 13; 37:30–32; and others. The pattern of citations seems to focus on several major issues, including the distinction between the righteous and the wicked among the people; the pilgrimage of the nations to Zion in order to return the exiled people of Israel and Judah; the imagery of the three in relation to the new growth of the "seed"; YHWH's readiness to accept the people in contrast to the people's unwillingness to accept YHWH and YHWH's sovereignty. Overall, the citations indicate a major interest in reading the book of Isaiah in order to point to the rebirth of the "seed" of Israel in a new creation centered at Zion. Furthermore, the nature of the citations changes within the text of Isaiah 65–66. Isaiah 65 makes brief scattered allusions to various Isaianic texts, whereas Isa 66:5–24 tends to develop a series of texts and motifs at length.

This has implications for understanding the composition and hermeneutics of the passage.

The interrelationship between Isaiah 1 and Isaiah 65–66 is well-documented. In general, Isaiah 1 points to the rebellious nature of the people who reject YHWH (vv. 2–9); the abuse of cultic sacrifice without sufficient attention to acts of justice (vv. 10–17); the need to purify the people from their sins (vv. 18–20); the need to purify Jerusalem by removing the corrupt elements among the people in its midst (vv. 21–26); the distinction among the people between the righteous who will be redeemed and the wicked who will be destroyed (vv. 27–28); and the use of imagery pertaining to withered trees and gardens to portray the destruction and shame of the wicked (vv. 29–31). Isaiah 65–66 likewise points to the distinction between the righteous and the wicked among the people (65:8–12; 66:1–4); the presence of cultic abuse, which serves as a major indicator for wrongdoing among the people (65:1–7; 66:3–4, 17); the need to preserve the righteous seed of the people that will posses Jerusalem in the future and the need to destroy the wicked among them (65:8–25; 66:18–24); the use of tree and garden imagery to illustrate the pruning process that must take place (65:8–25).

These thematic connections are reinforced by a number of lexical associations. The reference to the people's abandonment of YHWH in Isa 65:11, *'ōzĕbê yhwh*, "those who abandon YHWH," echoes the language of Isa 1:4, *'āzĕbû 'et yhwh*, "they have abandoned YHWH," and 1:28, *wĕ'ōzĕbê yhwh yiklû*, "and those who abandon YHWH will perish." The reference to the rebellious nature of the people in Isa 65:2, *'am sôrēr*, "rebellious people," takes up language from 1:4, *'am kebed 'āwōn*, "a people heavy with sin," and 1:5, *tôsîpû sārâ*, "they continue rebellion." The statements in Isa 65:12 and 66:4 that the people have chosen to act in a manner that YHWH does not want, *ûba' ăšer lō'-ḥāpaṣtî bĕḥartem/bāḥārû*, "and in what I did not delight you have chosen/they have chosen." The references in Isa 65:3 to the people sacrificing in the gardens, *zōbĕḥîm baggannôt*, "sacrificing in the gardens," and in 66:17 to their sanctifying themselves in the gardens, *hammitqaddĕšîm wĕhammiṭṭahărîm 'el-haggannôt*, "those who sanctify themselves and purify themselves unto the gardens," combine the language of sacrifice in Isa 1:11, *lāmmâ-lî rōb-zibḥêhem*, "why multiply to me your sacrifices?" with the reference in 1:29 to cultic apostasy in the gardens, *wĕtaḥpĕrû mēhaggannôt*, "and you were embarrassed by the gardens." The reference to the shame of the apostates appears again in Isa 1:29, *kî yēbōšû mē'êlîm*, "for they will be ashamed from the oaks," and in Isa 66:5, *wĕhem yēbōšû*, "and they will be ashamed," and in 65:13, *wĕ'attem tēbōšû*, "and you will be ashamed." The reference in Isa 66:17 to the destruction of the apostates together, *yaḥdāyw yāsupû*, "together they will be brought to an end," corresponds to the statements that the wicked will be destroyed together in 1:28, *wĕšeber pōšĕ'îm wĕḥaṭṭā'îm yaḥdāyw*, "and the breaking of the rebellious and sinners together," and 1:31, *ûbā'ărû šĕnêhem yaḥdāyw*, "and the two of them shall burn together." Likewise, the statement in Isa 66:24 that the fire that consumes the rebels will not be quenched, *wĕʾiššēm lōʾ tikbeh*, "and their fire will not be quenched," takes up the language of Isa 1:31, *wĕʾên mĕkabbeh*, "and there is no quenching." The passage also contains elements of reversal. In contrast to the reference in Isa 1:15 to people who spread their hands to YHWH in unwanted sacrifice, *ûbĕpāriśkem kappêkem*, "and when you spread your hands," Isa 65:2 indicates that YHWH's hands were spread to the people all along, *pēraśtî yāday kol hayyôm*, "I spread my hands all day." In contrast to the reference in Isa 1:15 that YHWH would be unwilling to hear unwanted prayer, *gam kî-tarbû tĕpillâ ʾênēnnî šōmēʿa*, "indeed, when you multiply prayer, there is no one listening," Isa 65:24 indicates that YHWH will listen when the people call, *waʾănî ʾešmāʿ*, "and I will listen."

Although these correspondences demonstrate the interrelationship between Isaiah 1 and 65–66, they do not explain all of the intertextual allusions between First Isaiah and Isaiah 65–66. For example, Isa 1:4 refers to the rebellious people as *zerʿa mĕrēʿîm*, "rebellious seed," whereas Isa 65:9 refers to the "seed" that YHWH will bring out from Jacob, *wĕhôṣēʾtî miyyaʿăqōb zeraʿ*, "and I will bring out from Jacob a seed." The association between these verses has little meaning unless it is considered in relation to Isa 6:13, which draws upon the imagery of a burnt tree to speak of the emergence of the "holy seed" (*zeraʿ qōdeš*) that will emerge from its stump to constitute the remnant of Israel. This likewise informs the reference in Isa 65:22 that the days of YHWH's people will be like the days of a tree, *kîmê hāʿēṣ yĕmê ʿammî*, "for the days of the tree are like the days of My people," which expresses the longevity of the restored people. It also aids in establishing the analogy between YHWH's statement of readiness in Isa 65:1 to accept the people, *ʾāmartî hinnēnî hinnēnî*, "I said, 'here I am, here I am,'" and the statement by the prophet in Isa 6:8 that he was prepared to accept YHWH's call, *wāʾōmar hinĕnî šĕlāḥēnî*, "and I said, 'here I am, send me.'"

The interrelationship between Isaiah 6 and Isaiah 65–66 likewise points to other textual associations. For example, YHWH's reference to the desolation of the land in Isa 6:11, *ʿārîm mēʾên yôšēb ûbātîm mēʾên ʾādām*, "cities without inhabitant and houses without a person," appears to stand behind the statement in Isa 65:21–22, *ûbānû bātîm wĕyāšābû wĕnāṭĕʿû kĕrāmîm wĕʾākĕlû piryām lōʾ yibnû wĕʾaḥēr yēšēb lōʾ yiṭṭĕʿû wĕʾaḥēr yōʾkēl*, "and they shall build houses and dwell in them and they shall plant vineyards and eat their fruit, they shall not build and another inhabit, they shall not plant and another eat." The fact that this statement appears immediately prior to the above mentioned analogy between the days of the tree and the days of the restored people aids in establishing the association. But the language and imagery of Isa 65:21–22 also presupposes that of Isa 5:1–7, which contains the vineyard allegory, and that of vv. 8–10, which contain the first of the woe oracles. Isa 5:1–7 points to YHWH's destruction of the "vineyard" (*kerem*) which produced poor fruit, and Isa 5:8–10 condemns those who appropriate the houses of the poor so that "surely many houses will be left desolate, great and good without inhabitant" (*'im-lō' bātîm rabbîm lĕšammâ yihyû gĕdōlîm wĕṭôbîm mē'ên yôšēb*). The reference to "the work of their hands" (*ûmaʿăśēh yĕdêhem*) in Isa 65:22 likewise takes up a phrase that appears in Isa 5:12 (*ûmaʿăśēh yādāyw*, "and the work of his hands") and elsewhere throughout the book (cf. 2:8; 17:8; 19:25; 29:23; 37:19; 60:21; 64:7).

The relationship between the "tree" and "seed" imagery of Isaiah 6 and 65–66 likewise points to other texts that play a role in Isaiah 65–66. For example, scholars have long noted that Isa 65:25 contains a condensed version of the paradisial imagery of Isa 11:6–9, in which the "wolf" (*zĕ'ēb*) and "lamb" (*ṭāleh*) will graze together, the "lion" (*'aryēh*) and "cattle" (*bāqār*) will eat chaff, and the serpent (*nāḥāš*) will be included with all of the others on YHWH's holy mountain. In fact, two statements from both passages are identical, *wĕ'aryēh kabāqār yō'kal-teben*, "and the lion shall eat chaff like cattle," and *lō'-yārē'û wĕlō'-yašḥîtû bĕkol-har qodšî*, "and no one will harm them and no one will destroy them in all of My holy mountain." The term *har qodšî*, "My holy mountain," is sufficiently important in Isaiah 65–66 that it appears in Isa 65:11 and 66:20 in reference respectively to "those who have abandoned YHWH, forgetting my holy mountain," and to the return of the exiles "upon my holy mountain Jerusalem." Many have supposed that this phrase refers back to Isa 56:7 and 57:13, which employ similar language and express similar concepts, but the association with other texts in Trito-Isaiah masks the role that Isaiah 11 plays in Isaiah 65–66. Like Isaiah 6, Isaiah 11 employs tree imagery to express the potential regrowth of the people after they have been cut down. Thus, Isa 11:1 states that "a new shoot shall go forth from the stump of Jesse and a shoot shall sprout from his roots." Not only does this new growth lead to the idyllic picture of the animals grazing together in Isa 11:6–9, it also leads to the scenario in 11:10–16 in which the nations will return the exiles of Israel to the land. This, of course, is a major motif of Isa 66:18–24, which portrays the nations bringing the exiled people of Israel back to Zion. The passage must be read in relation to other texts that express the same motif, such as Isa 2:2–4 and 60–62, but scholars often overlook the association with Isa 37:30–32, which conveys Isaiah's sign that Jerusalem will be saved from Sennacherib. Isa 37:30–32 calls for the remnant of the people to "take root below and make fruit above," in comparison to the new root of Jesse mentioned in Isa 11:1. But the sign also calls for the people to plant new vineyards in the third year after the siege: *wĕnāṭĕʿû kĕrāmîm wĕ'ākĕlû piryām*,[15] "and they shall plant vineyards and eat their fruit," which corresponds precisely to Isa 65:21. The preceding command to "sow seed and harvest" (*zirʿû wĕqiṣrû*) likewise aids in establishing the relationship of this text with the reference to "seed" in Isa 6:13 and 65:9.

---

[15] Read with *qere*; see BHS.

This survey of textual and motific references shows an extensive relationship between Isaiah 1; 5; 6; 11; and 37 with Isaiah 65–66. But with the exception of minor references to "my holy mountain" in Isa 66:20, to the impossibility of quenching the fire that burns the wicked in 66:24, and to the apostasy of the wicked in the gardens in 66:17, the bulk of the references pertain to Isa 65:1–66:4, but not to Isa 66:5–24. Nevertheless, Isa 66:5–24 also makes extensive reference to earlier Isaianic texts, but it does so in a manner different from Isa 65:1–66:4 in that it tends to develop motifs at length rather than simply to cite or to allude to an earlier textual tradition. Furthermore, in citing earlier texts and motifs, it builds on statements from Isa 65:1–66:4.

This is evident first of all in Isa 66:7–9. The passage describes the birth of a new land and nation, and Zion's giving birth to new sons. The characteristic language of this passage includes the verbs *ḥwl*, "to be in labor" (vv. 7, 8) and *yld*, "to give birth" (vv. 7, 8 [2x], 9 [2x]) and the noun *ḥbl*, "labor pain" (v. 7). A recent study by Katheryn Darr treats the motif of birthing in the book of Isaiah, particularly as it relates to the present passage.[16] She points to birthing imagery as a motif that appears throughout the book of Isaiah, noting especially the role of Hezekiah's proverb in Isa 37:3, "babes are positioned for birth, but there is no strength to deliver." In the context of the narrative concerning Sennacherib's siege of Jerusalem, the proverb signifies the imperilment of Jerusalem which is ultimately delivered by YHWH after Hezekiah turns to YHWH in the Temple. Darr also notes the appearance of this motif in Isa 26:17–18, in which the distressed people appeal to YHWH to deliver them by describing themselves in analogy to a woman in childbirth who brings forth nothing. Because they are unable to deliver themselves, they appeal to YHWH. The passage continues with a reference to the resurrection of the dead in v. 19 and to YHWH's approach to punish the wicked, who have brought about the distress of the people. She likewise notes the use of the imagery in Isa 66:7–9, but concludes that it is impossible to know whether the author of Isa 66:7–9 wrote with Isa 37:3 specifically in mind. Nevertheless, it is clear that Isa 66:7–9 takes up a major motif that is developed throughout the book of Isaiah. Isaiah 3:25–4:1, for example, portrays the defeated Jerusalem as a mother whose sons have all been killed around her. Isaiah 7:1–9:6 portrays the birth of Isaiah's sons as important signs concerning YHWH's deliverance of the city of Jerusalem. Isaiah 13 portrays the downfall of Babylon to YHWH's holy warriors as a symbol for the birth of a new world. Especially noteworthy is Isa 13:8 which descries the agony of the city's defenders with imagery of childbirth: "and they are dismayed, pangs and labor pains seize them, like a birthing woman they give birth." Likewise, Isa 13:5 employs a word play on the verb *ḥbl* to portray YHWH destruction of the land: "YHWH

---

[16] Katheryn Pfisterer Darr, *Isaiah's Vision and the Family of G-d* (Louisville: Westminster John Knox, 1994) 205–25, esp. 221–4.

and the weapons of his wrath (come) to destroy/give labor pain to (*lĕḥabēl*) all the earth." Finally, Isaiah 54 portrays Zion as a barren mother whose children will now be gathered around her as a means to announce the restoration of Jerusalem that YHWH is bringing about. It would seem that Isa 66:7–9 draws upon these themes in its own portrayal of the restoration of Zion. In this regard, it seems to have a precursor in Isa 65:23, "They will not labor in vain, and they will not give birth for disaster, because they are seed blessed of YHWH, and their offspring are with them." Here it is noteworthy that Isa 65:23 combines the imagery of childbirth as a metaphor for the restoration of Zion with that of the seed from Isa 6:13; 37:30–32; and 65:9.

The second example is Isa 66:10–14. This section extends the metaphor of childbirth from Isa 66:7–9 by portraying the redeemed people as the babies of mother Jerusalem who suck at her breast. This imagery appears in v. 11, "in order that you may suck and be sated from her consoling breast, in order that you may suck and be delighted from the fullness of her glory," and vv. 12aβb–13abα, "and you will suck, upon the hip you will be carried, and upon the knees you will be played with, like a man whose mother comforts him, I will comfort you." But Isa 66:10–14 also shifts its intertextual references from the childbirth imagery that appears in Isaiah 13 and other texts to the imagery of rejoicing and flowing water that appears in Isa 8:6–8. Although the commands to rejoice in Isa 66:10 draw upon the language and imagery of Isa 35:1–2,[17] the phrase *śîśāh ʾittâ māśôś*, "rejoice with her in exultation," draws explicitly on Isa 8:6 in that it is the only other instance in the Hebrew Bible in which the verb *śwś* and the noun *māśôś* are employed together with the particle *ʾet*, "with." Isa 8:6 reads, *ûmāśôś ʾet-rĕṣîn ûben-rĕmalyāhû*, "and exultation with the son of Rezin and the son of Remaliah." Furthermore, Isa 66:10–14 draws on other vocabulary from Isa 8:6–8 in order to present the image of YHWH's glory restored to Jerusalem.[18] Thus, Isa 66:12aβ reads *hinĕnî nōṭeh-ʾēlêhā kĕnāhār šālôm ûkĕnaḥal šôṭēp kĕbôd gôyim*, "behold, I am extending unto her peace like a river and the glory of the nations like an overflowing stream." This draws especially on the language and imagery of Assyrian conquest as a flood that "overflows and passes by" (*šāṭap wĕʿābar*), and it presents the Assyrian king as one who "extends his wings/skirts" to fill the land. As the present writer demonstrates elsewhere, the portrayal of overflowing waters and the "spreading of his wings/skirts"[19] in Isa

---

[17] Compare Isa 66:10, *śimḥû ʾet-yĕrûšālayim wĕgîlû bāh kol-ʾōhăbeyhā śîśû ʾittāh māśôś kol-hammitʾabĕlîm ʿāleyhā*, "rejoice with Jerusalem and be glad for her all who love her, rejoice with her (in) rejoicing all who were mourning over her," with Isa 35:1aα, *yĕśuśûm midbār wĕṣiyâ wĕtāgēl ʿărābâ wĕtipraḥ kaḥăbaṣṣālet pārōaḥ tipraḥ wĕtāgēl ʾap gîlat wĕranēn*, "Let the wilderness and desert rejoice and the Arabah will be glad and will blossom! Like a crocus it will indeed blossom and be glad, indeed, rejoicing and merriment."

[18] See Sweeney, "On *ûmĕśôś*," esp. 48–52.

[19] Note that *muṭṭôt*, "spreading," is derived from the same verb root, *nṭh*, "extending," in Isa 66:12.

8:7b–8 conveys the imagery of sexual intercourse – or more precisely rape.[20] Although it employs the vocabulary and imagery of Isa 8:6–8, Isa 66:10–14 reverses the imagery of rape by the Assyrian monarch to the imagery of YHWH as the father who brings about the new birth in Jerusalem and thereby provides the cause for rejoicing. Furthermore, it appears to build upon the statement Isa 65:18–19a, "Indeed, rejoice and be glad (*śîśû wĕgîlû*) forever (over) what I am creating, for behold, I am creating for Jerusalem gladness (*gîlâ*) and for her people exultation (*māśôś*), and I will be glad (*wĕgaltî*) with Jerusalem and I shall rejoice (*wĕśaśtî*) with her people."

The final example is Isa 66:15–24. Scholars have noted that this passages seems to draw upon the pilgrimage imagery of Isaiah 60–62 and other texts from Deutero- and Trito-Isaiah, but texts from First Isaiah appear to play the constitutive role. As noted above, the portrayal in v. 17 of illicit worship in the gardens draws upon Isa 1:29–31. The imagery in vv. 15–16 of YHWH's coming in fire to judge the apostates draws upon the imagery of the burning gardens/tree of Isa 1:29–31 as well. The passage also depends upon Isa 5:28 insofar as its imagery of the approach of YHWH's chariots "like a whirlwind" (*kĕsûpâ*) corresponds to the imagery and language of Isa 5:28, "their horses hooves are like flint, and his wheels like the whirlwind (*kĕsûpâ*)." But the "flowing river" imagery of Isa 66:10–14 appears to be operative here as well in that it establishes a connection between the portrayal of the pilgrimage of the nations to Zion in Isa 66:18–24 and a similar portrayal in Isa 2:2–4. In portraying the imagery of the nations' pilgrimage to Zion, Isa 2:2b employs the language of flowing waters, "and all the nations shall flow (*wĕnāhărû*) unto it." The verb "flow" (*wĕnāhărû*) is based on the same root as river (*nāhār*) in Isa 66:12, "peace like a river (*kĕnāhār šālôm*)." Many scholars see Isa 66:18–24 as a prophecy that the nations will come to Zion and that YHWH will choose priests and Levites from them (see esp. vv. 20–21), but as Schramm's recent analysis of this passage demonstrates, the passage refers to YHWH's choosing priests and Levities from the exiled Israelite who are returned by the nations to Zion.[21] This is completely consistent with the perspective of Isa 2:2–4 in the context of Isaiah 2–4 as a whole; Isa 2:5 invites Jacob to become a part of the procession, and Isa 2:6–22 portrays YHWH's destruction of evil in the land. The ultimate result is a cleansed Jerusalem in which the

---

[20] See Sweeney, "On *ûmĕśôś*," esp. 50–2.

[21] Schramm, *The Opponents of Third Isaiah* 172–3. Schramm notes that the grammatical antecedent for *mēhem*, "from them," in v. 21 can refer either to the "fugitives" from the nations in v. 19 or to "your brothers" from Israel in v. 20. He states that most commentators chose the former based on the conviction that the passage promotes the role of Gentiles as worshippers of YHWH. Nevertheless, the statement must be read in the literary context of Isaiah 65–66 so that "your seed and your name shall stand" in v. 22 refers to the establishment of the seed and name of the righteous among Israel and Judah (cf. 65:8–9, 15b–16).

remnant of Israel will be established in Jerusalem (4:2–6).²² The reference to the establishment of "your seed and your name" in v. 22 indicates that the passage draws upon Isa 65:8–9, which portrays YHWH's intentions to preserve a "seed" from Jacob (and Judah) to possess the holy mountain, and Isa 65:15b–16, which indicates that YHWH's servants will have another name.

IV

Isaiah 65–66 serves as the conclusion for the book of Isaiah. The concluding position of these chapters at the end of the book of Isaiah, their literary character as an announcement of YHWH's judgment of the wicked and restoration of the righteous, and their interrelationship with texts throughout First Isaiah, all demonstrate that Isaiah 65–66 serve not only as the conclusion to Trito-Isaiah or Deutero-Isaiah, but as the conclusion for the book of Isaiah as a whole. In this regard, it is noteworthy that the initial address to the heavens and earth in Isa 1:2–31 becomes the basis for the announcement in Isaiah 65–66 that YHWH will create a new heavens and earth. Overall, Isaiah 65–66 point to the purging of Zion that dominates the presentation of the book of Isaiah, and indicates that the righteous who hold fast to YHWH will stand at the center of the new creation whereas the wicked will perish.²³

It is doubtful that these chapters were composed in their entirety for such a role however. As the above discussion demonstrates, the structure of the passage points to a composite text in which Isa 65:1–66:4 may have stood as an earlier text that was expanded by the addition of Isa 66:5–24. Isaiah 65:1–7 takes up concern with the wicked, and Isa 65:8–25 addresses the wicked to announce to them that they will perish. Insofar as Isa 66:1–4 addresses an unidentified audience, rehearses the formulation of Isa 65:12, and rehearses the theme of cultic propriety with which the unit begins, it appears to be original to Isa 65:1–25. Isaiah 66:5–24 is clearly later, in that its primary concern is with the fate of the righteous, a concern that does not appear in 65:1–7. It is addressed to the righteous in marked contrast to Isa 65:1–66:4, and the nature of its textual references to the book of Isaiah differs markedly from the references in Isa 65:1–66:4. Furthermore, Isa 66:5–24 builds upon statements from Isa 65:1–25 in developing its own intertextual hermeneutics. Altogether, it appears to be an expansion of Isa 65:1–25 designed to exhort the righteous to become part of YHWH's plans for the future of Jerusalem. Insofar as Isa 66:1–2 questions the building of the

---

²² For a full discussion of this material, see Sweeney, *Isaiah 1–4* 134–84; idem, *Isaiah 1–39* ad loc.

²³ For a full discussion of this perspective, see Sweeney, *Isaiah 1–4* 96–9; idem, *Isaiah 1–39*, ad loc, on the introduction to the book of Isaiah.

Temple, it would appear that Isa 65:1–66:4, with the questions it raises about proper cultic action, belongs to the late sixth century when the Second Temple was built. Insofar as Isa 66:5–24 points to instability and conflict in the eastern Mediterranean, especially in the area of Greece, the Greek islands, Asia Minor, and other territories within the general orbit of Greece, it would appear that Isa 66:5–24 stems from some point later in the 5th century when the Persian empire was severely challenged in these regions.[24] Further evidence of composition in the fifth century appears in the address to the *ḥārēdîm*, "those who tremble," at YHWH's word (66:5; cf. 66:2). As Blenkinsopp indicates, this corresponds to the self-designation of the community under Ezra (cf. Ezra 9:3; 10:4).[25] As the present writer argues elsewhere, this is one element that dates the final form of the book of Isaiah to the late-fifth century in the period of Ezra's reforms.[26]

Finally, this study points to the literary character of prophecy in Isaiah 65–66. As Lau notes, the literary forms employed in these chapters are those of oral prophetic announcement, but the references to earlier parts of the book of Isaiah as scripture demonstrates that this material is a form of literary prophecy.[27] Such literary activity is consistent with the practice of prophecy and divination throughout the ancient Near East, in that the prophet or diviner was expected to be competent in writing in order to formulate and compose his oracles and to examine past texts in order to come to conclusion about the present.[28] It is also consistent with the various references to recording and reading prophecy in the book of Isaiah,[29] indicating that the authors of Isaiah 65–66 worked in full consciousness of the commands to read the book of Isaiah in order to determine YHWH's plans, "Seek and read from the book of YHWH: Not one of these shall be missing; none shall be without its mate, for the mouth of YHWH has commanded, and his spirit has gathered them. He has cast the lot for them, his hand has portioned it out to them with the line; they shall possess it forever, from

---

[24] For a convenient summary of Persian reverses in the Mediterranean during the 5th century B.C.E., see P. Briant, "Persian Empire," *ABD* 5:236–44, esp. 240–2. On the identification of Tarshish, Pul (=Put; cf. LXX), Lud, Moshke Qeshet, Tubal, Greece, and the islands, see Bonnard, *Le Second Isaïe* 492.

[25] Joseph Blenkinsopp, *Ezra-Nehemiah: A Commentary* (OTL; Philadelphia: Westminster, 1988) 178–9.

[26] Sweeney, *Isaiah 1–39* ad loc.

[27] Lau, *Schriftgelehrte Prophetie* 1–21, esp. 12–14.

[28] See now Frederick H. Cryer, *Divination in Ancient Israel and its Near Eastern Environment: A Socio-Historical Investigation* (JSOTSup 142; Sheffield: Sheffield Academic Press, 1994), who argues that ancient divination is a form of empirical science in which the practitioner must be trained in specific skills, including writing.

[29] See Isa 8:1–4, 16–18; 29:11–12; 30:8; 34:16–17. The references to recording Isaiah's prophecies and the commands to read it indicate the basis on which inner biblical exegesis within the book of Isaiah would proceed. For treatment of this issue, see Sweeney, *Isaiah 1–39* ad loc; H. G. M. Williamson, *The Book Called Isaiah: Deutero-Isaiah's Role in its Composition and Redaction* (Oxford: Clarendon, 1994) 94–115.

generation to generation they shall dwell in it" (34:16–17). It would appear that in following this command, the authors of Isaiah 65–66, and many who preceded them, treated the earlier Isaianic writings as a source of revelation that stood as the basis of the creation of new prophecy in the final form of the book.[30]

---

[30] For a full treatment of inner-biblical interpretation, see Michael Fishbane, *Biblical Interpretation in Ancient Israel* (Oxford: Clarendon, 1985) esp. 443–524, which treats the "mantological exegesis" of dreams, visions, oracles, etc.

Part 2: Jeremiah

5. The Masoretic and Septuagint Versions of the Book of Jeremiah in Synchronic and Diachronic Perspective

I

The study of the book of Jeremiah is both complicated and enhanced by the existence of two distinct and yet interrelated versions of the book in the Masoretic Hebrew and Septuagint Greek traditions.[1] Although both versions contain much of the same material, the Masoretic text (MT) is about one eighth longer than the Septuagint text (LXX). Many scholars maintain that the MT appears to be an expanded version of the Hebrew *Vorlage* underlying the Greek LXX, although some evidence in the texts suggests the possibility that both texts have undergone extensive editing since the times of their respective origins. The earliest complete manuscripts of the LXX text are Codex Vaticanus and Codex Sinaiti-

---

[1] For introductory discussion of the MT and LXX versions of the book of Jeremiah (as well as the Qumran manuscripts and other versions), see Robert P. Carroll, *Jeremiah* (OT Guides; Sheffield: JSOT Press, 1989) 21–30; William L. Holladay, *Jeremiah* (Hermeneia; Minneapolis: Fortress, 1989) 2:2–10; Jack R. Lundbom, "Jeremiah, Book of," *ABD* 3:706–21, esp. 707–9; idem, *Jeremiah 1–20* (AB 21A; New York: Doubleday, 1999) 57–63; William McKane, *Jeremiah* (ICC; Edinburgh: T & T Clark, 1986) 1:xv–xli; Marvin A. Sweeney, "Jeremiah," *Eerdmans Dictionary of the Bible* (ed. D. N. Freedman et al.; Grand Rapids and Cambridge: Eerdmans, 2000) 686–9. For more detailed discussion, see P.-M. Bogaert, "De Baruch à Jérémie. Les deux redactions conserves du livre de Jérémie," *Le Livre de Jérémie. Le prophète et son milieu. Les oracles et leur transmission* (BETL 54; Leuven: Peeters; Leuven University Press, 1981) 168–73; Yohanan Goldman, *Prophétie et royauté au retour de l'exil. Les origines littéraires de la forme massorétique du livre de Jérémie* (OBO 118; Freiburg: Universitätsverlag; Göttingen: Vandenhoeck & Ruprecht, 1992; J. Gerald Janzen, *Studies in the Text of Jeremiah* (HSM 6; Cambridge: Harvard University Press, 1973; Andrew G. Shead, *The Open and the Sealed Book. Jeremiah 32 in its Hebrew and Greek Recensions* (JSOTSup 347; London: Sheffield Academic Press, 2002); Hermann-Josef Stipp, *Das masoretische und alexandrinische Sondergut des Jeremiabuches. Textgeschichtlicher Rang, Eigenarten, Triebkräfte* (OBO 136; Freiburg: Universitätsverlag; Göttingen: Vandenhoeck & Ruprecht, 1994); Emanuel Tov, "Some Aspects of the Textual and Literary History of the Book of Jeremiah," *Le Livre de Jérémie* 145–67; idem, *The Septuagint Translation of Jeremiah and Baruch: A Discussion of an Early Revision of the LXX of Jeremiah 29–52 and Baruch 1:1–3:8* (HSM 8; Missoula: Scholars Press, 1976); Shirley Lal Wijesinghe, *Jeremiah 34,8–22. Structure and Redactional History of the Masoretic Text and of the Septuagint Hebrew Vorlage* (Colombo, Sri Lanka: Centre for Society and Religion, 1999); Bernard N. Zlotowitz, *The Septuagint Translation of the Hebrew Terms in Relation to G-d in the Book of Jeremiah* (New York: KTAV, 1981).

cus, both of which are early Christian manuscripts that date to the fourth century C.E. Most scholars maintain that the shorter LXX version of the text must be the earlier version of the text that was composed in the Jewish community of Egypt, sometime during the third or second century B.C.E., although the underlying Hebrew *Vorlage* likely dates to a much earlier time in the Second Temple period. Interpreters generally maintain that the earliest Masoretic manuscripts, such as the Leningrad Codex of the Bible (1009 C.E.), the Aleppo Codex of the Bible (925 C.E.), and the Cairo Codex of the Prophets (896 C.E.), presuppose a version of the book produced in the Jewish community of Babylonia at some point during the Second Temple period. [2]

Examples of both versions of the text have been discovered among the four fragmentary Jeremiah manuscripts found by the Dead Sea at Qumran Caves 4 and 2.[3] The oldest Qumran manuscript is 4QJer^a, which dates to 225–175 B.C.E., and includes Jer 7:1–2, 15–19; 7:28–9:2 (minus 7:30–8:8); 9:7–15; 10:9–23; 11:3–20; 12:3–16; 12:17–13:7; 13:27–14:8; 15:1–2; 17:8–26; 18:15–19:1; 20:15–18; 22:3–16; and 26:10. This manuscript corresponds to the MT, although it contains many corrections. 4QJer^{bde} dates to the mid-second century B.C.E., and it includes Jer 9:22–10:18; 43:3–9; and 50:4–6. The text of the first fragment corresponds to the shorter text of the LXX version of this passage, which indicates that 4QJer^b represents the Hebrew *Vorlage* that underlies the LXX text. Although the three fragments were originally identified as a single manuscript, they are now considered as three separate manuscripts. 4QJer^c dates to the Herodian era (30–1 B.C.E.), and it contains a proto-MT version of Jer 4:5, 13–16; 8:1–3; 8:20–9:5; 10:12–13; 19:8–9; 20:2–5, 7–8, 14–15; 21:6–10; 22:4–6, 10–28; 25:7–8, 15–17, 24–26; 26:10–13; 27:1–3, 14–15; 30:6–31:14; 31:16–26; and 33:16–20. Finally, 2QJer dates to the first century C.E., and contains a proto-MT version (with some variations) of Jer 42:7–11, 14; 43:8–11; 44:1–3, 12–14; 46:27–47:7; 48:7, 25–39, 43–45; and 49:10.

Interpreters have long noted these differences in their analyses of the respective forms of the LXX and MT forms of the book of Jeremiah. In considering the significance of these materials, however, early research tended to focus on the question of establishing the earliest form of the text. Although early work tended to presuppose a relatively mechanical process of textual transmission, interpreters have increasingly come to appreciate the roles of translation technique in shaping

---

[2] See esp. Tov, "Some Aspects"; Janzen, *Studies*; Goldman, *Prophétie*; Stipp, *Sondergut*; Shead, *Open Book*.

[3] For discussion of the Qumran evidence, see Janzen, *Studies*; George J. Brooke, "The Book of Jeremiah and its Reception in the Qumran Scrolls," *The Book of Jeremiah and its Reception* (ed. A. H. W. Curtis and T. Römer; BETL 128; Leuven: Peeters and Leuven University Press, 1997) 183–205. The text of Jeremiah from Qumran Cave 2 appear in M. Baillet, J. T. Milik, and R. de Vaux, *Les 'Petites Grottes' de Qumran* (DJD 3; Oxford: Clarendon, 1962) 62–69, and the texts of Jeremiah from Qumran Cave 4 appear in Eugene Ulrich et al, *Qumran Cave 4.X: The Prophets* (DJD 15; Oxford: Clarendon, 1997) 145–207.

the Greek text, the role that redactional expansion and reinterpretation play in shaping both the Masoretic and the Septuagint versions of the text, and the essential role of textual reading and hermeneutics that must be presupposed in both the translation of the Greek text and the redactional reworking of both editions.

In the case of the former, the rendition of the text into Greek frequently takes account of both aesthetic factors and hermeneutical perspective. We can no longer presuppose that every Greek phrase, syntactical construction, or choice of individual lexemes can be mechanically retroverted to establish the purported Hebrew *Vorlage* of the Greek text. Instead, interpreters must attempt to reconstruct the hermeneutical perspectives that inform the current reading and translation of the Greek text.

Much the same might be said of the redaction-critical process that must stand behind the two distinctive and yet interrelated forms of the book. Despite the wide consensus that the LXX form of the text likely represents an earlier edition that the MT, there is also widespread agreement that both versions of Jeremiah have undergone extensive editing, reworking, and even expansion beyond the projected original forms of their respective Hebrew *Vorlagen*. In the course of their analyses of each form of the text, interpreters have also noted that distinctive readings in each text appear to reflect distinctive hermeneutical perspectives or agendas that point in turn to efforts to read and interpret the underlying Hebrew *Vorlagen*.

Such work demonstrates that each form of the book of Jeremiah, or at least individual pericopes within each form of the book, is not simply the result of a relatively mechanical process of textual transmission. Instead, such readings demonstrate that each form of the text also presupposes a process of textual reading and reflection upon the underlying *Vorlage* that plays an important role in shaping and transmitting the present form of each respective version of the book.

And yet such work has tended to proceed for the most part at the level of individual pericopes or blocks of text within the larger structure of each form of the book. This is striking, given the major differences in form that we have already observed in each edition of the book and the increasingly important role that assessments of the overall structures of prophetic books play in interpretation of prophetic literature. Recent studies of works such as Isaiah, Ezekiel, and the Book of the Twelve – both in relation to the Book of the Twelve as a whole and in relation to the individual books that comprise the book of the Twelve – demonstrate that each prophetic book has been shaped to convey a particular perspective based upon a particular understanding of the material contained within.[4] Indeed, consideration of the clearly different forms of the Book of the

---

[4] For discussion see Marvin A. Sweeney, *Isaiah 1–39, with an Introduction to Prophetic Literature* (FOTL 16; Grand Rapids and Cambridge, 1996); idem, "Ezekiel: Zadokite Priest and Visionary Prophet of the Exile," *OPIAC* 41 (2001); idem, "Sequence and Interpretation in

Twelve in the MT and LXX traditions indicates that we cannot presuppose a single agenda behind both forms of the book.[5] Rather, each is shaped by a different set of concerns that must be identified by the interpreter. Insofar as Jeremiah appears in two very different forms in the MT and LXX editions of the book, interpreters are obligated to consider the hermeneutical significance of each of these forms as well.

II

Apart from the expanded form of the MT, both versions are substantially the same through Jeremiah 25:13a, but they differ markedly after this point. The MT form of Jeremiah includes the largely oracular material in chapters 1–25; the largely narrative material about the prophet in chapters 26–45; the oracles concerning the nations in chapters 46–51; and the historical narrative concerning the Babylonian siege and destruction of Jerusalem, which appears to be drawn from 2 Kings 25, in Jeremiah 52. The LXX version, however, begins with Jeremiah's oracular material in LXXJer 1:1–25:13a, and continues with the oracles concerning the nations in LXXJer 25:14–31:14 (=MTJer 46–51); the narrative materials concerning the prophet in LXXJer 32–51 (=MTJer 25:13b–45:5); and it concludes once again with the narrative concerning the fall of Jerusalem in LXXJer 52 (=MTJer 52). For the most part, scholars have been unable to determine the significance of the differences in this arrangement.[6] Some have argued that the LXX structure represents a common tripartite pattern in the organization of prophetic books which announce judgment against Israel, judgment against the nations, and restoration for both Israel and the nations.[7] But such a pattern is not well represented in the prophetic books, and it appears to be a pattern derived in part from the concerns of Christian systematic theology that are imposed upon the reading of the prophetic books with insufficient justification. Of course, the

---

the Book of the Twelve," *Reading and Hearing the Book of the Twelve* (ed. J. D. Nogalski and M. A. Sweeney; SBLSym 15; Atlanta: Society of Biblical Literature, 2000) 49–64; cf. Erich Bosshard-Nepustil, *Rezeptionen von Jesaja 1–39 im Zwölfprophetenbuch. Untersuchungen zur literarischen Verbindung von Prophetenbüchern in babylonischer und persischer Zeit* (OBO 154; Freiburg: Universitätsverlag; Göttingen: Vandenhoeck & Ruprecht, 1997).

[5] See esp. Sweeney, "Sequence and Interpretation."

[6] For discussion of the significance of the structure of the book of Jeremiah, see esp. Holladay, *Jeremiah* 2:10–24; Lundbom, *Jeremiah 1–20* 68–102. For a detailed overview of critical discussion of Jeremiah, see Siegfried Herrmann, *Jeremia. Der Prophet und das Buch* (Erträge der Forschung 271; Darmstadt: Wissenschaftliche Buchgesellschaft, 1990) 38–181.

[7] E. g., Otto Kaiser, *Introduction to the Old Testament: A Presentation of its Results and Problems* (Minneapolis: Augsburg, 1975) 239 (cf. his remarks on Isaiah 1–39, p. 223; Zephaniah, p. 230; and Ezekiel, p. 250); cf. my critical discussion of the alleged tripartite pattern in Zephaniah, "A Form-Critical Reassessment of the Book of Zephaniah," *CBQ* 53 (1991) 388–408.

proposed tripartite pattern does little to explain the structure of the Masoretic version of Jeremiah.

We must note that past attempts to explain the structure of both versions of the book of Jeremiah have been unsuccessful because they employ diachronic criteria, which are better suited to explaining the history of the literary growth of the text than its final literary structure. Because both the LXX and MT versions of the book begin with a very similar structure in chapters 1–25, most interpreters presuppose that they represent the first major unit within the literary structure of the book.[8] And yet such a view overlooks the role of the most fundamental markers of literary structure within both versions of the book, i. e., the superscriptions that appear throughout the book to introduce and characterize the individual blocks of material that comprise both versions of the book of Jeremiah. The book of Jeremiah begins with the superscription in Jer 1:1–3, which identifies the contents of the book as "the words of Jeremiah ben Hilkiah ..." It is noteworthy that a standard version of this formula, "the word that came to Jeremiah from YHWH," and slight variations appear at the beginning of textual sub-units in Jer 7:1; 11:1; 14:1; 18:1; 21:1; 25:1; 30:1; 32:1; 34:1; 34:8; 35:1; 40:1; 44:1; 45:1; 46:1; 46:13; 47:1; 50:1; and 51:59 in the MT version of the book. In addition, a number of examples of this formula begin with the conjunction, "and," which indicates that they introduce sections that are subsumed structurally into the preceding material. The result is a general statement of the superscription of the book as "the words of Jeremiah" in Jer 1:1 followed by a succession of individual words given by YHWH to the prophet throughout the balance of the book. The narrative concerning the fall of Jerusalem in Jeremiah 52 lacks such a formula, however, and therefore stands outside this structure as a concluding appendix. A similar phenomenon may be observed in the LXX form of the book, which likewise begins with the phrase, "the word of G-d, which came to Jeremiah the son of Hilkiah," in LXXJer 1:1, and continues with individual examples in LXXJer 1:4; 1:11; 11:1; 14:1; 18:1; 21:1; 25:1; 25:1; 37:1; 39:1; 41:1; 41:8; 42:1; 47:1; 50:8; 51:5. Again, the narrative in LXXJeremiah 52 concerning the fall of Jerusalem stands outside of this structure as an appendix.

The sequence of superscriptions cuts through the major blocks of material, including the oracles concerning Judah and Israel in MTJeremiah 1–25, the narratives in MTJeremiah 26–45, and the oracles concerning the nations in MTJeremiah 46–51. They likewise cut through the oracles concerning Israel and Judah in LXXJeremiah 1–25 and the narratives in LXXJeremiah 37–51, but the oracles concerning the nations in LXXJeremiah 25–36 appear together with the

---

[8] For a recent attempt to examine the literary structure of MTJeremiah that self-consciously attempts to avoid the pitfalls of classic, diachronic literary analysis, see Louis Stuhlman, *Order Amid Chaos: Jeremiah as Symbolic Tapestry* (BibSem 57; Sheffield: Sheffield Academic Press, 1998). Despite his attempt, however, his discussion of literary structure in Jeremiah remains heavily influenced by diachronic considerations.

narratives concerning Jeremiah's warnings to submit to Babylon (=MTJeremiah 26–29) as a single block of text within the structure of the book. Both versions present a sequence of events in the prophet's career, but the differences in the respective sequences indicate a substantive difference in the overall historical and theological perspective of each.

The structure of LXXJeremiah indicates an interest in presenting YHWH's plans for Israel/Judah and the nations, followed by a depiction of the consequences for Jerusalem for failing to abide by YHWH's will. The LXX sequence includes oracles that call upon Israel and Judah to observe YHWH's will in chapters 1–25 and a block of oracles that announce YHWH's judgment against the nations together with Jeremiah's warnings to submit to Babylon in LXXJeremiah 26–36. The following sequence in LXXJeremiah 37–51; 52 then presents a scenario for future restoration followed by a sequence of sub-units that recount Jerusalem's destruction and its aftermath. Such a structure indicates a retrospective perspective for the book, insofar as it is designed to explain the destruction of Jerusalem as a consequence of the people's failure to heed the prophet's warnings. The structure of LXXJeremiah appears as follows:

The Words of Jeremiah Son of Hilkiah
Concerning YHWH's Judgment against Jerusalem

I.	Superscription	1:1–3
II.	Call of the Prophet	1:4–10
III.	Oracles concerning Israel and Judah	1:11–10:25
IV.	Oracles concerning the rejection of YHWH's covenant	11:1–13:27
V.	Oracles concerning drought and marriage	14:1–17:27
VI.	Oracles concerning shattered pottery/judgment agst Judah	18:1–20:18
VII.	Oracles concerning Davidic kingship	21:1–24:13
VIII.	Oracles concerning the nations	25:1–36:32
IX.	Oracles concerning the future restoration of Jerusalem	37:1–38:40
X.	Narrative concerning the field at Anathoth	39:1–40:13
XI.	Narrative concerning YHWH's decision to deliver Jerusalem to Nebuchadnezzar	41:1–7
XII.	Narrative concerning reneging on the year of release	41:8–22
XIII.	Narrative concerning Babylonian siege of Jerusalem	42:1–46:18
XIV.	Narrative concerning aftermath of destruction	47:1–50:7
XV.	Narrative concerning Jeremiah in Egypt	50:8–13
XVI.	Narrative concerning Jeremiah's word to Baruch	51:1–5
XVII.	Appendix concerning destruction of Jerusalem	52:1–34

The structure of the Masoretic version of Jeremiah demonstrates a different concern. It, too, begins with a sequence in MTJeremiah 1–25 in which the prophet warns Israel and Judah to abide by YHWH's will, and it presents the consequences for the people's failure to do so together with a portrayal of future restoration in the narrative sequence of MTJeremiah 26–45. The placement of the individual oracles concerning the nations in MTJeremiah 46–51, in which the oracle concerning Babylon concludes the sequence, points to a concern to demonstrate the future realization of YHWH's plans to bring about the downfall of the nations, culminating in Babylon. Such a structure indicates a prospective, hopeful interest in the book, insofar as it is designed to point to the rise of the Persian empire as the agent of YHWH's restoration for Jerusalem and punishment against Babylon and the nations that oppressed Judah. The structure of the Masoretic version of Jeremiah appears as follows:

The Words of Jeremiah Ben Hilkiah
Concerning the Restoration of Jerusalem and the Downfall of Babylon

I.	Oracles concerning Israel and Judah	1:1–6:30
	A. Superscription	1:1–3
	B. Commissioning of the prophet	1:4–10
	C. Signs concerning YHWH's purpose	1:11–19
	D. Oracles calling for Israel and Judah to return to YHWH	2:1–6:30
II.	Account concerning Jeremiah's Temple sermon	7:1–10:25
III.	Oracles concerning rejection of YHWH's covenant	11:1–13:27
IV.	Oracles concerning drought and marriage	14:1–17:27
	A. Drought	14:1–15:21
	B. Marriage	16:1–17:27
V.	Oracles concerning shattered pot/judgment against Judah	18:1–20:18
VI.	Oracles concerning Davidic kingship	21:1–24:10
VII.	Narratives concerning Jeremiah's warnings to submit to Babylon	25:1–29:32
VIII.	Oracles concerning restoration of Israel and Judah	30:1–31:40
IX.	Narrative concerning field at Anathoth	32:1–33:26
X.	Narrative concerning YHWH's decision to give Jerusalem to Nebuchadnezzar	34:1–7
XI.	Narrative concerning reneging on year of release	34:8–22
XII.	Narrative concerning fall of Jerusalem	35:1–39:18
XIII.	Narrative concerning Jeremiah's removal to Egypt	40:1–43:13
XIV.	Narrative concerning Jeremiah's oracles in Egypt	44:1–30
XV.	Narrative concerning word to Baruch	45:1–5
XVI.	Oracle concerning Egypt	46:1–12
XVII.	Oracle concerning Babylonian conquest of Egypt	46:13–28
XVIII.	Oracle concerning small nations	47:1–49:39
XIX.	Oracle concerning Babylon	50:1–51:58
XX.	Narrative conc. Jeremiah's instructions about Babylon	51:59–64
XXI.	Appendix concerning fall of Jerusalem	52:1–34

The synchronic analysis of the respective forms of both versions of the book points to their distinctive theological perspectives. Both are concerned with the issue of theodicy because both attempt to argue that the destruction of Jerusalem was caused by the failure of the people to observe YHWH's Torah. Both also point to future restoration in which YHWH's Torah will be inscribed upon the hearts of the people. But the retrospective perspective of the LXX form of the book places greater weight on explaining the destruction of Jerusalem as an act of YHWH as part of a more general pattern of divine punishment for the nations. The LXX version likewise gives greater emphasis to comparing Jerusalem's fate to that of the northern kingdom of Israel (see esp. LXXJeremiah 2–6; 11; 37–38[=MTJeremiah 30–31]),[9] and the inclusion of only one royal oracle together with the prophet's diatribe against false prophets (LXXJeremiah 23) indicates that it places less emphasis on the restoration of Davidic kingship.[10] Such concerns would be typical of those of the early Persian period in which books such as Isaiah and Ezra-Nehemiah would call for the restoration of Judah under the authority of the Persian empire.[11] The Masoretic version of Jeremiah, however, places much more emphasis on the downfall of the nations, particularly Babylon, after the destruction of Jerusalem is complete.[12] It also places far greater emphasis on the restoration of righteous Davidic kingship by including a second oracle concerning the restoration of the Davidic king that is not qualified by its proximity to a concern with false prophecy (Jeremiah 33).[13] Indeed, it appears together with the narrative concerning Jeremiah's attempt to redeem land in Anathoth (Jeremiah 32), and it follows upon Jeremiah's oracles of restoration (Jeremiah 30–31). Such a perspective has far more in common with the Book of the Twelve Prophets, which frequently challenges Isaiah's notions of submission to the nations by positing the downfall of the oppressor and the rise of a new Davidic king.[14] Such sentiments were known in the Persian period (see Haggai), but did not achieve their realization until the rise of the Hasmonean state in the second century B.C.E. (see Daniel).

---

[9] Both Jeremiah 2–6 and 30–31 appear to reflect earlier texts concerned with the punishment and restoration of the northern kingdom of Israel that were reworked to account for Judah as well. See my studies, "Structure and Redaction in Jeremiah 2–6," *Troubling Jeremiah* (ed. A. R. Diamond et al; JSOTSup 260; Sheffield: Sheffield Academic Press, 1999) 200–18; idem, "Jeremiah 30–31 and King Josiah's Program of National Restoration and Religious Reform," *ZAW* 108 (1996) 569–83.

[10] For discussion of the significance of the royal oracles in both the MT and LXX versions of Jeremiah, see Goldman, *Prophétie*.

[11] Note that the present form of the book of Isaiah names the Persian monarch Cyrus as YHWH's messiah and temple builder in Isa 44:28; 45:1. For consideration of the conceptualization of Cyrus in the formation of Isaiah, see Reinhard Gregor Kratz, *Kyros im Deuterojesaja-Buch* (FAT 1; Tübingen: Mohr Siebeck 1991), although Kratz limits his treatment to the Deutero-Isaiah tradition, the conceptualization of Cyrus has implications for understanding the book of Isaiah as a whole. Ezra-Nehemiah portrays the restoration of Jerusalem and Judah under the authority of Nehemiah the governor and Ezra the priest, two Persian-appointed officers.

[12] See now, John Hill, *Friend or Foe? The Figure of Babylon in the Book of Jeremiah MT* (BibInt 40; Leiden: Brill, 1999).

[13] Goldman, *Prophétie*.

[14] See my studies, "Micah's Debate with Isaiah," *JSOT* 93 (2001) 111–24; "Zechariah's Debate with Isaiah," *The Changing Face of Form-Criticism for the Twenty-First Century* (ed, M. A. Sweeney and E. Ben Zvi; Grand Rapids and Cambridge: Eerdmans, 2003) 335–50.

III

Consideration of the synchronic or final forms of the Masoretic and Septuagint editions of the book of Jeremiah also has important implications for the diachronic interpretation of this material. It is axiomatic that interpretation must first account for the final form of a biblical work – or in this case, the two final forms of the book of Jeremiah – before taking up the diachronic questions of the socio-historical setting and the compositional history of the work in question.[15] We have already had a hint of such diachronic possibilities in the assertions above that the concerns with the destruction of northern Israel and the restoration of exiles evident in the purportedly earlier Septuagint form of the book seem to reflect concerns expressed in the books of Isaiah and Ezra-Nehemiah during the Persian period for understanding the restoration of Judea under Persian rule. Likewise, concerns with the downfall of Babylon and the rise of a Davidic monarch evident in the purportedly later Masoretic form of the book seem to reflect concerns expressed in the Book of the Twelve Prophets during the Persian period or in the book of Daniel during the Hasmonean period with the downfall of the oppressor and the restoration of righteous Judean rule. Of course, there is much more to do – both with demonstrating these assertions and in carrying a diachronic interpretative agenda well beyond these basic claims. Due to the lack of space, we will simply lay out some possibilities that arise from the preceding consideration of Jeremiah's two final forms.

In a climate dominated by concerns for establishing which of the two forms of the book of Jeremiah represents the earliest form of the Jeremian tradition – and therefore which form of the book best represents the words of the prophet himself and perhaps of his earliest tradents (Baruch ben Neriah?) – interpreters tended to note that the supposed tripartite form of LXXJeremiah, which included punishment against Israel/Judah/Jerusalem (LXXJeremiah 1–24); punishment against the nations (LXXJeremiah 25–36=MTJeremiah 25; 46–51; 26–29); and restoration for Israel/Jerusalem and the nations (LXXJeremiah 37–51=MTJeremiah 30–45), corresponded to the tripartite pattern that allegedly informed the ideal structure of prophetic books in general, such as Isaiah 1–39; Ezekiel; and Zephaniah.[16] Subsequent research reveals that this alleged pattern hardly exists in the prophetic books. Detailed analysis of each example demonstrates that the pattern represents a far too simplified reading of the prophetic books in which it

---

[15] For discussion of the need to consider the final redactional form of the text prior to any attempt at diachronic reconstruction of textual history, see Rolf Knierim, "Criticism of Literary Features, Form, Tradition, and Redaction," *Reading the Hebrew Bible for a New Millennium: Form, Concept, and Theological Perspective* (ed. W. Kim et al; SAC; Harrisburg: Trinity International, 2000) 2:42–71.

[16] Kaiser, *Introduction* 239, 302–5; cf. Georg Fohrer, "Die Struktur der alttestamentlichen Eschatologie," *Studien zur alttestamentlichen Prophetie (1949–1965)* (BZAW 99; Berlin: Alfred Töpelmann, 1967) 32–58.

allegedly appears and that the pattern itself owes more to the concerns of later Christian systematic theology than it does to patterns that actually exist in the prophets.

Nevertheless, the parallel with Isaiah 1–39 is an especially interesting point of comparison, especially since intertextual study of Isaiah and Jeremiah demonstrates that so many pericopes in the book of Jeremiah appear to draw upon, cite, allude to, and argue with elements of the Isaian tradition.[17] Other misconceptions of the past discussion must also be cleared away. Isaiah 1–39 can hardly be viewed as a self-standing prophetic book to which the works of Second and Third Isaiah are mechanically joined. Isaiah 1–39 is itself heavily influenced by exilic and post-exilic redactional reworking that appears to have taken place in conjunction with the literary and hermeneutical process that saw the combination of the work of First, Second, and Third Isaiah.[18] Indeed, a pre-exilic form of the work of First Isaiah appears to have been produced during the reign of King Josiah of Judah, in which the earlier oracles of Isaiah ben Amoz were read in relation to the program of religious reform and national restoration led by King Josiah during the latter half of the seventh century B.C.E.[19] Given Jeremiah's alleged prophetic activity from the thirteenth year of Josiah's reign (Jer 1:1–3) and the many citations of Isaian texts and traditions in Jeremiah, especially in texts that many scholars maintain represent some of Jeremiah's earliest oracles, it becomes necessary to consider the relationship between Isaiah and Jeremiah as an important interpretative question in assessing the books of Jeremiah.

My own earlier work has already identified a number of key intertextual relationships between Jeremiah and Isaiah.[20] Jeremiah's famed Temple sermon in Jeremiah 7 rejects the Isaian notion, based in the Davidic/Zion covenant tradition expressed in Isaiah 7; 36–37; and elsewhere, that YHWH will defend unconditionally Jerusalem, the Davidic monarchy, and the Jerusalem Temple. Jeremiah's letter to the exiles in Jeremiah 29 builds upon the Isaian remnant tradition that will represent the seed of a restored Israel/Jerusalem in Isa 6:12–13; 7:1–9; 10:20–26; and elsewhere. Jeremiah's depiction of a future righteous Davidic monarch in Jer 23:1–8 draws upon the Isaian oracle in Isa 11:1–16. Jeremiah's description of the approach of an enemy come to destroy Judah echoes Isaiah's

---

[17] See Ute Wendel, *Jesaja und Jeremia. Worte, Motive und Einsichten Jesajas in der Verkündigung Jeremias* (Biblisch-Theologische Studien 25; Neukirchen-Vluyn: Neukirchener, 1995); Marvin A. Sweeney, "The Truth in True and False Prophecy," *Truth: Interdisciplinary Dialogues in a Pluralist Age* (ed. C. Helmer and K. De Troyer; Studies in Philosophical Theology 22; Leuven: Peeters, 2003) 9–26.

[18] For full discussion, see my *Isaiah 1–39*.

[19] In addition to my *Isaiah 1–39*, see esp. Hermann Barth, *Die Jesaja-Worte in der Josiazeit* (WMANT 48; Neukirchen-Vluyn: Neukirchener, 1977); Jacques Vermeylen, *Du prophète d'Isaïe à l'apocalyptique* (EB; Paris: Gabalda, 1977–78); Ronald E. Clements, *Isaiah 1–39* (NCeB; Grand Rapids: Eerdmans, London: Marshall, Morgan, and Scott, 1980).

[20] See Sweeney, "Truth."

earlier oracle concerning the approach of the Assyrian army in Isa 5:26–29. Jeremiah's concern with false prophecy in the depiction of his encounter with the prophet Hananiah, whose message of Babylon's impending fall echoes Isaiah, demonstrates Jeremiah's contention that Isaiah's promises of unconditional deliverance of Jerusalem constitute a form of false prophecy. And there are many others as well. Overall, Jeremiah shows a consistent engagement with the Isaian tradition, which was apparently read as an announcement of the end of the period of Assyrian oppression and the restoration of a righteous Davidic monarchy over all Israel. But whereas Isaiah announced the downfall of northern Israel and looked forward to the rise of Jerusalem/Judah in the aftermath of that punishment, Jeremiah contended that the period of Jerusalem's and Judah's punishment had not yet come to an end. Jerusalem and Judah would suffer destruction and exile much like northern Israel if they did not observe YHWH's will, and restoration would take place only after the experience of a lengthy exile.

It is with this in mind that we must consider the interrelationship between the forms of Isaiah 1–39 (or at least the Josianic form of the tradition in Isaiah 5–12; 14–23; 28–32; 36–37) and LXXJeremiah. Isaiah 1–12 (or 5–12 in the reconstructed Josianic text) presents a scenario of judgment for Jerusalem, Judah, and Israel; the downfall of the Assyrian oppressor; and restoration for Jerusalem in the aftermath of the punishment. Isaiah 13–27 (or 14–23 in the reconstructed Josianic text) presents a scenario of punishment against the foreign nations, including Jerusalem. Isaiah 28–33 (or 28–32 in the Josianic edition) focus especially on Jerusalem's punishment and restoration in contrast to the more general focus on Israel, Jerusalem, and Judah in the first part of the book. Finally, Isaiah 36–39 (or 36–37 in the Josianic edition) relates YHWH's deliverance of Jerusalem from the Assyrian threat.

LXXJeremiah displays a somewhat parallel set of concerns. Jeremiah 1–24 portrays the punishment of Jerusalem and Judah on the model of the experience of the northern kingdom of Israel. Unlike Isaiah 1–12, however, Jeremiah 1–24 provides far less emphasis on the possibility of restoration. LXXJeremiah 25–36 (=MT Jeremiah 25; 46–51; 26–29) emphasizes the punishment of the nations as in Isaiah 13–27, although it also emphasizes Jerusalem's and Judah's exile to Babylon. LXXJeremiah 37–51 (=MTJeremiah 30–45) raises the hope of the restoration of Israel and Judah to Jerusalem prior to recounting the fall of Jerusalem to the Babylonians. LXXJeremiah 52 (=MTJeremiah 52) concludes the book with an account of the exile of Jerusalem, which contrasts markedly with the deliverance of Jerusalem in Isaiah 36–37/39.

Such a parallel – and the contrasts that are highlighted during the course of the parallel presentation – hardly seems to be accidental. LXXJeremiah follows the lead of Isaiah 1–39, but whereas Isaiah 1–39 is presented to anticipate YHWH's restoration of Jerusalem at the center of a restored Israel and the nations, LXXJeremiah contends that Jerusalem will suffer punishment along with the nations – and it leaves the question of restoration to a very distant future. Indeed, LXXJeremiah appears designed to prepare its readers to accept a long period of exile as the will of YHWH. The notion of restoration is included, but it receives only minimal attention when compared to Isaiah. Such a portrayal of divine will in Jeremiah well suits the picture in Ezra-Nehemiah, viz., the exile took place because the ancestors sinned, and it is up to the present generation to heed YHWH's – and Jeremiah's! – call for observance of divine Torah to ensure that punishment will not be suffered once again.

The Masoretic form of Jeremiah clearly builds upon the shorter LXX form of Jeremiah, and like LXXJeremiah it too draws upon the Isaian tradition. But unlike the LXX form of the book, the overarching motific structure of MTJeremiah indicates that the redactors of the book drew more heavily on the Isaian scenario of restoration than did those of LXXJeremiah.[21] By placing the oracles concerning the nations at the end of the book and portraying the downfall of Babylon as the culmination of both the oracles concerning the nations and the book as a whole, MTJeremiah provides a very different reading of the Jeremian tradition that displays a much greater interest in the question of Babylon's downfall – and thus with Judah's restoration – in the aftermath of the Babylonian exile. MTJeremiah 1–45 provides an extended account of Jerusalem's punishment, with brief glimpses in Jeremiah 25 of the downfall of the nations and in Jeremiah 30–31 of the restoration of Israel. The addition of a second oracle concerning the restoration of the Davidic monarchy – albeit under the control of the Levitical priests – provides even greater emphasis on the motif of Jerusalem's and Israel's restoration following the exile. The oracles concerning the nations, culminating in the downfall of Babylon, then constitute YHWH's final judgment against the nations that carried out the punishment of Jerusalem and Judah.

When considered in diachronic perspective, we should not be surprised that the Jeremian tradition wrestles with the question of Jerusalem's and Judah's punishment and restoration as expressed in the book of Isaiah. Indeed, several blocks of material, including Jeremiah 2–6; 11; 23:1–8; 30–31, with their emphasis on Israel's restoration to Jerusalem and righteous Davidic rule, suggest that Jeremiah may once have supported Josiah's program of religious reform and national restoration early in his prophetic career.[22] But Josiah's early death at Megiddo in 609 B.C.E., the subsequent failure of Josiah's reform, and the ensuing collapse of Judah, forced the prophet to rethink the optimism of his

---

[21] See also J. Edward Wright, *Baruch ben Neriah: From Biblical Scribe to Apocalyptic Seer* (Studies on Personalities of the Old Testament; Columbia: University of South Carolina, 2003) 26–39, who notes that the placement of Jeremiah 45, which portrays Jeremiah's entrusting his prophetic word to Baruch, after the oracles against the nations and prior to the destruction of Jerusalem in LXXJeremiah gives greater emphasis than does MTJeremiah in presenting Baruch as a prophetic figure in his own right who succeeds Jeremiah.

[22] See Marvin A. Sweeney, *King Josiah of Judah: The Lost Messiah of Israel* (Oxford and New York: Oxford University Press, 2001) 208–33.

early years under Josiah and to accept the reality that Jerusalem and Judah would suffer greatly – as Israel had suffered a century earlier – before any restoration such as that posited by Josiah would ever take place.

Our two extant forms of the book of Jeremiah reflect the continued grappling by the prophet's tradents with these questions and with the Isaian tradition as they sought to make sense of the Jeremian tradition in relation to the later experience of the Persian and Hellenistic periods.

IV

Overall, this study points to the importance of two crucial factors in reading the books of Jeremiah. First, is the importance of assessing the final, synchronic literary form of both the MT and LXX versions of the book of Jeremiah as a means to understand the perspectives and concerns of the later tradents of the Jeremian tradition who produced the *Vorlagen* of our present texts. Such work serves as the necessary prelude to diachronic analysis of the setting in which each version was produced, the function each might serve, and the respective compositional history of each text. Second, is the importance of the inter-textual dimensions of the books of Jeremiah and other biblical works, most notably the book of Isaiah. Although the books of Jeremiah were very clearly related to other works of biblical literature as well, its citations of and allusions to the Isaian tradition demonstrates that Jeremiah – both as prophet and as book – was in close conversation with the work of the prophet Isaiah in articulating a new understanding of divine purpose and earlier prophetic tradition in relation to the circumstances and needs of a much later period.

6. The Truth in True and False Prophecy

I

The epistemological question of truth must lie, explicitly or implicitly, at the very core of any attempt to engage in theological interpretation of the Bible. By its very nature, biblical theology must presuppose that the notion of G-d be accepted as an absolute truth, although the criteria by which to define G-d as such are lacking. This is deliberate – at least in the Hebrew Bible – insofar as the Bible forbids attempts to define or delimit G-d as expressed in the fundamental prohibitions against the making of idols to represent G-d (Exod 20:4–6; Lev 19:4; Deut 5:8–10) or the uttering of G-d's holy name (see Lev 24:10–16; cf. Exod 20:7; 22:27; Lev 19:12; Deut 5:11). The wisdom of such a prohibition should be clear, insofar as physical or audial representations of G-d necessarily limit the conceptualization of G-d and renders G-d as something less than the absolute, eternal, infinite, omnipotent, and omniscient author of all creation.

The Bible therefore does not attempt to prove the existence of G-d strictly speaking, i.e., it does not seriously entertain the possibility that G-d does not exist. Rather, it asserts the existence of G-d by portraying creation and events that take place therein as acts of G-d. Because G-d is beyond definition in the Bible, it cannot present G-d as an absolute truth other than by the statement, "I am what I am," as indicated in the etymology of the divine name offered in Exodus 3:14. Otherwise, the Bible is left to present G-d as a contingent truth, insofar as it asserts that worldly phenomena and events must metaphorically represent divine action and intent.[1]

Although all of the books of the Bible represent G-d to some extent or other, interpreters generally understand the prophets or the prophetic books as those that most fully represent human apprehension of the divine. After all, it is Moses, the Levite and prophet, who serves as G-d's agent for the revelation of Torah at

---

[1] This is true even if relation to books such as Esther or the Song of Songs, which never mention G-d (with the possible exception of ʾēš šalhebetyâ in Song 8:6. The expression means literally, "a fire which blazes [of/like] YH," but refers basically to "a blazing fire." For discussion, see, Roland Murphy, *Song of* Songs [Hermeneia; Minneapolis: Fortress, 1990] 191–2. Because they function as part of a larger biblical canon or canons that represent Israel's or Judah's testimony to the reality of G-d, they function as exceptions to the rule, i.e., they are understood to provide insight into the nature and actions of G-d even when G-d appears to be absent or uninvolved.

Sinai; prophets such as Elijah the Tishbite, Micaiah ben Imlah, Isaiah ben Amoz, Jeremiah ben Hilkiah, Ezekiel ben Buzi, and others, who reportedly experience visions of or from G-d, and certainly all of the other prophets presuppose some direct experience of the divine. Consequently, later interpreters or theologians look to prophetic experience as the epitome of human apprehension of the divine. The 12th–13th century Spanish-Egyptian philosopher and halakhic scholar, Moses ben Maimon, for example, states, "Prophecy is, in truth and reality, an emanation sent forth by the Divine Being through the medium of the Active Intellect, in the first instance to man's rational faculty, and then to his imaginative faculty; it is the highest degree and the greatest perfection that man can attain; it consists in the most perfect development of the imaginative faculty."[2]

And yet, both the Bible and Maimonides are well aware of the problem of false prophecy, whether by those who employ the standard prophetic linguistic formulae to claim prophetic authority (Deut 18:9–22; 1 Kgs 13:11–32; Jer 23:9–40; 29:15–23) or by those to whom YHWH actually does communicate a false message (1 Kgs 22:1–38; Ezek 14:9). Primary examples of false prophets appear in the narratives concerning the deception of an unnamed prophet from Judah by the old prophet from Beth El (1 Kgs 13:11–32); Micaiah ben Imlah's contention that YHWH had deliberately lied to Zedekiah ben Canaanah concerning King Ahab's upcoming battle with the Arameans (1 Kgs 22:1–38); and Jeremiah's confrontation with Hananiah ben Azzur, who claimed that YHWH would deliver Jerusalem from Babylon (Jeremiah 27–28). Indeed, Deut 18:9–22 provides criteria by which to determine whether or not prophecy is false, i.e., if the prophet speaks a word from YHWH that does not come true, then it is false prophecy.

Of course, interpreters well recognize that such a criterion can not serve as an absolute standard by which to judge prophecy; it may conceivably take years or even many millennia for a prophecy to be realized. Deuteronomy thereby provides a criterion by which prophecy is considered to be true, i.e., it comes to pass, but it does not provide a demonstrable criterion by which prophecy is considered to be false. The ultimate outcome of this situation is that the Bible does not in fact provide criteria for the recognition of unrealized prophecy as true or false other than the contention that a prophetic word is indeed given by YHWH. YHWH's indefineability therefore renders such a criterion both absolute and meaningless, i.e., of course a prophecy is true if YHWH gives it (and does not lie in doing so), but how can one possibly prove such a claim? Micaiah ben Imlah and Jeremiah both argue that the true prophet receives the prophetic

---

[2] Guide for the Perplexed 2:36. Cited from M. Friedländer, translator, *The Guide for the Perplexed, by Moses Maimonides* (2nd edition; London: Routledge and Kegan Paul, 1951) 225. For an introductory discussion of Maimonides' views on prophecy in the Bible, see David Bakan, *Maimonides on Prophecy: A Commentary on Selected Chapters of the Guide of the Perplexed* (Northvale, NJ, and London: Jason Aronson, 1991).

word while standing in the presence or council of YHWH (1 Kgs 22:17-23; Jer 23:18-22), but like claims for the existence of YHWH, such a contention cannot be demonstrated by absolute standards of empirical observation. The validity of such a claim is then contingent upon the willingness of the prophet's audience to accept it.

Most interpreters therefore focus upon the question of defining criteria for the identification of false prophecy, but they are necessarily limited to those whose prophecies are demonstrably incapable of fulfillment, such as Hananiah's claim that Jerusalem would be delivered from Babylon in two years' time.[3] As a result, the Septuagint in LXXJer 35:1 can label him as *ho pseudoprophētēs*, "the false prophet," although the Masoretic text in MTJer 28:1 nonjudgmentally refers to him simply as *hannābî'*, "the prophet." It is noteworthy then that, when considered in relation to such standards, the canonical books of the prophets cannot be considered as fully true. Insofar as many of their prophecies have not been realized, the prophetic books of Isaiah, Jeremiah, Ezekiel, and the Twelve Prophets (and in Christian Bibles, Daniel), constitute a combination of true and potentially false prophecy.

This presents a very serious problem. One might attempt to argue that the unfulfilled promises of the prophetic books were indeed fulfilled through the return of Jews to the land of Israel, the restoration of Jerusalem and the Temple, and the relative peace and cooperation of the Persian empire representing the nations, but this is only partial fulfillment at best. Indeed, the later experiences of destruction and exile at the hands of the Roman empire indicate that the whole process can repeat itself, albeit in a different time with a different set of historical characters, so that restoration might be anticipated once again in a cycle of suffering and redemption. In all cases, interpreters must dehistoricize the prophetic books to accept them as true by identifying the Assyrians with the Babylonians, the Romans, the Arabs, the Christians, the Nazis, etc., but this leads to wild and irresponsible claims concerning divine action in the world that potentially do far more harm than good, insofar as the prophetic books then

---

[3] For discussion of the issue of true and false prophecy in the Bible, see esp. Martin Buber, "False Prophets (Jeremiah 28) in Nahum N. Glatzer, ed., *On the Bible:* Eighteen Studies (New York: Schocken, 1982) 166-71; James Crenshaw, "Prophecy, False," *IDB[S]* 701-2; idem, *Prophetic Conflict* (BZAW 124; Berlin: Walter de Gruyter, 1971); F. L. Hossfeld and I. Meyer, *Prophet gegen Prophet* (BibB 9; Freiburg: Schweizerisches Katholisches Bibelwerk, 1973); Armin Lange, *Vom prophetischen Wort zur prophetischen Tradition. Studien zur Traditions- und Redaktionsgeschichtliche innerprophetischer Konflikte in der Hebräischen* Bible (FAT 34; Tübingen: Mohr Siebeck, 2002); Ivo Meyer, *Jeremia und die falschen Propheten* (OBO 13; Freiburg: Universitätsverlag; Göttingen: Vandenhoeck & Ruprecht, 1977); E. Osswald, *Falsche Prophetie im Alten* Testament (Tübingen: Mohr Siebeck, 1962); Thomas W. Overholt, *The Threat of Falsehood: A Study in the Theology of the Book of Jeremiah* (SBT 2/16; Naperville, IL: Alec Allenson, 1970); G. Quell, *Wahre und falsche Propheten* (Gütersloh: Bertelmann, 1952); James A. Sanders, "Hermeneutics in True and False Prophecy," in George W. Coats and Burke O. Long, eds., *Canon and Authority* (Philadelphia: Fortress, 1977) 21-41.

become weapons employed by those who irresponsibly claim identification with the divine. Otherwise, interpreters are left to look to some sort of an eschatological fulfillment beyond the current course of historical events. The results are the same: the prophetic books may be regarded only partially as true. Alternatively expressed, this means that the prophetic books must be regarded potentially as false prophecy. Having proposed that canonical prophets may be considered as potentially false, I would like to address three issues: 1) disagreement among the canonical prophets and the potential charge of falsehood; 2) Jeremiah's disagreement with Isaiah; and 3) Jeremiah's reading of Isaian tradition as examples of the contingent nature of truth in prophetic tradition.

II

Although clearly provocative, the contention that the prophetic books are potentially false should come as no surprise. We have already seen examples of prophetic conflict, but each case involves a prophet whose prophecy is demonstrably false, i.e., 1 Kgs 13:18 states bluntly that the old prophet from Beth El was lying; Micaiah ben Imlah cites a visionary experience to claim that YHWH lied to Zedekiah ben Canaanah in 1 Kgs 22:1–38; Hananiah's prophecy that Jerusalem would be freed from the Babylonian threat in two years fails to materialize.

Insofar as these cases evoke prophetic response, it seems possible that other cases of unfulfilled – or potentially unfulfilled – prophecy would also elicit prophetic response and even conflict. This is especially the case as interpreters are coming increasingly to reject the notion of a single or monolithic prophetic message or theological standpoint and to appreciate the differences among them, i.e., Isaiah's prophecy is heavily informed by the royalist ideology of the centrality of Jerusalem and the house of David; Jeremiah is a Levitical priest whose oracles are informed by his role as a deuteronomistically-oriented teacher of Mosaic Torah; Ezekiel is a Zadokite priest, whose oracles are informed by a keen sense of the Jerusalem Temple as the holy center of all creation, etc.[4] With such divergent social and theological standpoints, it is inevitable that these canonically-recognized prophets, or their tradents, will disagree. One sees such disagreement, for example, in Jeremiah's contentions that the Jerusalem

---

[4] See esp. Gerhard von Rad, *Old Testament Theology. Volume II: The Theology of Israel's Prophetic Traditions* (translated by D. M. G. Stalker; New York: Harper and Row, 1965), who points to the unit of prophetic tradition but also to its diversity insofar as the perspectives of the individual prophets were rooted in distinctive sets of tradition within Israel. See now, Marvin A. Sweeney, "The Latter Prophets (Isaiah, Jeremiah, Ezekiel)," *The Hebrew Bible Today: An Introduction to Critical Issues* (ed. S. L. McKenzie and M. P. Graham; Louisville: Westminster John Knox, 1998) 69–94.

Temple does not guarantee the security of Jerusalem (Jer 7:1–8:3), which flies in the face of Isaiah's ideology of divine protection for Jerusalem and the house of David (Isa 7:1–9:6); Micah's contentions that the messages of peace cited in his book are wrong, and that war must break out when the new Judean messiah will destroy those who oppress Israel (Micah 4–5); or Ezekiel's contention that YHWH calls for individual accountability with regard to moral and cultic matters as opposed to the corporate accountability articulated in the Mosaic Torah (Ezekiel 18; contra Exod 20:5–6).

There is a reluctance on the part of interpreters to face the possibility that such disagreement entails the contention that canonical prophets may be regarded as false.[5] Such a contention would clearly undermine the authority of prophets, and indeed scripture as a whole. After all, the prophets play a foundational theological role in the Bible insofar as they represent the fundamental basis for divine revelation, whether through Moses or his successors. Indeed, the prophets play constitutive roles within the structures of both the Jewish Tanakh and the Christian Old Testament.[6] Within the Tanakh, the Prophets mark the transition between the dissolution of the Mosaic ideal in the Torah and its potential restoration in the Writings. Within the Christian Bible the Prophets sum up the Old Testament and point to the New Testament. Nevertheless, various factors enable interpreters to avoid identifying the Prophets as false, e. g., Hananiah may represent Isaiah's theology, but he is not Isaiah himself; Micah's opponents represent a nationalist ideology that could hardly represent authentic prophetic tradition; Ezekiel is a maverick insofar as his book is nearly rejected in Rabbinic tradition, and some even question his mental stability.[7]

---

[5] See, for example, Adam S. van der Woude, "Micah in Dispute with the Pseudo-Prophets," *VT* 19 (1969) 244–60; idem, "Micah IV 1–5: An Instance of the Pseudo-Prophets Quoting Isaiah, in M. Beek et al., ed., *Symbolicae et Mesopotamicae Fancisco Mario Theodoro de Liagre Böhl Dedicatae* (Leiden: Brill, 1973) 396–402, who argues that the tensions evident in the book of Micah are the result of (the authentic) Micah's dispute with false prophets who misapprehend Isaiah. Contra Marvin A. Sweeney, "Micah's Debate with Isaiah," *JSOT* 93 (2001) 111–24, who argues that the book of Micah is not in dispute with false prophets with the book of Isaiah itself.

[6] See my "Tanakh versus Old Testament: Concerning the Foundation for a Jewish Theology of the Bible, in H. T. C. Sun and K. L. Eades, with J. M. Robinson and G. I. Möller, ed., *Problems in Biblical Theology: Essays in Honor of Rolf Knierim* (Grand Rapids: Eerdmans, 1997) 353–72.

[7] For the tradition concerning R. Hanina ben Hezekiah's apparently successful attempt to reconcile the differences between Ezekiel and the Torah so that the former might be accepted as sacred scripture, see bShabbat 13b; bMenahot 45a. For the most recent discussion of Ezekiel's mental stability see David J. Halperin, *Seeking Ezekiel: Text and Psychology* (University Park, PA: Pennsylvania State University Press, 1993), and the literature cited there. See, by contrast, my "Ezekiel: Zadokite Priest and Visionary Prophet of the Exile," *OPIAC* 41 (2001), which argues that much of Ezekiel's strange actions and imagery may be attributed to his identity as a Zadokite priest.

Despite the efforts of past interpreters to identify the opponents of the canonical prophets as false prophets, there is considerable evidence that their opponents may indeed be identified with the traditions or written records of past prophets who were later recognized as canonical. I have attempted to point to this phenomenon in previous studies of Micah and Zechariah, whose books are constructed to challenge the prophetic tradition of Isaiah ben Amoz and his postulated successors, Deutero- and Trito-Isaiah.[8]

The book of Micah, for example, cites Isaiah's initial vision in Isa 2:2–4 of world peace and the turning of swords into plowshares, etc., and argues contrary to the Isaian tradition that such peace will be achieved only after the future Judean messiah defeats the nations which oppress Jerusalem, Judah, and Israel. Such a scenario runs contrary to that of the book of Isaiah, which holds that Jews must submit to the rule of the Persian monarchs as part of YHWH's plans to achieve world peace and the universal recognition of YHWH's sovereignty. The book of Isaiah even goes so far as to declare that King Cyrus of Persia, a foreign monarch, is YHWH's messiah and Temple builder (Isa 44:28; 45:1). Micah charges that Jerusalem's prophets divine only for pay and lead the people astray by crying, "peace!" when they have something to eat (Mic 3:5–12). Although he is a contemporary of the great Isaiah ben Amoz, who envisioned the possibility of peace for Jerusalem and Judah in the late-eighth century, few interpreters would think that Micah's charges were directed against one of the greatest prophets of biblical tradition.

The book of Zechariah, for its own part, reworks the prophet's name from Zechariah bar/ben Iddo to Zechariah ben Berechiah ben Iddo so that he might be identified with the witness to Isaiah's prophecy, Zechariah ben Yeberechiah, who is named in Isa 8:1–4. The book continues to cite Isaian statements, including the so-called swords into plowshares passage, as part of its overall vision of world peace and universal recognition of YHWH that is likewise achieved only after YHWH and Judah defeat the nations that threaten Jerusalem. The book once again rejects the Isaian contention that world peace will be achieved when Judah submits to the Persians. In light of these considerations, it is all the more striking that Zech 13:2–6 calls for the elimination of "false" prophets, who lie in the name of YHWH. Insofar as Isaiah is Zechariah's major target, this would imply that the book of Zechariah charges that Isaiah is a false prophet.

The evidence indicates that not only did Micah and Zechariah and their tradents disagree with Isaiah and his tradition, but that they were willing to charge their great colleague(s) with gross misconduct and deceit in carrying out their prophetic vocations. Insofar as prior treatment of Jeremiah points to exten-

---

[8] See Sweeney, "Micah's Debate with Isaiah"; idem, "Zechariah's Debate with Isaiah," *The Changing Face of Form Criticism for the Twenty-First Century* (ed. M. A. Sweeney and E. Ben Zvi; Grand Rapids and Cambridge: Eerdmans, 2003) 335–50.

sive conflict with supposedly false prophets, who may themselves be identified with the Isaian tradition, his case bears detailed examination.[9]

III

Jeremiah is especially well known for his diatribes against false prophecy. A variety of texts take up the issue of true and false prophecy in Jeremiah or convey his polemics against false prophets. Examination of these texts indicates that Jeremiah does not reject the Isaian tradition like his colleagues Micah and Zechariah, but that the issue turns upon differences in understanding the Isaian tradition. Jeremiah's understanding of false prophecy includes those who would follow the Isaian tradition by prophesying that YHWH would deliver Jerusalem and Judah from the Babylonians and bring about peace in keeping with Isaiah's understanding of the Zion or Davidic tradition. By contrast, Jeremiah consistently calls for submission to Babylon in keeping with his own interpretation of the Isaian tradition, i. e., that the Babylonians were brought by YHWH to subdue Jerusalem and Judah as a result of their failure to abide by YHWH's Torah. In short, Jeremiah debates with his contemporaries concerning the meaning of the Isaian tradition, and ultimately charges that those prophets who understand it to mean peace in his time must be considered as false.

We begin with the Temple sermon in Jeremiah 7, in which the prophet argues that the presence of the Temple does not guarantee the security of the nation, and the portrayal of his consequent trial for sedition in Jeremiah 26. Jeremiah's Temple sermon is generally considered to be one of the highlights of his prophetic corpus that best articulates his call for adherence to YHWH's Torah.[10] According to Jeremiah 7, the prophet stands at the gate of the Jerusalem Temple, where he delivers a sermon that calls upon the people to mend their ways because the presence of the Jerusalem Temple will hardly guarantee their security in the face of threat. In true Levitical fashion, he makes his point by drawing upon an exposition of Mosaic Torah and his understanding of past history. He demands that the people not trust in delusions by putting their trust in the Temple of YHWH, and he cites some of the Ten Commandments in vv. 9–10, "Will you steal and murder and commit adultery, and swear falsely and sacrifice to Baal, and follow gods whom you have not known, and then come and stand before

---

[9] For treatment of Jeremiah, see esp. the studies by Buber, Lange, Meyer, Overholt, and Sanders cited above.

[10] For recent discussion of the Temple sermon, see esp. Douglas Rawlinson Jones, *Jeremiah* (NCeB; London: Marshall Pickering; Grand Rapids: Eerdmans, 1992) 141–58; William L. Holladay, Jr., *Jeremiah 1* (Hermeneia; Philadelphia: Fortress, 1986) 241–74; Helga Weippert, *Die Prosareden des Jeremiabuches* (BZAW 132; Berlin and New York: Walter de Gruyter, 1973) 26–48. Most scholars correctly consider the present form of the text to be heavily edited by later tradents.

Me in this House which bears My name and say, 'We are safe?'" He continues by asking his audience to consider the destruction of his ancestral sanctuary at Shiloh, which serves as a demonstration that YHWH will punish the people for wickedness despite the presence of a sanctuary in their midst. On this basis he argues that just as YHWH destroyed the northern kingdom of Israel for wickedness, so YHWH would destroy Jerusalem and Judah if the people persist in rejecting YHWH's Torah.

It is noteworthy that the narrative concerning Jeremiah's trial for sedition in Jeremiah 26 indicates that true and false prophecy is a major issue in the prophet's speech. Jeremiah is charged with prophesying against the city, and he is defended by the claim that he speaks in the name of YHWH and is therefore not to be considered a false prophet. During the course of the trial evidence is brought forward, i.e., Micah prophesied that Jerusalem would be plowed as a field, but his words prompted Hezekiah to turn to YHWH so that the city was saved (cf. Mic 3:12). On the other hand, the prophet Uriah ben Shemaiah was executed by King Jehoiakim for similar statements. Ultimately, Jeremiah was saved by the intervention of Ahikam ben Shaphan, the son of one of the late King Josiah's chief administrators.

Interpreters generally consider the issue in relation to the terms presented in the narrative, i.e., does Jeremiah act to protect the city and will Jerusalem potentially be destroyed? Of course, the subsequent destruction of Jerusalem by the Babylonians validates his message. But one must consider the matter from the standpoint of those in late-seventh/early-sixth century Jerusalem, prior to the time when the destruction of Jerusalem was a demonstrable reality. The presumption that the Jerusalem Temple signaled YHWH's guarantee of security for the city of Jerusalem and the house of David is a basic tenant of Isaiah's prophetic message approximately a century before.[11] The book of Isaiah is clear throughout, i.e., if the Davidic monarchs would put their trust in YHWH, YHWH would protect Jerusalem and the Davidic line. Indeed, Isaiah's statement to Ahaz in Isa 7:9 at the time when the king was concerned with the threat to Jerusalem posed by the Syro-Ephraimitic coalition expresses the point succinctly with a pun in Hebrew, "If you will not trust (*'im lō' ta'ămînû*), indeed, you will not be secure (*kî lō' tē'āmēnû*)." Likewise, the narratives concerning Sennacherib's siege of Jerusalem in Isaiah 36–37 make it very clear that the city was saved when Hezekiah put his trust in YHWH. From the standpoint of late-seventh/early-sixth century Jerusalem, Isaiah's prophecies were understood to support the notion that YHWH would protect Jerusalem and the house of David. Although the historical details are debated, this premise was validated by the continuing existence of the city of Jerusalem and the house of David

---

[11] For treatment of the relevant text in Isaiah, see my *Isaiah 1–39, with an Introduction to Prophetic Literature* (FOTL 16; Grand Rapids and Cambridge, 1996) ad loc.

beyond the period when the Assyrian empire was destroyed. Furthermore, it accentuates the tenuous nature of Jeremiah's prophecy. On the one hand, his warning that the Temple and Jerusalem could be destroyed runs counter to the Isaian tradition and historical experience up to that time – Isaiah never states that Jerusalem or the Temple might be destroyed; on the other hand, Jeremiah's call to turn to YHWH stands directly in line with the Isaian tradition. Although the texts concerning Jeremiah's Temple Sermon broadly address the question of the people's adherence to divine expectations and the future of the city of Jerusalem, they do so by posing the question of true and false prophecy. Ironically, both are based to a certain extent in the Isaian tradition, albeit on fundamentally different understandings of that tradition.

The issue is addressed pointedly in the narratives concerning Jeremiah's confrontation with the prophet Hananiah ben Azzur in Jeremiah 27–28. The narrative focuses on Jeremiah's call to submit to the rule of the Babylonian empire at the beginning of the reign of Zedekiah ben Josiah in 597 B.C.E. In order to make his point, the prophet engages in a symbolic action in which he wears a yoke to symbolize his message of submission to Babylon as an expression of the will of YHWH. Throughout the chapter, the prophet repeatedly counsels the people not to follow the words of the false prophets who assure them that they should not submit to Babylon and that YHWH will see to the return of the Temple vessels that were taken away by the Babylonians. The second narrative in Jeremiah 28 relates Jeremiah's confrontation with Hananiah, in which Hananiah announces that YHWH would break the yoke of Babylon and that the sacred vessels of the Temple would be restored in two years. In order to symbolize his message, Hananiah breaks Jeremiah's yoke. Of course, Jeremiah later returns with an iron yoke that could not be broken, and declares that YHWH had placed the yoke of Babylon on all the nations. The narrative concludes with a notice of Hananiah's death, which apparently validates Jeremiah's message.[12]

Jeremiah's statements reflect the divisive political debate of the time in which the nation was considering its future course of action.[13] Zedekiah's father, King Josiah, was a staunch ally of the Babylonians who had been killed by the Egyptians in 609 B.C.E. while acting to support his Babylonian allies in their efforts to destroy the Assyrian empire. In the aftermath of Josiah's death, the Egyptians had removed Josiah's pro-Babylonian son Jehoahaz from the throne and installed in his place the pro-Egyptian Jehoiakim. After the Babylonians took control of Judah from Egypt in 605 B.C.E., Jehoiakim revolted in 598 B.C.E.

---

[12] N.b., Jeremiah makes similar claims in Jer 20:1–16, against the priest Pashḥur ben Immer, who imprisoned the prophet for declaring that YHWH would hand the nation over to the Babylonians. Again, the prophet charges Pashḥur with false prophecy, and declares that he will die in Babylonian captivity.

[13] See esp. Jay Wilcoxen, "The Political Background of Jeremiah's Temple Sermon," in A. Merrill and T. Overholt, ed., *Scripture in History and Theology* (Fest. J. C. Rylaarsdam; Pittsburg: Pickwick, 1977) 151–66.

Jehoiakim died during the revolt of unknown causes, and the Babylonians exiled his eighteen year old son Jehoiachin to Babylonia, leaving Jehoiakim's brother, Zedekiah ben Josiah, on the throne to act as a puppet regent. The pro-Babylonian party that once served Josiah was still strong at this time, and Jeremiah's calls for submission to Babylonian must be understood in this context; the prophet calls for the continuation of Josiah's foreign policy as an expression of the will of YHWH. Indeed, Jeremiah's position also follows Isaiah's reasoning, i.e., Isaiah holds that YHWH brought Assyria to punish Israel and Judah, but he never claims that Assyria would destroy Jerusalem (see esp. Isa 5:1–30; 7:1–9:6; 10:5–11:16; 14:24–27). Ultimately, YHWH would restore Jerusalem once the period of Assyrian punishment had ended. Jeremiah apparently envisions a similar scenario in which Babylon would dominate and oppress the city ostensibly for the sins of the people, but the city and people would survive in keeping with the Isaian scenario. At the same time, it is evident that Hananiah's position also reflects a reading of the Isaian tradition, i.e., YHWH would defend Jerusalem when the people turned to YHWH. Interestingly, Hananiah's position reflects the anti-Babylonian stance of Jehoiakim and his supporters, but it also appears to be based in part on Isaiah's own rejection of Hezekiah's alliance with Babylon as articulated in Isaiah 39. In sum, the question of true and false prophecy in relation to the confrontation between Jeremiah and Hananiah appears points to differences in the means by which the prophets understand the older Isaian tradition.

Similar considerations may be brought to bear in the reading of Jeremiah 29, which relates Jeremiah's letter to the exiles, who were taken to Babylonia together with the young King Jehoiachin ben Jehoiakim in 597 B.C.E. Here, the prophet writes that the exiles should build houses, plant gardens, take wives, beget children, and seek the welfare of the city to which YHWH has sent them. Essentially, Jeremiah calls upon the exiles to accept their lot as the will of YHWH and to ignore the claims of false prophets who presumably predict a speedy return to Jerusalem. Jeremiah names the false prophets and calls for their punishment. He further claims that the exile will last for seventy years, and that YHWH will punish those who remain in Jerusalem during that period. The narrative clearly presupposes Jeremiah 24, in which the prophet identifies those who are exiled as the good figs that would be preserved by YHWH and ultimately returned to the land of Israel. Those left in the land are the bad figs that would suffer punishment. But Jeremiah also presupposes an essential Isaian point articulated in Isa 6:12–13; 7:1–9; 10:20–26; and elsewhere, i.e., although Jerusalem would not be destroyed, only a remnant of the people would survive the punishment leveled by YHWH against the people. Isaiah is not clear concerning the identity of the one-tenth of the people who will constitute the remnant. The position of the false prophets also appears to envision an Isaian restoration in which the exiles would return to Jerusalem. The difference lies in the timing, i.e., Jeremiah holds that the exiles will return only after seventy years when the returnees will include the children and grandchildren of those sent into exile. The basis for Jeremiah's seventy-year period is not clear – it does not stem from the Isaian tradition[14] – but it is clear that his understanding of the fate of the exiles differs from those whom he identifies as false prophets, and that both positions are ultimately rooted in an understanding of the Isaian tradition.

IV

Up to this point, we have seen narrative presentations of the prophet that broadly indicate his interaction with the Isaian tradition, including both his dependence upon the Isaian tradition and his understanding of it in relation to the circumstances of his own time. It is clear throughout that this material presents Jeremiah as differing from other prophets, whom he labels as false, in his understanding of the Isaian tradition. Nevertheless, we have not yet seen an instance in which Jeremiah actually cites or alludes to an Isaian text. There are, however, a number of instances in which such citations or allusions appear, and they frequently appear in relation to statements concerning true and false prophecy.[15] In order further to clarify Jeremiah's understanding of true and false prophecy and the relation of this understanding to the Isaian tradition, it is necessary to consider these passages as well.

Jeremiah 23:9–40 constitutes one of the most important texts concerning the issue of false prophecy in the book of Jeremiah.[16] The passage begins with the prophet's own lament concerning the misrepresentation of YHWH's words:

> My heart is crushed within me, all my bones are trembling;
> I have become like a drunken man, like one overcome by wine –
> Because of YHWH and because of his holy words (Jer 23:9).[17]

The prophet is clearly distressed by the matter, and he goes on to relate several statements by YHWH concerning the mourning of the land because both prophets and priests are godless and run to do wrong even in the Temple of YHWH. G-d announces that disaster will fall upon them, and charges that the prophets of Jerusalem are like the people of Sodom and Gomorrah in their efforts to encour-

---

[14] For discussion, see Holladay, *Jeremiah 1* 688–89.

[15] For discussion of Jeremiah's citation of or allusion to Isaian texts, see now Ute Wendel, *Jesaja und Jeremia. Worte, Motive und Einsichten Jesajas in der Verkündigung Jeremias* (BibThS 25; Neukirchen-Vluyn: Neukirchener, 1995).

[16] For critical treatment of this passage, see now Lange, *Vom prophetischen Worte* 106–31, 208–24.

[17] All English translations are from *The JPS Hebrew-English Tanakh* (Philadelphia: Jewish Publication Society, 1999).

age evil among the people. Ultimately, G-d calls upon the people not to listen to the prophets who delude them with prophecies spoken from their own minds.

There are several striking observations to be made concerning this oracle. The first is that it is directed against the prophets of Jerusalem, who are differentiated from Jeremiah insofar as Jeremiah is an Elide priest from the city of Anathoth – he is hardly a Jerusalem prophet like Isaiah before him. Although Isaiah lived a century before the time of Jeremiah, he does not hesitate to compare the Jerusalem prophets to the prophets of Samaria, who led their people astray in the time of Isaiah ben Amoz. Such a comparison of course suggests that Jeremiah is not concerned solely with the prophets of his own day, but with a tradition of prophecy that extends back over a century to one of the best-known of the Jerusalemite prophets, who in turn set the patterns for his successors. It is therefore noteworthy that Jeremiah claims that the Jerusalemite prophets delude the people with false promises that "all shall be well with you," and that, "no evil shall befall you." Such statements correspond to those of Isaiah, who assured Ahaz that all would be well with him if only he would put his trust in YHWH (Isa 7:1–9) and who assured Hezekiah that YHWH would take action against Sennacherib because Hezekiah had placed his trust in YHWH in a time of grave national crisis (Isaiah 37). But one hundred years later, again at a time of grave national crisis, Jeremiah holds that such prophecies are delusions and lies.

One might note Jeremiah's statement, "the anger of YHWH shall not turn back, till it has fulfilled and completed its purpose; in the days to come you shall clearly perceive it" (Jer 23:20). The statement clearly corresponds to Isaiah's oracular sequences in Isa 5:1–30; 9:7–10:4, in which the characteristic refrain, "in all this, His anger has not turned back, and His hand is outstretched still," appears repeatedly. These oracles call for the punishment of Israel and Judah in the Assyrian period, but they appear in the context of a much larger unit in Isaiah 2/5–12, which envisions the ultimate downfall of the Assyrian oppressor once the punishment is complete. In citing this refrain from Isaiah, Jeremiah apparently intends to announce that YHWH's anger and punishment is not complete. Jeremiah's contemporaries could point to the collapse of the Assyrian empire in the late-seventh century as an indication that YHWH's anger was concluded and that Isaiah's prophecies of peace were now at hand. Although Jeremiah lived a hundred years later than Isaiah, and the Assyrian oppressor was vanquished, the threat of divine punishment had not yet subsided in Jeremiah's estimation insofar as Babylon was rising to take Assyria's place. Perhaps Isaiah was wrong, i.e., Assyria's collapse did not entail Jerusalem's security.

Finally, it must be noted that Jeremiah's oracle concerning false prophets in Jer 23:9–40 relates to its literary context in that it immediately follows one of Jeremiah's oracles in Jer 23:1–8 concerning the "righteous branch" of the house of David, i.e., the righteous Davidic monarch who will rule at the time that Israel and Judah will live securely in the land. This oracle clearly builds upon the Isaian oracle concerning the righteous monarch or "shoot" that "shall grow out of the stump of Jesse" to preside over the restoration of the exiles of Israel and Judah to the land in the aftermath of the period of Assyrian oppression. Interpreters have been somewhat puzzled by this oracle because it is one of the few instances in which Jeremiah is presented as having something positive to say about the Davidic monarchy. Indeed, Jeremiah's anti-monarchical stance is so-pronounced that many interpreters regard this text as a late addition to the book of Jeremiah that was designed to express exilic or post-exilic hopes for the restoration of Jerusalem and the house of David at the time of the Persian-period restoration.[18] Although more recent commentators are inclined to see the oracle as Jeremiah,[19] there is a certain tension to be considered when it is read in relation to its immediate literary context, i. e., the preceding oracle in Jeremiah 22, which condemns the Davidic king Jehoiakim for self-indulgently building his own luxury palace while ignoring the needs of his people. Indeed, the concluding statements of this oracle claim that his son Jehoiachin will be left without a successor to sit on the throne of David and to rule once again in Judah.

What does it mean when the oracle concerning the future righteous branch of the house of David immediately follows an oracle that envisions the end of Jehoiakim's and Jehoaiachin's royal line? What does it mean when Jeremiah's major oracle condemning false prophecy appears immediately following a royal oracle that is dependent upon the Isaian tradition? Apparently, it means that Jeremiah does not anticipate a restoration of the monarchy in the lifetime of Jehoiachin, but that such a restoration would take place much later. This position is consistent with the claim in Jeremiah 25 and 29 that the exile would last for seventy years. It also indicates Jeremiah's interaction with the Isaian tradition, i. e., he accepts the Isaian claim that a righteous Davidic monarch will once again rule in Jerusalem, but in contrast to the claims of others, the realization of the Isaian claim would only take place well beyond the lifetime of Jehoiachin.

A similar perspective concerning delay in the realization of earlier Isaian prophecy appears in relation to Jeremiah's statements concerning false prophets in Jer 5:12–13.[20] Countering the claims of other prophets who stated that Israel and Judah would not be punished for their purported betrayal of G-d, Jeremiah states, "The prophets shall prove mere wind, for the word is not in them; so shall it (punishment) be done to them." This statement appears within the larger framework of Jeremiah's prophetic summons to repentance directed to Judah in Jeremiah 2–6 in which the prophet points to the example of northern Israel's punishment as a model for what will happen to Judah if the nation does not

---

[18] E. g., Winfred Thiel, *Die deuteronomistische Redaktion von Jeremia 1–25* (WMANT 41; Neukirchen-Vluyn: Neukirchener, 1973) 246–49.

[19] E. g., Jones, *Jeremiah* 296–98.

[20] See now Lange, *Vom prophetischen Wort* 189–93.

repent.²¹ The passage is particularly pertinent for our concern with Jeremiah's understanding of Isaian tradition insofar as his description of the coming punishment draws heavily on Isaian texts:

> Lo, I am bringing against you, O House of Israel, a nation from afar –
> declares YHWH;
> It is an enduring nation, it is an ancient nation;
> A nation whose language you do not know–you will not understand what they say.
> Their quivers are like a yawning grave – they are all mighty men.
> They will devour your sons and daughters, they will devour your flocks and herds,
> They will devour your vines and fig trees.
> They will batter down with the sword the fortified towns on which you rely
> (Jer 5:15–17).

This statement is remarkably reminiscent of Isaiah's prophecy in Isa 5:26–29 concerning the coming Assyrian invasion of Israel:²²

> He will raise an ensign to a nation afar, whistle to one at the end of the earth.
> There it comes with lightning speed!
> In its ranks, none is weary or stumbles, they never sleep or slumber;
> The belts on their waists do not come loose, nor do the thongs on their sandals break.
> Their arrows are sharpened, and all their bows are drawn.
> Their horses' hooves are like flint, their chariot wheels like the whirlwind.
> Their roaring is like a lion's, they roar like the great beasts;
> When they growl and seize a prey, they carry it off and none can recover it.

Both passages indicate YHWH's bringing of a nation from afar to punish Israel or Judah, both describe the arms, especially the arrows and bows of the approaching army, and both employ the metaphor of a devouring beast to portray the conqueror's devastation of the people. Indeed, further Isaian parallels appear later in the passage with references to the people's rejection of YHWH's Torah (Jer 6:19; Isa 5:24; 1:10); YHWH's rejection of the people's sacrifices (Jer 6:20; Isa 1:10–17); YHWH's placing stumbling blocks before the people (Jer 6:21; Isa 3:8; 8:14); another description of the army from the north (Jer 6:22–26; Isa 5:26–30); the portrayal of Judah's suffering like that of a woman in childbirth (Jer 6:24; Isa 13:8; 26:17–18); and the portrayal of Judah's punishment as iron or copper ore which is purified when dross is removed (Jer 6:27–30; Isa 1:21–26). The cluster of parallels between Jeremian and Isaian texts is remarkable in this passage, all the more so because they all appear in the latter part of the passage. I have argued elsewhere that Jeremiah 2–6 is an updated version of an early text in Jeremiah 2:2–4:2 that originally called upon Israel to return to Jerusalem in

---

²¹ Marvin A. Sweeney, "Structure and Redaction in Jeremiah 2–6," *Troubling Jeremiah* (ed. A. R. Diamond et al.; JSOTSup 260; Sheffield: Sheffield Academic Press, 1999) 200–18; idem, *King Josiah of Judah: The Lost Messiah of Israel* (Oxford and New York: Oxford University Press, 2001) 215–35.

²² See Holladay, *Jeremiah 1* 188; Jones, *Jeremiah* 125.

keeping with Josiah's reform, but that the text was reworked in the aftermath of Josiah's unexpected death at the hands of Egypt to call for Judah's repentance as well.[23] It would appear that Jeremiah once supported Josiah's program of national restoration and religious reform, based in part on a Josian understanding that earlier prophecy in Isaiah and elsewhere anticipated the king's program. But Jeremiah was compelled by Josiah's death to change his mind about the timing of the restoration, and concluded that Judah would undergo a punishment much like that suffered by Israel. Insofar as Isaian texts concerning the upcoming invasion play such an important role in his portrayal of Judah's coming judgment, it would appear that Jeremiah came to the conclusion that Isaiah's earlier prophecies would not come to realization in Josiah's program of national reunification and restoration; rather, they would come to realization only after Judah had suffered a similar devastating punishment at the hands of Babylon, the new enemy from the north. Those prophets who looked forward to restoration based upon the Josian model must be considered as false.[24] Jeremiah anticipates that the Isaian scenario will overtake Judah, but unlike those who maintain that Isaiah's period of punishment is over and that the restoration is about to begin, Jeremiah maintains that Judah's own period of punishment is only now at hand. Restoration will come, but it will have to wait until the punishment is complete.

V

In sum then, it would appear that the issue of true and false prophecy turns upon Jeremiah's relationship to the older Isaian tradition. Indeed, both Jeremiah and his opponents appear to be reading some form of the Isaian tradition, which calls for a period of punishment at the hands of the Assyrians followed by a period of restoration once the punishment is complete. Jeremiah's opponents apparently maintain that the Isaian tradition has reached its fulfillment, i. e., now that the Assyrian empire has collapsed, the time for Judah's restoration is at hand. Although redaction critical arguments suggest that Jeremiah may once have held such a position himself, the present form of the Jeremiah tradition indicates that Jeremiah came to believe that Jerusalem and Judah were about to suffer punish-

---

[23] Sweeney, "Structure and Redaction in Jeremiah 2–6."

[24] We may arrive at similar conclusions concerning Jeremiah's diatribe concerning false prophets in Jer 14:13–22 in which he charges those who anticipate peace as lying prophets out a scenario in which the streets of Jerusalem are filled with the bodies of those who perished by sword and famine as YHWH rejects His own people. The following passage portrays YHWH's rejection of the prophet's intercession on behalf of the people and employs key Isaian motifs, such as the reference to YHWH's outstretched hand in Jer 15:6/Isa 5:25 and the portrayal of the remnant left to the people in Jer 15:11–14. Additional Isaian parallels appear throughout the book most notably in the book of consolation in Jeremiah 30–31 and in the oracle against Moab in Jeremiah 48.

ment at the hands of the Babylonians very much like that suffered by Israel at the hands of the Assyrians. Throughout the book, it seems clear that Jeremiah relies upon his own (or his tradents') reading of the Isaian tradition. It is upon this basis that Jeremiah charges many of his contemporaries as false prophets.

Truth in prophecy lies therefore not simply in the question of whether or not it will be fulfilled, but when and how. Indeed, even the prophets disagree among themselves concerning the veracity of their colleagues' prophecies and their respective understandings of divine intent. In this sense, the truth of earlier prophetic tradition is relative to the circumstances and means by which it is interpreted and by which it might ultimately be realized. And yet in the end, biblical theology must always reckon with the possibility that the canonically-recognized prophets might just be false, despite the presumption that each somehow represents the truth of the divine. In this respect, truth must be recognized as a debated or contingent category, both within the Bible itself and among its interpreters.

7. Structure and Redaction in Jeremiah 2–6[1]

I

Current discussion of the book of Jeremiah is heavily influenced by a methodological debate that emphasizes three major reading strategies: (1) author-centered approaches that attempt to read Jeremiah in relation to the historical settings and concerns of the purported author or authors of the text; (2) text-centered approaches that focus on the literary features of the text of Jeremiah irrespective of its supposed historical settings; and (3) reader-centered approaches that emphasize the biases, perspectives and concerns of the readers of Jeremiah as major elements in the interpretation of the book. Each of these approaches has its own strength and weaknesses. Author-centered approaches correctly emphasize the role that the author and historical setting of a text play in determining its formulation and the concerns that it addresses, but they suffer from the inherently hypothetical nature of the textual, authorial and historical reconstructions that constitute a necessary element of such reading strategies. Text-centered approaches correctly emphasize the literary features of a text as the basis for interpretation, insofar as they text is the only objective element that stands before the interpreter, but such analyses do not account adequately for the determinative roles of the context in which the text is formed or read. Likewise, reader-centered approaches correctly point to the role of the reader in setting the agenda and parameters for interpretation, but again they do not account adequately for the role of the writers and the historical contexts of composition and readings from later historical contexts.

Although it is important to identify these emphases in current interpretation, to some extent, their differentiation leads to a certain element of scholarly polarization as proponents of each approach tend to emphasize the benefits of their respective strategies and to critique alternative approaches. This is an indication of scholarly health in that it facilitates full discussion of the strengths and weaknesses of each strategy that ultimately serve biblical interpretation by

---

[1] This is an expanded version of a paper read at the Pacific Coast Regional Meeting of the Society of Biblical Literature, March 31, 1995, Redlands, CA. An earlier draft was prepared during my appointment as the 1993–94 Dorot Research Professor at the W. F. Albright Institute, Jerusalem, Israel. I would like to thank the Albright Institute, the Dorot Research Foundation, and the University of Miami for making this appointment possible.

7. Structure and Redaction in Jeremiah 2–6 95

pointing to previously unrecognized aspects of biblical literature. But one must also ask to what extent such strategies can be combined in an overall reading of a text. Indeed, all three strategies play an important and necessary role in biblical interpretation, and the insights gained by each approach must be considered in the interpretation of a biblical text. Biblical texts are written by authors with a unique set of concerns in specific historical settings; they display distinctive literary features; and they are read by interpreters, either in the present or in the past, who also bring their unique concerns in relation to their own settings.[2]

Jeremiah 2–6 is a particularly useful text for illustrating the interrelationship of these three reading strategies. Although Jeremiah 2–6 presently forms a major component of the book of Jeremiah that in its present form addresses the issue of the Babylonian exile, scholars have consistently maintained that an earlier form of this material from the reign of King Josiah may be reconstructed.[3] Attempts have been made to establish the literary structure of this text and to examine its literary features, but such attempts have frequently been overly influenced by redaction-critical concerns that have hampered such literary analysis. Nevertheless, a full understanding of the text in its present form is the necessary prerequisite for historical and redaction-critical reconstruction. Furthermore, the concerns of the reader must be considered as those concerns delimit and define the issues to be addressed in the interpretation of the text. In the present case, the reader of this text is interested in determining its relevance for reconstructing aspects of King Josiah's reign and reform program and for understanding the early career of the prophet Jeremiah in relation to Josiah's reign.[4]

---

[2] For methodological discussion, see esp. John Barton, *Reading the Old Testament: Method in Biblical Study* (Louisville: Westminster John Knox, 1996); Rolf Knierim, "Criticism of Literary Features, Form, Tradition, and Redaction," in D. A. Knight and G. M. Tucker, eds., *The Hebrew Bible and its Modern Interpreters* (Chico, CA: Scholars Press, 1985) 123–65; Robert Morgan with John Barton, *Biblical Interpretation* (Oxford Bible Series; Oxford: Oxford University Press, 1988); Marvin A. Sweeney, "Formation and Form in Prophetic Literature," in D. L. Mays et al., eds., *Old Testament Interpretation: Past, Present, and Future. Essays in Honor of Gene M. Tucker* (Nashville: Abingdon, 1995) 113–26; idem, "Form Criticism," *To Each Its own Meaning: An Introduction to Biblical Criticisms and their Application* (ed. S. McKenzie and S. R. Haynes; Louisville: KY: Westminster John Knox, 1999) 58–89.

[3] For a summary of research on Jeremiah 2–6, see Mark E. Biddle, *A Redaction History of Jeremiah 2:1–4:2* (ATANT 77; Zürich: Theologischer Verlag, 1990) 3–29; cf. Siegfried Herrmann, *Jeremia* (BKAT 12/2; Neukirchen-Vluyn: Neukirchener, 1990) 93–109; Klaus Seybold, *Der Prophet Jeremia: Leben und Werk* (Stuttgart: Kohlhammer, 1993) 68–80. For general overviews of research on the book of Jeremiah and the prophet, see R. P. Carroll, *Jeremiah* (OT Guides; Sheffield: Sheffield Academic Press, 1989); Siegfried Herrmann, *Jeremia. Der Prophet und das Buch* (Erträge der Forschung 271; Darmstadt: Wissenschaftliche Buchgesellschaft, 1990); Jack R. Lundbom, "Jeremiah, Book of," *ABD* 3:706–21; idem, "Jeremiah (Prophet)," *ABD* 3:684–98; Seybold, *Der Prophet Jeremia*.

[4] See also Jack Lundbom, *The Early Career of the Prophet Jeremiah* (Lewistoon, KY: Mellen Press, 1993), for discussion of research. Lundbom's proposal for an early dating of Jeremiah's oracles correctly notes thematic elements in various passages that point to Josiah's reign, but it is dependent on an overly literal reading of the reference to Jeremiah's eating of

This essay therefore proposes a redaction-critical analysis of Jeremiah 2–6 that accounts for the author of the text, its literary features and the concerns of its reader. It examines a recent proposal by Biddle for a redaction-critical analysis of the text[5] and argues that although Biddle's idea advances redaction-critical research on Jeremiah 2–6, it is limited by insufficient attention to the literary features of the text in its own right as literature. On the basis of a synchronic examination of the literary structure of these chapters, it argues that a basis for redaction-critical reconstruction emerges. The present form of the text points to an attempt to address the former northern kingdom of Israel with an accusation that its rejection of YHWH led to its punishment. This serves as the basis for a similar address to Judah that establishes an analogy between Israel's and Judah's actions and thereby points to the potential punishment of Judah. Insofar as the material directed to Israel appears in Jer 2:2–4:2* and that directed to Judah appears in Jer 2:1–2, 28; 3:6–11; and 4:3–6:30, the essay argues that a text addressed to Israel during the reign of King Josiah was reworked and expanded to address the kingdom of Judah in the face of the later Babylonian threat.[6] Such work indicates the dynamic nature of Jeremiah's oracles in that they are read and applied in relation to different historical contexts during the course of his career. It further indicates shifts in the prophet's thinking in relation to the changing sociopolitical and religious circumstances of Judah during his lifetime. This of course does not address subsequent readings and applications of the text – that is the topic of future research.

II

Scholars generally maintain that Jeremiah 2–6 constitutes a distinct collection of Jeremiah's oracles that stem from the earliest periods of the prophet's activity. The present form of this material is addressed to Jerusalem and Judah (cf. Jer 2:2; 4:3–4, 5–6), and it appears to presuppose the early reign of Jehoiakim, following the death of Josiah, when Judah was threatened by Egypt in the wake of the Assyrian collapse (cf. Jer 2:18, 36:3:6). These chapters portray the coming threat of punishment that YHWH is bringing against Judah and Jerusalem from

---

YHWH's words in Jer 15:16 as a reference to the discovery of the Torah scroll during the reign of Josiah reported in 2 Kgs 22:8–13.

[5] Biddle, *A Redaction History of Jeremiah 2:1–4:2*.

[6] See also Christof Hardmeier, "Die Redekomposition Jer 2–6: Eine ultimative Verwarnung Jerusalems in Kontext des Zidkijasaufstandes," *Wort und Dienst* 21 (1991) 11–42; idem, "Geschichte und Erfahrung in Jer 2–6: Zur theologischen Notwendigkeit einer geschichts- und erfahrungsbezogenen Ezegese und ihrer methodischen Neuorientierung," *EvT* 56 (1996) 3–29, who argues that these chapters may well contain material that dates to the reign of Josiah, but reads them in relation to the threat posed against Judah by Babylonia during the reign of Zedekiah.

the north for their lack of fidelity to their G-d. Insofar as the theme of repentance plays a major role in these chapters, they appear to constitute a parenetical composition that is designed to persuade Judah and Jerusalem to return to YHWH before the punishment is realized.

Although the present form of Jeremiah 2–6 is addressed to Judah and Jerusalem, scholars persistently argue that an earlier text form, addressed to the northern kingdom of Israel, lies behind the present form of the text in Jer 2:1–4:2. The reasons for this contention are quite clear. Although the text as a whole identifies Jerusalem and Judah as its addressee, Jer 2:1–4:4 frequently identifies "Israel" (Jer 2:4, 26; 3:20); "apostate Israel" (Jer 3:12); and the "the sons of Israel" Jer 3:21) as its addressee. In addition, it emphasizes the wilderness tradition (Jer 2:2, 6, 17, 31), typically associated with the northern kingdom of Israel; the return of the "rebellious sons" to Zion (Jer 3:14, 17); and the walking together of the "House of Judah" and the "House of Israel" (Jer 3:18). It likewise compares the apostasy of Israel with that of Judah (Jer 3:6–10, 11). Furthermore, the superscription of the book (Jer 1:1–3) states that the prophet was active during the reign of King Josiah, who attempted to bring the territory and people of the former northern kingdom of Israel back under Davidic rule. Finally, the text employs a variety of pronoun forms, including 2ms, 2mp, and 2fs, to designate its addressee, which suggests the hand of a redactor at work. Because of these considerations, many scholars argue that an earlier form of Jer 2:1–4:4 was composed by the prophet during the reign of King Josiah as part of an effort to convince the people living in the territory of the former northern kingdom of Israel to accept Davidic sovereignty and thus to return to YHWH.[7]

But this consensus can be challenged on a number of grounds. The most important objection involves the chronology of the book and the prophet's career. Although Jer 1:1–3 states that Jeremiah spoke during the reign of King Josiah, the book contains no text that appears unequivocally to derive from this period. In two instances, the text refers positively to Josiah (Jer 3:6; 22:15–17), but it views Josiah retrospectively and never suggests that the prophet spoke during his reign. Likewise, the two blocks of text that scholars identify as those that may derive from Josiah's reign are addressed to both Israel and Judah in their present

---

[7] Rainer Albertz, "Jer 2–6 und die Frühzeitverkündigung Jeremias," *ZAW* 94 (1982) 20–47; cf. William L. Holladay, *Jeremiah 1: A Commentary on the Book of the Prophet Jeremiah, Chapters 1–25* (Hermeneia; Philadelphia: Fortress, 1986) 2. Rüdiger Liwak, *Der Prophet und die Geschichte. Eine literarhistorische Untersuchung zum Jeremiabuch* (BWANT 121; Stuttgart: Kohlhammer, 1987) 303–31, argues that Jeremiah 2 contains prophetic words from various periods during the reign of Josiah (p. 304), but that the whole of Jeremiah 2–6 dates to shortly after 586 (p. 312). Contra. Taro Odashima, *Heilsworte im Jeremiabuch. Untersuchungen zu ihrer vordeuteronomistischen Bearbeitung* (BWANT 125; Stuttgart: Kohlhammer, 1989) 296, who dates the "pre-deuteronomistic" words of Jeremiah 2–6 to the early exilic period, and Robert Carroll, *Jeremiah: A Commentary* (OTL; Philadelphia: Westminster, 1986) 116–17, who maintains that it is possible to date this material to any period of Israelite history.

forms. This suggests either that they have been edited or composed to address a later period when Judah was also threatened. Other objections question the relationship of Jeremiah to Josiah's reform, the historical reliability or referents of these texts, and the meaning of the term "Israel" in Jeremiah.[8]

On the basis of these objections, Biddle's recent study of the redaction history of these chapters correctly challenges this consensus by pointing to the difficulties that scholars face in their attempts to posit Jeremiah's prophetic activity during the reign of Josiah.[9] Biddle maintains that there is no clear evidence that Jeremiah spoke during the reign of Josiah, and that the ideological character of Jeremiah 36 undermines the basis for reconstructing an *Urrolle* of the prophet's words that might be attributed, at least in part, to the reign of Josiah.[10] Nevertheless, he does not reject the possibility or need for redaction-critical work on the book as a means for reconstructing earlier text forms. He correctly argues that an analysis of the structure of the text must constitute the starting point for redaction-critical reconstruction, insofar as the present structure of these chapters points to various inconsistencies, such as shifts in the addressee, the status of the people, and the presence of smaller textual units on which the present text is based.[11] Following an analysis of the structure of Jeremiah 2:1–4:2, Biddle identifies four major stages in the composition of this text that encompass the entire period of the composition of the book of Jeremiah in the exilic and postexilic periods.[12]

---

[8] For a summary of the primary objections, see Biddle, *A Redaction History of Jeremiah 2:1–4:2* 16–23.

[9] Biddle, *A Redaction History of Jeremiah 2:1–4:2*.

[10] Biddle, *A Redaction History of Jeremiah 2:1–4:2* 16–25. On the ideological character of Jeremiah 36 which argues that the chapter was composed in order to contrast the "wicked" Jehoiakim with the "righteous" Josiah, see Charles D. Isbell, "2 Kings 22:3–23:24 and Jeremiah 36: A Stylistic Comparison," *JSOT* 8 (1978) 33–45. Against Albertz, Biddle (pp. 19–20, n. 53) maintains that the references to Israel in Jer 2:1–4:2 must be understood in relation to all the tribes of Israel, including Judah, in that the reference to "all the families of the House of Israel" in Jer 2:4 is an ambiguous term that frequently refers to both north and south in prophetic literature (cf. Amos 3:1), but this fails to account for the distinction between Israel and Judah in Jer 3:6–10, 11, 18. He further argues against Albertz's association of the salvation preaching in ch. 3 with that of Jeremiah 30–31, which is also concerned with the north, because Jeremiah 3 (and 4) portrays a people already in judgment, who are summoned to repentance whereas Jeremiah 30–31 announces salvation. But this overlooks the rhetorical force of Jeremiah 3–4, which is designed to motivate the audience to accept a call to return to Zion and YHWH, and that of Jeremiah 30–31, which announces and looks forward to the realization of that return. For a study of the structure, intention, and redaction history of Jeremiah 30–31, see my study, "Jeremiah 30–31 and King Josiah's Program of National Restoration and Religious Reform," *ZAW* 108 (1996) 569–83.

[11] Cf. Knierim, "Criticism of Literary Features, esp. 150–58.

[12] Biddle's stages include (1) the *Schuldübernahme* redaction, composed during the exilic period as a preamble to Jeremiah 4–6, which argues that the people of Jerusalem must recognize their guilt as the cause for their own predicament; (2) the repentance series, which calls for reconciliation based upon the people's repentance; (3) the generations redaction, composed during a later postexilic period when Deuteronomistic theology had become orthodox, which extended the indictment to later generations of all Israel and Judah as a means to account for

Altogether, these chapters constitute a theological treatise that introduces the entire book.[13]

Insofar as Biddle focuses on the final form of the text of Jeremiah as a basis for redaction-critical reconstruction, he advances the study of Jeremiah 2–6 considerably. But despite its methodological sophistication and well-considered challenge to past scholarship, two major difficulties appear in his work. The first is his contention that the 2fs address forms constitute the oldest layer of material within this text that the 2fs, *wattōměrî*, "but you said," verbal forms constitute the basis for the structure of the text. Unfortunately, this contention cannot be accepted in that it prejudges the historical and structural conclusions that the study attempts to achieve. Furthermore, past research demonstrates the difficulties in employing the address forms of this passage as a basis for textual reconstruction, which calls into question the employment of such a procedure as a major criterion for redaction-critical work on this text. The problem is especially evident in the observation that nowhere in this text is Israel identified with a feminine appellation, such as the *bětûlat yiśrā'ēl* of Jeremiah 30–31; rather, the text employs common forms for the designation of Israel as a people and alludes metaphorically to the role of Israel as a bride (cf. Jer 2:2–3). This suggests that the interplay between masculine and feminine address forms for Israel in this text may be deliberate, in that they refer respectively to the sociopolitical reality of Israel as a people and to the metaphorical portrayal of Israel as YHWH's bridge. In general, the address forms are relatively consistent within the constituent textual blocks of this passage, but at times they mix and demonstrate their rhetorical, but not redactional, significance. The phenomenon is evident in Jer 2:31–33, which begins with 2mp address forms directed to Israel as a people but shifts its imagery to that of a bride followed by 2fs address forms directed to Israel. This suggests that the shift in address forms cannot serve as reliable indicator of the redaction history this text or even of its structure.

The second difficulty pertains to his demarcation of this text, its relation to its literary context, and the relative meaning of the term, "Israel." Biddle does not fully justify the structural demarcation of Jer 2:1–4:2, although he does provide several hints to his thinking. He notes the occurrence of Jerusalem in Jer 2:1–2 and 4:3, 5, and argues that Jerusalem is otherwise unnamed through-out the body of the text. Because he maintains that these texts constitute framework materials for the whole, he discounts them as constituent elements of the text to be studied and posits that they facilitate a transition from a collection concerned with Israel's sin in Jeremiah 2–3 to one concerned with the "foe from the north" directed against Jerusalem in Jeremiah 4–6. Nevertheless, he treats chapters 2–3 and 4–6 as if they are separate textual blocks, overlooking the syntactical

---

continued hardships; and (4) the final framework redaction which places greater emphasis on the guilt of an earlier generation from whose sinful history Israel must distance itself.

[13] Cf. Liwak, *Der Prophet* 293–302.

connective *kî* which links Jer 4:3–4 to 4:1–2, and which effects the transition between two subunits of a larger text. Because Jacob/Israel is the addressee of Jeremiah 2–3 (cf. Jer 2:4), this forces him to discount the address to Judah in Jer 2:28 as contradictory. He therefore argues that Jer 2:1–3 is secondary "since it is difficult to imagine a redactor destroying an original unity between 2:2b–3 and 2:5 ff (p. 34), and he dismisses the structural significance of Jer 3:6–12 which distinguishes Israel and Judah. These texts are particularly important in defining the relationship between Judah (and thus Jerusalem) and Israel within Jer 2:1–4:2 in that they indicate that the distinction between Israel and Judah is fundamental to the concerns of this text. Such a distinction points to the larger literary context in which concern with Israel in chapters 2–3 prefigures concerns with Judah/Jerusalem in chapters 4–6. In short, redactional criteria influence his views on the structure and interpretation of the final form of the text and thereby aid in predetermining his results. This suggests that greater attention should be directed to the larger literary context of Jeremiah 2–6, the distinction between Israel and Judah within that context, and the role that the references to Jerusalem and Judah in Jeremiah 2–3 play in relating these chapters and their concerns to Jeremiah 4–6.

On the basis of these considerations, it is therefore necessary to reconsider the redaction history of Jer 2:1–4:2, both in relation to its internal referents and in relation to the larger literary context of Jeremiah 2–6. This reconsideration points to the need establish the structure of Jeremiah 2–6 together with the differing references to Israel and Judah, as the bases for the redaction-critical study of this text.

III

Jeremiah 2–6 is demarcated initially by the YHWH-word transmission formula in 2:1, *weyĕhî dĕbar-yhwh ʾēlay lēʾmōr*, "and the word of YHWH was unto me saying ..."[14] This occurrence of the formula is the third in a series of the same formula that appears also in 1:4 and 1:11. No such formula appears again until Jer 7:1, which reads, *haddābār ʾăšer hāyâ yirmĕyāhû mēʾēt lēʾmōr*, "the word which was unto Jeremiah from YHWH, saying ..." The correspondence between this formula and the superscription in Jer 1:1–3, *dibrê yirmĕyāhû ben-ḥilqîyāhû ... ʾăšer hāyâ dĕbar-yhwh ʾēlāyw ...*, "the words of Jeremiah ben Hilkiah ... which was the word of YHWH unto him ...," suggest that Jer 1:1–3 and 7:1 mark major divisions within the book. Insofar as the formulas in Jer 1:4; 1:11; and 2:1 are linked syntactically to Jer 1:1–3 by their *waw*-consecutive verbal forms,

---

[14] On the YHWH word transmission formula in Jeremiah, see Theodor Seidl, "Die Wortereignisformel in Jeremia," *BZ* 23 (1979) 20–47.

this suggests that a sequence of three interrelated textual blocks in Jer 1:4–10; 1:11–19; and 2:1–6:30, introduced by the superscription in 1:1–3, defines the structure of the initial subunit of the book of Jeremiah. As scholars note, these chapters introduce the reader to the major themes, concerns, and perspectives of the book.

Jeremiah 2–6 is defined as a distinct textual block within Jeremiah 1–7 not only by the introductory YWHWH-word transmission formulae in Jer 2:1 and 7:1, but as well by its concerns with both Israel and Judah, the threat of destruction or punishment leveled against them, and the call for repentance. Several observations are pertinent in attempting to define the internal structure of these chapters. First, the interchange between the various address forms (i.e., 2mp, 2ms, 2fs) cannot serve as an adequate criterion to establish the structure of this text; the various forms are simply too intertwined within the text which suggests that they constitute a rhetorical shift in the means to address Israel and Judah rather than a structural criterion.

Second, the shift in the addressee detected by scholars within the larger framework of Jeremiah 2–6 likewise cannot serve as an adequate structural criterion. The material addressed to Israel in Jer 2:1–4:2 focuses especially on repentance in the wake of punishment, and that addressed to Jerusalem/Judah in 4:3–6:30 focuses especially on the threat from the "foe from the north." But the distinction in addressee is not so clear. The Israelite material is placed within a framework that is initially addressed to Jerusalem in 2:2, and that reiterates this perspective with an address to Judah in 2:28. Likewise, material addressed to "the house of Israel" (5:15) appears in 5:14–19 within the context of that addressed to Jerusalem/Judah. The apostasy of both Israel and Judah are compared in 3:6–10, 11 with the aim of demonstrating that Judah is worse than Israel. Furthermore, both Israel[15] and Judah are addressed together in 5:20 (cf. 5:11), and Jerusalem is defined as "the remnant of Israel" (*šĕʾērît yiśrāʾēl*) in 6:8–9. Finally, the address to Jerusalem and Judah which begins in 4:3 is linked syntactically to material addressed explicitly to Israel in 4:1–2 by the connective, *kî*, "because." This demonstrates that a structural distinction can not be made at this point, and it suggests that a deliberate transition is made in the text which highlights the importance of the analogy between Israel and Judah made elsewhere in these chapters. Although the distinction between Israel and Judah is fundamental to the purposes of this text, the shift in address is not a criterion for establishing its structure.

Third, the fundamental significance of the analogy between Israel and Judah within this text points especially to Jer 3:6–10, 11, which establishes the analogy most clearly. Jeremiah 3:6–10, 11 is composed in narrative form, and the only other narrative material in this entire text appears in the YHWH-word transmis-

---

[15] Lit., "the house of Jacob."

sion formula in 2:1. Taken by itself, 2:1 establishes the generic character of this text as a report of YHWH's word to the prophet, insofar it describes objectively the transmission of YHWH word to Jeremiah. Furthermore, the 1cs pronoun suffix of *'ēlay*, "unto me," establishes that it is formulated as a first person statement by the prophet. Jeremiah 3:6–10, 11 is likewise formulated as 1cs statements by YHWH to the prophet. Likewise, both 2:2 and 3:12 contain commissioning formulae within the speech by YHWH to the prophet which instruct him to speak the following statements by YHWH to the people. These factors indicate that the narrative passages in Jer 2:1; 3:6–10; and 3:11, each formulated as a 1cs narrative report of YHWH's word to the prophet, mark the basic structural divisions of Jeremiah 2–6. These passages therefore characterize the whole as the prophet's report of YHWH's word to him concerning Israel and Judah.

This, of course, raises the issue of the interrelationship between Israel and Judah within the larger structure of this text. Jer 3:6–10, 11 plays an especially important role in establishing the analogy between Israel and Judah that defines an essential concern of this text. Because of its central position within the structure of the text, Jer 3:6–10 facilitates the transition from concern with Israel to concern with Jerusalem/Judah. Concern with Jerusalem/Judah appears in the context of concern with Israel in 2:1–3:5, and concern with Israel continues to be highlighted especially in 3:12–4:2, but also in the balance of 4:3–6:30. In both cases, concern with Jerusalem/Judah defines the context in which concern with Israel is raised. Jeremiah 2:2, 28 define the primary addressee of 2:2–3:5 as Jerusalem/Judah, and Jer 4:3–4 and the entire context of 4:5–6:30 define the primary addressee as Jerusalem/Judah as well, even though Israel is prominently mentioned.

Obviously, a thematic concern other than the distinction in addressee must define the interrelationship of the textual blocks Jer 2:1–3:5; 3:6–10; and 3:11–6:30. It is noteworthy that following the establishment of the analogy between Israel and Judah in 3:6–10, 11, the text immediately turns to a concern with the repentance of Israel that continues throughout the balance of the material directed to Israel in 3:12–4:2. In contrast, the material addressed directly to Jerusalem/Judah in 4:3–6:30 does not speak of repentance, but of the threat posed by the "foe from the north." At first sight, this appears to be unrelated to the repentance motif, but the nature of the analogy established between Israel and Judah in 3:6–10, 11 requires consideration of the interrelationship of these themes. Prior to the establishment of the analogy, the material directed to Israel in 2:2–3:5 focuses especially on YHWH's judgment against and punishment of Israel expressed metaphorically in terms of a divorce. Israel's guilt or abandonment of YHWH is established as the basis for the divorce decree. Likewise, Jer 4:5–6:30 focuses on Jerusalem's and Judah's guilt as the basis for the punishment at the hand of the "foe from the north" brought by YHWH. In this regard, the calls for the repentance of Israel in 3:12–4:2 play a very important role in relation to the following announcement of punishment directed to Jerusalem/Judah in that they provide the context for understanding the purpose of such judgment. Based on the analogy of Israel, which YHWH calls to repentance after its "divorce," Jerusalem/Judah will likewise be called to repentance in light of its upcoming punishment. This concern is hardly evident from 4:5–6:30; only the slightest hint of Jerusalem's repentance appears in 6:8, "be warned, O Jerusalem, lest my soul be thrust from you, lest I make you a desolation, an uninhabited land." Rather, it is evident from the literary context and structure of Jeremiah 2–6, in which Israel serves as an analogy for Jerusalem and Judah. It is also evident from the structural relationship between Jeremiah 2–6 and 1:4–10 and 1:11–19, in which the prophet is told respectively that YHWH will both destroy and rebuild (Jer 1:10) and that YHWH's punishment will come in the form of a threat from the north (Jer 1:13–19). Consequently, the call for repentance to Israel found in Jer 3:12–4:2 also serves as an indication of what YHWH expects from Jerusalem/ Judah once the punishment is completed.

The result is a three-part structure for Jeremiah 2–6. Jeremiah 2:1–3:5 constitutes "The Prophet's Report of YHWH's Word Concerning Israel" in the form of a trial speech or divorce proceeding. Jeremiah 3:6–10 constitutes "the Prophet's Report of YHWH's Word Concerning Both Israel's and Judah's Unfaithfulness in the Days of Josiah." Jeremiah 3:6–10 merely states the comparison or analogy between Israel and Judah, that is, both are unfaithful. Jeremiah 3:11 then asserts that the unfaithfulness of Judah is worse than that of Israel as the premise on which the following material will proceed. Jeremiah 3:11–6:30 therefore constitutes "The Prophet's Report of YHWH's Word Concerning Judah," which employs the analogy of Israel and Judah to call for repentance (Jer 3:12–4:4) as a basis for defining the purpose of the punishment announced in Jer 4:5–6:30.

IV

It is now possible to attempt a redation-critical reconstruction of an earlier form of Jeremiah 2–6. As noted above, the text identifies both the northern kingdom of Israel and the southern kingdom of Judah (or simply Jerusalem) as its addressees. Specific references for the northern kingdom include "Israel" (Jer 2:3, 14, 31; 4:1), the "house of Israel" (Jer 2:4, 26; 3:18, 20; 5:11, 15), the "sons of Israel" (Jer 3:21), the "house of Jacob" (Jer 2:4; 5:20), "apostate Israel" (Jer 3:6, 8, 11, 12), "repentant Israel" (Jer 3:23); specific references for the southern kingdom include "Judah" (Jer 3:18; 5:11), "treacherous Judah" (Jer 3:7, 8, 10, 11), "Jerusalem" (Jer 2:2; 4:3, 4, 5, 10, 11, 14, 16; 5:1; 6:6, 8), "Zion" (Jer 4:6), the "daughter of Zion" (Jer 4:31; 6:2, 23) and the "remnant of Israel" (Jer 6:9). Apart from the indirect references to the northern kingdom as the addressee that appear in various texts, all but one of the references to the northern kingdom as the addressee of the text (Jer 5:15) appear in Jer 2:2–4:2. Although the address to the northern kingdom is relatively consistent throughout Jer 2:2–4:2, it is set in a framework that identifies Jerusalem and Judah as the addressee.[16] This distinction in addressee is crucial for understanding the redactional character of this text in that the references to the southern kingdom appear primarily at the beginning and end of 2:1–4:4 and in the prose material in 3:6–11. This suggests that a text addressed to the northern kingdom of Israel has been reworked to address the southern kingdom of Judah.[17]

The redactional character of this text is evident in the relationship between the prose material in Jer 3:6–11, which establishes the analogy between the unfaithfulness of "apostate Israel" and that of "treacherous Judah," and the surrounding poetic material that is addressed to the northern kingdom. Since Mowinckel's early source-critical study identified poetic material in Jeremiah 1–25 as source A and the prose sermons as source C,[18] scholars have become accustomed to identifying the source A material as the work of Jeremiah himself and the prose material as the work of a Deuteronomistic redaction.[19] Although the distinction between poetry and prose is not in itself an adequate criterion to define the redactional character of a text, a recent study by McKane demonstrates the exegetical relationship between Jer 3:6–11 and both 3:1–5 and 3:12–13.[20] The prose material in 3:6–11 takes up vocabulary and develops themes from both 3:1–5 and 3:12–13 which demonstrates its redactional character. Thus, Jer 3:6–11 takes up the divorce theme from 3:1–5, the appellation *mĕšubâ yiśrā'ēl* from 3:12, and the phrase *taḥat kol 'ēṣ ra'ănān*, "under every green tree," from 3:13, all of which appear in contexts that are addressed to the northern kingdom of Israel, in order to create a text that establishes the analogy between the unfaithfulness of Israel and that of Judah. As noted above, the purpose of this text is to establish that the guilt of Judah is greater that that of Israel. It thereby creates the premise for the final form of this text which warns Judah of the coming punishment from YHWH in the form of an enemy from the north and thus calls for Judah's repentance just as Israel was called to repent. In this manner, the redaction apparent in

---

[16] Jer 2:2, 28; 3:6–10, 11, 18; 4:3–4.

[17] Note that in the bulk of Jer 2:1–2aα, including the reference to Jerusalem, is missing in the LXX, which reads only, *kai eipe*, "and he said," prior to the messenger formula in v. 2aα.

[18] See Sigmund Mowinckel, *Zur Komposition des Buches Jeremia* (Kristiana: Jacob Dybwad, 1914); cf. Bernhard Duhm, *Das Buch Jeremia* (Tübingen: Mohr Siebeck, 1901).

[19] See, for example, Winfried Thiel, *Die deuteronomistische Redaktion von Jeremia 1–25* (WMANT 41; Neukirchen-Vluyn: Neukirchener, 1981).

[20] William McKane, "Relations Between Poetry and Prose in the Book of Jeremiah with Special Reference to Jeremiah III 6–11 and XII 14–17," *Congress Volume: Vienna 1980* (ed., J. A. Emerton; VTSup 32; Leiden: Brill, 1981) 220–37, esp. 229–33; see also his *A Critical and Exegetical Commentary on Jeremiah. I. Introduction and Commentary on Jeremiah I–XXV* (ICC; Edinburgh: T & T Clark, 1986) 67–69. Cf. Thiel, *Jeremia 1–25* 83–93, who assigns Jer 3:6–13 to the basic deuteronomic redaction of the book of Jeremiah during the exile and Jer 3:14–18 to various postexilic expansions.

Jer 3:6–11 transforms a text that calls for the repentance of Israel following its punishment to one that announces the anticipated punishment of Judah as a basis for its subsequent repentance.

A similar concern is evident in the framework material that appears at the beginning (Jer 2:1–2) and end (4:3–4) of the material addressed to the northern kingdom of Israel. Following the narrative YHWH-word transmission formula in 2:1, Jer 2:2 contains a commissioning formula in which YHWH commissions the prophet to speak the following words "in the ears of Jerusalem" (*bĕʾoznê yĕrûšalayim*). This is remarkable in that the following material is addressed to the northern kingdom, not Jerusalem, as indicated by the address forms discussed in the analysis of the structure presented above. Nevertheless, such a distinction serves the purposes of the redaction evident in 3:6–11; that is, the experience of the northern kingdom of Israel will serve as an analogy and example for Judah.

The same may be said of the juxtaposition of the address to Israel in Jer 4:1–2, which states the conditions of Israel's repentance, and the address to Judah in 4:3–4, which is linked syntactically to 4:1–2 by the particle *kî*, "for, because." The address to Judah cannot be considered separately from that to Israel; the command for Judah and Jerusalem to "plow its own field" and to "circumcise itself" must be taken as a consequence of the instructions to Israel to remove its filth and to restore righteousness and justice; that is, just as Israel must repent so must Judah and Jerusalem. Again, the experience of Israel serves an analogy and model for Judah.

The framework passages in Jer 2:1–2 and 4:3–4 and the prose material in 3:6–11 appears to be redactional in that they transform material addressed to the northern kingdom of Israel into material addressed to the southern kingdom of Judah. Two exceptions appear, however, that must be considered. The first occurs in Jer 2:28 in the form of an address to Judah which appears unexpectedly in the context of an address to the northern kingdom. But v. 28b, *kî mispar ʿārêkā hāyû ʾĕlōhêkā yĕhûdâ*, "for the number of your cities were as the number of your gods, O Judah," appears to be a gloss in that it duplicates exactly the language of Jer 11:13 which addresses Judah's revolt against YHWH. Such an address is anomalous in an immediate context which addresses the northern kingdom (cf. 2:26, 31) with no indication of a transition. It would appear that the glossator or redactor of this text employed a statement form 11:13 to establish the context of an address to Judah in keeping with the purposes of the overall redaction of this text evident in 2:1–2; 3:6–11; 4:3–4. The second appears in Jer 3:18, which looks forward to the time when the "house of Judah" will walk together with the "house of Israel." But such a statement is consistent with expectations that the northern kingdom of Israel would be reunited with the southern kingdom of Judah under Davidic rule in Jerusalem as result of its repentance (cf. Jer 3:14–17). It need not be explained as a redactional expansion in this text.

From these considerations, it becomes apparent that the redaction has transformed a text addressed to the northern kingdom of Israel to one that is addressed to Jerusalem and Judah. Thus the anticipation of Judah's punishment and the expectation of Judah's repentance in the larger framework of Jeremiah 2–6 are based on Israel's experience of punishment and call for repentance evident in Jer 2:2–4:2.

The redactional material in Jer 2:1aα^1; 2:28; 3:6–11; and 4:3–4 establishes the analogy between Israel and Judah. Once this material is removed, a relatively coherent text remains in which the northern kingdom of Israel is called to repentance. The text begins with the trial speech or divorce proceeding identified earlier in Jer 2:1–3:5, which identifies Israel as YHWH's bride (2:1aα$^{2-3}$) and continues with the divorce proceeding proper in which YHWH states the grounds for divorce and argues that Israel has no basis on which to argue. The result is a call for repentance in Jer 3:12–4:2 in which Israel is given the chance to return to YHWH provided the filth is removed and Israel is "circumcised," or purified from previous wrongdoing.[21]

The setting of such a text must be placed in the reign of King Josiah, who attempted to restore the former northern kingdom of Israel to Davidic rule and thereby to reunite the twelve tribes of Israel. In this case, the repentance and purification of the former northern kingdom articulated in Jer 3:12–4:2 is equated with its reunification with Judah under Davidic rule (cf. Jer 3:14–18). Josiah's destruction of the former northern sanctuary at Beth El (2 Kgs 23:15–15–20), his attempts to centralize worship and royal authority in Jerusalem (2 Kgs 23:1–25), and his marriages to women from Libnah and Rumah (2 Kgs 23:31, 36; 24:18), all demonstrate his intention to bring the territory of the former northern kingdom of Israel under David rule and thereby to strengthen the authority of the Davidic dynasty.[22] Insofar as the superscription to the book of Jeremiah states

---

[21] It must remain uncertain whether Jer 5:15–17, which is also addressed to the northern kingdom, ever formed a part of this text. Note the address to *bêt yiśrā'ēl*, "the House of Israel," in v. 15. The vocabulary of this passage suggests that it may allude to Isa 5:26–30, which also addresses the northern kingdom of Israel in the context of the book of Isaiah. In this case, a warning to Israel would serve the purposes of the composer of the material addressed to Judah in Jer 4:3–6:30 who built upon the analogy between Israel and Judah established in the redaction of Jeremiah 2–6.

[22] For an overview of Josiah's policies during this period, see Jay Wilcoxen, "the Policitical Background of Jeremiah's Temple Sermon," *Scripture in History and Theology* (ed. A. Merrill and T. Overholt; Fest. J. C. Rylaarsdam; Pittsburgh: Pickwick, 1977) 151–66. See also R. Althann, "Josiah," *ABD* 3:1015–18 and the bibliography cited there; D. L. Christensen, "Zeph 2:14–15: A Theological Basis for Josiah's Program of Political Expansion," *CBQ* 46 (1984) 669–82; M. A. Sweeney, "A Form-Critical Reassessment of the Book of Zephaniah," *CBQ* 53 (1991) 388–408; W. E. Claburn, "The Fiscal Basis of Josiah's Reforms," *JBL* 92 (1973) 11–22; Naomi Steinberg, "the Deuteronomic Law Code and the Politics of State Centralization," *The Bible and the Politics of Exegesis* (ed. D. Jobling et al.; Fest. N. K. Gottwald; Cleveland: Pilgrim, 1991) 161–70, 336–39; N. Na'aman, "the Kingdom of Judah under Josiah," *Tel Aviv* 18 (1991) 3–71.

that the prophet was active during the reign of Josiah (Jer 1:1–3), it would appear that this address to the northern kingdom was written by Jeremiah as part of an attempt to support Josiah's policies of reform and restoration. Certainly, the favorable reference to Josiah in Jer 22:13–17 indicate the prophet's support for Josiah.

Likewise, the redaction that established the analogy between the call for Israel's repentance and the warning to Judah would also stem from Jeremiah. Following the death of Josiah in 609 B.C.E., Judah came under threat from Egypt and later from Babylon. The present text of Jeremiah 2–6 certainly indicates fear of a threat from both Egypt and Assyria (cf. Jer 2:16–18, 36–37), which suggests that, with its warning of punishment by an "enemy from the north," it is consistent with Jeremiah's advice to avoid alliance with Egypt and to submit to Babylon as an expression of YHWH's will (cf. Jeremiah 27–28; 29). Just as Israel was punished and called to repent for its rejection of YHWH, so Judah's attempts to ally with Egypt against Babylon during the early reign of Jehoiakim (609–598 B.C.E.) prior to the Babylonian defeat of Egypt at Carchemesh in 605 would provide an appropriate setting for this text.

V

In conclusion, this essay demonstrates that a synchronic literary evaluation of the structure and themes of Jeremiah 2–6 provides a basis for the redaction-critical reconstruction of an earlier text form. In the present case, it proves evidence for the activity of the prophet during the reign of King Josiah. It demonstrates that the prophet supported Josiah's policy of reunification of the former northern kingdom of Israel with Judah under Davidic rule. It further demonstrates the prophet's conclusion that, in light of Josiah's death and the failure of his program, the case of Israel provides an analogy with that of Judah. Just as Israel was called to repentance for its abandonment of YHWH, so Judah will also face punishment for abandoning YHWH. By analogy with Israel's experience in the view of this text, such punishment will also serve as the basis for Judah's repentance once the punishment is complete.

Appendix

Jeremiah 2–6: Structure Diagram

Prophetic Summons to Repentance directed to Judah	Jer 2:1–6:30
I. Prophet's report of YHWH's Word concerning Israel:	
Trial speech/Divorce proceeding	2:1–3:5
A. Narrative introduction: word transmission Formula	2:1

B. Report of YHWH's word proper: trial speech/divorce proceeding	2:2–3:5
1. commissioning speech concerning Israel as YHWH's bride	2:2–3
a. commissioning formula	2:2aα^1
b. content of commission: YHWH's reminiscence of Israel as bride: basis for trial/divorce proceeding	2:2aα^2–3
2. trial speech/divorce proceeding proper	2:4–3:5
a. call to attention directed to Jacob/Israel	2:4
b. messenger speech concerning basis for YHWH's continuing controversy against Israel	2:5–11
(1) concerning Israel's rejection of YHWH's benefits/actions for Israel	2:5–8
(2) announcement of continuing controversy	2:9–11
c. concerning YHWH's accusations against Israel: abandonment of YHWH	2:12–28
(1) YHWH speech accusing Israel of abandonment with call to attention directed to heavens	2:12–13
(2) prophet's elaboration speech concerning Israel's turn to Egypt/Assur	2:14–19a
(3) YHWH speech concerning Israel's pursuit of other lovers	2:19b–25
(4) prophet's elaboration concerning Israel's reliance on other gods	2:26–28
d. concerning Israel's lack of grounds for argument	2:29–3:5
(1) YHWH speech questioning Israel's ability to contend	2:29–30
(2) prophet's elaboration: confirmation of divorce proceeding/grounds for judgment	2:31–3:5
(a) prophet's quote of YHWH speech stating YHWH's rejection of Israel	2:31–37
(b) substantiation concerning law of divorce	3:1–5
II. Prophetic Report of Conversation with YHWH Concerning Israel's and Judah's Unfaithfulness in Days of Josiah	3:6–10
III. Prophet's Report of YHWH's Word Concerning Judah	3:11–6:30
A. Report of YHWH's call for repentance to Israel	3:11–17
1. report of YHWH's word that Israel is more righteous than Judah	3:11
2. commissioning speech to prophet to call for Israel's repentance	3:12–17
a. commissioning formula	3:12aα^1
b. two-fold call for repentance	3:12aα^2–17
(1) 1st call: premise	3:12aα^2–13
(2) 2nd call: repentance leads to restoration of Zion	3:14–17
B. concerning future realization of Judah's repentance	3:18–6:30
1. premise: Israel and Judah will walk together in land after repentance	3:18–25
2. conditions of repentance for Israel and Judah	4:1–4
3. warning to Judah/Jerusalem of YHWH's punishment in form of enemy from north	4:5–6:30

8. Jeremiah 30–31 and King Josiah's Program of National Restoration and Religious Reform

I

Jeremiah 30–31 constitutes the prophet's report of the word of YHWH concerning the establishment of a new covenant Israel with and Judah. As part of the present form of Jeremiah, these chapters presuppose the Babylonian destruction of Jerusalem and Judah the years 597–582 B.C.E. Although Jeremiah 30–31 stands by itself as a distinct literary unit, it is frequently considered as a component of a larger "Book of Consolation" in Jeremiah 30–33[1]; Jeremiah 30–33 in turn culminates in an announcement of the restoration of the House of David in Jer 33:14–26 that draws upon the language of Jer 23:5–8.[2] Jeremiah 31:28 likewise employs language from Jeremiah's vocation account to refer to the "building" and "planting" of the "uprooted" and "destroyed" kingdoms of Israel and Judah (Jer 1:1–19, esp. v. 10). These chapters therefore play an important role in defining the outlook of the book of Jeremiah concerning the restoration of Israel that will follow the Babylonian exile.

Although the present form of Jeremiah 30–31 addresses the restoration of Israel following the Babylonian exile, scholars generally maintain that these chapters represent an expansion or reworking of an earlier text form.[3] The basis

---

[1] Cf. Mark Biddle, "The Literary Frame Surrounding Jeremiah 30,1–33,26," *ZAW* 100 (1988) 409–13.

[2] On the redactional character and interrelationship of Jer 33:14–26 and 23:5–8, see Y. Goldman, *Prophétie et royauté au retour de l'exil. Les origins littéraires de la forme massorétique du livre de Jérémie* (OBO 118; Freiburg: Universitätsverg; Göttingen: Vandenhoeck & Ruprecht, 1992) 9–64, esp. 38–44, 45–52.

[3] For the history of research on these chapters, see S. Böhmer, *Heimkehr und neuer Bund. Studien zur Jeremia 30–31* (Göttingen: Vandenhoeck & Ruprecht, 1976) 11 ff; N. Lohfink, "Der junge Jeremia als Propagandist und Poet. Zum Grundstock von Jer 30–31," *Le Livre de Jérémie. Le prophète et son milieu. Les oracles et leur transmission* (ed. P.-M. Bogaert; BETL 54; Leuven: Peeters and Leuven University Press, 1981) 351–68, esp. 352–3; B. Bozak, *Life "Anew" A Literary-Theological Study of Jer. 30–31* (AnBib 122; Rome: Biblical Institute, 1991) 1–17; S. Herrmann, *Jeremiah. Der Prophet und das Buch* (Erträge der Forschung 271; Darmstadt: Wissenschaftliche Buchgesellschaft, 1990) 146–62; J. Lundbom, "Jeremiah, Book of," *ABD* 3:706–21. See also N. Kilpp, *Niederreissen und aufbauen. Das Verhältnis von Heilsverheissung und Unheilsverkündigung bei Jeremia und im Jeremiabuch* (Neukirchen-Vluyn: Neukirchener, 1990); G. Fohrer, "Der Israel-Prophet in Jeremia 30–31," *Studien zum Alten Testament (1966–1988)* (BZAW 196; Berlin and New York: Walter de Gruyter, 1991)

for this view is quite clear. Whereas the introductory and concluding material of Jeremiah 30–31 speaks of the restoration of *both* the "House of Israel" and the "House of Judah" (Jer 30:2–3, 4; 31:27–30, 31–34; cf. 31:37–40), the bulk of the material in these chapters speak of the restoration *only* of a devastated Israel to Judah and the House of David (e. g., Jer 30:5–11; 31:7–14; cf. 30:18–31:1; 31:16–22). Nevertheless, many scholars follow Volz in identifying the name "Israel" as an exilic or post-exilic designation for the restored people of Israel and Judah.[4]

The most cogent recent proposal for the reconstruction of this text is that of Lohfink who argues that the *Urtext* of Jeremiah 30–31 constitutes the prophet's statements in support of King Josiah's (640–609 B.C.E.) program of national reunification and religious reform during the early years of his prophetic activity.[5] Lohfink rejects the traditional critical view that these chapters comprise a variety of short, originally independent units, and maintains that a single, coherent composition stands behind the present form of Jeremiah 30–31. Employing a variety of arguments based on form and content to eliminate secondary material, he reconstructs the earliest form of these chapters comprising seven strophes: 30:5–7, 12–15, 18–21; 31:2–6, 15–17, 18–20, 21–22. The text presents a progression of thought that begins with the motif of the north in distress (strophes I and II), continues with the restoration in the land (strophes III and IV) and the return of the deportees (strophes V and VI), and concludes with a call for the return of the deportees (strophe VII). This text therefore demonstrates Jeremiah's role as a propagandist in support of Josiah's reform.

But there are problems with Lohfink's analysis.[6] One of his principle criteria for identifying material is the presence of redactional formulae, such as *wĕhāyâ bayyôm hahû'* in Jer 30:8; *lākēn* in Jer 30:16; *kî koh 'āmar yhwh* in 31:7; *koh 'āmar yhwh* in 31:23, 35, 37; and *hinneh yāmîm bā'îm* in 31:27, 31, 38. Unfortunately, this does not appear to supply a secure criterion in that the presence of such formulations does not *necessarily* demonstrate the presence of secondary

---

56–69; G. Fischer, *Das Trostbüchlein. Text, Komposition und Theologie von Jer 30–31* (SBB 26; Stuttgart: Katholisches Biblewerk, 1993). Note especially R. P. Carroll, *From Chaos to Covenant: Uses of Prophecy in the Book of Jeremiah* (New York: Crossroad, 1981) 198–225, esp. 201, who acknowledges Deuteronomistic influence in the redaction of Jeremiah 30–33 based on its emphasis on salvation in these chapters. According to Carroll, Jeremiah could not have been a prophet of salvation because he announced the destruction of Jerusalem. Rather, later circles concerned with the restoration of Jerusalem attached a message of salvation to the prophet as a means to express their theological outlook in the final form of the book.

[4] P. Volz, *Der Prophet Jeremia* (KAT X; Leipzig: A. Deichert, 1922) 274–98.

[5] Lohfink, "Der junge Jeremiah"; cf. W. L. Holladay, *Jeremiah 2: A Commentary on the Book of the Prophet Jeremiah, Chapters 26–52* (Hermeneia; Philadelphia: Fortress, 1989) 148–201.

[6] Cf. U. Schröter, "Jeremias Botschaft für das Nordreich. Zu N. Lohfinks Überlegungen zum Grundbestand von Jeremia XXX–XXXI," *VT* 35 (1985) 312–29; H. Leene, "Jeremiah 31:23–26 and the Redaction of the Book of Comfort," *ZAW* 104 (1992) 349–64, who attempt to modify Lohfink's analysis.

material; rather, such formulations frequently serve a rhetorical function as transitional markers within a coherent text. The problem is further complicated by inconsistent decision concerning the messenger formula in this text. Thus, *koh ʾāmar yhwh* is redactional in 31:23, but not in 30:18; 31:2, 15, 16. Likewise, *kî koh ʾāmar yhwh* is redactional in 31:7, but in 30:5 and 30:12. A second problem emerges in that Lohfink removes materials that contain promises directed specifically to the northern kingdom of Israel throughout the text. Jeremiah 30:8–11 and 30:16–17, for example, conflict with Lohfink's identification of the initial presentation of northern Israel's distress in strophes I and II, and Jer 31:35–36 and Jer 31:37 fall outside of his strophic structure. Obviously, these considerations raise questions concerning Lohfink's analysis.

Nevertheless, a consistent set of formal criteria appears within the structure of Jeremiah 30–31 that provides the key for distinguishing primary and secondary material within this text. The structure of Jeremiah 30–31 is defined by the interrelationship of the two basic formulae that introduce most of its constituent structural units: *koh ʾāmar yhwh / kî koh ʾāmar yhwh* in Jer 30:2, 18; 31:2, 15, 16, 23, 35, 37 / 30:5, 12; 31:7, and *hinneh yāmîm bāʾîm* in Jer 30:3; 31:27, 31, 38.[7] It is noteworthy that passages introduced by *hinneh yāmîm bāʾîm* uniformly take up the fate of *both* Israel and Judah, whereas passages introduced by *koh ʾāmar yhwh / kî koh ʾāmar yhwh* focus on the northern kingdom of Israel in a relatively consistent fashion. There are, of course, exceptions. Both formulas appear together in the context of Jer 30:1–4, but an analysis of the structure of Jeremiah 30–31 demonstrates that these verses constitute the introductory material that identifies the structural principles by which this text was composed. Likewise, Jer 30:12–17 addresses a wounded Zion rather than the northern kingdom of Israel, but the only identification of Zion in this text appears in v. 17, in which the statement *ṣîyôn hîʾ* appears to be a textual alteration from an original *ṣēdenû hîʾ*, "it is our food" (see BHS note), which corresponds to the imagery of devouring oppressors in vv. 16–17. Finally, Jer 31:23–26 appears to address the restoration of Judah in the present form of the text, but an examination of its vocabulary and contents in relation to the structure of the text demonstrates that it takes up the return of the northern kingdom of Israel to Judah.

II

Redaction critical work must begin with a clear understanding of the final form of the text as the basis for literary-historical reconstruction.[8] An analysis of the

---

[7] Cf. Bozak, *Life "Anew"* 18–26, who identifies the repeated messenger formulas as one of the basic structural principles of this text.

[8] See R. P. Knierim, "Criticism of Literary Features, Form, Tradition, and Redaction," in *The Hebrew Bible and its Modern Interpreters* (ed. D. A. Knight and G. M. Tucker; Chico: Scholars

structure of Jeremiah 30–31 provides the means to define the concerns and logical flow of the ideas contained within this text that calls for the restoration of *both* Israel and Judah following the collapse of the kingdom of Judah during the years 597–582 B.C.E. Unfortunately, a fully detailed discussion of the structure of Jeremiah 30–31 is not possible within the limits of the present context, but an analysis of the major features of the structure of these chapters provides the criteria for reconstructing an earlier form of the text that calls for the restoration of the former kingdom of Israel to Judah and Davidic rule. In so far as this concern was a primary feature of King Josiah's program of national restoration and religious reform, it demonstrates that the prophet Jeremiah was a supporter of Josiah's reform during the early stages of his prophetic career.

Jeremiah 30–31 is demarcated initially by the formula, *haddābār ʾăšer hāyâ ʾel yirmĕyāhû meʾet yhwh lēʾmor*, "the word which was to Jeremiah from YHWH, saying," which introduces the entire unit. A similar formula in Jer 32:1, *haddābār ʾăšer hāyâ ʾel yirmĕyāhû meʾet yhwh*, marks the beginning of the new unit in Jeremiah 32. These chapters are tied together thematically by their concern with the restoration of the fallen houses of Israel and Judah, indicated at the beginning (30:2–4) and the end (31:37–40) of the unit. They are united formally by the appearance of the formulas, *koh ʾāmar yhwh / kî koh ʾāmar yhwh*, "thus says YHWH / for thus says YHWH," and *hinneh yāmîm bāʾîm*, "behold the days are coming," throughout the text. The formulae appear together at the beginning of the unit in 30:2–3, and they appear individually in 30:18; 31:2, 15, 16, 23, 35, 37 / 30:5, 12; 31:7 and in 31:27, 31, 38 respectively.

The structure of Jeremiah 30–31 is defined initially by the appearance of the superscription in 30:1, which identifies the following material as "the word of YHWH which was to Jeremiah." Because superscriptions stand apart from the material which they identify and introduce,[9] the superscription in 30:1 and the body of the text in 30:2–31:40 constitute the two major structural elements of this text. Jeremiah 30:2–31:40 may then be characterized as the prophet's report of YHWH's word.

The structure of 30:2–31:40 is defined by the appearance of the formula *koh ʾāmar yhwh* in 30:2, 18; 31:2, 15, 16, 23, 35, 37, which introduces the constituent sub-units of this text and thereby specifies the components of "the word of YHWH" to Jeremiah mentioned in the superscription. YHWH's command to Jeremiah to write the words in a book appears in 30:2–3 together with an introductory statement in 30:4 that identifies the following materials as the words

---

Press, 1985) 123–65, esp. 156; M. A. Sweeney, "Formation and Form in Prophetic Literature," in *The Future of Old Testament Interpretation: Essays in Honor of Gene M. Tucker* (ed. J. L. Mays et al; Nashville: Abingdon, 1995) 113–26.

[9] See G. Tucker, "Prophetic Superscriptions and the Growth of the Canon," *Canon and Authority: Essays in Old Testament Religion and Theology* (ed. B. O. Long and G. W. Coats; Philadelphia: Fortress, 1977) 56–77.

of YHWH. Nevertheless, the initial sub-unit of the text comprises 30:2–17. Both 30:2–3 and 30:4–17 are formulated as the author's report of YHWH's words to the prophet, and they are linked together by the conjunctive *waw* at the beginning of 30:4. Successive appearances of the formula *kî koh 'āmar yhwh* in 30:5 and 30:12, linked syntactically by the conjunctive particle, *kî*, define the two specific words of YHWH that appear within 30:2–17. In contrast, the appearances of the formula *koh 'āmar yhwh* in 30:18; 31:2, 15, 16, 23, 35, 37 are not linked by syntactical connectives to Jer 30:2–17. Whereas Jer 30:2–17 constitutes the initial report of YHWH's word, the following appearances of the formula *koh 'āmar yhwh* define subsequent reports of YHWH's word in 30:18–31:1; 31:2–14; 31:15; 31:16–22; 31:23–34; 31:35–36; and 31:37–40. The successive reports of the word of YHWH to Jeremiah convey an image of Israel's and Judah's devastation, repentance, eventual restoration, and YHWH's guarantee of eternal security.

The initial report of YHWH's word in Jer 30:2–17 constitutes a report of YHWH's instruction to Jeremiah to write YHWH's words in a book. The structure of the passage includes two basic sub-units. The first is the report of the introduction proper in 30:2–3, defined by the objective reporting language that frames the statements by YHWH quoted by the author and by its focus on the instruction per se. The second is the report of YHWH's words concerning Israel and Judah that are to be recorded by the prophet in 30:4–17, linked to 30:2–3 by the initial conjunctive *waw*.[10] Two reports of YHWH's words appear in 30:5–11 and 30:12–17, as indicated by the introductory formula *kî koh 'āmar yhwh* in each. The references to Jacob (vv. 7, 10 [2x]) and to Israel (v. 10) in the context of 2ms address language demonstrate that 30:5–11 is addressed to Israel. It is formulated as a prophetic announcement of salvation with two basic elements. Jeremiah 30:5–7 constitutes a report of Jacob's distress, which focuses on the image of Israel's men suffering as if they were women in childbirth, and Jer 30:8–11 constitutes a report of YHWH's announcement of salvation, which states that YHWH will defeat the oppressor and restore Israel to Davidic rule and that Israel's punishment will be limited. The reference to Zion (v. 17) in the context of 2fs address language demonstrates that 30:12–17 is addressed to Judah or more specifically to Zion. Jer 30:12–15 constitutes a report of Zion's distress, which describes Zion's mortal wounds. Jeremiah 30:16–17, linked syntactically by the introductory *lākēn*, "therefore," reports YHWH's announcement of salvation to Zion, as demonstrated by the appearance of the oracular formula in v. 17 and the employment of the 2fs address language directed to Judah.

The report of YHWH's second word appears in Jer 30:18–31:1. The reference to "the return of the captivity of the tents of Jacob" in v. 18 and the 1st person

---

[10] Contra B. Becking, "'I Will Break His Yoke From Off Your Neck,' Remarks on Jeremiah xxx 4–11," *OTS* 25 (1989) 63–76, who defines Jer 30:4–11 as the primary unit based on the Masoretic divisions of the text.

announcement language addressed to a 2mp addressee (see v. 22) demonstrates that the passage is a report of YHWH's word of salvation for Israel. The word report in vv. 18–22 includes a series of five statements concerning the return of Jacob's captivity, the increase and honor of the people, the punishment of the oppressors, the restoration of Jacob's ruler, and a version of the covenant formula which states that the covenant relationship between Israel and YHWH will be restored. The prophet's evaluation of YHWH's word appears in Jer 30:23–31:1. This passage is introduced by *hinneh*, and it is formulated in 2mp address language (see v. 24) and objective announcement language that describes YHWH's anger and its effects. It includes a metaphorical description of YHWH's anger as a storm, a statement that YHWH's anger will end only when YHWH decides that it should, and the prophet's address to Israel stating that Israel will understand in the future and quoting YHWH's statement of the covenant formula directed to all the families of Israel. Altogether, 30:23–31:1 affirms YHWH's word of salvation in 30:18–22.

The report of YHWH's third word appears in Jer 31:2–14 is concerned with the restoration of Israel to Zion (see esp. vv. 6, 11–12). The appearance of the formula *kî koh ʾāmar yhwh* in 31:7 demonstrates that the passage comprises two reports of YHWH's word in 31:2–6 and 31:7–14 respectively. The initial word report in vv. 2–6 includes a 2fs address to *bĕtûlat yiśrāʾēl*, "the virgin Israel," concerning Israel's restoration. The address begins with an objective description of Israel's approach to YHWH in the wilderness[11] and a quotation of YHWH's address to *bĕtûlat yiśrāʾēl* (n.b. v. 4), indicated by 1cs speaker's forms and the 2fs address forms employed throughout these verses, which contains a series of statements that focus on YHWH's eternal love for the "maiden" Israel and

---

[11] Read *nirʾāh lî* in v. 3a as *nirʾāh lô* with LXX (see BHS notes). Verse 3a will then read, "from afar, YHWH appeared to him (i.e., Israel)," which is consistent with the description of Israel's approach to YHWH in v. 2αβ–b. In the MT, v. 3a is formulated as a 1cs statement, "from afar, YHWH appeared to me." Although the immediate context might suggest that Israel is the intended speaker here, there is nothing in the text to indicate to the scribe that a dialogue should take place between Israel and YHWH (cf. D. Barthélemy et al, *Critique textuelle de l'ancien testament.2.Isaïe, Jérémie, Lamentations* (OBO 50/2; Freiburg: Universitätsverlag; Göttingen: Vandenhoeck & Ruprecht, 1986) 603–4, who argue that the MT reading should be retained because it is the *lectio difficilior* and because it identifies Israel as the 1st person speaker in the dialogue of vv. 4–5). It is likely that the introduction of the 1cs reference was motivated by the statement in Jer 31:26, "Because of this, I awakened, and I saw, and my sleep was pleasant to me." This statement indicates that Jeremiah's prophecies appeared to him in a dream, and it is likely that the statement was intended to introduce the following material that is characterized by the formula *hinneh yāmîm bāʾîm* as a vision of the future. Unfortunately, there is no antecedent for such visionary experience in this text. By changing *nirʾāh lô* to *nirʾāh lî*, the scribe apparently provided such an antecedent within the text that then presents the word reports as the product of the prophet's vision in a dream. Note that *nirʾāh* is reflected in the verb *wāʾerʾeh*, "and I saw," and that *lî* is reflected in the statement *ûšnātî ʿārĕbāh lî*, "and my sleep was pleasant to me," in Jer 31:26. Contra Leene, *ZAW* 104 (1992) 349–64, who argues that Jer 31:23–26 builds upon the imagery of 31:21–22, but his analysis does not consider the structural criteria defined here nor the significance of the reading *nirʾāh lî* in 31:3.

her return to Zion. The second word report in Jer 31:7–14 substantiates the first by forward calls to rejoice over Israel's restoration to Zion (see esp. vv. 7, 10). The messenger formula *kî koh ʾāmar yhwh* links these verses to vv. 2–6, and the announcement of Israel's restoration presents two addresses. The first employs mp address forms directed to an unspecified addressee to call for rejoicing over the restoration of Israel. The second employs mp address forms directed to the nations (see v. 10a) to rejoice over YHWH's redemption and return of Israel to Zion.

The report of YHWH's fourth word in Jer 31:15 describes Rachel's weeping in Ramah for her lost sons.

The report of YHWH's fifth word in Jer 31:16–22 focuses on the repentance of Israel as the basis for the restoration of the relationship with YHWH. The word report proper appears in vv. 16–20, formulated as a mixed fs and mp address by YHWH to Ephraim. Presumably, the appearance of 2fs address forms in this context may be attributed to the metaphorical identification of Ephraim as *Rachel* in Jer 31:15. The word proper comprises three basic elements: the imperative command to stop weeping; the 1cs report by YHWH of Ephraim's repentance; and YHWH's assertion in the form of a rhetorical question that Ephraim's relationship is secure. The second major sub-unit of this text, Jer 31:21–22 constitutes the prophet's exhortation to *bĕtûlat yiśrāʾēl*, which personifies Ephraim, to return to her cities. It is formulated as a 2fs address which includes a command to set out on the journey and a statement of the reason for the command. The rhetorical question in v. 22a and the statement in v. 22b together assert that YHWH has done something new. The fact that a woman now "encompasses" or acts as a man becomes the basis for the command for the return of *bĕtûlat yiśrāʾēl*.[12]

---

[12] In this case, the phrase *nĕqebah tĕsôbeb gāber*, "a female encompasses a man," refers to the image of the female *bĕtûlat yiśrāʾēl* erecting highway markers and journeying back to her cities. Note the assonantal associate between the phrase *habbat haššobebāh*, "the wandering daughter," in v. 22a and *nĕqebah tĕsôbeb gāber* in v. 22b which associates the female figure with highway building and travel. Normally, such activities would pertain to a man rather than to a woman in Israelite society. Likewise, the reversal of gender role activities calls to mind the metaphorical reference in Jer 30:6 to the suffering of Israel's warriors (i. e., *geber*) in terms of childbirth (cf. Holladay, *Jeremiah 2* 194–5). Holladay's understanding of role reversal in terms of sexual and military activities, however, is mistaken; the assonantal association between vv. 21–22a and v. 22b indicates that in setting up highway markers and traveling alone, the female acts as a man, and thereby effects the restoration of Israel to Zion. Note also the reference to *ṣiyunîm*, "road markers," is a play on the Hebrew word *ṣiyôn*, "Zion," and indicates that Israel returns to Zion (Holladay, *Jeremiah 2* 193–4). Likewise, the reference *tamrûrîm*, "signposts," may well be a play on the Hebrew word *tomer*, "palm tree." The *tomer* designates Deborah's tree in Judg 4:5, which is identified as *ʾallôn bākût*, "oak of weeping," in Gen 35:8. Deborah's tree was located nearby to Rachel's tomb in Benjamin (cf. 1 Sam 10:2). The motif of weeping pervades the region south of nearby Beth El (cf Judg 2:1–5; cf. L. Luker, "Rachel's Tomb," *ABD* 5:608–9), which suggests that the motif of Rachel's weeping may be derived from the presence of Rachel's tomb on the highway between Beth El and Jerusalem. In any case,

The report of YHWH's sixth word appears in Jer 31:23–34 as an announcement of the new covenant between YHWH and Israel/Judah. The word report proper appears in vv. 23–25, which asserts YHWH's blessing for Judah and the return of Herdsmen to Judah, and it states that the basis for this situation lies in YHWH's restoration of the people. The reference to YHWH as G-d of Israel in v. 23 indicates that the restoration of Judah is effected by the return of Israel to Zion. The second major sub-unit of the passage is Jer 31:26–34, which builds upon the imagery of vv. 23–25 by presenting the prophet's announcement of his vision of a new covenant between YHWH and Israel/Judah in the future. The text comprises three basic sub-units demarcated by vv. 27 and 31. The first is the prophet's report of his visionary experience in v. 26, presumably the setting in which he received the preceding word of YHWH.[13] The second is the prophet's first announcement in vv. 27–30 that focuses on the restoration of the House of Israel and the House of Judah. Verses 27–28 portray the future restoration itself, and vv. 29–30 employ a proverb to state that only the guilty are punished, there by clearing the way for restoration once the guilty are removed. The third is the prophet's second announcement in vv. 31–34 that focuses on the institution of a new covenant between YHWH and Israel/Judah. The announcement is formulated as an oracular report of YHWH's word which states that the new covenant will not be like the old Exodus covenant in that YHWH's Torah is placed in the heart of the people so that all will know YHWH.

The report of YHWH's seventh word appears in Jer 31:35–36, as indicated by the expanded messenger formula in v. 35 and the standard messenger formula in v. 37. The unit focuses on YHWH's eternal promise to Israel. The expanded messenger formula delineates YHWH's role as creator of the universe in order to assert that Israel's existence is guaranteed as long as the laws that govern the creation of the universe.

Finally, the report of YHWH's eighth word appears in Jer 31:37–40. The unit focuses on YHWH's eternal promise to Jerusalem, and it comprises two basic sub-units as indicated by the messenger formula in v. 37 and the formula *hinneh yāmîm bā'îm* in v. 38. Verse 37 therefore constitutes the word report proper, which contains the report of YHWH's eternal promise to "all the seed of Israel." Verses 38–40 then shift the prophet's announcement of the future restoration of Jerusalem by describing the restoration of three districts of the city, emphasizing that they will not be torn down forever.

---

such an association would aid in defining the image of Rachel/*bĕtûlat yiśrā'ēl* or the "apostate daughter (*habbat haššobēbāh*) returning to Zion from Beth El.

[13] The introductory *'al-zō't*, "because of this," indicates that the prophet awoke because of the preceding word of YHWH. The portrayal of his awakening thereby indicates that the following material is his explanation of the meaning of the statements communicated to him by YHWH during his sleep (for the problems occasioned by this verse, see Holladay, *Jeremiah 2* 196).

III

The preceding analysis of the structure and formal features of Jeremiah 30–31 provides the basis for a reconstruction of an earlier form of this text. As noted above, there is a major inconsistency in this text in that the introductory and concluding materials speak about the restoration of *both* Israel and Judah (cf. Jer 30:2–3, 4; 31:27–28, 31–34; cf. 31:37–40), whereas the bulk of the intervening materials focus *only* on the restoration of Israel and its return to Zion (cf. Jer 30:5–11; 30:18–31:22). It is noteworthy that the formula *hinneh yāmîm bā'îm* appears consistently in relation to the introductory and concluding texts that address the restoration of *both* Israel and Judah (Jer 30:3; 31:27, 31, 38). Concerns for the restoration of Israel alone appear in texts introduced by the formula *koh 'āmar yhwh / kî koh 'āmar yhwh* (Jer 30:5–11; 30:18–31:1; 31:2–14; 31:15; 31:16–22; 31:35–36; cf. 31:37). Exceptions to this pattern appear in Jer 30:2–3, which includes both formulas in a context that addresses the restoration of Israel and Judah, and in Jer 30:12–17 and 31:23–25, which seems to address the restoration of Zion or Judah.

The correlation of the formula with the respective concerns for the restoration of *both* Israel and Judah or the restoration of Israel and Judah *alone* provides the primary criterion for the reconstruction of an earlier text form from Jeremiah 30–31. Jeremiah 30:2–3, 4, for example, combines both of the key formulas in an introduction to the entire passage that define the concern of this text with the restoration of both Israel and Judah. This concern appears again only in the concluding segments of the passage introduced by the formula *hinneh yāmîm bā'îm*. This suggests that the present form of the text is the product of a redaction which emphasizes the restoration of *both* Israel and Judah rather than either Israel or Judah alone. In this case, the introductory material in Jer 30:2–3, 4 combines the formulaic introductions that characterize both an earlier text form (*kî / koh 'āmar yhwh*) and the later supplementary materials (*hinneh yāmîm bā'îm*) in an attempt to facilitate a combination and integration of materials that will result in a fundamental change in the outlook and concern of this text.

Such a concern is apparent also in Jer 31:37–40. This text employs both formulas in a context that combines concerns for the restoration of *both* Israel and Jerusalem, viz., v. 37 is introduced by *koh 'āmar yhwh* and speaks of YHWH's guarantee of security to the "seed of Israel," and vv. 38–40 are introduced by *hinneh yāmîm bā'îm* and speak of YHWH's promise to rebuild Jerusalem. The statement promising security to Israel in v. 37 can stand entirely on its own, but its combination with the promises for the rebuilding of Jerusalem in vv. 38–40 changes the character of the passage from one concerned only with Israel to one concerned with *both* Israel and Jerusalem (i. e., Judah).

The materials concerned with the restoration of Judah alone in Jer 30:12–17; 31:23–25 appear to break a pattern of concern with the restoration of Israel associated with texts introduced by the formula *kî / koh 'āmar yhwh*. In the case of the former, the fs addressee of the passage is never made clear until the very end, when it is identified as *ṣîyôn hî'* in v. 17. The LXX reads, *thēreuma hēmōn*, "our prey," which presupposes the Hebrew *ṣēdenû*, "our sustenance," in place of *ṣîyôn*. The reading *ṣēdenû* makes perfect sense in the immediate context which employs the metaphorical imagery of enemies "eating" and "plundering" the victim (see esp. v. 16), but the reading *ṣîyôn* relates only to the larger literary context of the entire unit. Furthermore, *ṣîyôn* relates awkwardly to its present context in that there is little reason to delay identification of the victim in vv. 12–17 until the end of the passage. Because *ṣēdenû* and *ṣîyôn* are related assonantally, this suggests that *ṣîyôn* was introduced into the text secondarily into this text under the influence of the concern with Israel and Judah that characterizes its present form. If v. 17 is read as *ṣēdenû*, vv. 12–17 still make perfect sense in their present context in that they take up the suffering of Israel introduced in Jer 30:5–11 and prepare the reader for the announcement of Israel's restoration in 30:18–31:1.[14]

Jeremiah 31:23–25 then presents a somewhat anomalous case in that it is the only passage that appears to speak of the restoration of Judah alone. But it is noteworthy that this passage is introduced by an expanded version of the messenger formula which identifies YHWH as the G-d of Israel (*koh 'āmar yhwh ṣĕbā'ôt 'lhy yiśrā'ēl*). The significance of this formulation is enhanced by the observation that Jer 31:23–25 follows immediately after the phrase, "a female shall encompass a man," in 31:22. As noted above, the phrase "a female shall encompass a man in 31:22 brings to full circle the imagery of gender role reversal initiated in 30:5–6 with the portrayal of Israel's men suffering as if they were women in childbirth. The phrase likewise signifies the return of Israel, here portrayed as *bĕtûlat yiśrā'ēl* and the "wandering/apostate daughter," as indicated by the highway imagery in 31:21–22 (cf. Jer 2:2–4:2). Jeremiah 31:23–25 also appears prior to the statements of the prophet's vision of the future in 31:26–28, which assert YHWH's promises to guarantee the existence of Israel forever.

Jeremiah 31:23–25 clearly occupies a penultimate position within the structure of this text. This suggests that the reference to the restoration of Judah in this passage must be considered as the climactic act of the return to Zion in the text as a whole. It further suggests that the reference to YHWH as G-d of Israel in the introductory messenger formula in v. 23 must be understood in reference to *all* Israel, i.e., Israel and Judah centered around Zion, rather than only to the northern kingdom of Israel. The concept of a united Israel would then provide

---

[14] Contra Kilpp, *Niederreissen und aufbauen* 127, n. 125, who maintains that *ṣîyôn hî'* is a gloss because a nominal sentence has no place in the present text. Although the nominal form is awkward in the present context, the presence of a different nominal statement in LXX demonstrates one of the two constitutes a legitimate component of this text.

the basis for the promises for Israel's eternal safety and existence expressed in 31:35–36 and 31:37.[15]

Once the framework material in Jer 30:1–4; 31:27–34; and 31:38–40 is recognized as the product of later redaction and the meaning of the materials in Jer 30:12–17 and 31:23–25 concerned with Zion/Judah is clarified, it becomes possible to posit an earlier form of Jeremiah 30–31. The resultant text comprises Jer 30:5–31:26; 31:35–37. It cannot be certain that these passages constitute an exact version of an original text. Perhaps there was some other form of introduction, and it is possible that elements from Jer 31:28–30 were included. Nevertheless, the result is a relatively coherent text with a consistent message concerning the restoration of the downfall northern kingdom of Israel to Jerusalem/Judah and the Davidic dynasty. The text is formulated initially as a series of statements by the prophet of YHWH word, introduced by a form of the messenger formula *koh ʾāmar yhwh / kî koh ʾāmar yhwh*: 30:5–11, 12–17; 30:18–31:1; 31:2–6, 7–14, 15, 16–22, 23–25. This is followed by the prophet's statement in 31:26 that he awoke from a pleasant sleep in which he "saw," which indicates the following material concerning YHWH's promises of eternal security to Israel in 31:35–36, 37, likewise introduced by the messenger formula, represents the content of his dreams or vision. The resulting text makes the following points: 1) Jacob's distress will be followed by deliverance and return to the Davidic dynasty (30:5–11); 2) Israel's wound is severe, but it will be healed (30:12–17); 3) YHWH promises to return the captives of Israel and to restore the covenant relationship with them to Zion (30:18–31:1); 4) the fertility of Israel shall be restored as Israel returns to Zion (31:2–6); 5) YHWH's restoration of Israel will lead to rejoicing in the world (31:7–14); 6) the imagery shifts to Israel, personified as the matriarch Rachel, weeping for her lost sons (31:15); 7) Israel is comforted and instructed to cease wandering and return home by highway (31:16–22); 8) Israel's return results in the restoration of Judah (31:23–25); 9) the prophet announces that he has awakened in order to state his vision of the future (31:26); 10) YHWH promises that Israel's security is as secure as the created world (31:35–36, 37).

These considerations demonstrate that the major concern of this reconstructed passage is the reunification of the northern kingdom of Israel with Judah and its return to the rule of the Davidic dynasty. Reunification of Israel and Judah under Davidic rule in Jerusalem was the primary goal of King Josiah's policy of religious reform and national restoration.[16] This is evident both in his destruc-

---

[15] Cf. B. W. Anderson, "'The L-rd has Created Something New': A Stylistic Study of Jer 31:15–22," *CBQ* 40 (1978) 463–78; P. Trible, *G-d and the Rhetoric of Sexuality* (OBT; Philadelphia: Fortress, 1978) 31–59.

[16] For an overview of Josiah's reform, see R. Althann, "Josiah," *ABD* 3:1015–18, and the bibliography cited there. See also M. A. Sweeney, "A Form-Critical Reassessment of the Book of Zephaniah," *CBQ* 53 (1991) 388–408; N. Steinberg, "The Deuteronomic Law Code and the Politics of State Centralization," *The Bible and the Politics of Exegesis, Fest. N. K. Gottwald*

tion of the sanctuary at Beth El (2 Kgs 23:15–20), formerly the royal altar of the northern kingdom of Israel, and in prophetic texts from the period that call for the reunification of Israel and Judah as well as the extension of Davidic rule over other nations that formerly comprise the united empire of Kings David and Solomon (e. g., Isaiah 11; Zephaniah).[17]

When read in relation to Josiah's interests in reunited Israel and Judah, several other features of this text take on added significance. The first is the allusion to the Exodus and Wandering tradition and its themes of redemption. Jeremiah 31:2–4 refers to Israel's wandering in the wilderness and YHWH's betrothal of *bĕtûlat yiśrāʾēl* at this time. Likewise, Jer 31:11 refers to the redemption of Jacob. The motif apparently played a constitutive role in northern Israel's self-consciousness; both writing prophets associated with the territory of the former northern kingdom frequently employ the tradition in relation to the north. Hosea makes frequent references to the tradition, including YHWH's betrothal of Israel in the wilderness (Hos 2:14–15), the apostasy at Baal Peor (Hos 3:10; cf Num 25:1–18), YHWH's love for Israel as a child at the time of the Exodus from Egypt (Hos 11:1–4), and YHWH's redemption of Israel from Egyptian bondage (Hos 13:4–6), and Jeremiah elsewhere refers to YHWH's betrothal to Israel in the wilderness (Jer 2:2–3). Josiah's reform also emphasized observance of Passover, which celebrates the Exodus from Egypt (2 Kgs 23:21–23). According to 2 Kgs 23:21–23, Passover had not been celebrated in Judah since the days of Joshua, but Josiah's observance of the holiday certainly serves his interests in attempting to extend Davidic rule over the former northern kingdom. In the case, the use of the Exodus tradition in the *Urtext* of Jeremiah 30–31 would support Josiah's program.

The second is the figure of Rachel and the movement of the *bĕtûlat yiśrāʾēl* along the highway. Rachel is known in Israelite tradition as the mother of Joseph and Benjamin, who ultimately produced the tribe of Ephraim, the major tribe of the northern kingdom of Israel, and the Saulide dynasty, the first dynasty to rule the northern tribes as well as Israel as a whole. As the wife of the patriarch Jacob, eponymous ancestor of the northern kingdom of Israel, Rachel functions as one of the matriarchs of the northern kingdom. Although later tradition places her tomb in Ephrath in the vicinity of Bethlehem in the territory of Judah (cf. Gen 35:19; 48:7; Ruth 4:11), it apparently was originally located in the vicinity of Beth El in the territory of Benjamin (1 Sam 10:2; cf. Jer 31:15).[18] This is particularly important in light of Josiah's destruction of the sanctuary at Beth El

---

(ed. D. Jobling et al; Cleveland: Pilgrim, 1991) 161–70, 336–9; N. Na'aman, "the Kingdom of Judah under Josiah," *Tel Aviv* 18 (1991) 3–71.

[17] See M. A. Sweeney, "Jesse's New Shoot in Isaiah 11: A Josianic Reading of the Prophet Isaiah," in *A Gift of G-d in Due Season: Essays on Scripture and Community in Honor of James A. Sanders* (JSOTSup 225; ed. R. D. Weis and D. M. Carr; Sheffield: Sheffield Academic Press, 1996) 103–118. See also Sweeney, *CBQ* 53 (1991) 388–408.

[18] See L. Luker, "Rachel's Tomb," *ABD* 5:608–9.

(2 Kgs 23:15-20). Jeremiah 31:15, 16-22 portrays the weeping Rachel / *bĕtûlat yiśrā'ēl* being comforted and instructed to return to her cities by way of the roads mentioned in vv. 21-22. Although precise locations are not listed, the literary context of this instruction makes it clear that her return is ultimately directed to Jerusalem / Zion and the Davidic dynasty (Jer 30:9; 31:6, 12, 23-25). In this regard, the references to the highway signposts, *ṣiyunîm* and *tamrûrîm* in 31:21, are particularly important. The term *ṣiyun*, "monument, road marker," appears here and in 2 Kgs 23:1 where it marks the tomb of the man of G-d at Beth El who predicted Josiah's destruction of the sanctuary (cf. 1 Kgs 13:1-3). Likewise, *tamrûr*, "pillar, way-post," alludes to the tree of Deborah, designated as *tomer*, "tamarisk," in Judg 4:5 and *'allôn bākût*, "oak of weeping," in Gen 35:8, located just south of Beth El and north of Rachel's tomb. In light of these allusions, it becomes clear that the text portrays Rachel's, and therefore Israel's, movement from Beth El to Jerusalem. Such a movement would obviously correspond to Josiah's intentions in destroying the Beth El sanctuary as a means to effect the reunification of Israel and Judah under Davidic rule.

IV

In conclusion, it appears that an earlier version of Jeremiah 30-31 can be identified within the present form of the text. Rather than focus on the restoration of *both* Israel and Judah in the aftermath of the Babylonian destruction of Jerusalem and Judah during the years 597-582 B.C.E., the *Urtext* of Jeremiah 30-31 supports Josiah's efforts to return the territory and people of the former northern kingdom of Israel to Davidic rule and thereby to reunite Israel and Judah. Such a reconstruction has significant implications for the study of Jeremiah. It demonstrates that the prophet was active during the reign of King Josiah, and the he supported Josiah's reform. It further points to the redactional process that produced the present form of the book of Jeremiah, in that an earlier text concerned with the restoration of Israel and its reunification with Judah under Davidic rule was modified and updated to address the restoration of *both* Israel and Judah in light of the Babylonian catastrophe. In light of these conclusions, Jeremiah emerges as a prophet who did speak a message of salvation and return in the early years of his career.[19] The message was initially directed to the people

---

[19] Cf. Kilpp, *Niederreissen und aufbauen* 177-82, who argues that Jeremiah was a theologically reflective prophet who did proclaim salvation to Judah and the people of former kingdom of Israel. Contra J. Lust, "'Gathering and Return' in Jeremiah and Ezekiel," in *Le Livre de Jérémie. Le prophète et son milieu. Les oracles et leur transmission* (ed. P.-M. Bogaert; BETL 54; Leuven: Peeters and Leuven University Press, 1981) 119-42, who argues that the theme of return does not appear in the earliest layers of the book of Jeremiah (p. 136). His argument in relation to Jeremiah 30-31 depends entirely on his association of Jer 30:10-11 and 31:8-10 with passages and language from Deutero-Isaiah (esp. 131-3). He admits, however, that Deutero-

of the former northern kingdom of Israel in a bid to convince them to return to Davidic rule in Jerusalem. But in light of the catastrophe of the Babylonian exile, it provides the pattern for the late message of Israelite and Judean restoration and return to Zion that appears in the final from of the book.[20]

Isaiah may be dependent upon Jeremiah or that both writings may presuppose a common circle of writers. He argues that Jeremiah is dependent upon Deutero-Isaiah because the double name "Jacob" and "Israel" frequently appears in Deutero-Isaiah together with the description "my servant," but Israel and Jacob appear together in Jer 2:4 and the term "servant" is frequently employed to designate Moses (Josh 1:13, 15; 8:31, 33; 11:12; 12:6 [2x]; 13:8; 14:7; 18:7; 22:2, 4, 5; 2 Kgs 18:12; 2 Chr 1:3; 24:6) after whom Jeremiah is modeled in the present form of the book (C. R. Seitz, "The Prophet Moses and the Canonical Shape of Jeremiah," *ZAW* 101 [1989] 3–27; cf. Holladay, *Jeremiah 2* 173–4, 184–5, who points to the Jeremianic phraseology of Jer 30:10–11 and 31:7–9 in order to argue that Jeremiah represents the earlier text). Lust does not address the imagery of the return to Rachel or the *bĕtûlat yiśrā'ēl* in 31:16–17, 21, which he assigns to the earliest layer of the text, but it is this image that establishes the primary pattern of return in Jeremiah 30–31. His distinction between "conversion" (*šûb*) and "return" (*hēšîb*) does not apply as *wĕšābû* and *šûbî* are employed respectively in Jer 31:17 and 31:21 to describe the "return" of Israel's sons and the *bĕtûlat yiśrā'ēl* to the land.

[20] This is a revised version of a paper read before the Hebrew University Bible Department Symposium on March 15, 1994. I would like to thank Professors Simha Kogut, Shalom Paul, Alexander Rofé, and Emanuel Tov for their efforts in making my presentation possible. I would also like to thank the W. F. Albright Institute, Jerusalem, Israel, for its support of my research during my term as Dorot Research Professor.

Part 3: Ezekiel

9. Ezekiel: Zadokite Priest
and Visionary Prophet of the Exile[1]

I

Biblical scholarship has long labored within the literary and theological paradigms formalized by Julius Wellhausen, who posited a fundamental dichotomy between the prophets and the priests.[2] Because of his views that prophecy constituted the most direct and pure expression of human experience of the divine and that the priestly interests in institutional authority, law, and ritual, constituted a self-serving disruption of that relationship, Wellhausen reversed the historical paradigm of the Hebrew Bible, which presents Mosaic Torah as the foundation of Israelite religion and the predecessor of the prophets. Wellhausen's views found expression in the Graf-Wellhausen model for the composition of the Pentateuch, which maintains that the J source, with its model of direct divine-human interaction, constitutes the earliest layer in the Pentateuchal narrative, whereas the P source presents a model of divine inaccessibility that is mediated only through

---

[1] This is a revised version of the William H. Brownlee Memorial Lecture, Institute for Antiquity and Christianity, Claremont, CA, April 13, 2000. Earlier versions of this paper were presented at the Korean Bible Society with the support of the Methodist Theological Seminary, Seoul, Korea, May 18, 2000, and at the Society of Biblical Literature Seminar on "Theological Perspectives on the Book of Ezekiel, November 20, 2000. Two earlier versions were published as "Ezekiel: Zadokite Priest and Visionary Prophet of the Exile," in booklet form (with Korean translation) by the Methodist Theological Seminary, Seoul, and the *Society of Biblical Literature 2000 Seminar Papers* (Atlanta: Society of Biblical Literature, 2000) 728–51. I would like to thank the Brownlee family; Karen Torjesen and Dennis MacDonald, Co-Directors of the IAC; Tai-il Wang, Professor of Old Testament, MTS; Young-Jin Min, Professor of Old Testament and Deputy General Secretary, KBS; and Rev. and Mrs. John Chang, Seoul, for their invitations and support. In addition, I would like to thank Prof. John T. Strong, Southwest Missouri State University, and Dr. John F. Kutsko, Hendrickson Publishers, for their invitations to present this paper as part of the SBL Ezekiel Seminar and Dr. Baruch J. Schwartz, Hebrew University of Jerusalem, and Prof. S. Dean McBride, Jr., Union Theological Seminary, Richmond, for their responses as part of the seminar program.

[2] Julius Wellhausen, *Die Composition des Hexateuch und der historischen Bücher des Alten Testament* (3rd ed. Berlin: Georg Reimer, 1898; repr. Berlin: Walter de Gruyter, 1963); idem, *Prolegomena to the History of Israel* (Edinburgh: A & C Black, 1885). For discussion of Wellhausen and his impact upon biblical scholarship, see John H. Hayes, *An Introduction to Old Testament Study* (Nashville: Abingdon, 1979) 159–180; Jon D. Levenson, "The Hebrew Bible, the Old Testament, and Historical Criticism," *The Hebrew Bible, The Old Testament, and Historical Criticism* (Louisville: Westminster John Knox, 1993) 1–32, esp. 10–15.

the interrelated institutions of the Temple and the priesthood. The demise of the monarchy, founded with prophetic support, and the rise of a theocracy in the time of Nehemiah and Ezra point to the degeneration of Israelite religion in his understanding as law came to replace direct human experience of G-d. Of course, contemporary scholars have come to recognize that Wellhausen's work is informed by a polemical interest in undermining opponents within Christianity together with an antisemitic world view by which he apparently sought to point to a pietistic Lutheran model, with its inherent prophetic world-view and anti-institutional bias, as the earliest and therefore purest and most authentic form of religious expression in the Hebrew Bible. For this and other reasons, alternative models for reading the Pentateuch are now being explored.

Wellhausen's views have also had their impact on the reading of prophetic literature, with particular significance for the book of Ezekiel.[3] Whereas books such as Amos, Hosea, Isaiah, and Micah have received extensive scholarly treatment in part because they are perceived to represent the earliest works of prophetic literature and because they frequently critique temple priesthoods and their practices, Ezekiel has received less scholarly attention because of the relatively late setting of his work in the exilic period and because of his priestly descent and its influence on his world-view. The issue has been compounded by some rather strange or even bizarre facets of his claims and behavior, such as his visionary experiences and symbolic actions, his supernatural transport from Babylonia to Jerusalem, his prolonged periods of speechlessness, or his refusal to mourn for his deceased wife, which continue to provoke speculative claims that his personality is abnormal, that he employed mind-altering substances, or that he suffered from some form of mental disturbance.[4] Indeed, many interpreters point to a sort of "split-personality" in the prophet, i.e., a fundamental conflict between his priestly identity and his prophetic role, to explain some of the unusual features of his book and its message.

As the Wellhausenian paradigm has begun to wane, more recent research has shown far greater interest in the literature, history, and social characteristics of the Exilic and early Second Temple periods, particularly in the institutions of the Jerusalem Temple and its priesthood. Furthermore, critical scholarship has shown greater appreciation for the role of temples, priests, and their rituals

---

[3] For discussion of research on Ezekiel, see Bernhard Lang, *Ezechiel* (Erträge der Forschung 153; Darmstadt: Wissenschaftliche Buchgesellschaft, 1981); William H. Brownlee, *Ezekiel 1–19* (Word Biblical Commentary 19; Waco: Word, 1986) xix–xxiii; Lawrence Boadt, "Ezekiel, Book of," *ABD* 2:711–22; Henry McKeating, *Ezekiel* (OTG; Sheffield: Sheffield Academic Press, 1993); Katheryn Pfisterer Darr, "Ezekiel Among the Critics," *CR:BS* 2 (1994) 9–24; Marvin A. Sweeney, "The Latter Prophets (Isaiah, Jeremiah, Ezekiel)," *The Hebrew Bible Today: An Introduction to Critical Issues* (ed. S. L. McKenzie and M. P. Graham; Louisville, KY: Westminster John Knox, 1998) 69–94, esp. 88–94.

[4] See most recently David J. Halperin, *Seeking Ezekiel: Text and Psychology* (University Park, PA: Pennsylvania State University Press, 1993) esp. 7–38.

in earlier periods as well. A particularly striking facet of such interest is that many ancient Near Eastern texts, such as the Mari letters, and biblical models point to an interrelationship between ancient temples and oracular prophecy or divination, e. g., Mari prophets appear to have functioned especially within the temple of Ishtar of Arbela; prophets such as Moses, Jeremiah, and Zechariah were priests; and even Samuel is portrayed as an oracular prophet situated in the Shiloh Temple.[5] The Wellhausenian dichotomy between prophecy and priesthood can no longer be maintained: many prophets were indeed priests or were closely associated with temples even when their remarks were critical of temple practice.

This raises questions concerning the extent to which priestly identity influences prophetic identity – or vice versa – and even the extent to which prophetic identity might be an expression of priestly identity. The question of course has important implications for understanding Ezekiel, who is identified as both a Zadokite priest and as a visionary prophet during the period of the Babylonian exile. A recent study by Margaret Odell takes an important step in this line of inquiry, in so far as she argues that the portrayal of Ezekiel's commission as a prophet in Ezekiel 1–5 is modeled on the priestly ordination ceremonies presented in Leviticus 8–9, and therefore represents the transition of Ezekiel's identity as a priest to that of a prophet.[6] The purpose of this paper, therefore, is to examine Odell's contention and to build upon it. It argues that a great many features of the book of Ezekiel are dependent upon the world view and practices of the Zadokite priesthood. Indeed, a close examination of these features demonstrates that Ezekiel did not give up his priestly identity for a prophetic role; instead, his prophetic role is an extension of his priestly identity under the influence of the very radically changed circumstances of Ezekiel's life in the Babylonian exile. As a result, the book of Ezekiel presents a priestly vision or interpretation of the role of the Temple in relation to creation as part of a process in which the Temple itself is sacrificed in order to bring about the purification or even reconstitution of creation at large.

---

[5] See Frederick H. Cryer, *Divination in Ancient Israel and its Near Eastern Environment: A Socio-Historical Investigation* (JSOTSup 142; Sheffield: Sheffield Academic Press, 1994); Martti Nissinen, *State Archives of Assyria Studies, Volume VII: References to Prophecy in Neo-Assyrian Sources* (Helsinki: University of Helsinki, 1998); Simo Parpola, *Assyrian Prophecies* (State Archives of Assyria 9; Helsinki: University of Helsinki, 1997); Friedrich Ellermeier, *Prophetie in Mari und Israel* (Herzberg: Erwin Jungfer, 1968).

[6] Margaret S. Odell, "You are What You Eat: Ezekiel and the Scroll," *JBL* 117 (1998) 229–48.

II

Odell's recent study, "You Are What You Eat: Ezekiel and the Scroll," constitutes an important contribution to the interpretation of Ezekiel in that it points to the dynamics of his transformation from a Zadokite priest of the Jerusalem Temple to a visionary prophet of the Babylonian exile.[7] In contrast to earlier studies that employ genre analysis as a means to define separate narratives concerning Ezekiel's call in Ezek 1:1–3:15 and his symbolic actions in Ezek 3:16–5:17, Odell employs recent advances in form-critical method to argue that genres function within larger texts and that the accounts of Ezekiel's call and symbolic acts must therefore be read together as part of a larger narrative in Ezekiel 1–5 that depicts Ezekiel's transformation from priest to prophet. She points to analogies between Ezekiel 1–5 and the narratives concerning the ordination of priests for holy service in Leviticus 8–9, i.e., whereas priestly ordinands eat the ram of ordination (Lev 8:31), Ezekiel eats the scroll given to him by YHWH (Ezek 2:8–3:3); whereas priestly ordinands sit in seclusion for seven days (Lev 8:33), Ezekiel sits in silence among his people for seven days (Ezek 3:15); whereas priestly ordinands make atonement for the guilt of the people (Lev 9:1–21), Ezekiel bears the guilt of the people although he does not make sacrificial atonement (Ezek 4:4–8); whereas priestly ordinands are admitted to the sanctuary to see the glory of YHWH (Lev 9:23), Ezekiel sees the glory of YHWH as YHWH prepares to destroy Jerusalem and the Temple (Ezekiel 8–11). Furthermore, based upon her interpretation of Ezek 1:1, she argues that Ezekiel's visionary experience begins at the age of thirty, the age at which Levites begin active service in the sanctuary (Num 4:3, 23, 30; cf. Num 8:23–25, which states that Levitical service begins at twenty-five), and that his visions continue for twenty years until he reaches the age of fifty, the age at which Levites retire from active service. Because Ezekiel lives outside the Temple in an impure land and because he engages in activities that mark him as impure, e.g., he eats impure food, cuts his hair, and is addressed as *ben-'ādām*, "son of Adam/human," rather than as priest, he does not function as priest. Instead, Odell maintains that he assumes a new role as a prophet as indicated by YHWH's commands to speak as a prophet in Ezekiel 2; 6–7.

One may question various details of Odell's argument without invalidating the overall soundness of her basic theses and insights, i.e., the initial narrative concerning the definition of Ezekiel's role should encompass Ezekiel 1–7 rather than only Ezekiel 1–5 in so far as the date formulae in Ezek 1:1, 2–3 and 8:1 mark the boundaries of the initial literary unit; Ezekiel's actions in eating impure food and cutting his hair mark him as impure but do not indicate that he has given up his priestly status and role; Ezekiel not only bears the guilt of his people like a priestly ordinand, he does indeed offer a sacrifice as atonement in

---

[7] See note 5 above.

so far as he portrays the destruction of the Jerusalem Temple as a sacrifice that is designed to purify Jerusalem, the nation Israel, and creation at large. Altogether, these observations point to the contention that Ezekiel does not give up his role as a Zadokite priest to become a prophet. Instead, he acts as a Zadokite priest throughout his career, albeit in the impure and changed conditions of life in Babylonian exile outside of the Jerusalem Temple, and incorporates his prophetic role into his priestly identity. This results in a transformation of Ezekiel's role as both priest and prophet. To be sure, his statements and actions frequently deviate from standard priestly conceptualizations and practice,[8] but this is to be expected insofar as he envisions a transformation of all creation in which the Jerusalem Temple, the holy center of creation, is destroyed and replaced with a new Temple that signals the beginning of a new creation in the aftermath of the Babylonian exile. The following discussion treats several topics, including the portrayal of Ezekiel's priestly role in Ezekiel 1–7, the portrayal of Jerusalem's destruction in Ezekiel 8–11; Ezekiel's symbolic acts, use of tradition, and self-appointed role as watchman throughout the body of the book; and his portrayal of the restored Temple in Ezekiel 40–48, in an effort to support this contention.

III

Ezekiel 1–7 constitutes the initial narrative of the book in which the prophet's identity and role are defined.[9] The narrative is demarcated at the outset by the initial date formulae in Ezekiel 1:1–3, which place the prophet's initial visions and experiences in fifth day of the fourth month (5 Tammuz?) of the fifth year of King Jehoiachin's exile, ca. 593 B.C.E. The initial date formula in Ezekiel 8:1 marks the beginning of a new sub-unit of the book. The appearance of the formula, "the word of YHWH was unto me," in Ezek 3:16; 6:1; and 7:1 indicates that Ezekiel 1–7 is further sub-divided into narratives concerning Ezekiel's vision of YHWH's throne chariot (Ezek 1:2–3:15; his commission as a watchman

---

[8] N.b., Ezekiel is clearly innovative in his treatment of tradition priestly knowledge and practice. According to Talmudic tradition, Rabbi Hananiah ben Hezekiah burned three hundred barrels of oil working at night to reconcile the differences between Ezekiel's statements and those of Mosaic Torah so that his book could be accepted as sacred scripture (b. Shabbat 13b; b. Hagigah 13a; b. Menahot 45a). Other Talmudic sources note that Ezekiel is a halakhic innovator, ascribing various rulings to him rather than to Moses (b. Yoma 71b; b. Moʿed Qatan 5a; 27b; b. Sanhedrin 81a; 83b).

[9] For discussion of the methodological principles that stand behind the present analysis of Ezekiel, see Marvin A. Sweeney, "Form Criticism," *To Each its Own Meaning: An Introduction to Biblical Criticisms and their Applications* (ed. S. L. McKenzie and S. R. Haynes; revised and expanded edition; Louisville: Westminster John Knox, 1999) 58–85; idem "Formation and Form in Prophetic Literature," *Old Testament Interpretation: Past, Present, and Future. Essays in Honor of Gene M. Tucker* (ed. J. L. Mays, D. L. Petersen, and K. H. Richards; Nashville: Abingdon, 1995) 113–26.

with its associated symbolic acts (Ezek 3:16–5:17); his commission to prophesy against the hills of Israel (Ezek 6:1–14); and his commission to speak about the end of the land of Israel (Ezek 7:1–27). Throughout these narratives, Ezekiel's identity as a priest undergirds and defines his role as prophet.

This is evident at the outset of the book in Ezekiel 1:1, which states, "And it came to pass in the thirtieth year, in the fourth month, on the fifth day of the month, while I was in the midst of the exile by the River Chebar, the heavens were opened and I saw visions of G-d." This verse is not strictly speaking a superscription, but it functions as a narrative introduction to the book as a whole. Scholars have advanced various theories concerning the significance of the thirtieth year, i. e., that it refers to the anniversary of Josiah's reform, a jubilee year, the anniversary of Jehoiachin's birth, the reign of the Babylonian king Nabopolassar, or Ezekiel's age at the time of his initial vision.[10] That the reference appears to indicate the age of the prophet at the time of his initial vision appears to be confirmed by the overall chronology presented in the book of Ezekiel and its correspondence to the age of Levitical service. Beginning with the syntactically distinct reference to the fifth day of the fourth month in the fifth year of Jehoaiachin's exile in Ezek 1:2–3 which introduces the initial vision of the throne chariot, the book presents a series of chronological references in Ezek 8:1; 20:1; 24:1; 26:1; 29:1; 29:17; 30:20; 31:1; 32;1; 32:17; 33:21; and 40:1 that extends to the tenth day of the first month (10 Nissan) of the twenty-fifth year, i. e., 573 B.C.E.[11] The sequence is not strictly chronological as there are minor discrepancies. A major discrepancy appears in Ezek 29:17, which dates the oracle concerning Egypt in Ezek 29:17–21 to the first day of the first month (1 Nissan) of the twenty-seventh year, i. e., 571 B.C.E., although it should be noted that many scholars consider this to be a corrected date reference to account for the failure of Nebuchadnezzar's thirteen year siege of Tyre.[12] Apart from this reference, the chronology of the book of Ezekiel presents a twenty year period of visionary experience that would extend from his thirtieth to his fiftieth year. As noted above, this corresponds precisely to the period of active service for the Levites, who serve at the tent of meeting or the sanctuary for a twenty year period from the age of thirty to the age of fifty (Num 4:3, 23, 30; cf. Num 8:23–25). Thus, it would appear that Ezekiel's active career as a visionary

---

[10] For a brief summary of the proposals, see Walther Zimmerli, *Ezekiel 1: A Commentary on the Book of the Prophet Ezekiel, Chapters 1–24* (Hermeneia; trans. R. E. Clements; Philadelphia: Fortress, 1979) 113–14.

[11] For an assessment of these references, see Ernst Kutsch, *Die Chronologischen Daten des Ezechielbuches* (OBO 62; Freiburg: Universitätsverlag; Göttingen: Vandenhoeck & Ruprecht, 1985).

[12] E. g., Moshe Greenberg, *Ezekiel 21–37* (AB 22A; New York: Doubleday, 1997) 616–18; Zimmerli, *Ezekiel 1* 72; idem, *Ezekiel 2: A Commentary on the Book of the Prophet Ezekiel, Chapters 25–48* (Hermeneia; Philadelphia: Fortress, 1983) 118–19; Ronald M. Hals, *Ezekiel* (FOTL 19; Grand Rapids: Eerdmans, 1989) 210–11.

prophet coincides with the time and ages of the active career of a Levitical priest. It is noteworthy therefore that Ezekiel's birth would then coincide roughly with the inauguration of Josiah's religious reform in the eighteenth year of his reign, 622 B.C.E. (2 Kings 22:3; Chr 34:8) and that his final vision portrays the restored Temple in Jerusalem in Ezekiel 40–48. One might speculate that Ezekiel saw his life's work somehow as a fulfillment or continuation of the reform process that was initiated at his birth by King Josiah. As Odell, following J. E. Miller, notes, "the reference to the thirtieth year is part of a larger autobiographical structuring of the book in light of crucial moments in the life of a priest."[13]

Ezekiel's priestly identity and perspective is evident throughout the book in his use of the expression, *kĕbôd yhwh*, "glory of YHWH," to describe the divine presence in the context of the throne visions and the restoration of YHWH's presence to the Temple (see Ezek 1:28; 3:23; 8:4; 10:3–4, 19; 11:22–23; 43:1–5). Indeed, the expression serves as a technical term to describe the presence of YHWH among the people at the time of the wilderness wandering (Exod 16:7, 10–12), in the tabernacle (Exod 40:34–38), and in the Temple in Jerusalem (1 Kgs 8:10–11; 2 Chr 7:1–3; cf. 1 Sam 4:21–22). This is especially significant in that Ezekiel's vision of the throne chariot appears to be based upon the imagery of the ark of the covenant, which prior to the Babylonian exile was accessible only to the priests in the Holy of Holies of the Jerusalem Temple. Ezekiel's initial reference to "a great cloud with brightness around it and fire flashing forth continuously" recalls the pillar of fire and cloud that accompanied the people of Israel as they journeyed from Egypt through the Sinai wilderness. Of course, it also symbolizes the altar of the Jerusalem Temple from which would rise a column of fire and smoke as sacrifices are consumed upon it as well as the interior of the Temple that is filled with clouds of incense smoke as the lights of the Temple *mĕnōrôt* or lamp stands burn before the ark.

Other features also correspond to such Temple-based motifs. The imagery of "gleaming amber" within the cloud or the "polished bronze" of the four creatures recalls the portrayal of the ark and its cherubim as overlaid with gold (Exod 25:1–22; 37:1–9) as well as the later tradition that Pharaoh Shishak of Egypt stripped the Temple of gold following the death of Solomon so that it had to be replaced with bronze (1 Kgs 14:25–28; cf. 2 Kgs 18:14–16). The four living creatures that bear the ark in Ezekiel's vision correspond to the two cherubim that are placed upon the mercy seat of the ark in Exod 25:18–22 and the additional two built by Solomon within the Holy of Holies in 1 Kgs 6:23–28; 2 Chr 3:10–14. The burning coals in the midst of the living creatures symbolize the coals of the sacrificial altar or those of the incense altars within the Temple, and the enigmatic "wheels within wheels" may represent the rings used to carry the ark in the

---

[13] Odell, "Your are what you Eat," 239; J. E. Miller, "The 'Thirtieth Year' of Ezekiel 1:1," *RB* 99 (1992) 499–503.

wilderness period (Exod 25:12–15) or the wheels of the cart used to convey the ark from Kiryat Yearim to Jerusalem (2 Sam 6:3; 1 Chr 13:7). The shining crystal firmament above the heads of the four creatures corresponds to the mercy seat above the ark (Exod 25:17) or the clear pavement beneath the throne of G-d as portrayed in the narrative of the divine banquet in Exod 24:9–11, bearing in mind of course that the ark and its mercy seat symbolize the footstool of G-d above which G-d is enthroned (see Ps 132:7; Isa 66:1; 1 Sam 4:4). Finally, the imagery of the bow in the cloud recalls the rain bow that symbolizes YHWH's covenant with creation in the priestly account of the flood (Gen 9:8–17). Altogether, the imagery of Ezekiel's vision corresponds almost precisely to that of the Ark of the Covenant in the Holy of Holies, and represents what one might expect of a priest educated for service in the Jerusalem Temple.

Although the imagery of Ezekiel's eating the scroll given to him by YHWH is frequently understood as a prophetic image, particularly since it corresponds to similar imagery in Jeremiah 15:16, it must be considered in relation to Ezekiel's priestly role as well. According to Deut 31:9–13, the priests and Levites are expected to read the Torah to the people of Israel every seven years. Such an obligation appears to lie behind the image of the flying scroll in Zechariah 5:1–4.[14] It should be noted that both Zechariah and Jeremiah are themselves priests of the Zadokite and Elide lines respectively as well as prophets. In so far as Ezekiel consumes the scroll given him by YHWH so that he might communicate its contents to the people, he metaphorically fulfills this priestly obligation.

Similar considerations apply to the portrayal of Ezekiel's symbolic acts in Ezek 3:16–5:17. Although the narratives concerning Ezekiel's symbolic acts in Ezekiel 4–5 are frequently separated from the preceding material on generic grounds, the reports of Ezekiel's commissioning as a watchman in Ezek 3:16–21 and his dumbness in Ezek 3:22–27 must be read together with the following reports of symbolic actions, especially since they continue the reports of YHWH's speech that commence in Ezek 3:16–21 and 3:22–27. The narratives concerning Ezekiel's role as watchman and his dumbness introduce the reports of YHWH's instructions to engage in symbolic acts.

This observation is particularly significant since both the watchman role and dumbness are characteristic elements of priestly identity. One of the essential roles of the Levitical priesthood is to serve as the gatekeepers for the holy precincts of the Temple (1 Chr 9:17–27; 26:1–19), a role which appears to be represented in the statements of the moral qualifications of those who would enter the Temple in the so-called "Entrance Liturgies" of Psalms 15 and 24.[15]

---

[14] For discussion of this passage, see Marvin A. Sweeney, *The Twelve Prophets* (Berit Olam; Collegeville, MN: Liturgical, 2000) 614–18.

[15] For discussion of the Entrance Liturgies, see Klaus Koch, "Tempeleinlassliturgien und Dekaloge," *Studien zur Theologie der alttestamentlichen Überlieferungen* (Fest. G. von Rad; ed. R. Rendtorff and K. Koch; Neukirchen-Vluyn: Neukirchener, 1961) 45–60; Marvin A.

The role of the Temple gatekeepers and guards is to protect the sanctity of the Temple so that it might not be profaned by the entry of those who are not properly prepared or qualified for holy activity at the site. Ezekiel's role as watchman for the people appears to be based on this model, especially since his purpose is to warn the people of YHWH's words so that they might avoid sins and the resulting consequences of their impurity (cf. Ezek 33:1–20). His dumbness also appears to be a priestly attribute in so far as priests remain entirely silent while offering holy sacrifice at the Temple altar. Because the Temple worship ritual is believed to represent that of the heavenly realm, so that the priests are in effect acting as the angels of YHWH's court, human speech cannot express the divine voices of the angels and therefore would compromise the sacred character of the sacrifice.[16] Ezekiel's adaptation of this role in the changed circumstances of exile would provide a means for him and the people to express absolute shock and grief at the loss of his wife and the city of Jerusalem. In both cases, Ezekiel appears to have drawn upon aspects of his priestly identity in order to convey his prophetic role.

The symbolic actions also appear to presuppose priestly identity, but they depict the profanation of Ezekiel's priestly status. Odell is correct to point to their transformative nature, but they do not entail that Ezekiel gives up his priestly identity. Priestly status is after all a fact of birth, and one remains a priest whether or not one is pure. Ezekiel is simply a priest who, like the sanctuary in Jerusalem, has been profaned and will need to be purified. When he lies on his right side for three hundred and ninety days to symbolize the guilt of Israel, and when he lies on his left side for forty days to symbolize the guilt of Judah, he acts as a priest in that he symbolically bears the guilt of his people for whom he is expected to atone.[17] The symbolic portrayal of the city under siege of course symbolizes the reality of divine punishment for the sins of the people that are now born by Ezekiel. Nevertheless, his capacity to act as a priest and to atone for the people's sins is impeded by the impure status of the Temple itself and by his own impurity while living outside of the Temple in an impure land. His eating of common food rather than the sacred portions of the Temple sacrifices and the shaving of his hair and beard both symbolize his own loss of sanctity as priest during a period when the holy precinct of the Temple itself can no longer claim

---

Sweeney, *Isaiah 1–39, with an Introduction to Prophetic Literature* (FOTL 16; Grand Rapids and Cambridge: Eerdmans, 1996) 520. For discussion with full bibliography of Psalms 15 and 24, see esp. Erhard S. Gerstenberger, *Psalms, Part 1, with an Introduction to Cultic Poetry* (FOTL 14; Grand Rapids: Erdmans, 1988) 117–19. One might also compare the High Priest Jehoiada's posting of guards supervised by Levites during the coup against Athaliah (2 Chronicles 23, esp. vv. 6, 18–19).

[16] See Israel Knohl, *The Sanctuary of Silence: The Priestly Torah and the Holiness School* (Minneapolis: Fortress, 1994).

[17] Cf. Num 18:1, which states that the role of Aaron and his house is to "bear the guilt of the sanctuary."

pure or holy status while it stands under conditions of siege as a punishment for the profanation within.[18]

Odell correctly notes that Ezekiel does not atone for the people's guilt in these narratives; he cannot when even the Temple is compromised.[19] Such atonement requires the purification of the Temple itself. That does not commence until chapters 8–11, and it is Ezekiel the priest and prophet who shows the reader that process of purification. The prophetic oracles presented in Ezekiel 6 and 7 are a necessary part of that process, as indicated by their structural subordination to Ezekiel 1–7 as a whole and their contents. The oracles express verbally what Ezekiel is instructed to express through his symbolic actions, i.e., the land and people of Israel will be punished and brought to an end. Strictly speaking, the repeated references to the pestilence, sword, and famine, in Ezek 6:11–12 and 7:15 indicate that the oracles explain the symbolic actions in which pestilence, sword, and famine figure prominently (e.g., Ezek 5:12); Ezekiel thereby reflects the instructional role of the priesthood, which is to explain the teachings or Torah of YHWH to the people so that they might understand how they are to conduct themselves in conformity with divine expectations (Lev 10:10–11). In this case, however, the instruction speaks of the end of Israel's existence–at least as it was known up to that time–and the beginning of the process by which Israel, the Temple, and creation will be transformed as the Temple, Israel, and creation are destroyed and, ultimately, reestablished.

IV

The second major component of the book appears in Ezekiel 8–19. The structural boundaries of this sub-unit are indicated initially by the date formula in Ezek 8:1, "and it came to pass in the sixth year, in the sixth month, on the fifth day of the month (5 Ellul, 592 B.C.E.), while I was sitting in my house and the elders of Judah were sitting before me, that the hand of my lord YHWH fell upon me there," and by the date formula in Ezek 20:1 which marks the beginning of the next subunit of the book. Again, the appearance of the formula, "and the word of YHWH came to me saying ..." in Ezek 11:14; 12:1; 12:17; 12:21; 13:1; 14:1–2; 15:1; 16:1; 17:1; 17:11; and 18:1 mark the various sub-units of this section that follow from the initial portrayal of Ezekiel's vision concerning the departure of "the glory of YHWH" from the Temple in Jerusalem and its destruction. Each of these sub-units elaborates upon the significance of this departure/destruction, beginning in Ezek 11:14–24 with an oracle concerning YHWH's intention

---

[18] The priests were to trim their hair, but not shave it entirely (Lev 21:5; 19:27). The Talmud requires priests to cut their hair every thirty days (b. Ta'anit 17a), preferably in a layered cut worn by ben Elasha, the son-in-law of Rabbi Judah (b. Sanhedrin 22b).

[19] See her discussion in "You are what you Eat," 239–41.

to restore Israel with a new heart and culminating in Ezek 18:1–19:14 with a Levitical discourse on individual moral responsibility followed by allegorical lamentation concerning the punishment of Israel/Judah and its kings.

The initial presentation of Ezekiel's vision concerning the destruction of Jerusalem is particularly important for understanding the priestly character of his prophetic visions and discourse. Fundamentally, it presents the Temple as profaned by the sins or idolatry of the people, thereby requiring destruction that will purge it of impurity and begin the process of its restoration and resanctification.

The initial scenes of this text depict Ezekiel's supernatural transportation to the Temple by the agency of an angelic creature like those that bore the throne chariot of YHWH in the inaugural vision of chapters 1–3. The purpose of the journey is so that Ezekiel might see the abominations that are being carried out within the Temple, the holy center of Israel and creation that is supposed to be maintained as a sacred and pure site.[20] The vision depicts various abominations, i.e., the idols of the house of Israel and their worship by the elders; the mourning rituals performed by women for the Babylonian god, Tammuz; and the worship of the sun by a group of twenty-five men. In so far as the Temple is to serve as the holy center of Israel and creation, the vision depicts the violence that permeates the land at large as a result of the disruption of sanctity in the holy center. From the perspective of a priest, such profanity requires purification in order to remove the impurity and to restore the sacred character of the site.

Various narratives concerning the purification of the Temple or the community at large appear throughout the Bible, e.g., the Temple purifications carried out by Hezekiah (2 Kgs 18:1–8; 2 Chronicles 29–31), Josiah (2 Kgs 23:1–25), Judah the Maccabee (1 Macc 4:36–51), the Levitical purge of the nation at the golden calf incident in the wilderness (Exodus 32), and the purge of Achan and family for theft from the *ḥerem* or booty dedicated to YHWH in the time of Joshua (Joshua 7). Although the details vary among them, they point to a process in which the impurities are removed from the Temple and destroyed, those who are directly responsible for such abominations are liable for expulsion or execution, and sacrifices are made in order to bring about the resanctification of the Temple and the community. Ezekiel's vision of the destruction of Jerusalem and the Temple functions in like manner in so far as it employs the imagery of the purge of those who are considered to be impure together with the imagery of expiatory sacrifice at the Temple altar.[21]

---

[20] For discussion of the Temple as holy center of creation in ancient Judean thought, see Jon D. Levenson, "The Temple and the World," *JR* 64 (1984) 275–98; idem, *Sinai and Zion: An Entry into the Jewish Bible* (Minneapolis: Winston, 1985).

[21] For portrayals of expiatory sacrifice, including the *ḥaṭṭa'ṭ*, "sin," and *'āšām*, "guilt," offerings, see Lev 4:1–5:26; 6:17–7:10. For discussion of the roles and functions of these sacrifices, see Jacob Milgrom, "Sacrifices and Offerings, OT," *IDB[S]* 763–71, esp. 766–69.

The imagery of Temple purging and expiatory sacrifice is clear from the outset in the narrative portrayal of the six armed men supervised by a man dressed in white linen with a writing case at his side, who will carry out the execution of the guilty and the destruction of the city beginning with the Temple. The white linen garments of course are the characteristic dress of a priest serving at the Temple altar (Exod 28:29) as well as of angels who are frequently portrayed as the heavenly counterparts of the priests (Dan 10:5). The man in white linen is to mark the foreheads of those who lament idolatry in the city, apparently so that they might be spared. The other six then follow to put the rest of Jerusalem's population to death. Although such details are lacking in the Bible, Mishnah Tamid 1:2; 3:1–9 describe a procedure in which a priestly officer supervises the other priests who engage in sacrifice; likewise, the practice of marking animals that are fit for sacrifice is known in the ancient world.[22] There is a difference, however, in that those who are marked in Ezekiel are innocent and therefore to be spared.[23] Once the slaughter is completed, the throne chariot appears and YHWH instructs the man in white linen to take burning coals from under the cherubim and scatter them over the city. YHWH then commands the man in white linen to take fire from within the wheelwork of the throne as the throne chariot ascends and prepares to depart from the city. These images are those of a priest who takes coals and fire in order to ignite the sacrificial offerings at the Temple altar. The sacrificial imagery is further clarified by YHWH's statement in Ezek 11:7, "the slain whom you have placed within it are the meat, and this city is the pot," i.e., the destruction of the city is compared to a sacrifice in which the sacrificial meat is boiled in pots (cf. 1 Sam 2:12–17). This metaphor appears once again in Ezekiel 24:1–14 in which the destruction of Jerusalem is likened to a pot full of meat that is burned entirely until it is purified from rust and residue.

Ezekiel's use of sacrificial imagery to portray the destruction of Jerusalem and the Temple indicates the pervasive influence of his priestly identity in his conceptualization of the city's demise. Expiatory sacrifice at the Temple – and to some extent sacrifice in general – plays a necessary role in maintaining (or restoring) the holiness, purity, and stability of creation.[24] Insofar as even the

---

[22] For discussion of the marking of unblemished animals that are fit for sacrifice in the ancient world, see "Blemish," *Encyclopaedia Judaica* 4:1081–84.

[23] N.b., the interpretation of Ezek 9:4, "Go through the city, through Jerusalem, and put a mark on the foreheads of those who sigh and groan over all the abominations that are committed in it," is disputed as it is not entirely certain whether or not all of the persons in Jerusalem were to be sacrificed in Ezekiel's view. For discussion, see Moshe Greenberg, *Ezekiel 1–20* (AB 22; Garden City: Doubleday, 1983) 176–77; Zimmerli, *Ezekiel 1* 248.

[24] See Jacob Milgrom, "Sacrifices and Offerings, OT," *IDB[S]* 763–71, esp. 766–69. For overviews of sacrifice in ancient Israel and Judah, see Gary Anderson, *Sacrifices and Offerings in Ancient Israel: Studies in their Social and Political Importance* (HSM 41; Atlanta: Scholars Press, 1987); Jacob Milgrom, *Studies in Cultic Theology and Terminology* (Leiden: Brill, 1983).

Temple has become a place of profanation in Ezekiel's understanding, so the Temple and Jerusalem themselves must be purged in order to bring about their purification and restoration. The remaining sub-units of Ezekiel 8–19 make this clear in so far as they portray various aspects of the punishment and restoration of Israel (Ezek 11:14–24); the exile of Judah (Ezek 12:1–16); the immediacy of judgment (Ezek 12:17–28); the condemnation of false prophets (Ezek 13:1–23); YHWH's justification for the punishment and call for repentance (Ezek 14:1–23); the allegory of the useless vine that is consumed with fire (Ezek 15:1–8); the allegory of Israel as faithless bride who will be punished and then restored (Ezek 16:1–63); the allegory of the eagles and the vine (Ezek 17:1–10); the explanation of the allegory concerning the actions of Babylonia, Egypt, and the Judean kings and the projection of restoration of Israel once the process of punishment is complete (Ezek 17:11–24); and Ezekiel's discourse concerning the moral responsibilities of the individual and the lamentation concerning Israel's degradation (Ezek 18:1–19:14). Scholars have particularly noted Ezekiel's exposition of moral responsibility in relation to the priestly Holiness Code,[25] which illustrates the priestly role as teacher and expositor of divine Torah. But in fact, the entire sequence of oracles in this section illustrates the priestly vocation and responsibility to instruct the people as Ezekiel employs prophetic oracles, sermons, allegories, etc., to instruct his audience in the significance of YHWH's actions in bringing about the destruction of Jerusalem, i.e., the city is being purged, but YHWH intends to restore Israel once the purge is complete. The use of past traditions, such as the portrayal of Israel as YHWH's bride (cf. Hosea 1–3; Jeremiah 2), and illustrations from the natural world are noteworthy because they the roles of both tradition and creation in expressing Ezekiel's priestly instruction concerning the significance of contemporary events.

V

A series of further sub-units in the book of Ezekiel, each introduced by its own date formula, then follows in Ezekiel 20:1–23:49; 24:1–25:17; 26:1–28:36; 29:1–16; 29:17–30:19; 30:20–26; 31:1–18; 32:1–16; 32:17–33:20; 33:21–39:29. Each is further sub-divided by the appearance of the formula, "and the word of YHWH was unto me saying ...," which then introduces the following material. These texts treat a variety of topics, including oracles concerned with the fate of Israel/Judah as well as with the nations. A sampling of topics further dem-

---

For the conceptualization of the Temple, see Levenson, "The Temple and the World"; idem, *Sinai and Zion*; C. L. Meyers, "Temple, Jerusalem," *ABD* 6:350–69, esp. 359–60.

[25] Knohl, *Sanctuary of Silence*; cf. Gordon H. Matties, *Ezekiel 18 and the Rhetoric of Moral Discourse* (SBLDS 126; Atlanta: Scholars Press, 1990).

onstrates the role that Ezekiel's priestly identity plays in the formulation of his prophetic viewpoints.

The first is the sanctity of YHWH's divine name, which appears in Ezekiel's theological reflection on Israel's history in the wilderness in Ezekiel 20 and in his portrayal of the purification of Israel in Ezekiel 36:16–38. Both chapters place special emphasis on the sanctity of YHWH's divine name. In Ezekiel 20, YHWH repeatedly states that YHWH acted against Israel in the wilderness period so that the divine name would not be profaned among the nations. Likewise in Ezekiel 36:16–38 YHWH states that the restoration of Israel from exile is motivated by YHWH's concern with the sanctity of the holy name which Israel had profaned among the nations. Indeed, the sanctity of the divine name is the fundamental concern of the Zadokite priesthood. Deuteronomy, for example, designates the site of the Temple as the place where YHWH chooses to cause the divine name to dwell so that the divine name comes to express the sacred character of the Temple site. Furthermore, the divine name appears in the context of covenant stipulations both to identify YHWH as a party to the relationship with Israel and to designate its sacred character. Thus, the ten commandments begin with the divine self-identification formula, "I am YHWH, your G-d," as the foundation for the system of observance that follows (Exod 20:2; Deut 5:6). The formula also appears in YHWH's revelation to Moses in Exod 6:2, and efforts to assert and protect its sacred character appear in the burning bush narrative in Exodus 3, in which YHWH initially declines to reveal the divine name, and in the ten commandments which prohibit frivolous use of the name because of its sacred character (Exod 20:7; Deut 5:11; cf. Lev 19:12; 24:10–23). The formula plays a particularly important role in the Holiness Code of Leviticus 17–26 in which repeated statements, "I am YHWH, your G-d," or, "I am YHWH," presents YHWH's holy name as the basis for the action expected of the people in order to ensure their holiness as well as of the divine name. Indeed, the self identification formula plays an important role in Ezekiel where it appears throughout the book to authorize the prophet's oracles and to indicate their sacred content.[26] Furthermore, both Ezekiel 20 and 36:16–38 present concern with the sanctity of the divine name together with other issues of particular importance to the priesthood. The presentation of Israel's attempted rebellion against YHWH in the wilderness period emphasizes the profanation of the Shabbat and the rejection of YHWH's holy statutes and ordinances. It also expresses the restoration of Israel by use of the metaphor passing under the staff, an expression that is used in Lev 27:32 in reference to the tithes that are designated as holy to YHWH. Ezekiel's discussion of Israel's restoration for the sake of the divine name in Ezek 36:16–38 emphasizes issues of purity in so far as it compares

---

[26] See Walther Zimmerli, "I am YHWH," *I am YHWH* (trans. D. W. Stott; Atlanta: John Knox, 1982) 1–28.

Israel to a menstruous woman and portrays her purification through water (see Lev 15:19–30; cf. Lev 15:1–18; 14:5–6, 50–52; Num 19:17). Images of priestly sanctity permeate both of these texts.

The second is his allegory concerning the death of his wife in Ezekiel 24:15–27. This passage has been a frequent source of attention and charges that Ezekiel is unbalanced or misogynistic because of his refusal to mourn for the death of his wife and his use of this motif to portray YHWH's refusal to mourn for the loss of Jerusalem.[27] Interpreters generally do not recognize, however, that Ezekiel's actions are consistent with his identity as a priest. Priests are forbidden to have any contact with the dead. Priestly tradition emphasizes that it is the role of the priest to stand between YHWH and the people and thus to stand at the boundary of life and death as human beings cannot survive YHWH's holiness (see Numbers 16, esp. vv. 41–50; 2 Samuel 6; Isaiah 6). Leviticus 21:1–12 stipulates that the priests may not mourn for the dead unless it is a close blood relation such as a mother, father, brother, or sister. The high priest may not even mourn for these relations. In no instance is a priest permitted to mourn for his wife as she is not a close blood relation. Furthermore, the concluding command in the narrative that Ezekiel may speak only after the Temple is destroyed reflects the silence of the priests as they officiate at the Temple altar; once the Temple is destroyed, there is no further need for Ezekiel's silence. Ezekiel's actions throughout this narrative are entirely in keeping with his role as a priest. As noted above, Ezekiel adapts these characteristic priestly practices to provide a means for himself and the people to express their grief and shock at the losses of his wife and the city of Jerusalem.

The third is his portrayal of the valley of dry bones in Ezekiel 37 and the defeat of Gog and Magog in Ezekiel 38–39. Both employ priestly images of purification from contact with the dead to portray the restoration of Israel and creation at large. In the case of Ezekiel 37, Ezekiel sees a valley of dry bones, perhaps the remains of those killed in a battle, that are restored to life. Much of the discussion of this passage focuses upon its implications for understanding the motif of resurrection in the Hebrew Bible,[28] but its significance for issues of priestly purity must also be noted. Death is the fundamental cause of impurity in priestly thought; as noted above, priests stand between death and life, and they are to have very limited contact with the dead. Consequently, the restoration of life to the dead in Ezekiel 37 constitutes an important metaphor for the restoration and resanctification of Israel; it is no accident that following the image of Israel's restoration from the dead in Ezek 37:11–14, verses 15–28 then present a symbolic action in which he joins two sticks to symbolize the restoration and re-

---

[27] E. g., Halperin, *Seeking Ezekiel* 176–83; Julie Galambush, *Jerusalem in the Book of Ezekiel: The City as YHWH's Wife* (SBLDS 130; Atlanta: Scholars Press, 1992) esp. 140–41, whose reading of this text is heavily influenced by Ezekiel 16 and 20.

[28] E. g., Zimmerli, *Ezekiel 2* 253–66.

unification of Israel and Judah. The concluding reference to a covenant of peace draws upon the priestly covenant granted to Phinehas ben Eleazar ben Aaron in Num 25:10–13 as well as the image of YHWH's holy sanctuary placed in the midst of the people Israel. The Gog of Magog oracles in Ezekiel 38–39 fill a similar role, except that they represent the purification of the world or creation at large rather than only Israel. Although much of the discussion of these chapters focuses on various attempts to identify Gog and Magog,[29] the significance of the passage lies in the purification of the land once Gog is defeated. Ezekiel 39 portrays a process in which the corpses left from the battle defile the land and must be properly buried in order to restore its purity. Fires burn for seven years as part of the process of purification, which recalls the seven year sabbatical and agricultural cycle of the Temple Jubilee (see Lev 25:1–7; Exod 23:10–11; 21:1–6; Deut 15:1–18). At the end of this process, the land is cleansed and YHWH's name is profaned no more. Such purification enables the glory of YHWH to be displayed among the nations; it would appear then that the purification of Israel and the nations/world at large sets the stage for Ezekiel's vision of the restored Temple which follows in Ezekiel 40–48.

VI

The final section of the book appears in Ezekiel 40–48, which presents Ezekiel's vision of the new Temple to be established in Zion and the return of the glory of YHWH that will enable it to function as the holy center of Jerusalem, Israel, and the cosmos at large. Although many scholars have attempted to argue that these chapters are largely or entirely the work of writers other than Ezekiel, perhaps his own disciples, Levenson rightly points to these chapters as "the crown and consummation of Ezekiel's life work," insofar as these chapters recapitulate the concerns and forms of Ezekiel's initial visions in Ezekiel 1–3; 8–11.[30]

There is little question as to their priestly character. Set in the tenth day of the beginning of the twenty-fifth year of the exile, 573 B.C.E., these chapters present a detailed first person account of Ezekiel's vision concerning the structure and dimensions of the Temple and the return of YHWH's glory (Ezek 40:1–43:12), the structure and dimensions of the Temple courtyards and the holy activities that take place therein (Ezek 43:13–47:12), and the reestablishment of the land and people of Israel at the center of a newly constituted land and creation that

---

[29] E. g., Zimmerli, *Ezekiel 2* 281–324.

[30] Jon Levenson, *Theology of the Program of Restoration of Ezekiel 40–48* (HSM 10; Missoula: Scholars Press, 1976) 10; cf. e. g., Hartmut Gese, *Der Verfassungsentwurf des Ezechiel (Kap. 40–48). Traditionsgeschichtlich Untersucht* (Beiträge zur historischen Theologie 25; Tübingen: J.C.B. Mohr [Paul Siebeck], 1957); see now Steven Shawn Tuell, *The Law of the Temple in Ezekiel 40–48* (HSM 49; Atlanta: Scholars Press, 1992).

is watered and sustained by the new Temple. Many have noted that Ezekiel's Temple does not correspond to what is known of the structure and character of the Second Temple that was actually built in Jerusalem in the late-sixth century B.C.E.[31] Consequently, medieval exegetes such as Rashi and David Kimḥi have indicated that Ezekiel's vision portrays the Third Temple that will be established in the days of the Messiah.[32] Overall, these chapters represent Ezekiel's own understanding of the character and role of the Temple once the punishment of the Babylonian exile is complete and the order of creation is established once again.

There is little need to rehearse the priestly character of the details that are presented here concerning the structure of the Temple complex and its rituals; they demonstrate clearly the priestly identity and expertise of their author. Instead, the role of the Temple as holy center of creation demands attention because this motif points to the comprehensive priestly theological viewpoint that is articulated throughout the book of Ezekiel, i.e., as holy center of creation, the Temple is to be equated with both Mount Zion and the Garden of Eden, and therefore represents the source on which the viability of creation is based. Levenson has already pointed to the pervasive influence of the Garden of Eden imagery in Ezekiel's oracles concerning the king of Tyre in Ezek 28:1–19, which compares Tyre's beauty and wealth to that of Eden, and his oracle concerning Egypt in Ezekiel 31, which compares both Assyria and Egypt to the well-watered trees of the Garden of Eden.[33] One might note that various features of the construction of Solomon's Temple as presented in 1 Kings 6–7 also recall motifs from the traditions concerning Eden and creation at large, e.g., the cherubim, palm trees, and pomegranates that decorate the interior of the Temple to represent the cherubim and fruitfulness of the garden; the representation of lions, oxen, etc., to symbolize the animals of the garden; the bronze pillars that represent the foundations of the earth; the bronze sea that represents the sea from which creation proceeds; the Temple lamp stands apparently constructed with flowers to symbolize the trees of the garden as well as light; etc. Later texts of the Second Temple period likewise note that the priest in the Temple represents Adam in the Garden of Eden,[34] which may explain the appellation *ben-ʾādām*, "son of Adam" or "mortal," that is consistently applied by YHWH to Ezekiel throughout the book. The fact that only the high priest may enter the Holy of Holies, where

---

[31] Tuell, *The Law of the Temple* 1–2, who cites the Rabbinic tradition in bShabbat 13b; bHaggigah 13a; and bMenahot 13a that R. Hananiah ben Hezekiah burned three hundred barrels of oil in all-night attempts to reconcile Ezekiel's vision with the Torah of Moses.

[32] See both Rashi and Radak (i.e., Kimḥi) on Ezek 40:2, where they cite Isaiah 2 as part of their arguments that Ezekiel is brought to the future Temple.

[33] Levenson, *Theology* 25–36.

[34] See C. T. R. Hayward, *The Jewish Temple: A Non-Biblical Sourcebook* (London and New York: Routledge, 1996), who cites various Second Temple period texts (e.g., Aristeas, Philo, Jubilees, Josephus) that illustrate this point.

the Ark of the Covenant is guarded by cherubim much like the Garden of Eden, reinforces this image.

Indeed, the Eden-like role of the new Temple in relation to all creation appears in the portrayal of the Temple as the source of water that flows eastward to water the Aravah, or the Jordan rift that includes the Jordan River, the Dead Sea, and the dry divide that extends south to the Gulf of Aqaba and the Red Sea.[35] As depicted in Ezekiel 47, this water brings life to this dead region and effectively renews the creation of the world. The imagery appears to be based both on that of the Gihon spring that waters Jerusalem (see 1 Kgs 1:32–40; Isa 7:3; 2 Chr 32:4) and the river that flows out of the Garden of Eden to water all of creation (see Gen 2:10–14; Ps 46:4). The role of the Temple as sacred center of creation is also signaled by the designation of the base of the Temple altar as *ḥēq hāʾāreṣ*, "bosom of the earth," in Ezek 43:14 and the designation of the altar hearth as *harʾēl*, "mountain of G-d," in Ezek 43:15, which indicate the role played by the altar and Temple sacrifice in sustaining creation.[36] This portrayal of the significance of the Temple in relation to creation at large then provides the basis for placing the tribes of Israel at the center of creation in their assigned territories, with the priests and Levites (together with prince) at the center of Israel, and the Temple at the center of the whole. The theological significance of this centering is articulated in the assignment of gates for entry to the Temple for each of the tribes and in the concluding statement of the book, *yhwh šāmmâ*, "YHWH is there."

Altogether Ezekiel's vision clearly portrays the Temple as the sacred center of creation, Israel, and Jerusalem, and the source from which all three are sustained. In essence, this is a priestly perspective on the character of the world and the role of the Temple and its priesthood within it.

VII

In conclusion, this essay points to the constitutive character of Ezekiel's identity as a Zadokite priest in the formulation of his prophetic perspective concerning the theological significance of YHWH's actions in bringing about the Babylonian exile. Insofar as Ezekiel employs the imagery of purge and sacrifice to portray the destruction of the Temple and the city of Jerusalem, he articulates a perspective that identifies YHWH's actions as a purge that is designed to cleanse the world from impurity in order that creation might be restored with a new Temple and the people Israel at its center. Although Ezekiel's vision was

---

[35] See Katheryn Pfisterer Darr, "The Wall Around Paradise: Ezekielian Ideas About the Future," *VT* 37 (1987) 271–79, who notes that the depiction of restored creation in Ezekiel focuses on the land of Israel.

[36] Levenson, *Sinai and Zion* 139; idem, "The Temple and the World."

never implemented in detail, it remains an ideal description of the renewal of both the Temple and creation, that perhaps played a role in motivating efforts to rebuild the Temple in the early Persian period and that continues to play a role in defining expectations of the world to come in Jewish tradition from ancient through modern times.

10. The Destruction of Jerusalem as Purification in Ezekiel 8–11

I

Ezekiel's vision of the departure of the divine presence from Jerusalem in Ezekiel 8–11 is particularly enigmatic.[1] It portrays Ezekiel's divinely guided vision of the corruption of the Jerusalem Temple together with YHWH's commands to destroy the city immediately prior to departure of the divine throne chariot. YHWH commands in Ezek 9:4 a divine representative in white linen together with his assistants to mark the foreheads and to spare "those who sigh and groan over all the abominations that are committed in (the city)." The portrayal of the corruption of the Temple is clear enough as a rationale for the divine decision to destroy the city, but the decision to spare those so marked and to destroy those left unmarked is not clear. Although those who sigh and groan appear to lament the abominations, those killed include the old men, young men and young women, children, and women whose guilt is not specified.[2] Such a general listing leaves the reader wondering whether those unmarked are guilty of corruption or not.

Prior treatments of Ezekiel 8–11 have tended to focus on discerning the compositional integrity of these chapters, although most have expressed some

---
[1] For discussion of Ezekiel 8–11, see Leslie Allen, *Ezekiel 1–19* (WBC 28; Waco: Word, 1994) 114–69; Katheryn Pfisterer Darr, "Ezekiel," *The New Interpreter's Bible* (ed. L. E. Keck et al.; Nashville: Abingdon, 2001) 6:1172–91; Georg Fohrer, *Ezechiel* (HAT 13; Tübingen: Mohr Siebeck, 1955) 47–63; Moshe Greenberg, *Ezekiel 1–20* (AB 22; Garden City: Doubleday, 1983) 164–206; Ronald M. Hals, *Ezekiel* (FOTL 19; Grand Rapids: Eerdmans, 1989) 46–74; Karl-Friedrich Pohlmann, *Der Prophet Hesekiel/Ezechiel Kapitel 1–19* (ATD 22,1; Göttingen: Vandenhoeck & Ruprecht, 1996) 123–70; Walther Zimmerli, *Ezekiel 1: A Commentary on the Book of the Prophet Ezekiel Chapters 1–24* (Hermeneia; Philadelphia: Fortress, 1979) 215–64. In addition to the commentaries, see J. Becker, "Ez 8–11 als einheitliche Komposition in einem pseudepigraphischen Ezechielbuch," *Ezekiel and His Book* (BETL 74; ed. J. Lust; Leuven: Peeters and Leuven University Press, 1986) 136–50; F. Horst, "Exilsgemeinde und Jerusalem in Ez viii–xi: Eine literarische Untersuchung," *VT* 3 (1953) 337–60; F.-L. Hossfeld, "Die Tempelvision Ez 8–11 im Licht unterschiedlichen methodischer Zugänge," *Ezekiel and His Book* 151–65; Ka Leung Wong, *The Idea of Retribution in the Book of Ezekiel* (VTSup 87; Leiden: Brill, 2001) 158–78.

[2] See also Greenberg, *Ezekiel 1–20* 177, who notes the difficulties of this portrayal by observing that, although some persons are marked, the prophet's comment in v. 8 indicates that no one is to be spared.

perplexity over the nature of YHWH's command. The issue is bound up with the question of Ezekiel's identity as prophet or priest. Many have argued that tensions in the prophet's social identity are the result of literary tension in the text.[3]

A form-critical reassessment of this material, including its literary structure, generic characteristics, socio-literary setting, and conceptual underpinnings will aid in resolving the problems posed by the text. On the basis of such considerations, this paper argues that Ezekiel 8–11 presents a coherent literary structure in which the portrayal of the destruction of Jerusalem introduces a sequence of oracle reports in Ezekiel 12–19 concerning the significance of the city's destruction. It further argues that the narrative patterns in Ezekiel 8–11, which present a series of elements in Ezekiel's overall vision together with explanations concerning the significance of each element, reflect the generic characteristics of priestly instruction in which the priests instruct the people to distinguish between the sacred and the profane. Finally, the paper points to the scapegoat offering as portrayed in Leviticus 16 as the basis for understanding the purging of the city in Ezekiel 8–11. Ezekiel does not depict the destruction of the wicked and the sparing of the righteous. Rather, Ezekiel portrays the division of the people into two parts. One part will be destroyed and one part spared to go into exile. Just as the scapegoat offering calls for the sacrifice of one of the goats and the expulsion of the other into the wilderness as a means to purge the nation's sins at Yom Kippur, so Ezekiel's presentation of the fate of the people of Jerusalem points to the means by which he conceives the significance of the destruction of Jerusalem in relation to the projected restoration of the Temple at the conclusion of the book.

II

An assessment of the literary structure of Ezekiel 8–11 necessarily begins with the demarcation of the text.[4] The extensive lexical and conceptual links between Ezekiel's vision of the divine throne chariot might tempt some to read these chapters together with Ezekiel 8–11.[5]

Such a view is very problematic, however, for two fundamental reasons. First, even a cursory reading of Ezekiel 1–11 indicates that these chapters are hardly limited to narrative reports of Ezekiel's visions, which appear only in Ezekiel

---

[3] See esp. the commentaries by Fohrer, Pohlmann, Zimmerli noted above. See also Hossfeld, "Methodischer Zugänge."

[4] For the methodological principles employed here, see Marvin A. Sweeney, "Form Criticism," *To Each Its Own Meaning: Biblical Criticisms and their Application* (ed. S. L. McKenzie and S. R. Haynes; Louisville: Westminster John Knox, 1999) 58–89.

[5] See the discussion in Zimmerli, *Ezekiel 1* 231–4.

1:1–3:15 and 8–11. Indeed, Ezekiel 1–11 includes a series of oracular reports in Ezekiel 3:16–5:17; 6:1–14; and 7:1–27 as well. The identification of Ezekiel 1–11 as a basic textual unit unfortunately does little to explain the interrelationship between the visionary accounts and the oracular reports. Second, it overlooks the role of the date formula in establishing the literary structure of the book as a whole.[6] The initial date formula appears in Ezek 1:1–3, which places Ezekiel's initial vision of YHWH in the fifth day of the fourth month of the thirtieth year, identified as the fifth year of Jehoiachin's exile, i. e., 592 B.C.E. Successive date formulae appear in Ezek 8:1; 20:1; 24:1; 26:1; 29:1; 29:17; 30:20; 31:1; 32:1; 32:17; 33:21; and 40:1, which establish a twenty year chronology for Ezekiel's prophetic career from his initial vision of the presence of YHWH, his subsequent vision of YHWH's departure from the corrupted Temple, his oracles concerning the destruction of Jerusalem and the punishment of the nations, and finally through his vision of the return of YHWH to the reestablished Temple at the center of creation. As noted in my earlier study, "Ezekiel: Zadokite Priest and Visionary Prophet of the Exile," such a chronology corresponds to the years of active service in the central sanctuary or tent of meeting by priests, viz., from the age of thirty until the age of fifty (see, e. g., Num 4:23). By contrast, those Levites who assist Aaron and his sons in the sanctuary serve from the age of twenty five until the age of fifty. Such a chronology in Ezekiel points to the book's portrayal of Ezekiel's social role as a Zadokite priest, insofar as the book places his prophetic career within the chronological framework of the years of active service at the Temple by a Zadokite priest.

Such a structural principle for the organization of the book of Ezekiel has implications for establishing the literary structure of Ezekiel 8–11, i. e., these chapters cannot form the conclusion of a unit defined as Ezekiel 1–11; rather they form the introduction to a unit defined as Ezekiel 8–19. Thus, the vision account in Ezekiel 8:1–11:25 relates Ezekiel's vision of YHWH's departure from Jerusalem on the fifth day of the sixth month of the sixth year, from his initial setting in his home in Babylonia, through his divinely-guided visionary journey to Jerusalem and the Temple, and finally through his return to Babylonia in Ezek 11:24–25, where he proceeded to tell the exiles what YHWH had shown to him. The series of oracle reports in Ezekiel 12–19, each introduced by the prophetic word transmission formula[7] in Ezek 12:1; 12:8; 12:17; 12:21; 12:26; 13:1; 14:1; 14:12; 15:1; 16:1; 17:1; and 18:1, then relates the various oracles that were prompted by Ezekiel's vision of YHWH's departure from Jerusalem. Each oracle in the series takes up an aspect of the significance of YHWH's departure from the

---

[6] See my "Ezekiel: Zadokite Priest and Visionary Prophet of the Exile," published in this volume.

[7] For discussion of the prophetic word formula, see now Samuel M. Meier, *Speaking of Speaking: Marking Direct Discourse in the Hebrew Bible* (VTSup 46; Leiden: Brill, 1992) 314–19.

initial depiction of the Exile as a reversal of the Exodus through the emphasis on the responsibility of the current generation and the monarchy for the debacle.

III

The internal structure of the vision account in Ezekiel 8–11 is based on Ezekiel's successive locations throughout the visionary experience. The text begins with a portrayal of Ezekiel's initial setting in Ezek 8:1-2 in his own house in Babylonia. Following the appearance of Ezekiel's divine guide, Ezek 8:3-6 portrays Ezekiel's visionary transport to the inner gate on the north side of the city. Here he sees the so-called "offensive image," perhaps a Babylonian idol or victory stele, which indicates the defilement of the city. He is then transported to the entrance of the Temple court in Ezek 8:7-13, where he sees a hole in the wall, perhaps the work of Babylonian sappers, that allows him to enter the Temple complex and to see the abominations practiced there. Ezekiel is then transported to the north gate of the Temple in Ezek 8:14-15, where he sees the women wailing for Tammuz in a typical mourning ritual for the dead Mesopotamian vegetation god. Ezekiel is then transported to the entrance of the Temple structure itself in Ezek 8:16-10:22 where he witnesses YHWH's instructions concerning the destruction of the city and the disposal of its inhabitants immediately prior to the departure of the divine presence. He is then transported to the east gate of the Temple in Ezek 11:1-23 where YHWH commands him to speak oracles concerning the ultimate restoration of Israel to the land as a result of the exile. Finally, Ezek 11:24-25 portrays Ezekiel's return to Babylonia where he speaks to the exiles concerning what YHWH has shown him.

The internal structure of each sub-unit in Ezekiel 8–11 must also be considered.

The report of the initial date and setting of the vision account in Ezek 8:1-2 displays a simple three-part structure based upon its *waw*-consecutive verbs, including a description of the initial setting in v. 1a, an autobiographical report concerning the fall of YHWH's hand upon Ezekiel in v. 1b, and the vision of the divine guide in v. 2.

The account of Ezekiel's vision of the offensive image by the north gate of Jerusalem in Ezek 8:3-6 includes a brief statement of Ezekiel's transport to the gate in v. 3 and an account of his vision of the glory or presence of YHWH in vv. 4-6. This vision account includes Ezekiel's initial report of the glory of YHWH in v. 4, a report of his compliance with YHWH's command to observe the offensive image in v. 5, and a report of YHWH's rhetorical question in v. 6 that asserts that such abominations will continue and that they will drive YHWH away. Thus, the basic pattern of Ezekiel's vision of YHWH is an attempt to explain the significance of the image shown to Ezekiel.

The account of Ezekiel's vision of the apostasy in the Temple in Ezek 8:7–13 displays a similar pattern based in an attempt to explain the significance of a scene shown to Ezekiel as a case of abomination. Again, the sub-unit includes a brief statement of Ezekiel's transport in v. 7a and a vision report in vv. 7b–13. The vision report itself includes five elements: the portrayal of the hole in the wall in v. 7b; an account of Ezekiel's compliance with the instruction to dig a hole in the wall in v. 8; an account of Ezekiel's compliance with the command to observe the abominations taking place in the Temple in vv. 9–11; an account of rhetorical question in v. 12 that asserts the elders' belief that YHWH has abandoned the land; and another account of a rhetorical question in v. 13 that asserts that more abominations will follow. Again, the sub-unit is designed to demonstrate the defilement of the Temple as the cause of YHWH's departure.

The account of Ezekiel's vision of the women wailing for Tammuz shows a somewhat truncated but similar pattern. The notice of Ezekiel's transport appears in v. 14a, and the vision report follows in vv. 14b–15. The components of the vision report include Ezekiel's observing the wailing women in v. 14b and the rhetorical question in v. 15 that asserts that he will see more such abominations.

The lengthy sub-unit in Ezek 8:16–10:22 devoted to Ezekiel's vision of the destruction of Jerusalem and the departure of YHWH again displays a similar structure to those of the preceding subunits, although the vision report is far more extensive. A transport notice appears in Ezek 8:16aα^{1-7}, and the vision report follows in Ezek 8:16aα^{8}–10:22. The vision report itself follows the typical pattern of its predecessors. The initial visionary episode of twenty-five men worshipping the sun appears in Ezek 8:16aα^{8}–b. The report of the rhetorical question in Ezek 8:17–18 asserts that YHWH will show them no pity as a result of this provocation.

The second visionary episode in Ezek 9:1–10:22 breaks the pattern of its predecessors by its detailed account of the destruction of Jerusalem and the departure of YHWH. Its length and subject matter indicates that this vision constitutes the primary concern of the unit as a whole. The unit begins in Ezek 9:1 with a report of YHWH's summons to the appointed officials of the city. They are not identified at this point, apart from the notice that each appears with a weapon in hand, but the following material suggests that they play a quasi-priestly role. Three episodes then follow in Ezek 9:2–11; 10:1–8; and 10:9–22, each of which is introduced by an introductory visionary formula, *wĕhinneh*, "and behold," in 9:2 and *waʾerʾeh wĕhinnēh*, "and I looked, and behold," in 10:1, 9. The first depicts the entrance of six men armed with clubs in v. 2, the leader of whom is dressed in the white linen of a priest and carries a scribal case at his side, who comply with YHWH's instructions to defile the city by killing all inhabitants not marked on the forehead by the priest. When Ezekiel protests that YHWH might wipe out the entire remnant of Israel, YHWH responds that the land and city have been defiled because the people contend that YHWH has abandoned the land and does not see. The second episode in Ezek 10:1–8 depicts the compliance of the priestly figure with YHWH's command to take fire from the cherubim so that he might destroy the city. The third episode in Ezek 10:9–22 then depicts the departure of the divine presence to the east gate of the Temple complex. The episode concludes with Ezekiel's observation that the cherubim were the creatures that he had seen earlier at the Chebar canal.

The account in Ezek 11:1–23 of Ezekiel's vision by the east gate of the Temple complex of YHWH's oracles concerning the restoration of Israel provides rationale for the destruction of the city and YHWH's departure from it. The first sub-unit in this passage in vv. 1–12 relates YHWH's oracle in the form of a disputation speech[8] concerning the sacrificial role of the city and its people, although YHWH is careful to note that the leaders of the people will be executed by the Babylonians at the borders of Israel. The second subunit in vv. 13–21 employs a disputation[9] in vv. 14–17 to provide YHWH's answer to Ezekiel's protest that all Israel might be destroyed. YHWH carefully notes that the ultimate goal of the punishment and exile is the purging of the land when the people are returned to it and the restoration of the relation between YHWH and the people of Israel. Finally, vv. 22–23 note YHWH's departure from Jerusalem by the east gate of the Temple complex.

The final unit of the vision appears in Ezek 11:24–25, which reports Ezekiel's return to Babylonia where he could then tell the exiles all that YHWH had shown him.

IV

In considering the generic characteristics of Ezekiel 8–11, interpreters generally stress the prophetic elements that inform this text, most notably its overall generic character as a vision report as well as the elements of the disputation and the prophecy of salvation that appear respectively in Ezek 11:1–12 and Ezek 11:14–21. And yet the narrative displays other generic elements that are rooted in the social matrix of the Judean priesthood.

First to be considered are the vision accounts of the offensive image in Ezek 8:3–6; apostasy in the Temple in Ezek 8:7–13; the women weeping for Tammuz in Ezek 8:14–15; and the initial elements of the destruction of Jerusalem prior to the departure of YHWH in Ezek 8:16–10:22. Each sub-unit is distinct, insofar as each takes place at a different location and portrays Ezekiel's observation of a different scene, but they are remarkably consistent in form. Each includes a

---

[8] Adrian Graffy, *A Prophet Confronts His People: The Disputation Speech in the Prophets* (AnBib 104; Rome: Biblical Institute Press, 1984) 42–47.

[9] Graffy, *A Prophet Confronts His People* 47–52.

notice of Ezekiel's transport to a new location and a vision report of what he sees upon arrival. The vision reports include a report of the vision per se followed by instructional elements that employ rhetorical questions to assert the abominable character of the scenes that Ezekiel observes.[10]

Although the instructional concerns and rhetorical questions might normally be related to the sphere of the wisdom literature and schools by classical form critics, such genres do indeed appear frequently in the contexts of other social matrices. In the present instances, we may note that the ultimate functions and concerns of these elements with the abominations are displayed or practiced within the Temple precincts. Indeed, the objects and actions observed by the prophet all make the case that the Temple has become ritually defiled, which in turn prompts the departure of YHWH's holy presence. In other words, the divine guide instructs Ezekiel concerning the holiness or ritual purity of the Temple in order to demonstrate the necessity for YHWH's departure. That such a concern is rooted in the typical experience or role of the priesthood should be evident from repeated assertions that one major role of the priesthood is to instruct the people in matters of holiness and defilement. Leviticus 10:10–11, for example, states that the role of Aaron and his descendants is "to distinguish between the holy and the profane, between the defiled and the pure, to teach the children of Israel all the statutes which YHWH their G-d spoke by the hand of Moses." Ezekiel 44:23 likewise states that "they (the Zadokite priests) shall teach my people the difference between the holy and the profane, and they shall know the difference between the defiled and the pure." Hosea upbraids the priests in Hos 4:6 for failing to teach the people knowledge of G-d. An example of priestly instruction appears in Hag 2:11–13 in which Haggai asks the priests for a ruling concerning the purity or holiness of meat carried in a garment and other foodstuffs with which it might come into contact. These examples demonstrate that instruction is an integral part of priestly activity and social identity.[11] The appearance of instructional elements in the present narrative demonstrates the defilement of the Temple, and points decidedly to a priestly role in instruction and its concomitant concern with the sanctity of the Temple itself.

The vision report of the destruction of Jerusalem in Ezek 9:1–10:22 must also be considered. Although it too constitutes a typical example of the vision reports,[12] the vision itself includes a number of priestly elements that inform

---

[10] For discussion of instruction genres and rhetorical questions, see Marvin A. Sweeney, *Isaiah 1–39, with an Introduction to Prophetic Literature* (FOTL 16; Grand Rapids and Cambridge: Eerdmans, 1996) 522, 537. See also, Deborah Sweeney, "What's a Rhetorical Question?" *Lingua Aegyptia* 1 (1991) 209–24.

[11] See J. Begrich, "Die priesterliche Tora," *Werden und Wesen des Alten Testaments* (BZAW 66; ed. P. Volz et al; Berlin: Töpelmann, 1936) 63–88, although he takes a characteristically narrow view of the concerns of priestly instruction.

[12] For discussion of vision reports, see F. Horst, "Die Visionsschilderungen der alttestamentlichen Propheten," *EvT* 20 (1960) 193–205; B. O. Long, "Reports of Visions among the

Ezekiel's overall understanding of the character and significance of the destruction of the city.

First is the portrayal of the six officials, who will execute the inhabitants of the city. Particularly noteworthy is the officer dressed in white linen. White linen is the characteristic dress of priests who serve at the altar (Exod 28:39). The white linen dress of the officer, the role of the others to carry out the execution of the inhabitants of the city, and their initial position by the bronze altar, suggest that Ezekiel portrays a scene informed by the typical priestly role of sacrifice at the Temple altar.

Second is the description of the glory of the G-d of Israel which is preparing to depart the city following its destruction. As noted in my earlier study,[13] the imagery is based on the ark of the covenant, which would have been housed in the Holy of Holies of the Jerusalem Temple. The throne imagery, the sapphire firmament above the cherubim, the wheelwork, and even the cherubim themselves – which are only identified here for the first time with the four creatures of Ezekiel's inaugural vision in Ezek 1:1–3:15 – all point to the identification of the divine glory with the ark. Because the ark is the central icon of the Jerusalem Temple, its central role in Ezekiel's vision demonstrates the priestly character of the scene and Ezekiel's fundamental priestly identity.

Finally, we may note the presentation of the destruction of the city. The presence of the priestly figures, their initial location by the bronze altar, and the command to ignite the city with fire taken by the figure in white linen from between the wheelwork of the cherubim suggests the imagery of sacrifice. And yet it is difficult to identify the destruction of the city with the standard sacrifices of Temple times, e. g., the whole burnt offering, the sin offering, the guilt offering, the peace offering, etc. In such sacrifices, the slaughter and burning of the sacrificial animal symbolizes the purification of those on whose behalf the offering is made. We might note the several instances of Temple purification, i. e., Hezekiah' purification of the Temple in 2 Kgs 18:1–8 and 2 Chronicles 29–31; Josiah's purification of the Temple in 2 Kgs 23:1–25; and Judah the Maccabee's purification of the Temple in 1 Macc 4:36–51, in which the *ḥaṭṭa'at* offering of seven bulls, seven rams, seven lambs, and seven goats plays a central role. We might also note instances in which the nation Israel is purged by the Levites' killing of those who worshipped the golden calf in Exodus 32–34; YHWH's killing of the wilderness generation in Numbers 14; the killing of Koraḥ, Dathan, and Abiram for presenting improper offerings in Numbers 16; the killing of Achan and his family for theft from booty devoted to YHWH in Joshua 7; and Elijah's killing of the four hundred fifty prophets of Baal in 1 Kings 18.

Prophets," *JBL* 95 (1976) 353–65; M. Sister, "Die Typen der prophetischen Visionen in der Bibel," *MGWJ* 78 (1934) 399–430.

[13] "Ezekiel: Zadokite Priest and Visionary Prophet of the Exile."

Although we have many examples of such sacrifices and purges, the model does not fit precisely because each instance presupposes that the guilty party is killed or that the sacrifices are made on behalf of those who are guilty. And yet the description of the killing in Ezek 9:1–10:22 does not make it clear that those who are killed are guilty and those who are spared are not. The divine officers are told to mark the foreheads of "the men who moan and groan over all the abominations that are done in your midst" (Ezek 9:4), presumably to indicate their disapproval. The divine agents are then ordered to kill "old men, young men, young women, little children, and women" throughout the city without pity. Curiously, the men of the city are not included, and we are hard pressed to argue that those listed for execution are those who are considered guilty and thereby responsible for the defilement and destruction of Jerusalem. The execution of these classes of people appears to presuppose a corporate understanding of guilt. They suffer their fates only because they are inhabitants of a defiled Jerusalem.

But we must observe that the survivors designated for exile in the concluding oracle of salvation in Ezek 11:14–21 are those who will form the basis for the restoration of the nation to the land of Israel. It is at this point that we must consider the role of the scapegoat ritual from Leviticus 16 in the portrayal of the destruction of Jerusalem. Leviticus 16 portrays the scapegoat ritual as a means to represent the purification of the people on Yom Kippur. The high priest, dressed in white linen, offers a sin offering for himself and his house, and then takes two goats to the entrance of the tent of meeting or sanctuary. After casting lots, one goat is designated for YHWH and the other for Azazel. He offers incense that forms a cloud of smoke to symbolize the divine presence. The goat designated for YHWH is sacrificed as a sin offering for the sanctuary and the people, and its blood is sprinkled before the ark and upon the altar. The priest then lays his hands on the goat designated for Azazel, and symbolically transfers the sins of the people to it. The goat is released into the wilderness in order to purify the nation by carrying its sins off into the wilderness. Indeed, the arbitrary selection of the two goats, the one killed and the other expelled into the wilderness to purify the sanctuary and the nation, provides a model for understanding Ezekiel's portrayal of the destruction of Jerusalem in Ezek 9:1–10:22. Some are killed in the destruction of the city itself; the others are sent off into exile where they will atone for the defilement of Jerusalem and ultimately form the basis by which Israel will be restored.

V

In conclusion, we may observe that the account of Ezekiel's vision concerning the destruction of Jerusalem in Ezekiel 8–11 stands as the basis for a series of oracles that speak to the significance of that event. Furthermore, although the vision report itself constitutes a prophetic genre, it is infused with a variety of generic elements, most notably of priestly origin, that indicate the priestly social role of instruction in matters pertaining to the sacred and profane and a priestly conceptualization of the destruction of Jerusalem as an act of purification. Although one might justifiably challenge such a theological viewpoint, insofar as it charges that the victims of the Babylonian assault are somehow corporately guilty and responsible for their own deaths, it points to the characterization of Ezekiel as both a prophet and a Zadokite priest, who employed his own priestly background and perceptions to offer an interpretation of the destruction of Jerusalem.[14]

Appendix

Formal Analysis: Ezekiel 8–19

Presentation of Ezekiel's Oracles following upon his Vision of
Jerusalem's Destruction/YHWH's Departure from
Jerusalem   Ezekiel 8:1–19:14

I. Autobiographical vision account: sixth year (592–1),
   sixth month, fifth day (5 Elul: late-August/early-September)   8:1–11:25
  A. Initial date and setting: Ezekiel's house; Elders; Angelic guide   8:1–2
    1. initial setting: date and location   8:1a
    2. inauguration of action/vision report   8:1b–2
      a. hand of YHWH   8:1b
      b. vision of guide   8:2
  B. New setting: North gate of Jerusalem: Ezekiel's vision of
    the offensive image (Babylonian victory stele?)   8:3–6
    1. transport to north gate by hand/wind (4 *waw*-consecutive verbs) 8:3
      a. and it sent/reached   8:3aα
      b. and it took me   8:3aβ
      c. and it carried me   8:3aα^{1-7}
      d. and it brought me   8:3aα^{8}–β
    2. vision report: Glory/Presence of G-d   8:4–6
      a. initial report of Glory/Presence   8:4
      b. report of Ezekiel's compliance with divine instruction   8:5
        1) instruction report: look north   8:5a
        2) compliance report: vision of offensive image   8:5b
      c. instruction report: rhetorical question asserts that
        abomination will drive divine Presence away   8:6
  C. New setting: North gate of inner court: Hole in wall;
    Ezekiel's vision of apostasy in the Temple
    (analogous to hole dug by Babylonian sappers?)   8:7–13

---

[14] This paper was presented at the annual meeting of the Theological Perspectives on the Book of Ezekiel Group, Society of Biblical Literature, Atlanta, November 24, 2003.

1. transport to Temple courtyard gate	8:7a
2. vision report: abominations in Temple	8:7b–13
a. initial report of hole in wall	8:7b
b. report of Ezekiel's compliance with divine instruction	8:8
1) instruction: dig	8:8a
2) compliance	8:8b
c. report of Ezekiel's compliance with second divine instruction	8:9–11
1) command: enter and see	8:9
2) compliance	8:10–11
a) compliance formula	$8:10a\alpha^{1-2}$
b) vision of abominations in Temple	$8:10a\alpha^{3}-11$
i. wall decorated with pagan images	$8:10a\alpha^{3}-b$
ii. 70 elders, incense, etc.	8:11
d. instruction report: rhetorical question asserts people's view that YHWH has abandoned them	8:12
e. instruction report: rhetorical question asserts great abominations	8:13
D. New setting: North gate of Temple; Ezekiel's vision of Women weeping for Tammuz (Babylonian mourning rite for late summer)	8:14–15
1. transport to north gate of Temple	8:14a
2. vision report of abomination in Temple precincts by women	8:14b–15
a. vision report: women weeping for Tammuz	8:14b
b. instruction report: rhetorical question asserts abominations	8:15
E. New setting: Entrance to Temple main hall: Ezekiel's vision of the destruction of Jerusalem and Departure of YHWH (exile of king[?] et al; destruction for those who remain)	8:16–10:22
1. transport to Temple entrance	$8:16a\alpha^{1-7}$
2. vision report of abomination in the Temple and its consequences	$8:10a\alpha^{8}-10:22$
a. 1st episode: 25 men facing east to worship sun	$8:10a\alpha^{8}-b$
b. instruction report: rhetorical question answered to assert provocation against YHWH	8:17–18
i. rhetorical question: provoke YHWH	8:17
ii. answer: YHWH will show no pity	8:18
c. 2nd episode: destruction of Jerusalem and departure of divine glory/Presence	9:1–10:22
i. YHWH's summons to officials	9:1
ii. killing of Jerusalem's inhabitants by six armed figure	9:2–11
iii. preparation to destroy city with fire	10:1–8
iv. preparation for departure of divine presence	10:9–22
F. New setting: East gate of Temple; Ezekiel's prophecy Concerning ultimate restoration as result of exile	11:1–23
1. YHWH's disputation oracle concerning sacrificial role of city	11:1–12

       2. YHWH's disputational answer to Ezekiel: purge/exile
          anticipates restoration   11:13–21
       3. YHWH's departure from Jerusalem   11:22–23
    G. New setting: Return to Babylonia; commence speaking
       to exiles   11:24–25
 II. Oracle: symbolic act conc. Exile as reversal of exodus   12:1–7
III. Oracle: Ezekiel's explanation of symbolic act   12:8–16
IV. Oracle: symbolic act conc. Eating and drinking (Exodus reversal)   12:17–20
 V. Oracle: conc. efficacy of vision   12:21–25
VI. Oracle: conc. imminent fulfillment of Ezekiel's oracle   12:26–28
VII. Oracle: conc. false prophets   13:1–23
VIII. Oracle: Threats against false prophets and diviners   14:1–11
IX. Oracle: conc. individual righteousness   14:12–23
 X. Oracle: Allegory of useless vine   15:1–8
XI. Oracle: Allegory of Jerusalem as G-d's adulterous wife   16:1–63
XII. Oracle: Allegory of eagles, vine, and cedar   17:1–24
XIII. Oracle: conc. responsibility of individual and demise of monarchy   18:1–19:14

11. The Assertion of Divine Power in Ezekiel 33:21–39:29

I

Interpreters generally accept as axiomatic the claim that the literary structure of the book of Ezekiel comprises three major components, including a message of judgment against Jerusalem and all Israel in Ezekiel 1–24; oracles against the foreign nations in Ezekiel 25–32; and a message of restoration for Jerusalem and all Israel at the center of the nations in Ezekiel 33–48.[1] This view is based on a broad thematic assessment of the contents of each of the three presumed sub-units of the book together with the belief that this so-called tripartite eschatological pattern is characteristic of prophetic books in general. Other examples brought forward to demonstrate such a contention include Isaiah 1–39; the Septuagint version of the book of Jeremiah; and the book of Zephaniah.[2]

Nevertheless, there are grounds to question such a widely-held view. The examples of such a tripartite pattern noted above hardly demonstrate the case. The present form of Isaiah 1–39 does not constitute a full prophetic book.[3] Even though elements of Isaiah 1–39 may once have constituted a self-contained preexilic edition of Isaiah's prophecies, they now appear as part of the full form of the book of Isaiah. Furthermore, these chapters include a great deal of exilic and post-exilic material that facilitates the formation of the book as a whole. The Septuagint edition of the book of Jeremiah is only one of two extant editions of the book.[4] The Masoretic Hebrew edition of the book of Jeremiah displays a very different arrangement that calls into question assertions that the alleged tripartite pattern is the standard form of a prophetic book. Indeed, a comparative examination of the Septuagint and Masoretic forms of Jeremiah demonstrates

---

[1] E.g., Otto Kaiser, *Introduction to the Old Testament* (Minneapolis: Augsburg, 1977) 250–51; Rolf Rendtorff, *The Old Testament: An Introduction* (Philadelphia: Fortress, 1986) 209–10; Henry McKeating, *Ezekiel* (OTG; Sheffield: Sheffield Academic Press, 1993) 15–6; cf. Brevard S. Childs, *Introduction to the Old Testament as Scripture* (Philadelphia: Fortress, 1979) 365–7, who presents a variation of this structure in four parts comprising chapters 1–24; 25–32; 33–39; and 40–48.

[2] Kaiser, *Introduction* 250–1, 239, 230–1, 223–4.

[3] See my *Isaiah 1–39, with an Introduction to Prophetic Literature* (FOTL 16; Grand Rapids and Cambridge: Eerdmans, 1996).

[4] See my, "The Masoretic and Septuagint Versions of Jeremiah in Synchronic and Diachronic Perspective," published in this volume.

that the respective structure of each version is determined by their very different concerns with presenting the prophets oracles in relation to earlier prophetic traditions or with the ultimate downfall of Babylon. Finally, close examination of Zephaniah demonstrates that assertions of the tripartite pattern represent a misreading of the book, which is fundamentally structured to call for repentance following an announcement of the impending "Day of YHWH."[5]

Interpreters have noted that there are problems with the view that the structure of Ezekiel comprises the alleged tripartite eschatological pattern. Greenberg, for example, observes that the fundamental pattern of the book may well be bipartite, insofar as Tannaitic tradition observes that "Ezekiel begins with doom, but ends with consolation."[6] Even so, he notes that this view is oversimplified insofar as the first half of the book in chapters 1–24 includes calls for repentance and oracles of restoration as well as oracles of doom and the second half of the book in chapters 25–48 includes oracles of doom against the nations and condemnations of Jerusalem and Israel together with its focus on restoration. Although he acknowledges that chapters 25–32 focus on the nations, he notes that concern with the nations appears in both chapters 1–24 and 33–48 as well, which calls into question the rather simplified view of Ezekiel's structure. Despite these observations, Greenberg is at a loss to explain fully the present order of the book or the interrelationships between its constituent oracles. In the end, he settles for a presentation of the book as the typical tripartite collection of the prophet's oracles that represents an inconsistently applied editorial attempt to place similar materials together.[7]

My own work notes the importance of the chronological framework in the presentation of the book as a sequence of dates that comprises what would have been Ezekiel's active years as a priest had he remained in Jerusalem.[8] The sequence begins in Ezek 1:1–3 with the fifth year of Jehoiachin's exile, which coincides with Ezekiel's thirtieth year, i.e., the year in which Zadokite priests would begin their service at the altar, and it continues through Ezek 40:1 with the twenty-fifth year of Jehoiachin's exile, which coincides with Ezekiel's fiftieth year, the normal year of retirement for a priest. The one exception to this pattern appears in Ezek 29:17, which dates the following oracle concerning Tyre to the twenty-seventh year, but interpreters generally agree that this oracle has been updated to account for the actual year of Tyre's fall to Nebuchadnezzar in 571 B.C.E.[9] The result is a presentation of the prophet's oracles, which represents his attempt to redefine and fulfill his priestly role by interpreting the fall of Jerusa-

---

[5] See my *Zephaniah* (Hermeneia; Minneapolis: Fortress, 2003) for full discussion.

[6] Moshe Greenberg, *Ezekiel 1–20* (AB 22; Garden City: Doubleday, 1983) 3.

[7] Greenberg, *Ezekiel 1–20* 5–6.

[8] See my "Ezekiel: Zadokite Priest and Visionary Prophet of the Exile," published in the present volume.

[9] E.g., Moshe Greenberg, *Ezekiel 21–37* (AB 22A; New York: Doubleday, 1997) 616–18.

lem and the projected restoration of the Temple in the midst of a restored and resanctified creation from the standpoint of his Zadokite priestly perspective.

Such a contention entails a radical rereading of the structure of the book of Ezekiel and its constituent sub-units. In the case of Ezekiel 33–39, which is generally read as a collection of previously independent restoration oracles immediately prior to Ezekiel's vision of the restored Temple, it calls for a fundamental redefinition and reinterpretation of the sub-unit. We must first observe that the chronological formula that introduces this sub-unit appears in Ezek 33:21 and not in Ezek 33:1, the classic watchman oracle of Ezek 33:1–20 does not constitute an element of this block. The sub-unit begins instead in Ezek 33:21–22, which announces the fall of Jerusalem. Closer attention must be paid to the so-called prophetic word formula, which appears to mark the boundaries of the various sub-units that comprise Ezek 33:21–39:29. Consideration of Ezekiel's structure as a literary work rather than as a collection of the prophet's oracles requires that the so-called apocalyptic text in Ezekiel 38–39, which so many scholars judge to be secondary,[10] must be integrated into the reading of this sub-unit. Second, the generic elements of this text also require reconsideration, particularly since they contribute to the text's argumentative or rhetorical character. The appearance of the prophetic word formula at the head of the major sub-units of this text points to an argumentative interest in validating the prophet's message as a prophetic word from YHWH that must therefore be accepted as true. Other prophetic genres likewise play an important role in validating Ezekiel's contentions. The appearance of the so-called prophetic proof saying in every constituent sub-unit of this text calls for a fundamental rethinking of the role of this genre within Ezek 33:21–39:29. Its presence in the midst of oracles that express concerns with both judgment and restoration challenges past contentions that the genre must be viewed simply in relation to divine judgment. Overall, consideration of the rhetorical functions of the genre in this text points to its overall disputational character, insofar as the text is designed to assert YHWH's power and thereby to challenge a widely held belief in YHWH's weakness in the aftermath of Jerusalem's destruction. Finally, the intertextual relationships of Ezek 33:21–39:29 must be examined to determine their function within the respective sub-units as well as in relation to Ezek 33:21–39:29 as a whole. The intertextual relationships in this text indicate Ezekiel's dependence on earlier tradition in addressing the crisis of the destruction of Jerusalem and collapse of confidence in YHWH.

On the basis of such redefinition and reconsideration, this paper argues that Ezekiel 33:21–39:29 can hardly be viewed simply as an announcement of restoration prior to the restoration of the Temple. Rather, it represents a fundamental reflection on the question of YHWH's role in relation to the destruction of Jerusalem and the Temple. It is disputational in character insofar as it is designed to

---

[10] See, e.g., McKeating, *Ezekiel* 114–22.

refute assertions of divine impotence or immorality. Instead, Ezek 33:21–39:29 employs the prophetic proof formula to assert that the destruction of Jerusalem demonstrates YHWH's power and righteousness as the author of creation who deliberately sought to remove the impurity of the desecrated Temple from the midst of creation, to purify the land of its impurity, and to reestablish a new Temple in the midst of a restored and purified creation. In the end, such a presentation represents a Zadokite interpretation of the destruction of the Jerusalem Temple and YHWH's role as the holy author of creation.

II

The first task is a redefinition of the textual unit at hand and a reassessment of its formal literary structure.[11] Although past interpreters have tended to employ thematic grounds to define the formal unit as Ezekiel 33:1–39:29, recent studies point to the role of the chronological notices in the book of Ezekiel as the key markers of the formal literary structure of the book.[12] In the case of Ezekiel 33:1–39:29, no chronological notice appears in Ezek 33:1, but such a notice does appear in Ezek 33:21, which dates the following material to the twelfth year of the exile, i.e., "And it came to pass in the twelfth year, on the tenth day, on the fifth month of our exile, the fugitive from Jerusalem came to me, saying, 'the city is stricken.'" The next chronological notice appears in Ezek 40:1, which introduces the report of the prophet's vision of the restored Temple in Ezekiel 40–48. Insofar as the chronological notices in Ezek 33:21 and 40:1 mark the formal boundaries of the unit our text comprises Ezek 33:21–39:29.

The oracular report concerning Ezekiel's role as watchman does not appear within our unit. It functions instead as the concluding sub-unit of Ezek 32:17–33:20, which employs the chronological notice in Ezek 32:17 to introduce the announcement of Ezekiel's role as watchman following its portrayal of Pharaoh's descent to Sheol to join the dead of the nations. Ezek 32:17–33:20 thereby asserts Ezekiel's role as watchman, whose task is to ensure the purity of the nation following the downfall of the last of the nations that threaten Jerusalem and Israel. The way is now clear for the process of purification and restoration that will follow from the destruction of the city of Jerusalem.

An assessment of the internal literary structure begins with the observation that the notice in Ezek 33:21–22 concerning the downfall of the city of Jerusalem introduces the unit. The thematic and syntactical features of these verses clearly

---

[11] For discussion of the methodological principles employed in the analysis of textual structure, see Marvin A. Sweeney, "Form Criticism," *To Each its Own Meaning: Biblical Criticisms and their Application* (ed. S. L. McKenzie and S. R. Haynes; Louisville: Westminster John Knox, 1999) 58–89.

[12] See my "Ezekiel: Zadokite Priest," noted above.

indicate that this sub-unit comprises two components. The first is the initial report concerning Ezekiel's reception of the news of Jerusalem's downfall in verse 21, and the second is the *waw*-conjunctive notice in verse 22 that YHWH's hand fell upon the prophet and ended his speechlessness. Both elements of this sub-unit are crucial for understanding the following material. Jerusalem's downfall becomes the premise that informs the sequence of oracular reports that then follow throughout the balance of the sub-unit, and the notice that YHWH has ended Ezekiel's speechlessness thereby introduces the following oracular sequence. The downfall of Jerusalem thereby constitutes the issue that each oracular report addresses or responds to, and the portrayal of Ezekiel's newly acquired ability to speak provides the means by which he is able to address this issue in the following oracular sequence.

The second observation concerning the conspicuous role of the so-called prophetic word transmission formula follows immediately from these considerations. The prophetic word transmission formula is a stereotypical formula that introduces narrative reports of a prophetic oracle.[13] In the present sub-unit, it reads consistently as, *wayĕhî dĕbar-yhwh ʾēlay lēʾmōr*, "and the word of YHWH was unto me, saying ..." This form of the prophetic word formula appears consistently throughout the present sub-unit in Ezek 33:23; 34:1; 35:1; 36:16; 37:15; and 38:1 to introduce the constituent sub-units of the following text in Ezek 33:23–39:29. Altogether, Ezek 33:23–39:29 constitutes a block of material that reports the prophet's oracles that follow from the initial notice concerning Jerusalem's fall and the end of Ezekiel's speechlessness in Ezek 33:21–22. Ezekiel 33:23–39:29 thereby constitutes the second major sub-unit of our text, and it includes a sequence of oracular reports in Ezek 33:23–33; 34:1–31; 35:1–36:15; 36:16–37:14; 37:15–28; and 38:1–39:29.

Each of the oracular reports in this sequence conveys an oracle from YHWH that builds upon the initial premise of Jerusalem's downfall.

The oracular report in Ezekiel 33:23–33 disputes the claims made by the people that they are entitled to possession of the land because they are more numerous than Abraham to whom the promise of land is made.[14] The oracle instead asserts that the people are being punished for the abominations that deny them their right to the land. It concludes by noting that although the people will ignore Ezekiel, the realization of YHWH's word of judgment will force them to recognize YHWH and that a prophet has been among them. Overall, the oracle

---

[13] For discussion of the prophetic word formula, see now, Samuel M. Meier, *Speaking of Speaking: Marking Direct Discourse in the Hebrew Bible* (VTSup 46; Leiden: Brill, 1992) 314–19.

[14] For discussion of the disputational character of this text, see Adrian Graffy, *A Prophet Confronts His People: The Disputation Speech in the Prophets* (AnBib 104; Rome: Biblical Institute Press, 1984) 78–82.

asserts that YHWH has brought about the destruction of Jerusalem and that the people can therefore not expect protection.

The oracular report in Ezekiel 34:1–31 addresses the "shepherds" of the people, which functions as a metaphorical reference to the leaders of the people.[15] The oracle charges the leaders with neglecting their responsibility to care for the people and with using their positions to benefit only themselves. It asserts that YHWH will take direct control of the people in order metaphorically to rescue the people from the mouths of predators. The coming scenario is not entirely idyllic, however, as YHWH will select from among the "sheep" those that will suffer punishment, i.e., the leaders who have abused their positions, and those that will be rescued, i.e., their victims who have suffered from the lack of responsible leadership. The oracle concludes with a promise of a restored Davidic ruler, a restored covenant of peace, and the restoration of security and prosperity in the land and in creation at large. Once again, the people will recognize YHWH as a result of these actions.

The oracular report in Ezekiel 35:1–36:15 comprises YHWH's instructions to Ezekiel to speak a number of oracles first to Edom in Ezek 35:2–15 and then to the mountains of Israel in Ezek 36:1–15. Although some earlier interpreters consider these texts to be two distinct units,[16] most contemporary interpreters recognize that they are united by the instructional framework in which they are presented and by the deliberate contrast made between the downfall of Edom and the restoration of the mountains of Israel (see esp. Ezek 36:5–12; cf. 35:12).[17] The presentation of YHWH's instructions begins with YHWH's announcement of judgment against Edom for their attack against Israel as a prelude for YHWH's announcements concerning the restoration of Israel. In this case, the oracular report presupposes the destruction or at least the suffering of the land of Israel, but it points to the restoration that follows from the conclusion of that suffering. Once again, it employs the prophetic proof formula to assert that Edom will know YHWH (see Ezek 35:15; cf. 35:12) and that Israel will likewise know YHWH (Ezek 36:11).

The oracular report in Ezekiel 36:16–37:14 provides an overview and rationale for the entire process of punishment and restoration outlined in the book of Ezekiel at large and within Ezekiel 33:21–39:29 in particular. It returns to the earlier assertions that the people had defiled the land through their actions and

---

[15] For discussion of this text, see esp. Walther Zimmerli, *Ezekiel 2: A Commentary on the Book of the Prophet Ezekiel 25–48* (Hermeneia; Philadelphia: Fortress, 1983) 203–23; Greenberg, *Ezekiel 21–37* 693–709; Ronald M. Hals, *Ezekiel* (FOTL 19; Grand Rapids: Eerdmans, 1989) 245–54.

[16] E.g., G. A. Cooke, *Ezekiel* (ICC; Edinburgh: T & T Clark, 1936) 381–96; Georg Fohrer, *Ezechiel* (HAT 13; Tübingen: Mohr Siebeck 1955) 197–202.

[17] E.g., Zimmerli; Greenberg; and Hals; cf. Karl-Friedrich Pohlmann, *Der Prophet Hesekiel/Ezechiel Kapital 20–48* (ATD 22,2; Göttingen: Vandenhoeck & Ruprecht, 2001) 471–82, who recognizes their present redactional unity, but posits a complex process of literary growth.

that YHWH had brought punishment upon them as a result of their actions. In this respect, it employs typical priestly images of impurity, e.g., pouring blood out on the land and the use of idols. In classical priestly fashion, the rationale for restoration of the land is the restoration of the holiness of the divine Name, i.e., YHWH will act to resanctify the land in the aftermath of its defilement. The restored, Eden-like land then becomes a testimony to the nations of the world that YHWH has spoken and acted (see Ezek 36:36). Although the account of the vision of dry bones is frequently read as a separate unit – and indeed, it may have been composed independently of its present context – the formal organization of our text incorporates it into the oracular report beginning in Ezek 36:16 so that it functions as a means to illustrate the portrayal of defilement and restoration in Ezek 36:16–38.[18] Dead corpses are the epitome of defilement in priestly thought, and their restoration to life illustrates the resanctification of the land that is outlined in Ezek 36:16–38. Both elements of the passage emphasize that, based upon the resanctification of the land, the people will recognize YHWH (Ezek 36:38; 37:13).

The oracular report in Ezekiel 37:15–28 portrays the restoration of Davidic kingship over a reunited and restored nation of Israel. The oracular report employs the metaphor of a broken stick, one part of which signifies Joseph or Ephraim and the other part of which signifies Judah, that are rejoined into one stick. Quite clearly, this oracle envisions the reunification of northern Israel and southern Judah. In addition to reunification, it envisions the restoration of Davidic kingship and the restoration of YHWH's covenant of peace with the people, and the restoration of YHWH's sanctuary and divine presence in their midst. In effect, this oracle addresses the restoration of the major institutions of Israel, the twelve tribes, the monarchy, the covenant, and the Temple, that will follow from the restoration of the land announced in the previous sub-unit. A variation of the recognition formula in Ezek 37:28 announces that the nations will know that YHWH sanctifies Israel.

The oracular report in Ezekiel 38:1–39:29 constitutes the concluding sub-unit in the oracular sequence of our passage. Although many interpreters remove this text from consideration as a later, proto-apocalyptic text, it is clearly placed within the oracular report framework evident in our text and it must therefore be read in relation to its present literary context.[19] The report relates the downfall of Gog from Magog, a mythologically-informed enemy of Israel that invaded the

---

[18] N.b., Zimmerli; Greenberg; Hals; Pohlmann; and Fohrer all read Ezek 36:16–38 and 37:1–14 as separate units.

[19] See, e.g., McKeating, *Ezekiel* 114–22, who views Ezekiel 38–39 as a later proto-apocalyptic text, but see Zimmerli, *Ezekiel 2*, 302–4, who concludes that it could well be Ezekiel's work following a thorough analysis of style and themes. See now, Stephen L. Cook, *Prophecy and Apocalypticism: The Post-Exilic Social Setting* (Minneapolis: Fortress, 1995) 85–121, who attributes this text to a priestly millennial group that would be considered disciples of the prophet.

land but was ultimately defeated by YHWH. Although a great deal of ink has been spilled in attempts to identify the invader, such efforts miss the point that Gog represents the stereo-typical oppressor who threatens Israel and is defeated by YHWH. Ezekiel 38:17 in particular notes that Gog is the enemy spoken of by the prophets in earlier times, which functions as a means to claim that earlier oracles concerning Assyria, Egypt, and others, are now fulfilled in the scenario laid out in our text. Several key elements must be noted. Following YHWH's defeat of Gog, our text portrays images of the restoration of creation, a common motif in priestly thought and in the book of Ezekiel as an element of the sanctification of creation. It also portrays the burial and burning of the corpses of the fallen enemy, which revisits the motif of purification of the land observed in Ezek 36:16–37:14. Such an act is a necessary prelude to the restoration of the holy Temple at the center of the land (cf. Ezekiel 37:24–38; 40–48). Finally, YHWH's actions testify to YHWH's role as the author of creation and the one who brought about the entire process of punishment and restoration. Once again, the nations will observe YHWH's glory (Ezek 39:21), and Israel will know that YHWH is their G-d (Ezek 39:22).

The formal structure of Ezekiel 33:21–39:29 may be diagramed as follows:

Disputation: YHWH is the Author of Creation who Brings Punishment and Restoration to Resanctify the Land	Ezek 33:21–39:29
I. Introduction: Report of Jerusalem's Fall and the End of Ezekiel's Speechlessness; 12th year, 10th day, 5th month	33:21–22
II. Report of Oracles spoken by YHWH to Ezekiel concerning destruction and restoration of Jerusalem	33:23–39:29
A. First oracular report: YHWH brings punishment to the land	33:23–33
B. Second oracular report: YHWH will punish Israel's leaders and restore Davidic rule	34:1–31
C. Third oracular report: YHWH will punish Edom and restore Israel 35:1–36:15	
D. Fourth oracular report: YHWH will resanctify the land of Israel for the sake of the divine Name	36:16–37:14
E. Fifth oracular report: YHWH will reunify Israel, restore Davidic kingship, and restore the Temple at Israel's center	37:15–28
F. Sixth oracular report: YHWH will fulfill earlier prophecy by defeating Gog and purifying the land	38:1–39:29

III

The preceding discussion of the formal literary definition and structure of Ezekiel 33:21–39:29 helps us to understand the passage and the inter-relationships among the various elements that comprise it. It provides a foundation for answering several other questions as well, such as the role of the chronological statement in defining the boundaries of the text, the role of the prophetic word transmission formula within the structure of the text, and the place and role of Ezekiel 38–39 within the larger unit Ezekiel 33:21–39:29.

But in order fully to understand this text, we must also examine its generic elements and overall character. As noted above, several important genres appear within the text that aid in defining its overall structure. Insofar as generic elements in a text also play a constitutive role in defining its presuppositions, rhetorical strategies, and overall interpretation, it is crucial that we examine them as well. Interpreters will easily recognize the prophetic oracles of judgment and restoration as well as the instructional elements that appear throughout this text, but there is little need to reexamine them because they are so well known. It is far more important to examine those genres that contribute to the overall rhetorical strategy of this text, insofar as the text appears to be designed to make claims to its readers or hearers and to convince them to accept its claims.[20] Generic elements that play such a role in this text include the prophetic word transmission formula, the prophetic messenger formula, the oracular formula, the oath formula, the prophetic proof saying, and the disputation genre. To a certain degree, the prophetic word transmission formula, the messenger formula, the oracular formula, and the oath formula, are already well understood, but they must be considered in relation to the prophetic proof saying and the disputational character of the text in order to enable us to best understand its rhetorical or argumentative strategy.

The prophetic word transmission formula is well known to biblical interpreters.[21] Its stereotypical formulation includes a combination of the phrase, *dĕbar yhwh*, "word of YHWH," a form of the verb, *hāyâ*, "to be, happen," the preposition, *ʾēl*, "to, unto," and the name of the prophet or a pronoun that refers to the prophet. In our present text, the prophetic word transmission formula appears as the phrase, *wayĕhî dĕbar yhwh ʾelay lēʾmōr*, "and the word of YHWH was unto me, saying ..." and it appears at the head of each of the oracle reports within the structure of our text as defined above. The function of this formula is obviously to identify the following material as a prophetic oracle from YHWH. In this respect, the formula plays an important argumentative or rhetorical role in that its identification of the following material as an oracle from YHWH is intended to convince the reading or listening audience of the authenticity of the oracle.

---

[20] For discussion of the rhetorical or argumentative dimensions of texts, see now Phyllis Trible, *Rhetorical Criticism: Context, Method, and the Book of Jonah* (Minneapolis: Fortress, 1994); Patricia K. Tull, "Rhetorical Criticism and Intertextuality," *To Each Its Own Meaning: Biblical Criticisms and their Application* (ed. S. L. McKenzie and S. R. Haynes; Louisville: Westminster John Knox, 1999) 156–80.

[21] See Meier, *Speaking of Speaking* 314–19.

Much the same might be said of the prophetic messenger formula that appears so frequently in this text (see Ezek 33:25; 27; 34:2, 10, 20; 35:1, 14; 36:2, 4, 5, 6, 7, 13, 22, 33, 37; 37:5, 9, 12, 19, 21; 38:2, 10, 14, 17; 39:1, 17, 25).[22] The messenger formula typically employs the phrase, *kōh ʾāmar yhwh*, "thus says YHWH," again to identify the following material as an oracle from YHWH. The function of this formula differs somewhat from the prophetic word transmission formula, however, in that it introduces direct quotes of YHWH's oracles, whereas the prophetic word transmission formula often includes YHWH's instructions to the prophet to deliver the oracle, which is introduced by the messenger formula. In this regard, we might note Ezek 38:1–3, "the word of YHWH was unto me, saying, 'O Ben Adam, turn your face to Gog of the land of Magog, the chief prince of Meshech and Tubal, and prophesy unto him, and you shall say, "Thus says my L-rd, YHWH, 'Behold, I am coming to you, O Gog, chief prince of Meshech and Tubal ...'"'" The formula presupposes the social setting of the delivery of a prophetic oracle, but it also plays an important rhetorical role in that it attempts to convince the reading or listening audience of the text that the following oracle is indeed an oracle from YHWH. In this respect, it functions much like the prophetic word formula in claiming legitimacy for alleged statements from YHWH within the text.

Other prophetic genres that appear less consistently throughout our text likewise aid in attempting to convince the audience that the material in this text represents authentic oracles from YHWH. Two genres in particular stand out, i. e., the oracular formula,[23] *nĕʾum yhwh*, "utterance of YHWH," which appears in Ezek 34:15, 30, 31; 35:6, 11; 36:23, 32; 38:18, 21; 39:5, 10, 13, 29, and the oath formula,[24] *ḥāy-ʾānî*, "as I live," which appears in Ezek 33:8; 35:6, 11, likewise function rhetorically to convince the audience of the authenticity of the prophetic oracles within this text.

Perhaps one of the most noteworthy genres in this text is the prophetic proof saying, which appears in each of the oracular reports that constitute the basic elements our text (see Ezek 33:29; 34:27; 35:4, 9, 15; 36:11, 23, 38; 37:6, 14, 28; 38:23; 39:7, 22).[25] The prophetic proof saying is identified as a subgenre of the prophetic announcement. Its typical elements include the prophetic announcement of punishment and the so-called recognition formula, which typically reads, "and they shall know that I am YHWH," or some variation of this statement. Some might view Hals' definition as a suggestion that the proof saying is to be regarded as a form of judgment speech, but Zimmerli's foundational discussion

---

[22] For discussion of the Messenger Formula, see now, Meier, *Speaking of Speaking* 273–98; Claus Westermann, *Basic Forms of Prophetic Speech* (Cambridge: Lutterworth; Louisville: Westminster John Knox, 1991) 98–115.

[23] For discussion of the oracular formula, see Meier, *Speaking of Speaking* 298–314.

[24] For discussion of the oath formula, see Sweeney, *Isaiah 1–39* 525–6, 546.

[25] See esp. Walther Zimmerli, "The Word of Divine Self-Manifestation (Proof Saying): A Prophetic Genre," *I am YHWH* (Atlanta: John Knox, 1982) 99–110; Hals, *Ezekiel* 353–4.

of the genre indicates that it is associated with assertions of the acts of YHWH, whether they are judgmental or restorative. Indeed, our passages indicate a predominance of judgment, either against Israel or against its enemies. In the case of the latter, however, judgment against Israel must be recognized as acts that benefit Israel and lead to its restoration. The genre is basically concerned with witnessing the actions of YHWH, either against or on behalf of the people of Israel that will result in recognition of an act of YHWH, either by Israel or by the nations, or even by both.

It is with respect to this concern with recognition of YHWH that the rhetorical dimensions of our text become evident, i.e., our text is designed to point to major events, whether realized or projected, and argue that they are acts of YHWH. Thus, each of the major oracular reports presents an act that will result in the recognition of YHWH, viz., the punishment of the land; the punishment of Israel's leaders and the restoration of Davidic rule; the punishment of Edom and the restoration of the mountains of Israel; the resanctification of the land; the reunification of Israel around a restored Davidic monarch and Temple; and the defeat of Gog from Magog and the purification of the land. Each of the oracular reports makes a claim to its reading or hearing audience that the act in question will lead to the recognition of YHWH as the actant or the cause of the act by either the nations or by Israel. Such an agenda points to an argumentative character in this text, i.e., it is trying to convince its audience of YHWH's power to act, both in judgment against Israel and the nations that threaten it and in restoration on behalf of Israel.

Such an argumentative character in turn points to the essential generic definition of this text. Ezekiel 33:21–39:29 appears to be constituted as a disputational text, i.e., it is designed to argue a point, in this case the power or efficacy of YHWH to act in judgment and in restoration and to be recognized for such action.[26] But the disputational character of this text points to a premise that it is designed to challenge. Indeed, studies of the disputational genre point to its essential characteristics. It is designed to examine contrasting viewpoints, and it plays an important role in attempting to resolve the conflict by demonstrating that one of the claims is correct and that the other is not. It generally states a thesis that is to be disputed, the counter thesis for which the text is designed to argue, and the dispute or argumentation proper. The analysis of the oracle reports identify the case that is to be argued in this text, viz., YHWH is acting in the world and will be recognized based upon the realization of those actions. But what is the thesis that is to be disputed?

It is at this point that we must reconsider the initial sub-unit of this text in Ezek 33:21–22. As noted above, this sub-unit presents the report of Jerusalem's

---

[26] For discussion of the disputation genre, see Graffy, *A Prophet Confronts his People*; and esp., D. F. Murray, "The Rhetoric of Disputation: Re-examination of a Prophetic Genre," *JSOT* 38 (1987) 95–121.

fall to Ezekiel and YHWH's action to end Ezekiel's speechlessness. The report of the fall of Jerusalem is especially important with regard to the disputational character of Ezekiel 33:21–39:29, especially when it is considered in relation to the theological perspectives of a Zadokite priest like Ezekiel. As a Zadokite priest, Ezekiel would hold to the Zion/Davidic conceptualization of the covenant between YHWH and Israel.[27] King and Temple go hand in hand in the Zadokite understanding of the covenant. Both represent the eternal nature of YHWH's covenant, not only with Israel but with creation at large, so that YHWH promises that the house of David will rule forever and that the Temple stands as the tangible symbol of that promise. Insofar as David and the Temple stand forever under YHWH's protection, the city of Jerusalem will also enjoy YHWH's eternal protection in the Zadokite understanding of the covenant.

And yet, the Zadokite conceptualization of an eternal covenant based in creation is precisely what is challenged in the book of Ezekiel. The Babylonian exile and the destruction of the Temple call the fundamental postulates of that tradition into question so that Ezekiel had to redefine his role as a priest, his understanding of divine presence, the character of the Temple, and the nature of the world in which he lived to posit ultimately that the destruction of Jerusalem and the Temple was an act of YHWH that would result in the purification of creation at large, the reestablishment of Israel, and the reestablishment of a new Temple in Jerusalem. By noting the destruction of Jerusalem at the outset of Ezekiel 33:21–39:29, our text presents the reader with a fundamental challenge to the Zadokite conceptualization of the covenant between YHWH and Israel. One might conclude – as many likely did at the time – that the destruction of Jerusalem meant that YHWH had been defeated by the Babylonian gods and that YHWH was impotent, uninvolved, unwilling, or otherwise unable to do anything to save the city that allegedly stood under YHWH's eternal protection.[28] The series of oracular reports that follow the initial report in Ezek 33:21–2, however, is designed to counter such a supposition by demonstrating in every case that YHWH will act, first to punish Israel, then to punish the nations that threaten Israel, and finally to purify the land, restore the nation, the house of David, and the Temple. As indicated in our text, the ultimate goal is to defend the sanctity of YHWH's holy name. Although many have recognized that agenda, it must be recognized as an agenda, i.e., the rhetorical goal of the text is to convince the reading and hearing audience that YHWH is indeed the actor that stands behind

---

[27] For discussion of the Davidic/Zion covenant tradition as understood by the Zadokite priesthood, see esp. Moshe Weinfeld, "Zion and Jerusalem as Religious and Political Capital: Ideology and Utopia," *The Poet and the Historian: Essays in Literary and Historical Biblical Criticism* (ed., R. E. Friedman; HSS 26; Chico: Scholars Press, 1983) 75–115.

[28] For discussion of this concern in Ezekiel, see now John F. Kutsko, *Between Heaven and Earth: Divine Presence and Absence in the Book of Ezekiel* (BJS 7; Winona Lake: Eisenbrauns, 2000).

both the punishment and restoration of Israel and that YHWH is therefore G-d of all creation.

This enables us to specify the generic character and rhetorical function of Ezekiel 33:21–39:29. Given the prominent role of the proof sayings in this text, it appears that Ezek 33:21–39:29 is a disputation text that argues that YHWH is the author of creation who brings both punishment and restoration in an effort to resanctify the land.[29] Each element of the text contributes to this argument. Ezekiel 33:21–22 announces the fall of Jerusalem and the end of Ezekiel's speechlessness so that he might address the significance of this event. The six oracular reports define the significance of this event. Ezekiel 33:23–33 asserts that YHWH brought about the punishment of Israel. Ezekiel 34:1–31 asserts that YHWH will punish Israel's leaders and restore Davidic rule. Ezekiel 35:1–36:15 asserts that YHWH will punish Edom and restore Israel. Ezekiel 36:16–37:14 asserts that YHWH will resanctify the land. Ezekiel 37:15–28 asserts that YHWH will reunite the people and restore both Davidic kingship and the Temple at its center. Ezekiel 38:1–39:29 asserts that YHWH will defeat Gog and purify the land as prophesied in the past. Each element includes a version of the prophetic proof saying that asserts that YHWH is the party who accomplishes this entire scenario.

IV

The third dimension of Ezekiel 33:21–39:29 to consider is its intertextual relationships, either by way of direct citation of or allusion to other texts and traditions in the Hebrew Bible.[30] Such work demonstrates an interest in drawing upon past tradition to address the questions and issues raised in Ezek 33:21–39:29, most notably the question of YHWH's power and willingness to act in the face of a fundamental challenge to the traditional views of YHWH as power and willingness to act as G-d and protector of Israel and indeed of all creation. Ezekiel is portrayed throughout the book as a prophet and Zadokite priest, who frequently employs elements from elsewhere in biblical literature – and to a certain degree from extrabiblical literature and traditions – to inform his oracles and ideas. The present text, with its reliance on Pentateuchal traditions concerning creation and priestly sanctity, particularly the priestly blessings and curses of Leviticus 26,[31] as well as prophetic traditions concerning the divine punishment of Israel and the

---

[29] Cf. Ka Leung Wong, *The Idea of Retribution in the Book of Ezekiel* (VTSup 87; Leiden: Brill, 2001).

[30] For discussion of intertextuality, see Tull, "Rhetorical Criticism and Intertextuality"; Benjamin D. Sommer, *A Prophet Reads Scripture: Allusion in Isaiah 40–66* (Stanford: Stanford University Press, 1998), esp. 6–31.

[31] See now Wong, *Idea of Retribution* 79–87.

downfall of its oppressors, demonstrates Ezekiel's reliance on past tradition in an effort to craft an argument that YHWH is responsible for both the destruction of Jerusalem and the projected restoration of Israel.

We have already noted the role that the Zadokite traditions concerning YHWH's covenant and commitment to protect Jerusalem and the house David play in relation to the report of Jerusalem's downfall in Ezek 33:21–22. We may now turn to the prophet's disputational refutation of beliefs in divine impotence in relation to the downfall of Jerusalem with the assertions of the divine role in Jerusalem's/Israel's destruction in Ezek 33:23–39:29.

The first instance appears in Ezek 33:23–33, which begins with Ezekiel's quotation of a view apparently common among the people that they have been granted possession of the land because they are more numerous than Abraham to whom the land is promised. This assertion of course depends upon the various statements in Genesis 12:1–9; 15; 17; and elsewhere concerning YHWH's promise to grant the land of Israel to Abraham and his descendants. Such a statement presupposes the security indicated in the Zadokite tradition of divine protection of Israel, but Ezekiel presents an argument, again based in Zadokite tradition, to challenge this presupposition. Employing images of priestly purity concerning the need to protect the land from defilement with blood, idolatry and sexual misconduct that are drawn from the Holiness Code in Leviticus 17–18, Ezekiel charges that the people have defiled the sanctity of the land by their conduct. Within the Holiness Code, such defilement likewise results in the defilement of the sanctuary (see Leviticus 16), and it results in curses against the people in which YHWH will loose wild animals and human enemies to devastate the land (see Leviticus 26). This is precisely the scenario described in our text. The rhetorical import, however, is not simply to identify covenant curses. It is to identify YHWH as the party responsible for the destruction of the city, and thereby to assert YHWH's power and control over an event that many would have understood to reveal YHWH's lack of power and control.

The second is the oracle against Israel's leaders, metaphorically portrayed as shepherds, in Ezekiel 34. Overall, the oracle charges Israel's leaders with neglect of their people, which is portrayed metaphorically as sheep scattered upon the hills without the proper protection of a shepherd. Such a portrayal depends of course on the royal Davidic tradition in which the house of David is divinely chosen to protect and lead the people on YHWH's behalf (see 2 Samuel 7; Psalms 2; 89; 110; 132). The tradition makes it clear that the Davidic monarch rules the people on YHWH's behalf. Although the tradition asserts repeatedly that the Davidic monarch will rule forever, it envisions times when the king will do wrong and suffer punishment from YHWH as a result. Ezekiel's oracle apparently presupposes such a situation, insofar as it castigates the "shepherds" for their neglect and promises restoration of the covenant of peace, which will see the restoration of Davidic leader to the throne. The idyllic images of a land freed of the ravages of wild beasts and human enemies recall the blessings of Leviticus 26.[32] Again, the prophet makes his point based on earlier tradition, viz., YHWH brought the punishment against the house of David, and YHWH will restore the house of David upon completion of the punishment.

The third example appears in Ezek 35:1–36:15, which presents Ezekiel's oracles of judgment against Edom and restoration for the hills and land of Israel. Oracles against Edom are well known in biblical tradition, particularly since Edom is charged with complicity in the destruction of Jerusalem by the Babylonians (see Obadiah 11–14; Ps 137:7–9; cf. Isaiah 34; Jer 49:7–22). Our present oracle adds to this condemnation, but it draws upon the Pentateuchal tradition of conflict between Jacob, the eponymous ancestor of Israel, and his older brother Esau, the eponymous ancestor of Edom. The tradition of Esau's enmity against Jacob is well known, particularly after Jacob deceived Isaac into giving him the blessing of the father that was intended for Esau (Gen 27:41–46). Edom's refusal to grant Israel passage through their territory is also well known (Num 20:14–21). Ezekiel's allusion to Edom's ancient hatred of Israel draws upon this tradition, becomes the basis for Ezekiel's application of the covenant curses from Leviticus 26 against Edom (n.b., Jacob and Esau are brothers and presumably would share in the covenant). But while Esau suffers, Ezekiel invokes the blessings and curses of Leviticus 26 once again to announce the impending restoration of the hills of Israel.

The oracle concerning the resanctification of the land for the sake of YHWH's divine name in Ezek 36:16–37:14 draws upon the concerns of Holiness Code in Leviticus 17–26 with the sanctity of the people of Israel and thus with the sanctity of the land of YHWH's holy name.[33] The oracle employs the image of a menstruous woman (v. 17) and her purification with clean water (v. 25) to provide an image of the resanctification of the land and thus the sanctification of YHWH's name that will symbolize the restoration of the land in keeping with the blessings articulated in Leviticus 26. The second part of the oracle, which presents Ezekiel's vision of the restoration of the dry bones, draws upon the priestly understanding of death as the ultimate form of defilement (cf. Lev 21:1–4; Numbers 19; 31:19–24). The argumentative character of the oracle is evident in Ezek 37:11, in which the prophet challenges the popular contention that the bones, i.e., the whole house of Israel, are dead and therefore doomed.

The royal oracle in Ezek 37:15–28 again draws upon past conceptualizations of the eternal Davidic covenant (see 2 Samuel 7; Psalms 2; 89; 110; 132). It adds to this concern, however, by taking up the ideal of the restoration of Davidic rule over a reunited Israel and Judah (see Isa 11:1–16; Hos 3:1–5; cf. Amos 9:11–15).

---

[32] Cf. Wong, *Idea of Retribution* 106–11.
[33] Cf. Wong, *Idea of Retribution* 179–84, 187–9.

Finally, the oracle concerning Gog of Magog in Ezekiel 38–39 expressly notes its dependence on earlier prophetic literature in Ezek 38:17. Indeed, it draws on a variety of texts and traditions.[34] The portrayal of the devastation of the land of Israel in Ezek 38:18–23 draws on the traditions of blessings and curses in Leviticus 26, the portrayal of the animals of all creation in Genesis 1, and the image of the destruction of creation in the flood tradition of Genesis 6–9. The image of Gog's warriors fallen upon the mountains and fields in Ezek 39:4–5 recall the downfall of the oppressor as portrayed in Isa 14:3–23 and the killing of the Assyrian tyrant on the mountains of Israel in Isa 14:24–27. The images of fires burning for seven years to purify the land of corpse contamination draws on the above-mentioned texts concerned with the impurity of death combined with the seven sabbatical cycle necessary to maintain the purity of the land (see Lev 25:1–7; Exod 23:10–11; Deut 15:1–18). The feast of the wild birds and animals on the corpses of Gog and his warriors in Ezek 39:17–21 again invokes the curse imagery of Lev 26:22 (see also Deut 28:26), but it is now directed to Israel's enemies. Altogether, these intertextual references build to a concluding argument in Ezek 39:22–29 that YHWH is restoring Israel to the land as part of a larger restoration of covenant.

The concluding argument for Israel's restoration constitutes both the culmination of both Ezekiel 38–39 and of the entire sequence in Ezekiel 33:23–39:29. The intertextual references demonstrate Ezekiel's dependence on past tradition in formulating the argument that YHWH has employed divine power to purify or resanctify Israel in keeping with the covenant curses and blessings of Leviticus 26.

V

This reconsideration of Ezekiel 33:21–39:29 points to several fundamental conclusions. First, it undermines traditional claims for a tripartite eschatological literary structure for the book of Ezekiel by pointing instead to a chronological structure of which our text is one component. This observation entails the redefinition of the literary unit, not as Ezekiel 33–39 as traditionally conceived, but as Ezekiel 33:21–39:29 as indicated by the introductory chronological statement in Ezek 33:21. Second, close attention to the formal features of this text points to a literary structure that is determined in large measure by a question that is implicitly posed by the announcement of Jerusalem's fall in Ezek 33:21–22, and answered in the following sequence of prophetic oracular reports. Third,

---

[34] For analysis of the intertextual relationships in Ezekiel 38–39, see esp. Cook, *Prophecy and Apocalypticism* 84–121; Marvin A. Sweeney, "The Priesthood and the Protoapocalyptic Reading of Prophetic and Pentateuchal Texts," *Knowing the End from the Beginning* (ed. L. L. Grabbe and R. D. Haak; JSPSup 46; London: Continuum, 2003) 167–78.

consideration of the prophetic genres, particularly prophetic word transmission formulas and the prophetic proof sayings, points to the rhetorical or disputational character of this text. Finally, consideration of the intertextual relationships in this text points to a concern to draw upon earlier tradition, particularly the priestly tradition of covenant curses and blessings in Leviticus 26, to support the argument of the text. Altogether, these considerations demonstrate that Ezekiel 33:21–39:29 is more than simply a collection of oracles that announce restoration. Indeed, it is a disputational text that is organized and presented to challenge notions of YHWH's impotence in the aftermath of the fall of Jerusalem and to argue instead that the fall of Jerusalem was an act of YHWH that demonstrates a divine concern to purify Israel and to resanctify Jerusalem at its center. Given the placement of this textual block immediately prior to Ezekiel 40–48, it demonstrates an interest in purifying Jerusalem, Israel and creation in anticipation of the reestablishment of the Temple at the center of each of these entities.

Part 4: The Book of the Twelve Prophets

12. Sequence and Interpretation in the Book of the Twelve

I

Recent years have seen a major shift in discussion concerning the Twelve Prophets, in that scholars are now beginning to move beyond the older literary-critical paradigm, which treats the Twelve Prophets as individual prophetic books, to a new literary-critical paradigm, which examines the Book of the Twelve as a coherent literary whole.[1] Whereas the older paradigm examines the distinctive literary forms, perspectives, and compositional histories of each of the twelve prophetic books, the new paradigm treats the Twelve as a single book and thereby raises questions concerning its literary form, theological or ideological perspective, and the history of its composition. This is not to say that the newer paradigm supplants the older paradigm; studies of the individual books of the Twelve Prophets continue to produce significant and innovative results. Nevertheless, the new paradigm introduces an important dimension into the study of the Twelve Prophets in that it considers the presentation of the Twelve Prophets as a single prophetic book – one the major forms in which the Twelve is encountered by its audience – to be a constitutive element in its interpretation.

---

[1] For discussion of the issue, see Karl Budde, "Eine folgenschwere Redaktion des Zwölfprophetenbuchs," *ZAW* 39 (1921) 218–29; Roland Emerson Wolfe, "The Editing of the Book of the Twelve," *ZAW* 53 (1935) 90–129; Peter Weimer, "Obadja: Eine redaktionskritische Analyse," *BN* 27 (1985) 35–99; Erich Bosshard-Nepustil, "Beobachtungen zum Zwölfprophetenbuch," *BN* 40 (1987) 30–62; Paul R. House, *The Unity of the Twelve* (Bible and Literature Series 27; JSOTSup 97; Sheffield: Almond Press, 1990); Erich Bosshard-Nepustil and Reinhold Gregor Kratz, "Maleachi im Zwölfprophetenbuch," *BN* 52 (1990) 27–46; Odil Hannes Steck, *Abschluss der Prophetie im Alten Testament. Ein Versuch zur Frage der Vorgeschichte des Kanons* (Biblisch-Theologische Studien 17; Neukirchen-Vluyn: Neukirchener Verlag, 1991); Terence Collins, *The Mantle of Elijah: The Redaction Criticism of the Prophetical Books* (Biblical Seminar 20; Sheffield: JSOT Press, 1993) 59–87; James D. Nogalski, *Literary Precursors to the Book of the Twelve* (BZAW 217; Berlin and New York: Walter de Gruyter, 1993); idem, *Redactional Processes in the Book of the Twelve* (BZAW 218; Berlin and New York: Walter de Gruyter, 1993); R. J. Coggins, "The Minor Prophets – One Book or Twelve?" in *Crossing the Boundaries: Essays in Biblical Interpretation in Honour of Michael D. Goulder* (ed. S. E. Porter et al; Biblical Interpretation Series 8; Leiden: Brill, 1994) 57–68; Barry Alan Jones, *The Formation of the Book of the Twelve: A Study in Text and Canon* (SBLDS 149; Atlanta: Scholars Press, 1995); John Barton, "The Canonical Meaning of the Book of the Twelve," in *After the Exile* (ed. J. Barton and D. J. Reimer; Macon, Ga.; Mercer University Press, 1996) 59–73; James W. Watts and Paul R. House, eds., *Forming Prophetic Literature: Essays on Isaiah and the Twelve in Honor of John D. W. Watts* (JSOTSup 235; Sheffield: Sheffield Academic Press, 1996).

This new paradigm, of course, introduces tension into the discussion in that the interpretation of the Twelve as individual prophetic books is not entirely or even necessarily compatible or consistent with the interpretation of the Twelve as a single work of literature. Ben Zvi treats this issue in a recent study in which he challenges "writer/redactor-" or "production-centered" interpretative approaches that posit the "Book of the Twelve" as a deliberate composition, and calls for an "audience-" or "reception-centered" approach that points to the emergence of the "Book of the Twelve" by default.[2] Ben Zvi points first to the variety of forms in which the Book of the Twelve appears and the absence of a superscription for the book as a whole, and he asks whether it is appropriate to speak of the book as an intentional composition or simply as a fluid collection of individual prophetic writings that crystallized into its various forms. He employs Obadiah to raise questions concerning the lexical associations between the various books. Must they be considered deliberate attempts by the "authors" of the Twelve to create a single literary work, or examples of a "default model" in which textual links are the result of their secondary juxtaposition and association within the literary context of the Book of the Twelve?

Overall, Ben Zvi finds little evidence that the Book of the Twelve was deliberately composed as such by writers or redactors, and opts instead for a reader-centered strategy, which focuses on the educated writers and readers who ascribed meaning to the individual books in relation to their own social and intellectual matrices by reading and rereading them in relation to each other. Ben Zvi is certainly correct to emphasize the role of the ancient readers or implied audience in the interpretation of the so-called Book of the Twelve, but his proposal raises a methodological question that requires further examination, that is, the extent to which one can distinguish between the writer/redactor/producer and the reader/recipient in such a scenario.[3] The anonymous readers act as recipients of the text and interpret it accordingly, but in the act of interpreting the texts of the Twelve Prophets and defining their places within the larger Book of the Twelve, these readers become authors and redactors as well. This is implied in Ben Zvi's designation of these readers as "writers," but in his reluctance to ascribe to them any demonstrable role in the composition of the individual prophetic books that comprise the "Book of the Twelve" he provides little guidance as to their "authorial" or "productive" activities or to their interpretation of the Twelve Prophets.

---

[2] E. Ben Zvi, "Twelve Prophetic Books or 'The Twelve': Some Preliminary Considerations," in Watts and House, *Forming Prophetic Literature* 125–56.

[3] For discussion of the methodological issues, see Rolf Knierim, "Criticism of Literary Features, Form, Tradition, and Redaction," in *The Hebrew Bible and Its Modern Interpreters* (ed. D. A. Knight and G. M. Tucker; Chico, Calif.; Scholars Press, 1985) 123–65, esp. 150–58; Marvin A. Sweeney, *Isaiah 1–39, with an Introduction to Prophetic Literature* (FOTL 16; Grand Rapids and Cambridge: Eerdmans, 1996) 10–15.

12. *Sequence and Interpretation in the Book of the Twelve*   177

There are various criteria by which such guidance may be found, such as the intertextual allusions within the Twelve that constitute instances of inner-biblical exegesis and composition,[4] the commentaries on the Twelve Prophets and citations that appear among the writings from Qumran and other Second Temple-period literature, and the ancient translations of the Twelve Prophets[5] that provide the basis for discerning the hermeneutical perspectives of the translators. Nevertheless, these criteria must be qualified in relation to the overall conception of the Book of the Twelve. Intertextual allusions have loomed large in the current discussion, but they do not always provide reliable criteria by which to establish the conception and composition of the Book of the Twelve.[6] The commentaries, citations, and translations may well provide valuable hermeneutical perspectives with regard to this issue, but they generally presuppose an already fixed composition.

A fourth criterion that has not been sufficiently examined, however, is the arrangement of the twelve prophetic books within the larger Book of the Twelve. This criterion is especially important in that it points to the overall conception and composition of the Book of the Twelve as an autonomous literary work. Sirach 49:10 demonstrates that there was a conception of the "Twelve Prophets" as early as the mid-second century B.C.E., although it provides no clue as to its arrangement. Other ancient sources indicate at least five different sequences for the Book of the Twelve, which demonstrates that the arrangement was quite fluid but that the concept of the book as a whole was secure.[7] Two of these sequences, that of the Septuagint (Hosea; Amos; Micah; Joel; Obadiah; Jonah;

---

[4] See esp. Nogalski, *Literary Precursors*; idem, *Redactional Processes*; and idem, "Intertextuality in the Twelve," in Watts and House, *Forming Prophetic Literature* 102–24, for discussion of intertextual factors in the formation of the Book of the Twelve.

[5] For discussion of the formation of the Twelve in relation to the Septuagint and versions extant among the scrolls from the Judean wilderness, see Jones, *Formation of the Book of the Twelve*.

[6] See Ben Zvi, "Twelve Prophetic Books," 140–42 for a critique of Nogalski on this point.

[7] See Ben Zvi, "Twelve Prophetic Books," 134, n. 24. The sequences include the (1) MT, 8HevXIIgr, and MurXII (Hosea; Joel; Amos; Obadiah; Jonah; Micah; Nahum; Habakkuk; Zephaniah; Haggai; Zechariah; Malachi); (2) LXX, *4 Ezra* 1:39–40 (Hosea; Amos; Micah; Joel; Obadiah; Jonah; Nahum; Habakkuk; Zephaniah; Haggai; Zechariah; Malachi); (3) *Martyrdom and Ascension of Isaiah* 4:22 (Amos; Hosea; Micah; Joel; Nahum; Jonah; Obadiah; Habakkuk; Haggai; Zephaniah; Zechariah; Malachi); (4) *Lives of the Prophets* (Hosea; Micah; Amos; Joel; Obadiah; Jonah; Nahum; Habakkuk; Zephaniah; Haggai; Zechariah; Malachi); and (5) 4QXII, which contains fragments of nine books (Joel; Obadiah; Jonah; Nahum; Habakkuk; Zephaniah; Haggai; Zechariah; Malachi), some of which show books in sequence: 4QXII[a] contains fragments of Zechariah and a sequence of Malachi-Jonah; 4QXII[b] contains a sequence of Zephaniah-Haggai; 4QXII[g] contains sequences for Amos-Obadiah and Nahum-Habakkuk. For discussion of 4QXII[a] and the other manuscripts from Cave 4 at Qumran and elsewhere in the Judean desert, see Russell Earl Fuller, "The Minor Prophets Manuscripts from Qumran, Cave IV" (Ph.D. diss., Harvard University, 1988); idem, "The Form and Formation of the Book of the Twelve: The Evidence from the Judean Desert," in Watts and House, *Forming Prophetic Literature* 86–101.

Nahum; Habakkuk; Zephaniah; Haggai; Zechariah; Malachi) and that of the Masoretic Text (Hosea; Joel; Amos; Obadiah; Jonah; Micah; Nahum; Habakkuk; Zephaniah; Haggai; Zechariah; Malachi) have dominated conceptions of the Book of the Twelve within Judaism, Western Christianity, and modern critical scholarship.

Attempts to explain the rationale for these sequences have emphasized chronological principles, even when lexical associations or analogies with other works, such as the book of Isaiah, are taken into account.[8] Scholars have observed that some synchronically based chronological principle is clearly discernable in the arrangement of both versions of the Book of the Twelve, in that each begins generally with prophets that are explicitly placed by their contents in the eighth century B.C.E. and then proceeds to prophets of the seventy and sixth centuries B.C.E. There are problems with the chronological sequence of both versions, particularly in relation to Joel, Obadiah, and Malachi, the contents of which make them difficult to place chronologically. Obadiah would have to be the first of the prophets in that the book presupposes a ninth-century setting, insofar as traditional sources identify Obadiah with Elijah's associate, who announced the presence of the prophet to the Israelite king Ahab (1 Kings 18).[9] The reference to the Valley of Jehoshaphat indicates that Joel alludes to the same general period in the ninth century, even though its own historical setting must remain uncertain.[10]

---

[8] See Nogalski, *Literary Precursors* 3–4; Paul Redditt, "Zechariah 9–14, Malachi, and the Redaction of the Book of the Twelve," in Watts and House, *Forming Prophetic Literature* 245–68, esp. 261–63, for discussion and critique of this view.

[9] See Paul R. Raabe, *Obadiah* (AB 24D; New York: Doubleday, 1996) 49. The superscription of the book of Obadiah provides little basis for establishing its historical setting, identifying it simply as "the vision of Obadiah." The book calls for the downfall of Edom at the Day of YHWH, and charges Edom with having gloated over the defeat of Jerusalem by foreigners. It looks to the reestablishment of Zion and Israelite/Judean control over all the land of Israel, the Phoenician coast, the Negev, the Shephelah, and the Transjordan. Based on analogies with exilic and postexilic texts such as Psalm 137; Lamentations 4; Isaiah 34; 63:1–6; and Ezek 25:12–14, many argue that the portrayal of Jerusalem's defeat must be understood in relation to the Babylonian exile. Although the Babylonian exile clearly influences the reading of the book, the figure of Obadiah has traditionally been identified with the ninth-century prophet Elijah's associate, who announced the presence of the prophet to the Israelite king Ahab (869–850 B.C.E.; see 1 Kings 18), a contemporary of Jehoshaphat. In the aftermath of the reigns of these kings, 2 Kings reports that Jerusalem was threatened and perhaps taken by Hazael of Aram (2 Kgs 12:17–18); it was later taken by Jehoash of northern Israel (2 Kgs 14:8–14). Insofar as Edom was expected to be a vassal and ally of Judah during this period (2 Kgs 8:20–22; 14:7), the charges against Edom detailed in Obadiah could well be read in relation to events from the ninth and early eighth centuries B.C.E. Even if they must be read in relation to the Babylonian exile, the identification of Obadiah with Elijah's associate establishes that the book presupposes a ninth-century setting, which would present Obadiah as the earliest of the Twelve Prophets.

[10] The superscription of Joel provides no basis for establishing the historical setting of the book, identifying it simply as "the word of YHWH that came to Joel ben Pethuel." The prophet is otherwise unknown. The book presents a scenario in which the land is devastated by locusts and an unidentified nation that has come against it, and the people are lamenting at the altar of the Temple (Joel 1). It anticipates the Day of YHWH, in which YHWH will act to restore

Of the eighth-century prophets, Jonah and Amos would have to come first in that they are placed only in the reigns of Jeroboam ben Joash and Uzziah,[11] followed by Hosea, whose setting ranges from the time of Jeroboam ben Joash through Hezekiah,[12] and then Micah, who is placed in the reigns of Jotham, Ahaz, and Hezekiah.[13] Of the seventh-century prophets, Zephaniah would have to be the first, although some would argue that Nahum must precede.[14] In any case, Habakkuk would have to be the last in that the book presupposes the period fol-

the fertility of the land (Joel 2) and to conduct holy war against the nations in the Valley of Jehoshaphat, thereby restoring the security of Judah, Jerusalem, Israel, and all creation (Joel 3–4) [MT]). The reference to the Valley of Jehoshaphat apparently recalls the Judean king Jehoshaphat's defeat of Moab, Ammon, and the men of Mount Seir (Edom) in the Valley of Berachah near Teqoa, which is recorded in 2 Chronicles 20. Jehoshaphat ruled 873–849 B.C.E., but this does not define the historical setting envisioned in the book. The mention of the Greeks (Joel 4:6 [NRSV, 3:6]) and Sabaeans (Joel 4:8 [NRSV, 3:8]) suggests settings ranging from the late eighth century through the Persian period and beyond, but the precise setting must remain uncertain.

[11] The contents of the book of Jonah clearly presuppose the period of Assyrian ascendancy as its historical setting, and the identification of Jonah ben Amittai with the prophet mentioned in 2 Kgs 14:25 likewise establishes the reign of Jeroboam ben Joash (786–746 B.C.E.) as the setting presupposed in the book. This would portray Jonah as a contemporary of Amos. The superscription of Amos clearly identifies the historical setting as the reigns of the Judean king Uzziah (783–742 B.C.E.) and the Israelite king Jeroboam ben Joash (786–746 B.C.E.). The book thereby presents Amos as an eighth-century prophet, but chronologically he must be considered prior to Hosea.

[12] The superscription of the book of Hosea identifies its historical setting in the reigns of the Judean kings Uzziah (783–742 B.C.E.), Jotham (742–735 B.C.E.), Ahaz (735–715 B.C.E.), and Hezekiah (715–687/6 B.C.E.) and the Israelite king Jeroboam ben Joash (786–746 B.C.E.), which establishes a historical range from 786 B.C.E. through 687/6 B.C.E. Basically, it presents Hosea as a prophet from the eighth and perhaps the early seventh century B.C.E.

[13] The superscription of Micah identifies the historical setting of the book as the reigns of the Judean kings Jotham (742–735 B.C.E.), Ahaz (735–715 B.C.E.), and Hezekiah (715–687/6 B.C.E.), which would make him a younger contemporary of Hosea. It looks forward to the Babylonian exile, in that it argues that ultimately Israel will return together with the nations to Zion to acknowledge YHWH's sovereignty in the aftermath of Babylonian captivity (Micah 4–5; N.B., 4:10). Nevertheless, it presents Micah as an eighth-century prophet.

[14] The superscription of Zephaniah identifies the reign of King Josiah (640–609 B.C.E.) as the setting of the book, which places the prophet prior to the time of Habakkuk and potentially prior to the time of Nahum. The date of Zephaniah's composition is disputed, and many see the book as an eschatological portrayal of world judgment. Nevertheless, the book is formulated as an exhortation to seek YHWH. The contents of the book, which call for the purification of Jerusalem and judgment against Judah's enemies on the Day of YHWH, fit well with the early years of Josiah's reform. For discussion of Zephaniah, see Marvin A. Sweeney, "A Form-Critical Reassessment of the Book of Zephaniah," *CBQ* 53 (1991) 388–408. The superscription of Nahum provides no overt historical setting for the book, but the prophet's vision concerning Nineveh clearly presupposes the downfall of the city, whether realized or impending. Although Nineveh fell in 612 B.C.E., many argue that the book may be dated earlier in the seventh century because of the reference to the fall of Thebes in 664 B.C.E. (Nah 3:8–9), so that the announcement of Nineveh's downfall must be read as anticipation of the event. In either case, the book presents Nahum as a seventh-century prophet. For discussion of Nahum, see Marvin A. Sweeney, "Concerning the Structure and Generic Character of the Book of Nahum," *ZAW* 104 (1992) 364–77.

lowing the reign of Josiah.[15] Of the sixth-century prophets, the setting of Haggai in the second year of Darius requires that he precede Zechariah, who is placed in Darius' second through fourth years.[16] The setting of Malachi is uncertain.[17]

A chronological principle does not provide the full rationale for the sequence of the Twelve Prophets in either the LXX or the MT. Nevertheless, the work of previous scholars on both versions suggests not a random, but a deliberate sequence of prophets within the whole. Much of this work, however, has been based in redaction-critical questions or other diachronic presuppositions that have unduly influenced the interpretation of the book. In an effort to identify the principle or principles that help determine the sequence of each version, it is necessary to examine the sequence of the prophets within both the LXX and MT versions of the Book of the Twelve from an exclusively synchronic perspective. In this regard, the sequence of books within both the LXX and MT versions may well address diachronic questions concerning the formation of the Book of the Twelve, in that the sequence points to hermeneutics by which the individual books are both received and presented as constitutive components of the "Book of the Twelve" as a whole.

---

[15] The two superscriptions of the book of Habakkuk (Hab 1:1; 3:1) provide no overt reference to the historical setting. The reference to the rise of the Neo-Babylonian empire in Hab 1:5–11 and the threat that it poses to Judah clearly places the setting in the late seventh or early sixth centuries B.C.E., in the aftermath of the reign of Josiah, when the Babylonians ultimately established hegemony over Judah.

[16] The date formulas of the book of Haggai clearly identify the second year of the Achaemenid king Darius (521–485 B.C.E.) i.e., 520 B.C.E., as the historical setting of the book, which places it at the beginning of Temple construction carried out by Zerubbabel and Joshua ben Jehozadak in 520–515 B.C.E. Hence, the book presents Haggai as a late sixth- century prophet. The date formulas of Zechariah identify the second through fourth years of Darius (520–518 B.C.E.) as the historical setting. Although scholars agree that Zechariah 9–14 must date to a period much later than the late sixth-century, the lack of overt indicators that these chapters constitute a separate book subsumes them to the message and setting of Zechariah 1–8. The entire book thereby presents Zechariah as a late sixth-century prophet, who must be viewed as contemporary with Haggai but who continued speaking after Haggai had ceased.

[17] Finally, Malachi provides no overt indication of its historical setting, and many have questioned whether "Malachi" constitutes a proper name or merely the designation "my messenger," perhaps in reference to the prophet Elijah who is to return (Mal 3:1; 4:5–6). Some have argued that its identification as a *maśśā'* indicates that it is to be read in sequence with the *maśśā'ôt* defined in Zechariah 9–11 and 12–14, so that it might not even constitute a distinct prophetic book. Despite its compositional prehistory, the present expanded form of the superscription in Mal 1:1 identifies it as a distinct book in the present form of the Twelve. Many see the concern with the priests as evidence of a postexilic setting, but, indeed, Malachi provides no overt evidence for such claims. The concern with purity and proper functioning of the Temple could be placed in many different periods of Judah's existence. For an overview of discussion concerning Malachi, see R. J. Coggins, *Haggai, Zechariah, Malachi* (OTG; Sheffield: JSOT Press, 1987).

II

Although it seems evident that chronological considerations may at some point have influenced the sequence in both versions of the Book of the Twelve, other criteria must be identified. In order to establish the rationale for the sequence of both the LXX and MT versions of the Book of the Twelve, it is necessary to examine the twelve individual prophetic compositions that constitute the book. The Book of the Twelve, apart from its presentation as a single assemblage, lacks overt indicators that the twelve individual prophetic works are to be read as a coherent whole. Each of the twelve individual works therefore constitutes a potentially self-standing composition that can be read independently of the current literary context of the Book of the Twelve. Each conveys its own unique contents, literary structure, generic characteristics, socio-historical setting, and theological or ideological outlook, so that each of the component prophetic works of the Book of the Twelve potentially constitutes a distinctive and autonomous literary communication. This helps to account for the variety of versions in which the book appears. Nevertheless, the placement of the individual books within the Book of the Twelve necessarily compromises their communicative autonomy and subsumes them to the overall communicative outlook of the book as a whole; that is, when the individual books are read in relation to each other, their communicative functions and outlooks change. In this respect, it is noteworthy that both the LXX and MT versions of the Twelve each begin with Hosea and end with Malachi; indeed, the sequence of the last six books, Nahum, Habakkuk, Zephaniah, Haggai, Zechariah, and Malachi, is identical in both versions.

Hosea seems particularly well suited to its introductory role. It begins by raising the question of the disrupted relationship between YHWH and Israel by comparing it to the disrupted marriage of the prophet to his wife Gomer. The nature of the analogy is spelled out throughout the book, which charges Israel with having abandoned its covenant relationship with YHWH throughout its history. It is noteworthy, however, that the book calls for a reconciliation, both between Hosea and his wife and between YHWH and Israel. The book ends with an appeal by the prophet for Israel to return to YHWH so that the relationship might be restored. The book thereby stands as a programmatic introduction to a major issue posed by the Twelve, the restoration of Israel and its relationship with YHWH following punishment at the hands of various nations. The statements in Malachi concerning YHWH's distaste for divorce take on new meaning when read in relation to Hosea, especially since Malachi also calls for the restoration of the covenant between YHWH and Israel.

The LXX sequence of the Twelve then continues with Amos and Micah.[18] They are not presented in chronological order, but according to thematic con-

---

[18] For studies of the interrelationship of Hosea and Amos, see Jörg Jeremias, "Die Anfänge

cerns. Amos is designed as a polemical discourse that ultimately calls for the destruction of the royal sanctuary of the northern kingdom of Israel at Beth El and the restoration of Davidic rule over all Israel.[19] Amos is clearly Judean and employs a Judean perspective as he attacks the northern kingdom and its rulers throughout the book. Ultimately, Amos must be recognized as a book that calls for the downfall of the northern monarchy and the reunification of the people of Israel around the house of David and the Jerusalem Temple. Micah follows naturally in this sequence. It begins by establishing that Samaria's and Israel's punishment would provide the model for the anticipated punishment of Judah and Jerusalem. But once the punishment of Jerusalem and Judah is complete, the people of Israel would be returned from their exile and reunited with Judah at Zion under the rule of YHWH. The nations are also included in the scenario; they recognize YHWH and come to Zion as the exiles are gathered from their midst. Likewise, a (Davidic) ruler will arise from Bethlehem and defeat the Assyrian enemy as part of the general restoration. The book concludes with statements of YHWH's expectations of the people for the future and a liturgical composition that expresses confidence in YHWH's mercy and capacity to forgive.

The initial LXX sequence of Hosea, Amos, and Micah expresses concern with the disruption and ultimate restoration of Israel's relationship with YHWH, as well as with restoring the unity of the people of Israel and Judah around the house of David and the Jerusalem Temple. The next four books in the LXX sequence, Joel, Obadiah, Jonah, and Nahum, shift their concern to the nations. Joel is especially well suited to begin this section in that it presents people mourning at the Temple over an unidentified nation and a locust plague that threaten the land–whether the land is Israel or Judah or both is uncertain. The book envisions a response to this threat on the Day of YHWH, in which YHWH brings a heavenly host to turn back the threats, defeats the nations that have attacked Jerusalem and Judah, and restores the natural vitality and fertility of the land. The lack of historical specificity enables the book of Joel and its presentation of the Day of YHWH to take on a programmatic character much as Hosea does; the enemy is not identified, and the threat is expressed against creation as well as against Judah and Jerusalem. Joel can therefore speak to any period in Judah's and Israel's history in which an enemy threatened the existence of YHWH's people and in which that threat was removed.

The book of Obadiah, by contrast, is quite specific about the identity of the nation that threatens Jerusalem. The book is a diatribe against Edom for standing

---

des Dodekapropheton: Hosea und Amos," in *Congress Volume: Paris, 1992* (ed. J. A. Emerton; VTSup 61; Leiden: Brill, 1992) 87–106; idem, "The Interrelationship between Amos and Hosea," in Watts and House, *Forming Prophetic Literature* 171–86.

[19] See Marvin A. Sweeney, "Formation and Form in Prophetic Literature," *Old Testament Interpretation: Past, Present, and Future* (ed. J. L. Mays et al; Nashville: Abingdon, 1995) 113–26.

by, gloating, and rendering assistance as foreigners ravage Jerusalem. Obadiah is generally read in relation to the Babylonian exile, but nothing in the book requires this context. It employs the motif of the Day of YHWH and makes it clear that the judgment is directed against all the nations, not just Edom, so that Edom easily stands as a symbol for all nations that threaten Jerusalem. This becomes especially important within the overall context of the Book of the Twelve as Joel defines a programmatic understanding of the Day of YHWH in relation to the nations at large,[20] and Malachi begins with a notice of Edom's destruction. The book envisions the restoration of Zion and calls for the subjugation of surrounding nations in much the same pattern as Zephaniah or Zechariah.

The book of Jonah reverses course in relation to Obadiah in that it presents a scenario in which even Nineveh can be forgiven and granted mercy by YHWH. The LXX sequence has already made clear that Israel can be forgiven and restored if it repents; the same possibility is envisioned for Assyria. By analogy with the model of Edom in Obadiah, such forgiveness perhaps can be extended to the other nations as well. The following book of Nahum, however, makes clear that no such forgiveness will be granted in the absence of repentance. Nahum argues that YHWH has been in control of events from the beginning, including the punishment of Judah by Assyria, and is now taking action against Assyria for its arrogance in abusing the people of Judah and Israel. Insofar as Nahum also looks forward to the restoration of Israel, it prepares for the books that follow.

Whereas the LXX version of the Twelve is organized first to address concerns with Israel and Judah and then with the nations, the MT version appears to adopt a different principle of organization, in which these concerns are mixed. The MT places both of the programmatic books at the beginning. Hosea again raises the question of the disrupted relationship between Israel and YHWH and calls for Israel's repentance and return. Likewise, the book of Joel outlines the threat posed against Israel by the unspecified enemy nation, and envisions the defeat of the threatening nation and the restoration of the people in Jerusalem at the Day of YHWH. The portrayal of cosmic upheaval and restoration feeds on the imagery of Hosea, which portrays natural upheaval of the land as a correlate to the disruption of Israel's relationship with YHWH (Hosea 4) and thereby expresses the cosmic dimensions of the scenario that will come to the forefront again in Zechariah.

The book of Amos follows and begins to spell out the implementation or realization of the scenarios set down in the programmatic books of Hosea and

---

[20] Note also that Joel cites extensively from Obadiah, indicating that it was composed to stand in relation to Obadiah. See Siegfried Bergler, *Joel als Schriftinterpret* (BEATAJ 16; Frankfurt/Main: Peter Lang, 1988). Joel quotes extensively from other prophetic books as well, indicating the late date of its composition. Particularly noteworthy in the present instance is the reversed citation of Mic 4:1–5/Isa 2:2–4 in Joel 4:10 (NRSV, 3:10), which suggests that Joel was designed to follow Micah, as in the LXX sequence. The citation would make little sense unless the reader had already encountered Mic 4:1–5.

Joel. It charges abuse against the northern kingdom of Israel, again calling for the destruction of the Beth El temple, the death of Jeroboam ben Joash, and the reestablishment of Davidic rule over Israel. Although these specific proposals were never realized, the book does point to the destruction of the northern kingdom of Israel in the late eighth century. The concluding call for possession of Edom may well speak to eighth-century Judean concerns with dominating its neighbor, but in the context of the Book of the Twelve, it provides a suitable transition to the book of Obadiah. Although Obadiah, when read in isolation from the other books of the Twelve, appears to be set in the ninth century, its placement may indicate Edom's seizure of Elat and other attacks against Judah during the Syro-Ephraimitic War (2 Kgs 16:5–6; 2 Chr 28:16–17) and perhaps Edom's failure to join Hezekiah's revolt or to support Jerusalem during Sennacherib's siege. Again, the condemnation of Edom and restoration of Zion presages YHWH's defeat of enemy nations later in the Twelve (e. g., Nahum; Zeph 2:4–15; Zechariah 9–14), and serves as the premise in Malachi for the call to observe YHWH's covenant.

That Jonah precedes Micah in the MT version of the Book of the Twelve is noteworthy in that Micah speaks clearly about Jerusalem's demise. When viewed within the sequence of the Book of the Twelve, Jonah's articulation of YHWH's potential forgiveness for Assyria may suggest an offer of mercy to Nineveh prior to its assaults against Jerusalem and Judah during the reign of Hezekiah. Insofar as Micah points to Israel as a model for the fate of Judah and Jerusalem, it may presuppose Sennacherib's invasion of Judah as the beginning of YHWH's punishment of Jerusalem. Israel's restoration to Zion presupposes return from the Babylonian exile, but it points to the defeat of the Assyrians as the first stage of the restoration in which a new king from Bethlehem will arise to defeat Israel's enemies. In the present MT form of the Book of the Twelve, Micah clearly looks toward the Babylonian exile, but it does so from the perspective of the Assyrian period.

Indeed, Micah's concern with the defeat of Assyria provides a suitable introduction for the book of Nahum in the MT sequence of the Twelve.[21] Nahum argues that YHWH has been in control of events from the beginning and was responsible for Assyria's punishment of Judah, but Nahum also argues that YHWH is punishing Nineveh for its arrogant treatment of Judah. Although there is little evidence that Nineveh was deliberately portrayed as a symbol for the nations in Nahum, its placement in the Book of the Twelve suggests this role, especially when Nahum is read in the aftermath of books like Joel, Obadiah, and Micah, which speak in nonspecific terms about the nations or mix their references so

---

[21] Note also the intertextual relationship defined by Nogalski, "The Redactional Shaping of Nahum 1 for the Book of the Twelve," *Among the Prophets: Language, Image, and Structure in the Prophetic Writings* (ed. P. R. Davies and D. J. A. Clines; JSOTSup 144; Sheffield: Sheffield Academic Press, 1993) 193–202.

that Edom and Assyria appear as models for enemy nations in general. As noted above, Nahum also occupies a similar position in the LXX version, although it is directly preceded by Joel, Obadiah, and Jonah so that the symbolic character of the book is even more clearly emphasized. Indeed, the actual downfall of Nineveh would help to validate the following prophetic books in both versions.

Beginning with Nahum, the sequence of the LXX and MT versions of the Book of the Twelve is identical. Habakkuk immediately follows Nahum's presentation of Nineveh's demise with its own portrayal of the threat posed to Judah by the rise of the Neo-Babylonian Empire. The book portrays a dialogue between the prophet and YHWH in which Habakkuk protests the evil done to Judah by the Babylonians.[22] As in Nahum, YHWH claims responsibility for bringing the Babylonians and then argues that they, too, will be brought down on account of their greed and arrogance in treating their subjects. The book calls for patience in waiting for YHWH to act, outlines the atrocities of the evil, and concludes with a liturgical psalm that expresses confidence in YHWH's defeat of the enemy.

The book of Zephaniah may well be set historically during the reign of Josiah, but its placement in the Book of the Twelve indicates a somewhat different conception of the chronology and role of the book.[23] It calls for the purge of evil from Jerusalem and Judah, and looks forward to the defeat of Philistia, Ammon, and Moab, Ethiopia, and Assyria prior to Jerusalem's restoration. Insofar as Zephaniah follows Habakkuk, which is concerned with temple reconstruction, the book apparently represents the defeat of Jerusalem, Judah, and the other nations by the Babylonian empire as an expression of the Day of YHWH. It thereby presents that defeat as YHWH's means of purging the city from evil and of preparing it for the role outlined in Micah 4. The placement of Zephaniah within the Twelve helps prompt the many eschatological understandings of the book in the history of interpretation.

The book of Haggai presupposes Temple reconstruction in the early post-exilic or Persian period. It argues that the reconstruction will bring recognition of YHWH by the nations and the return of exiles, events previously articulated in various books of the Twelve Prophets. Likewise, its portrayal of Zerubbabel as the "signet ring" of YHWH builds on the portrayals of the rise of righteous Davidic rule that appear throughout the Twelve. The book of Zechariah continues this theme, although it does not envision the rise of a Davidic monarch until the eschatological manifestation of YHWH in the world. It employs the visions of the prophet to portray the reconstruction of the Temple in cosmic terms, as a sign of YHWH's universal sovereignty, and argues that the priests will rule until the new Davidic king and YHWH appear. It recaps the vision in Micah 4 of the nations streaming to Zion with Israel, and then describes the eschatologi-

---

[22] See Marvin A. Sweeney, "Structure, Genre, and Intent in the Book of Habakkuk," *VT* 41 (1991) 63–83.

[23] See also Collins, *Mantle of Elijah* 76–7.

cal scenario whereby the new king appears, the cosmos is transformed, and the nations defeated as YHWH establishes sovereignty at Zion.

Finally, Malachi, in its call for the renewed observance of the covenant, rehearses various themes from the Twelve, such as the destruction of Edom/Esau, the disrupted covenant between YHWH and Israel, the polluted state of the Temple and the priesthood, and the Day of YHWH. In projecting YHWH's appearance, Malachi calls for observance of Mosaic Torah, and thereby recalls the instruction in YHWH's Torah that will be given in Zion (Micah 4); it looks forward to the appearance of Elijah, who is perhaps associated with the allusions to Jehoshaphat in Joel and Obadiah, when Israel turns its heart back to YHWH. Insofar as Malachi expresses YHWH's distaste for divorce and calls for the return of Israel to YHWH, it rounds out the themes introduced in the book of Hosea.

III

On the basis of the preceding discussion, several observations and conclusions can be made. First, it is clear that a chronological principle does not fully explain the sequence of books in either the LXX or the MT versions of the Book of the Twelve. Chronology is influential in that the books are grouped roughly by the eighth, seventh, and sixth centuries, but various problems appear. Joel and Malachi present no chronological setting. Obadiah may relate to the ninth century, but it does not begin either the LXX or the MT sequence. Within the various centuries, the sequence does not appear to be chronological; Jonah and Amos should be the earliest of the eighth-century books, and Habakkuk should be the last of the seventh-century books. The placement of the books in each sequence may reflect a different concept of chronology from that present in the individual book. Within the MT sequence, Obadiah may presuppose Edom's actions against Jerusalem and Judah in the late eighth century, and in both sequences, Zephaniah apparently expresses the purging of Jerusalem during the Babylonian exile. Nevertheless, chronological principles provide some basis for the organization of both LXX and MT versions insofar as they follow a general sequence of centuries, but such principles are skewed in placing individual books within each century.

Second, thematic factors appear to play a role in the organization of the Book of the Twelve, but these factors differ in the LXX and MT versions. The LXX presents a sequence that, in Hosea, Amos, and Micah, first emphasizes YHWH's judgment against the northern kingdom (Israel), the implications of judgment for Jerusalem and Judah, and the potential for Israel's restoration in Zion. The LXX in Joel, Obadiah, Jonah, and Nahum then turns to the nations; it points to the Day of YHWH as a programmatic day of judgment against the nations and of restoration for Zion. It then lays out the specifics of YHWH's plans by portraying Edom's punishment as a model for the other nations, by articulating the principle that repentance will result in mercy and forgiveness, and by demonstrating that punishment will ensue if nations continue to abuse the roles to which YHWH assigns them. The LXX then turns in Habakkuk, Zephaniah, Haggai, and Zechariah to Jerusalem and the Babylonian exile. It first points to Babylon as a power established by YHWH that will fall when it abuses its position, and then outlines the process by which Jerusalem and various nations will be purged by the Babylonians prior to restoration. Restoration involves rebuilding the Temple as a sign of YHWH's sovereignty over the nations, the restoration of Davidic rule, and the nations' submission to YHWH as indicative of the restoration's cosmic significance. Finally, the book of Malachi rehearses the themes of the Twelve and presents a renewed call for Israel's repentance and observance of the covenant, thereby recapping the themes introduced by Hosea.

Although the last six books of the MT employ the same sequence as the LXX, the first six are arranged according to a different principle. Instead of first presenting the books concerned with Israel and then those concerned with the nations, the MT mixes books together. The result is the placement of two programmatic books at the beginning – Hosea outlines the disrupted relationship between YHWH and Israel and calls for Israel's repentance; Joel outlines YHWH's defense of Jerusalem and Israel on the Day of YHWH, emphasizing the transformation of the cosmos as YHWH manifests sovereignty over the nations. The following books then lay out the details of these two programmatic books. Amos, as an expression of the Day of YHWH, takes up the punishment of northern Israel, the destruction of Beth El, and the reinstatement of the house of David, and Obadiah does the same for the punishment of Edom and other nations. Jonah expresses the principle – applied to Israel in Hosea – that the nations, exemplified by Assyria, might also repent and receive mercy from YHWH. Micah then portrays Israel's punishment as a means by which Jerusalem will be prepared for its role as the holy center, where all the nations of the earth will join Israel in acknowledging YHWH's sovereignty. Nahum outlines the consequences for Assyria when it refuses to repent, and the rest follows as in the LXX version with an outline of the punishment and restoration of Jerusalem during the course of the Babylonian exile and its aftermath. Whereas the LXX version distinguishes stages, focusing first on Israel and then the nations prior to presenting Jerusalem's punishment and restoration, the MT presents the process as a continuum, emphasizing Jerusalem from the outset. In calling for the return of Israel, Hosea makes clear that Israel must return to Jerusalem and David as well as to YHWH, and Joel emphasizes Jerusalem's defense as the primary concern of the Day of YHWH.

These differences point to different conceptions of the Book of the Twelve that may relate to the theological concerns of the circles in which each version was transmitted. The LXX organization of Israel, nations, and Jerusalem also appears in the LXX version of Jeremiah and in Ezekiel. Many have argued that the LXX originated in the Alexandrian Jewish Diaspora and reflects the concerns of an exiled Jewish community living among the nations.[24] Unfortunately, no manuscript evidence confirms this point; the earliest LXX manuscripts of the Twelve are Christian manuscripts that date to the third and fourth centuries C.E. Indeed, the concern with Israel, the nations, and the restoration of the nations in Jerusalem fits well with Christian theology and its understanding of the role of prophecy as a means to predict the fulfillment of Israel's destiny in the revelation of Christ to the nations. The MT sequence, on the other hand, focuses especially on the role of Jerusalem, including the punishment of Israel and the nations, and the implications these developments have for the purging of Jerusalem and its place as the center of YHWH's world sovereignty. Such concern would be particularly characteristic of an indigenous Jewish community centered in Jerusalem. It could easily derive from either the Persian or the Hellenistic period, when Jerusalem was subject to foreign rule.[25] In this respect, it is noteworthy that the second-century B.C.E. Wadi Murabbaʿat manuscript and the mid-first century B.C.E. Naḥal Ḥever Greek manuscript both derive from Judah, and present the same order of books that later appears in the MT.[26]

Further research and discussion is necessary in order to test the validity of the proposals outlined here. In any case, this essay points not only to the fluidity of conceptions of the Book of the Twelve in antiquity, but to the fluidity of interpretation of the individual books, once they became parts of the whole.

---

[24] For overviews, see H. B. Swete, *An Introduction to the Old Testament in Greek* (repr., New York: KTAV, 1968); Sidney Jellicoe, *The Septuagint and Modern Study* (Oxford: Oxford University Press, 1968); Emanuel Tov, *The Text-Critical Use of the Septuagint in Biblical Research* (Jerusalem: Simor, 1981); Melvin K. Peters, "Septuagint," *ABD* 5:1093–1104.

[25] Cf. Steck, *Abschluss* (see n. 1 above), who argues that the Book of the Twelve derives from the period of the Diadochi wars.

[26] For discussion, see Fuller, "Form and Formation in the Book of the Twelve"; Jones, *Formation of the Book of the Twelve*.

13. The Place and Function of Joel in the Book of the Twelve

I

Recent scholarly discussion of the so-called "Minor Prophets" has begun to recognize that these twelve prophetic compositions can no longer be treated exclusively as twelve discrete prophetic works. Their consistent appearance as a single book in all canonical forms of the Jewish and Christian Bibles, where they are known respectively as *těrê ʿāśār* or "Dodekapropheton," as well as in three distinct manuscripts from the Judean wilderness (MurXII; 4QXII^a; 8HevXIIgr), and finally their collective citation in several apocryphal and pseudepigraphical sources (Sirach 49:10; 4 Ezra 1:39–40; Martyrdom and Ascension of Isaiah 4:22; Lives of the Prophets), demonstrate that ancient readers from as early as the second century B.C.E. understood them as a single unit or collection. Although the bulk of modern critical treatment of the Twelve Prophets focuses on their interpretation as individual compositions, scholars increasingly address both the literary form and compositional history of the Book of the Twelve as a whole.[1] Especially noteworthy are the attempts to employ intertextual refer-

---

[1] For discussion of the issue, see Karl Budde, "Eine folgenschwere Redaktion des Zwölfprophetenbuchs," *ZAW* 39 (1921) 218–29; Roland Emerson Wolfe, "The Editing of the Book of the Twelve," *ZAW* 53 (1935) 90–129; Peter Weimer, "Obadja. Eine redaktionskritische Analyse," *BN* 27 (1985) 35–99; Erich Bosshard, "Beobachtungen zum Zwölfprophetenbuch," *BN* 40 (1987) 30–62; Paul R. House, *The Unity of the Twelve* (JSOTSup 97; BLS 27; Sheffield: Almond, 1990); Erich Bosshard and Reinhold Gregor Kratz, "Maleachi im Zwölfprophetenbuch," *BN* 52 (1990) 27–46; Odil Hannes Steck, *Der Abschluss der Prophetie im alten Testament. Ein Versuch zur Frage der Vorgeschichte des Kanons* (BibThSt 17; Neukirchen-Vluyn: Neukirchener, 1991); Terence Collins, *The Mantle of Elijah: The Redaction Criticism of the Prophetical Books* (BibSem 20; Sheffield: JSOT Press, 1993) 59–87; James D. Nogalski, *Literary Precursors to the Book of the Twelve* (BZAW 217; Berlin and New York: Walter de Gruyter, 1993); idem, *Redactional Processes in the Book of the Twelve* (BZAW 218; Berlin and New York: Walter de Gruyter, 1993); Barry Alan Jones, *The Formation of the Book of the Twelve: A Study in Text and Canon* (SBLDS 149; Atlanta: Scholars Press, 1995); R. J. Coggins, "The Minor Prophets – One Book or Twelve?" *Crossing the Boundaries* (BibInt 8; Fest. M. D. Goulder; eds. J. Barton and D. J. Reimer; Macon, GA: Mercer University Press, 1996); James W. Watts and Paul R. House, editors, *Forming Prophetic Literature: Essays on Isaiah and the Twelve in Honor of John D. W. Watts* (JSOTSup 235; Sheffield: Sheffield Academic Press, 1996); Erich Bosshard-Nepustil, *Rezeptionen von Jesaia 1–39 im Zwölfprophetenbuch* (OBO 154; Freiburg: Universitätsverlag; Göttingen: Vandenhoeck & Ruprecht, 1997); Burkhard M.

ences as well as generic and thematic similarities within the Twelve and with Isaiah to reconstruct a multi-staged redactional history of the book. Steck and Bosshard-Nepustil, for example, argue that the Book of the Twelve appears to have been deliberately composed in stages in relation to the basic theological outlook, chronological progression, and compositional history of the book of Isaiah.[2] Nogalski and Schart note the similarities in form and outlook of several sub-collections within the Book of the Twelve, i. e., Hosea, Amos, Micah, and Zephaniah; Nahum and Habakkuk; and Haggai, Zechariah, and Malachi, as well as other features of materials within the Twelve, such as the lack of historical specificity in Joel, Obadiah, and Jonah and the numerous intertextual citations in Joel, particularly of the other books of the Twelve. On this basis, they attempt to reconstruct the redactional development of the Twelve through several stages as collections are formed and redactionally expanded into the present form of the book. Although the details of their respective models differ, both posit early collections in Hosea/Amos/Micah/Zephaniah; Nahum/Habakkuk; and Haggai/ Zechariah that are brought together and organized by a late redaction based upon a collection that includes Joel and Obadiah and other writings, such as Jonah; Zechariah 9–14; and Malachi.[3]

For the most part, these studies presuppose the priority of the Masoretic text, which presents the books of the Twelve according to the order Hosea; Joel; Amos; Obadiah; Jonah; Micah; Nahum; Habakkuk; Zephaniah; Haggai; Zechariah; and Malachi. Other orders are extant, however, such as the LXX (Hosea; Amos; Micah; Joel; Obadiah; Jonah; Nahum; Habakkuk; Zephaniah; Haggai; Zechariah; and Malachi) and 4QXII[a] (Hosea; Joel; Amos; Obadiah; Micah; Nahum; Habakkuk; Zephaniah; Haggai; Zechariah; Malachi; and Jonah). B. Jones notes that the differing orders of these versions of the individual prophets contained within the Twelve may have some bearing on the compositional history of the book as a whole.[4] Based upon his assessment of the differing orders of books in the MT; LXX; and 4QXII[a], he likewise argues that Joel and Obadiah entered the book of the Twelve at a relatively late stage (but prior to Jonah), and play a constitutive role in shaping the final form of the book in all three of these textual versions. He further contends that the original order of books within the Twelve is that of 4QXII[a], which is in turn a variation of the LXX order. Jones' position is based especially on the observations that Joel, Obadiah, and Jonah

---

Zapff, *Redaktionsgeschichtliche Studien zum Michabuch im Kontext des Dodekapropheton* (BZAW 256; Berlin and New York: Walter de Gruyter, 1997) Aaron Schart, *Die Entstehung des Zwölfprophetenbuchs* (BZAW 260; Berlin and New York: Walter de Gruyter, 1998); James D. Nogalski and Marvin A. Sweeney, editors, *Reading and Hearing the Book of the Twelve* (SBLSym 15; Atlanta: Society of Biblical Literature, 2000); Marvin A. Sweeney, *The Twelve Prophets* (Berit Olam; 2 vols.; Collegeville: Liturgical, 2000).

[2] Steck, *Der Abschluss der Prophetie*; Bosshard-Nepustil, *Rezeptionen von Jesaia 1–39*.
[3] Nogalski, *Literary Precursors*; idem, *Redactional Processes*; Schart, *Entstehung*.
[4] Jones, *The Formation*.

appear in different positions within the respective orders of these three versions of the book of the Twelve, that Joel and Obadiah provide little indication of their historical settings, and that Joel contains a large number of intertextual references to other books among the Twelve.

Jones' work in particular points to the need for an assessment of the overall form or arrangement of books in each version of the Book of the Twelve, both as a means to understand the hermeneutical perspective of each and as a basis for reconstructing the compositional history of the book. Indeed, he makes some pertinent observations concerning the overall form of the various versions of the Twelve, particularly when he notes that Joel introduces a concern with foreign nations that is carried through in Obadiah, Jonah, and Nahum in the LXX version of the Twelve, but he does not provide a full analysis of the rational underlying the sequence of books in any version of the Twelve. The present writer has made a preliminary attempt for the MT and LXX versions of the book in a recently published paper.[5] It argues that the LXX version of the Twelve is based on a concern to demonstrate that the experience of the northern kingdom of Israel in the Assyrian period provides the paradigm for the experience of Jerusalem and Judah in the Babylonian period and beyond. This is evident in the first three books, Hosea, Amos, and Micah, all three of which provide the rationale for the punishment of northern Israel prior to addressing the future of Jerusalem, Judah, and the nations in Micah. Joel then focuses on the fate of Jerusalem in relation to the nations that occupies the attention of the balance of the book. In contrast, the MT introduces Joel immediately after Hosea and places Micah after Jonah so that concern with Jerusalem, Judah, and the nations appears throughout the Twelve. Nevertheless, the paper provides only an overview, and a more detailed analysis is needed.

This paper attempts to meet the need for such a detailed analysis in relation to Joel. Clearly, the book of Joel plays a key role in the overall form and compositional history of the Book of the Twelve,[6] but a full assessment of Joel in relation to the overall form of both the LXX and MT versions of the Twelve is necessary. Several aspects require treatment. First is an assessment of the overall form of the book of Joel, including its literary structure and generic characteristics in order to determine its intention as a discrete unit within the Twelve. Second is an assessment of its intertextual relationships, particularly with other books from the Twelve, in order to define its interrelationships with the other individual units that form the Twelve and to determine further its intention. Third, is an assessment of the place and function of Joel within the sequence of books in each version of the Twelve in order to determine the distinctive outlook of each.

---

[5] Marvin A. Sweeney, "Sequence and Interpretation in the Book of the Twelve," *Reading and Hearing the Book of the Twelve* 49–64; see also idem, *The Twelve Prophets* xxvii–xxxv.

[6] See James D. Nogalski, "Joel as 'Literary Anchor' for the Book of the Twelve," *Reading and Hearing* 91–109.

II

Scholarly assessment of the overall form and function of the book of Joel has been unduly influenced by concern with establishing the compositional history of the text and the socio-historical setting or settings in which the book or its major components were composed.[7] It has also been heavily influenced by the theological presupposition that authentic prophets must somehow speak a message of judgment against the people of Israel; messages of restoration or divine favor for Israel must be the work of later priestly or apocalyptic writers, who sought to transform the prophetic message of judgment into one of salvation. As a result, scholars have generally followed the early works of Rothstein and Duhm, who argue that the key to the structure of the book lies in the distinction between the authentic words of prophetic judgment in Joel 1–2 and later "apocalyptic" additions in Joel 3–4.[8] Indeed, Duhm argues that the shift actually takes place in Joel 2:18, which turns to YHWH's jealousy on behalf of Israel and marks the beginning of the second half of the book. Although many later scholars have argued for the unity of the book on various grounds, particularly in relation to its cultic or liturgical character, the shift from judgment to salvation in Joel 2:18 continues to serve as the basis for claims that Joel comprises two basic structural components, i. e., prophetic or liturgical calls to lamentation and repentance in Joel 1:2–2:17 and apocalyptic oracles predicting salvation in Joel 2:18–4:21.[9] The contention that the book of Joel is, at least in part, an apocalyptically-oriented composition that looks beyond the concerns of the historical present to posit eschatological salvation has frequently resulted in dismissal of the book's significance.[10] Such an evaluation of the book is no doubt fueled in part by the difficulties in establishing its historical setting.

Nevertheless, there are grounds to question this assessment of the book of Joel as scholars increasingly point to the need for a systematic synchronic analysis

---

[7] See the overviews of research on Joel in Theodore Hiebert, "Joel, Book of," *ABD* 3:873–80; Rex Mason, *Zephaniah, Habakkuk, Joel* (OTG; Sheffield: JSOT Press, 1994) esp. 103–12.

[8] For discussion of Rothstein's position in his 1896 annotated German translation of S. R. Driver's *Introduction to the Literature of the Old Testament*, see Mason, *Joel* 105; B. Duhm, "Anmerkungen zu den Zwölf Propheten," *ZAW* 31 (1911) 1–43, 81–110, 161–204, esp. 184–8.

[9] E. g., Arvid S. Kapelrud, *Joel Studies* (UUÅ 4; Uppsala: A.-B. Lundequist; Leipzig: Otto Harrassowitz, 1948); Hans Walter Wolff, *Joel and Amos* (Hermeneia; trans. W. Janzen et al; Philadelphia: Fortress, 1977) 6–12.

[10] See, e. g., the assessment of Joel by Wilhelm Rudolph, *Joel – Amos – Obadja – Jona* (KAT XIII/2; Gütersloh: Gerd Mohn, 1971) 24–29.

of texts as communicative entities, which in turn provides the necessary prerequisite for diachronic literary analysis.[11] The standard two-part division of Joel is not based on a full assessment of its synchronic textual linguistic form, including its syntactic and semantic forms of expression; rather, it is based largely upon the book's most basic thematic motifs, i.e., judgment and restoration, which are conveyed by its linguistic form. Indeed, such motifs likely play a role in the so-called "deep" or "conceptual" structure of the book, but they do not define the formal literary structure of the text as presented to the reader. The proposed transition between Joel 2:27 and Joel 2:18, for example, is marked by a *waw*-consecutive formation, *wayĕqannēʾ yhwh lĕʾarṣô*, "and YHWH is jealous for his land," which indicates a syntactical relationship with the preceding material that must be taken into account. Other linguistic features, such as the commands to "hear this, O elders" (*šimĕʿû-zōt hazzĕqēnîm*) in Joel 1:2 or to "blow the shofar in Zion" (*tiqʿû šôpār bĕṣîyôn*) in Joel 2:1 and 2:15, indicate an effort to address a listening or reading audience from the outset of the book that must also be considered. Such features point to a need to consider the rhetorical function of this text, i.e., is it designed merely to convey an expectation of salvation in some distant, undefined future that can be safely ignored by its contemporary audience, or is it designed to have an impact on the perspectives of its audience that will prompt it to some sort of decision or action?[12]

In considering the formal literary structure of the text,[13] the first observation concerns demarcation. The book of Joel is clearly identified within the Book of the Twelve by its initial superscription in Joel 1:1, "The word of YHWH which was unto Joel ben Pethuel," which introduces and identifies the following material.[14] No other superscription appears until the following book, Amos 1:1 in the

---

[11] Rolf Knierim, "Criticism of Literary Features, Form, Tradition, and Redaction," *The Hebrew Bible and its Modern Interpreters* (eds., D. Knight and G. M. Tucker; Chico: Scholars Press, 1985) 123–165 (reprinted in *Reading the Hebrew Bible for a New Millennium: Form, Concept, and Theological Perspective. Volume 2: Exegetical and Theological Studies* [SAC; eds. W. Kim, D. Ellens, M. Floyd, and M. A. Sweeney; Harrisburg, PA: Trinity Press International, 2000] 1–41); idem, "Old Testament Form Criticism Reconsidered," *Int* 27 (1973) 435–48 (Reprinted in *Reading the Hebrew Bible for a New Millennium* 42–71; Marvin A. Sweeney, "Formation and Form in Prophetic Literature," *Old Testament Interpretation: Past, Present and Future* (eds. J. L. Mays, D. L. Petersen, and K. H. Richards; Nashville: Abingdon, 1995) 113–26; idem, "Form Criticism," *To Each Its Own Meaning: Biblical Criticisms and their Application* (eds. S. L. McKenzie and S. R. Haynes; Revised and expanded edition; Louisville: Westminster John Knox, 1999) 58–89.

[12] See the recent analysis of Joel by Stephen L. Cook, *Prophecy and Apocalypticism: The Post-Exilic Social Setting* (Minneapolis: Fortress, 1995) 167–209, who argues that Joel is designed to mobilize the Judean community to support the programs of the Zadokite priesthood.

[13] For full discussion of the formal literary structure of Joel, see my commentary, *The Twelve Prophets* 1:145–87.

[14] For discussion of the formal character and role of superscriptions, see Gene M. Tucker, "Prophetic Superscriptions and the Growth of the Canon," *Canon and Authority* (eds., G. W. Coats and B. O. Long; Philadelphia: Fortress, 1977) 56–70.

sequence of the MT and Obadiah 1a in the sequence of the LXX. The superscription marks the book of Joel as a discrete unit within the Book of the Twelve.

The second observation concerns the generic character and function of the superscription in relation to the rest of the book. The objective third person form of the superscription clearly indicates that the narrator of the book is the speaker, and its reference to the word of YHWH that was unto Joel ben Pethuel clearly indicates that the following material must be identified as that word. At no point in the rest of the book is there a clear indication that the narrator of the book appears once again. Consequently, the superscription is generically distinct from the following material. It stands apart from Joel 1:2–4:21 in that it introduces and identifies that material as the word of YHWH that was unto Joel ben Pethuel. The superscription in Joel 1:1 therefore constitutes the first major structural component of the book, and the word of YHWH that was unto Joel ben Pethuel in Joel 1:2–4:21 then constitutes the second major component.

In assessing the literary structure of Joel 1:2–4:21, it must be observed at the outset that this text is formulated as an imperative address to its audience. This is clear from the initial commands in Joel 1:2, "Hear this, O elders, and give ear, all inhabitants of the land." This command then introduces statements throughout Joel 1:3–20 that are concerned with a plague of locusts that threatens the land and that identify that threat as a manifestation of the "Day of YHWH" (v. 15). Indeed, a series of imperatives in vv. 2, 5, 8, 11, and 13 appear to define the basic literary structure of this text. Joel 1:2–4 introduces the basic premise of the entire passage, i.e., that a plague of locusts threatens the land that the audience must tell their children and future generations about it. Joel 1:5–7 addresses the audience as drunkards who must weep because an enemy nation has invaded the land and laid waste to the vines, fig trees, etc., of the land. Inherent in this section is the metaphorical portrayal of the enemy as locusts that would strip the land bare of its agricultural growth. Joel 1:8–10 calls upon the audience to lament like a young woman who has lost her husband, because this disaster threatens the grain and drink offerings of the Temple and indeed the entire crop of grain, wine, and oil that support life in the land. Joel 1:11–12 then calls upon the farmers and vintners to wail over the loss of the grain and fruit crops. Finally, Joel 1:13–20 culminates in a call to the priests to declare a fast and solemn assembly in the Temple to mourn and to petition YHWH concerning the disaster that the land has suffered. It is clear that the text presupposes that the disaster comes from YHWH as vv. 15–18 identify it as the "Day of YHWH," which brings destruction and famine as food is cut off from the land. Verses 19–20 specify that the fast is designed to appeal to YHWH to put a stop to such suffering. In short, Joel 1:2–20 constitutes a distinct literary sub-unit that must be identified as "a call to communal complaint concerning the threat of the locust plague on the Day of YHWH."

Imperative formulations appear to play key roles in the balance of the book as well. Joel 2:1, "Blow the shofar in Zion, and raise a shout on my holy mountain," introduces a second address that also warns of the coming "Day of YHWH" (v. 1b), but it employs theophanic language to characterize the threat to the land as a military invasion that is led by YHWH. Joel 2:1–14 calls upon the people to return to YHWH (v. 12) so that the threat might cease. It therefore builds upon Joel 1:5–7, which metaphorically compares the locust plague to the invasion of an enemy nation, but it drops the metaphor entirely. The passage therefore presents military invasion as the human counterpart to the locust plague described in Joel 1:2–20. The structure of the passage appears to be defined by the presence of quotations by YHWH in vv. 1a, "blow the shofar in Zion, raise a shout on my holy mountain," and 12–13aα, "'And also now,' utterance of YHWH, 'return to me with all your heart and with fasting and with weeping and with mourning, and tear your heart and not your garments,'" which then serve as the basis for the prophet's own statements that build upon YHWH's words. Thus, Joel 2:1–11 constitutes the prophet's theophanic portrayal of the threat against the land posed by YHWH's invading army on the "Day of YHWH." Joel 2:12–14 then comprises the prophet's call to the people to appeal to YHWH for relief, particularly as he reiterates YHWH's own appeal for return in v. 13aβ–b, "and return to YHWH, your G-d, because he is gracious and merciful, slow to anger and full of loyalty, and he relents concerning evil." To a certain extent, Joel 2:1–14 is parallel to Joel 1:2–20 in that it calls upon the audience to appeal to YHWH for deliverance from the threat of military invasion on the Day of YHWH. Joel 2:1–14 must therefore be identified as "a call to communal complaint concerning the threat of invasion of the Day of YHWH."

A third major imperative appears in Joel 2:15 that is initially parallel to that in Joel 2:1, "Blow the shofar in Zion, sanctify a fast, call a solemn assembly." Verses 15–17 then build upon this command by calling upon the entire people to gather for cultic assembly in which the priests will appeal to YHWH to spare the people from YHWH's threat. This call culminates in a rhetorical question, "Why should they say among the nations, 'Where is their G-d?'" that is obviously designed to provoke YHWH's response. The report of that response begins in Joel 2:18 and continues throughout the balance of the book.

Most interpreters view the structure of this sub-unit quite differently.[15] Joel 2:15–17 is frequently viewed as the conclusion to the previous material because it calls upon the people to gather at the Temple to appeal to YHWH for deliverance, much like Joel 1:19–20 and 2:15–17 that also call for the people to cry out to YHWH. Joel 2:18–4:21, however, focuses specifically on YHWH's response and promises to deliver the people. Several factors call for a reconsideration of

---

[15] For an overview of the discussion, see most recently, James L. Crenshaw, *Joel* (AB 24C; New York: Doubleday, 1995) 29–39.

this view. First, the initial imperatives in Joel 2:15–17, "blow the shofar in Zion," "sanctify a fast," "gather the people," etc., take up not only the initial call of Joel 2:1, "blow the shofar in Zion," but language in Joel 1:2–20 as well, i.e., "hear this, O elders, give ear, all inhabitants of the land" (1:2) and "sanctify a fast, call a solemn assembly. Gather the elders and all the inhabitants of the land" (1:14). Joel 2:15–17 does not simply provide a rhetorical inclusio for Joel 2:1–14, but it recapitulates the major concerns of Joel 1:2–20. Second, in recalling elements from the previous units of the book, Joel 2:15–17 does not simply sum up the preceding text, but it also looks forward so that it constitutes an introduction to the following material. It does not call the people together for the purpose of lamentation; that has already been accomplished in Joel 1:2–20 and 2:1–14. Rather, it calls the people together so that they may hear YHWH's answer to their complaint in Joel 2:18–4:21. Whereas Joel 2:1–14 announced the "Day of YHWH" as a day of coming threat to the people, the question posed YHWH in Joel 2:15–17 points to YHWH's anticipated action to deliver the people from that threat, viz., "spare your people, O YHWH, and do not make your heritage a mockery, a byword among the nations. Why should they say among the nations, 'Where is their G-d?'" Furthermore, the beginning of the announcement of YHWH's response in Joel 2:18 is linked syntactically to Joel 2:15–17 by a *waw*-consecutive formulation, "then YHWH became jealous for his land and had pity on his people ..." The material beginning in Joel 2:18 is meant to be read together with Joel 2:15–17, whereas the disjunctive imperatives in Joel 2:15–17 indicate that it is the beginning of a new unit. Finally, Joel 2:1–14 concludes with the call to "return" to YHWH and the speculation that YHWH will show mercy for such a request. Joel 2:15–4:21 constitutes precisely such an attempt to appeal to YHWH for mercy together with YHWH's answer.

The structure of Joel 2:15–4:21 is defined by a succession of syntactically disjunctive introductory imperatives in Joel 2:15–16, "Blow a shofar in Zion ..."; 2:21–22, "Do not fear, O land, celebrate and rejoice because YHWH has prepared to act. Do not fear, O beasts of the field, for the pastures of the wilderness are green; for the tree bears its fruit, the fig tree and vine give their yield; 4:9–11, "Proclaim this among the nations, sanctify/prepare for war, rouse the warriors, ..." Joel 2:15–20 therefore begins the sub-unit with the prophet's presentation of YHWH's response to the people's appeal for mercy in which YHWH promises to send grain, wine, and oil, and to remove the northern threat against the people, i.e., the army that had threatened them.[16] Joel 2:21–4:8 conveys YHWH's reassurance to restore the natural world of creation and to deliver the nation from its oppressors. Indeed, this passage is tied together by syntactical conjunctives in 3:1 (*wĕhāyâ ʾaḥărê-kēn*), "and it shall come to pass afterwards") and 4:1

---

[16] For discussion of the significance of YHWH's response to national lament in Joel, see Graham S. Ogden, "Joel 4 and Prophetic Responses to National Laments," *JSOT* 26 (1983) 97–106.

(*kîhinnēh bayyāmîm hāhēmmâ ûbāʿēt hahîʾ ʾăšer*), "for behold, in those days and at that time when ..."), and specifies that YHWH will restore the fortunes of Judah and Jerusalem (4:1). Finally, Joel 4:9–21 presents the prophet's call to the nations to assemble themselves at the Valley of Jehoshaphat for YHWH's judgment, which in turn will lead to the restoration of fertility in the natural world together with Judah's and Jerusalem's eternal security. Altogether, Joel 2:15–4:21 constitutes "the prophet's announcement of YHWH's response to protect the people from threats."

The structure of the passage may be outlined as follows:

The Book of Joel: YHWH's Response to Judah's Appeals for Relief
from Threat   Joel 1:1–4:21

I. Superscription   1:1
II. Body of Book: YHWH's Response to Judah's Appeals for
    Relief from Threat   1:2–4:21
    A. Prophet's Call to Communal Complaint concerning the
       Threat of the Locust Plague   1:2–20
       1. The basic premise: threat posed by locusts   1:2–4
       2. The threat to the grape harvest and wine   1:5–7
       3. The threat to the people of the land and the offerings
          at the Temple   1:8–10
       4. The threat to the grain crop   1:11–12
       5. Appeal for fasting and mourning on the Day of YHWH   1:13–20
    B. Prophet's Call to Communal Complaint concerning the
       Threat of Invasion   2:1–14
       1. Theophanic portrayal of the threat posed to the land by
          YHWH's army   2:1–11
       2. The call to appeal to YHWH for mercy   2:12–14
    C. Prophet's Announcement of YHWH's Response to Protect
       People from Threats   2:15–4:21
       1. Presentation of YHWH's response to the people:
          deliverance from threat   2:15–20
       2. Presentation of YHWH's reassurance to restore
          creation and to deliver the nation from oppressors   2:21–4:8
       3. Announcement concerning YHWH's response to protect
          the people from threats   4:9–21

Several conclusions may be drawn from this analysis of the literary structure and generic characteristics of Joel. First, the book is identified by the superscription as "the word of YHWH that was to Joel ben Pethuel," which lends it a certain truth claim to its status as divine revelation, even if Joel ben Petheul is otherwise unknown. Second, the body of the book is identified as the prophet's presentation of YHWH's response to Judah's appeals from threat. Insofar as that response promises deliverance for Judah and Jerusalem and punishment of the nations that threaten Jerusalem/Judah, it must be taken as YHWH's pledge to undertake such action. Third, insofar as the response is delivered in relation to the prophet's calls to communal complaint to YHWH concerning the threat, YHWH is also viewed as responsible for bringing or allowing the threats in the first place. In this sense, YHWH is portrayed as exercising absolute control over the fate of Jerusalem, Judah, and the nations. Furthermore, the threat posed against Jerusalem/Judah and its agricultural produce is portrayed simultaneously as the armies of enemy nations and as locusts or sheaves of grain that are cut down. This suggests a certain mythological dimension in the conceptualization of the entire scenario in which the events of the human world are also conceived as events in the natural world of creation and in the heavenly realm. The entire scenario is presented in relation to the Day of YHWH, as both a day of threat against Jerusalem/Judah and as a day of deliverance for Jerusalem/Judah. Insofar as the Day of YHWH is portrayed elsewhere as a cultic event that portends both threat and deliverance for the people, Joel must be considered as an expression of the patterns of thought inherent in the ancient Jerusalemite/Judean cult and liturgy, i.e., threat and deliverance appear successively as a cyclical pattern much like the seasons of the year, and both stem from YHWH. In short, YHWH will take action to remove a threat to Jerusalem in response to the appeals of the people. Such a contention plays a major role in defining Jerusalem's/Judah's expectations of YHWH in time of crisis, i.e., YHWH may bring the crisis, but YHWH has the capacity to end it based upon the repentance and appeal of the people. Finally, Joel presents its scenario of threat and deliverance in anonymous terms; it therefore constitutes a basic pattern of threat and divine response to threat that can be read in relation to any particular historical situation in which the same patterns apply.

III

The second major facet of Joel to be treated is its intertextual relationships, particularly in relation to the other constituent books of the Book of the Twelve. Several intertextual relationships require examination.[17] Apart from those pertaining to the Book of the Twelve, they include first of all the use of the Exodus tradition, particularly the plagues of locusts in Exodus 10:1–20 and darkness in Exodus 10:21–29. The use of the Exodus tradition includes the Sharav or Ḥamsin, the dry desert wind that brings locusts and perhaps the darkness to depict YHWH's defeat of threats against the people (Exod 10:13, 19; cf. Exodus 14–15; Isa 11:11–16). Other traditions employed include the "Day of YHWH" tradition that depicts punishment against Israel's enemies as well as against Israel itself (Isaiah 2; 13; see also Amos 5:18–20; Obadiah; Zephaniah; Zechariah)

---

[17] For a full study of the intertextual relationships in Joel, see Siegfried Bergler, *Joel als Schriftinterpret* (BEATAJ 16; Frankfurt/Main: Peter Lang, 1988).

and 2 Chronicles 20, which portrays King Jehoshaphat's defeat of the nations, Ammon, Moab, and Edom, that threatened Jerusalem. Intertextual references with the book the Book of the Twelve include the citation of Amos 1:2 and 9:13 in Joel 4:16, 18; the use of Micah 4:1–5 (cf. Isaiah 2:2–4) in Joel 4:10; and citations from the book of Obadiah that appear throughout Joel 3–4.

The use in Joel of the locust plague from Exodus 10:1–20 has already been noted by scholars. Bergler's recent dissertation studies the extensive intertextual relationships between Joel and the Exodus narrative, including parallels in Joel 1:3; 2:26–27 and Exodus 10:1, 2 concerning YHWH's self-identification and the instruction to the people to tell their children about YHWH's actions; Joel 2:19, 25 and Exodus 10:4 concerning the motif of "sending"; Joel 1:4; 2:25 and Exodus 10:5, 12, 15 concerning the devouring of the remnant or what is left over; Joel 1:2; 2:2 and Exodus 10:6, 14 concerning the threat posed by the locusts to houses that has not been seen since the days of the people's ancestors; Joel 2:20 and Exodus 10:17, 19 concerning YHWH's capacity to remove the threat from the land; and Joel 3:3–4 and the general pattern of signs and wonders in the Exodus.[18] Bergler's examination of these intertextual relationships stresses that Joel creates an Exodus typology in which the specific setting of the locust plague against Egypt in the Exodus account is removed so that the pattern of the locust plague may be applied to the situation of threat that is articulated in Joel. It should be noted, however, that Joel does not present a particular situation of threat, i.e., no specific enemy is identified, rendering it impossible to tie Joel's depiction of threat to any specific historical situation or event. The presentation of threat against Jerusalem and Judah in Joel is almost entirely anonymous. Apparently, this is deliberate in that the creation of such an Exodus typology enables the book of Joel to be read in relation to any threat, whether real or potential, that might be posed against Jerusalem and Judah. In this respect, Joel draws upon past tradition to assert that YHWH has the capacity to bring a threat against Jerusalem and Judah and to deliver Jerusalem and Judah from that threat, just as YHWH did at the time of the Exodus from Egyptian slavery.

It is noteworthy, therefore, that Joel 3:1–5 employs the motif of YHWH's "wind" or "spirit" that will be poured out over all flesh so that all the people, including slaves and maidservants, will prophesy and Jerusalem and Judah will be saved. It is not insignificant that this passage follows immediately the reference in Joel 2:27 in which YHWH states, "and you shall know that I am in the midst of Israel; and I am YHWH your G-d and there is no other, and my people shall not be ashamed forever." As noted above, the motif of YHWH's self-identification and the instruction to tell the children constitutes one of the key intertextual connections between Joel and the Exodus narrative of the locust plague. Although many interpreters correctly read the reference to YHWH's

---

[18] Bergler, *Joel als Schriftinterpret* 247–94.

pouring out of the divine "spirit" or "wind" (Hebrew, *rûaḥ*) on the people in relation to the following statements concerning their ability to prophesy (cf. Num 11:16–20; 1 Sam 10:6; 19:20–24), the statement also relates to the Exodus locust narrative in that the locusts are brought upon Egypt by an "east wind" (Exod 10:13) and later removed by a "west wind" that was changed by YHWH (Exod 10:19). The east wind in particular is a frequent motif in the Hebrew Bible that is to be identified with the Sharav (Hebrew) or Ḥamsin (Arabic), a strong dry desert wind, much like the Santa Ana winds of Southern California, that blows in from the desert at times of seasonal transition in Israel, either from the dry summer to the wet winter in October or from the wet winter to the dry summer in April. These winds can be very destructive as they reach high velocities, and they frequently blow in a great deal of dust and debris that blocks out the sun, thus darkening the land and causing the moon to appear as a deep red or blood-like color as described in Joel 3:3–5. In this respect, the imagery of Joel 3 also relates to that of the plague of darkness as described in Exodus 10:21–29, which is variously understood in relation to a solar eclipse or the Sharav/Ḥamsin that is common to the region.[19]

The use of the image of the Sharav/Ḥamsin once again speaks to a concern to portray YHWH's actions of threat and deliverance in relation to the cosmic patterns of nature, i.e., YHWH brings destruction as well as deliverance, and the cyclical nature of such events, i.e., just as YHWH brought about such actions at the time of the Exodus, so YHWH is capable of bringing them about once again. Indeed, the use of the Sharav/Ḥamsin as a symbol for YHWH's deliverance is known in Exodus 14–15 and Isaiah 11:11–16 in which the wind divides the water of the Red Sea or the River of Egypt, and enables Israel to return from exile in Assyrian as well as in Egypt. Joel's images of the portents in heaven and earth, blood, fire, and columns of smoke are also noteworthy in that they combine the images of the natural phenomenon of creation in the Sharav/Ḥamsin with those of sacrifice at the Temple altar. Indeed, the cyclical pattern of threat and deliverance that is conveyed by the Sharav/Ḥamsin also appears in Temple sacrifice in which the images of blood, fire, and columns of smoke speak to the act of destruction in the killing and consumption of the sacrificial animal as well as the deliverance or the restoration of cosmic order that such an action embodies. The imagery of the Sharav/Ḥamsin and the Temple sacrifice are both transformative in that both mark the transition from threat to order or security that underlies the basic pattern of Joel.

Such a concern also underlies the use of the "Day of YHWH" motif in Joel. The "Day of YHWH" is mentioned explicitly in Joel 1:15; 2:1; and 4:14, and it appears to underlie the entire scenario of threat and deliverance in the book.

---

[19] For discussion of the Sharav or Ḥamsin, see "Israel, Land of (Geographical Survey)," *Encyclopaedia Judaica* 9:189–93.

Although the "Day of YHWH" is not well understood in that it is variously identified in relation to the holy war, cultic/Sukkot, royal, or eschatological/ apocalyptic traditions,[20] it is clear that the "Day of YHWH" elsewhere signifies both a day of threat against Israel and a day of deliverance for Israel from its enemies. Thus, Amos 5:18–20 indicates that the people of Israel might desire the Day of YHWH as a day of light or deliverance, in fact it is to be a day of darkness and threat. Isaiah 2:6–21 portrays it as a day of threat against all the arrogant of the earth or land; Isaiah 13 portrays it as a day in which YHWH's warriors will bring down Babylon; and Isaiah 34 presents it as a day of YHWH's vengeance against the nations, especially Edom. Ezekiel 30 presents it as a day of judgment against Egypt; Obadiah presents it as a day of judgment against Edom; and Zechariah 14 presents it as the day that YHWH will defeat the nations and bring them to Zion to worship YHWH at the festival of Sukkot. Like Amos, Zephaniah portrays it as a day of judgment against those in Jerusalem/Judah and the nations who resist YHWH's sovereignty. As the various images of the day demonstrate, it is present as a day of cultic sacrifice at the Temple (Zeph 1:7–9; Zech 14:20–21; cf. Isa 34:5–7) in which theophanic images of warfare, darkness, gloom, thick clouds, and shofar blast predominate (Ezek 30:3; Amos 5:18–20; Zeph 1:14–16; cf. Isa 13:10; 34:8–10). Insofar as the "Day of YHWH" motif permeates the entire book of Joel, it appears to define the entire scenario of threat against Jerusalem/Judah by the nations and deliverance from that threat throughout the book of Joel as a whole. Again, the general scenario is anonymous in that it can be applied to various nations.

The motif of the Day of YHWH especially appears to define the use in Joel 4:9–21 of the tradition concerning King Jehoshaphat's defeat of the Moabites, Ammonites, Meunites, and Edomites from 2 Chronicles 20. Scholars have already noted Joel's dependence upon some form of this tradition in that Jehoshaphat's defeat in the Valley of Berachah of the nations that threatened Jerusalem underlies Joel's call to prepare for war against the nations in the "Valley of Jehoshaphat" or the "Valley of Decision."[21] The reason for the use of this particular tradition in Joel is unclear, but it does seem to play on the name of the valley where Jehoshaphat won his victory in that the Valley of Berachah (Hebrew, *'ēmeq běrākâ*) means "valley of blessing," which of course calls to mind the motif of YHWH's deliverance in a time of threat. More importantly for the present purposes, the text in Joel initially renders the nations anonymous so that the scenario may be applied once again to any situation of threat against Jerusalem. Furthermore, Joel introduces both the motifs of the Day of YHWH and the cosmic transformation of the sun and the moon that darken in keeping with the previously discussed use of the Sharav/Ḥamsin from the Exodus plague

---

[20] See the discussion by K. J. Cathcart, "Day of YHWH," *ABD* 2:84–5.
[21] E. g., Nogalski, *Redactional Processes* 30–7.

narratives. Again, the agricultural motifs from the first part of the book of Joel appear as YHWH's deliverance ensures the harvest of grain and wine that were previously threatened by the locusts. By the end of the passage, however, the general threat against the nations that threatened Jerusalem and Judah is directed specifically against Egypt and Edom. The basis for the mention of Egypt is clear since Joel makes such extensive use of the Exodus tradition. The mention of Edom likewise becomes clear when one considers the use of Obadiah, which is formulated as an oracle of judgment against Edom, throughout Joel 3–4.

Indeed, scholars have long noted the extensive allusion to texts from Obadiah in Joel 3–4.[22] The allusions include Joel 3:5 and Obadiah 17–18 concerning the remnant for Jerusalem/Judah in Zion and the lack of one for Esau; Joel 4:17 and Obadiah 17, 11 concerning the foreigners who threaten YHWH's mountain in Zion; Joel 4:3 and Obadiah 11 concerning the lot cast against Jerusalem; Joel 4:3 and Obadiah 16 concerning the nations who drink at Zion; Joel 4:4, 7 and Obadiah 15 concerning recompense for deeds against YHWH/Zion; Joel 4:6 and Obadiah 18 concerning YHWH's speaking; Joel 4:19 and Obadiah 10 concerning Edom's slaughter of Judah or Jacob; Joel 4:9, 11 and Obadiah 1 (cf. Jer 49:14) concerning the call to war; Joel 4:11 and Obadiah 9 concerning warriors; Joel 4:14 and Obadiah 19–20 concerning the sale or exile of Jerusalem/Judah to Greece or Sepharad; and Joel 4:12, 17 and Obadiah 21 concerning YHWH's judgment against Esau and the nations. Based upon his analysis of the allusions to Obadiah in Joel 3–4, Bergler argues that Joel typologizes Edom so that it becomes a representative of the nations at large. This is in contrast to Obadiah, which condemns Edom specifically for wrongs done against Jacob and Jerusalem. He maintains that the typologization of Edom thereby provides the link in Joel between the initial locust plague of the book and its later judgment against the nations. This is apparent especially from Joel 4:19 where Egypt and Edom are placed together and condemned for the violence that they have done against Judah in shedding innocent blood. Clearly, Joel is dependent upon Obadiah, and employs Obadian texts to build its typological portrayal of YHWH's bringing nations against Jerusalem for judgment and then delivering Jerusalem from the threat when the people repent. The use of Obadiah is apparently linked to the use of 2 Chronicles 20 with its portrayal of Jehoshaphat's defeat of the nations, including Edom/Esau, that threatened Jerusalem. Whereas 2 Chronicles 20 depicts the defeat of Edom and the other nations, Obadiah provides a prophet's condemnation of Edom for its crimes against Jerusalem.

The concern with the threat against Jerusalem and YHWH's deliverance of the city from that threat also appears to motivate the use of Amos 1:2 and 9:13 in Joel 4:16 and 18 respectively.[23] In portraying YHWH's actions against the

---

[22] See Bergler, *Joel als Schriftinterpret* 295–333.
[23] Cf. Nogalski, *Redactional Processes* 42–8.

nations, Joel 4:16 states, "and YHWH will roar from Zion, and from Jerusalem he will give his voice, and heaven and earth will tremble (*wĕrā'ăšû*)," which draws directly from Amos 1:2, "YHWH will roar from Zion, and from Jerusalem he will give his voice," which appears immediately following the reference to the earthquake (*hārā'aš*) in Amos 1:1. Likewise, in portraying the coming day of YHWH's deliverance, Joel 4:18 states, "and it shall come to pass in that day that the mountains will drip fresh wine, and the hills shall flow with milk," which draws upon the portrayal of Israel's fecundity in Amos 9:13, "and the mountains shall drip fresh wine, and all the hills shall flow (literally, 'melt, dissolve') with it." The use of these verses clearly supports Joel's attempt to portray Jerusalem's deliverance from threat by YHWH as well as the overall portrayal of the threat against Jerusalem and its deliverance in cosmic imagery or natural terms. It must also be noted that these verses respectively introduce and conclude the words of Amos as presented in his book so that they encapsulate Amos' message of judgment against various nations and northern Israel and the restoration of Israel under Davidic kingship or Jerusalemite rule as the goal of that punishment. In short, Joel apparently reads Amos as an expression of its own scenario in which Jerusalem is under threat, this time from northern Israel, and YHWH takes action to remove that threat and to restore Jerusalem to its rightful state of existence.

Finally, scholars have also long noted the use of Micah 4:1–5 or Isaiah 2:2–4 in Joel 4:10.[24] As part of the general call to battle against the nations, Joel 4:10 states, "beat your plowshares into swords and your pruning hooks into spears (*rĕḥāmîm*)," whereas Micah 4:3/Isaiah 2:4 state, "and they shall beat their swords into plowshares and their spears (*ḥănîtôtêhem/ḥănîtôtêhem*) into pruning hooks," as part of the overall scenario of world peace that will ensue when the nations recognize YHWH's sovereignty at Zion. Although the reference to spears differs slightly as *ḥănît* may refer to a lighter javelin whereas *rōmaḥ* may refer to the heavier lance, the passage clearly draws upon some version of the text that appears in Micah or Isaiah. It is impossible to determine upon which text it is dependent, or even if it is dependent upon a third text. Nevertheless, it draws its power of expression from the reversal of the motif of world peace depicted in these texts, and thereby serves Joel's agenda of declaring YHWH's judgment against the nations that threaten the security of Jerusalem, the city of peace that stands at the center of the cosmos. Again, no specific nations are singled out, but they are treated as a whole to serve Joel's interests in depicting typologically the resolution of a threat to the cosmos.

---

[24] E. g., Wolff, *Joel and Amos* 80.

IV

Clearly, Joel depends heavily upon other biblical texts, including texts from the Book of the Twelve as well as other biblical writings. Although Joel's use of other biblical texts has implications for establishing the date of Joel, Joel's use of other texts from the Book of the Twelve also has implications for understanding Joel's place or setting within the major versions of the Twelve. Insofar as the Twelve appears within different sequences of books in its MT and LXX versions, the sequence of Joel's appearance in relation to the other books that it cites appears to have some bearing in understanding the arrangement of the Twelve in both versions.

The use of Micah 4:3/Isaiah 2:4 in Joel 4:10 is particularly noteworthy. This citation appears at the outset of the last discrete sub-unit of the book in Joel 4:9–21 in which the prophet calls for the gathering of warriors who will enforce YHWH's judgment against the nations that threaten Jerusalem in the Valley of Jehoshaphat. The reversal of this statement makes for a particularly powerful rhetorical impact upon the audience because the Mican/Isaian text was apparently very well known (see Zech 8:20–23; Isa 37:32/2 Kgs 19:31; Isa 51:4), which presuppose the Mican/Isaian oracle) and because it conveyed a very compelling image of peace among the nations that is shattered in Joel. One can account for its function in Joel even if Joel appears prior to Micah in the sequence of the Twelve as is the case in the MT. If Joel is read first, then the reversal of the image actually occurs in Micah 4:1–5 as Joel's image of judgment among the nations is resolved when the nations voluntarily stream to Zion for YHWH's judgment and rework their weapons in the Mican text. But this sequence does create problems in that Micah defines an ideal situation in the middle of the Twelve that is not resolved until nearly the end of the sequence. Zechariah 8:20–23 portrays the nations grasping onto the garments of Jews in Zechariah 8:20–23 so that they might come to Jerusalem and suffer YHWH's punishment before finally celebrating Sukkot in Zechariah 14. In such a sequence, it is not clear why the judgment should be mentioned near the outset of the Twelve, only to point to an ideal in the middle of the sequence, and then to return once again to judgment and its resolution near the end of the sequence. The MT order highlights the experience of Jerusalem throughout, but it does not present a smoothly flowing sequence for the definition and realization of Jerusalem's ideal state of being in relation to the nations. The LXX order, which places Micah prior to Joel, appears to make much better sense. Insofar as the LXX sequence of the Twelve treats the experience of northern Israel as a paradigm for that of Jerusalem and Judah,[25] Micah points to the ideal future of Jerusalem as the sequence makes the transition from Israel to Jerusalem. Joel then imitates the scenario of judgment against the

---

[25] See Sweeney, "Sequence and Interpretation."

nations with typological portrayal that is specified with successive treatment of Edom (Obadiah), Assyria (Jonah; Nahum), Babylon (Habakkuk), and Jerusalem (Zephaniah) prior to the images of Jerusalem's restoration in the midst of the nations (Haggai; Zechariah) and a concluding book that calls for the realization of this scenario (Malachi). In short, the ideal is defined, and then the process by which that ideal is to be achieved follows in a logical progression.

Similar considerations apply to the citation of Amos 1:2 and 9:13. Once again, the citation of these texts appears in the concluding sub-unit of the book of Joel, which portrays the prophet's summons of the warriors to the Valley of Jehoshaphat for YHWH's judgment against the nations. As noted above, these verses appear at the beginning and end of the book of Amos. Amos in turn presents its own scenario of YHWH's judgment against the nations and the northern kingdom of Israel that culminates in the call for the destruction of the Beth El altar and the restoration of Davidic kingship, and thus Jerusalem's central role, over all Israel. In this respect, Amos 1:2 and 9:13 encapsulate the message of the book of Amos as a whole, and thus provide Joel with an abbreviated reference to that message that points to YHWH's capacity for judgment from Zion and the resolution of that judgment in a restored state of fecundity and order in creation. Naturally, this reference can be lost if Joel appears prior to Amos as it does in the MT. Although this problem might be resolved by the recognition that biblical books are intended to be read and reread,[26] the MT sequence nevertheless creates tension in that the book of Amos addresses a fundamental judgment and transformation of the northern kingdom of Israel which has an impact on Jerusalem, whereas Joel is concerned with Jerusalem and Judah throughout. If Amos is read first, as is the case in the LXX sequence of the Book of the Twelve, then the situation of the northern kingdom of Israel is addressed first, with its implications for Jerusalem, and Joel subsequently treats the issue of Jerusalem as a next stage in the sequence. In this case, the citation of Amos 1:2 and 9:13 in Joel provides a cryptic reference to the scenario of judgment that recalls the experience of northern Israel just as Jerusalem and Judah undergo their own experience of judgment and transformation. Once again, the LXX sequence appears to make a great deal of sense whereas the MT sequence appears to create tension.

Finally, the use of the Obadian passages in Joel also appears to make greater sense when read in the LXX sequence of the Twelve. As noted above, Obadiah apparently portrays the judgment against Edom as an actual historical situation whereas Joel employs Edom together with Egypt as a typological portrayal of the nations at large. In both the MT and LXX sequences of the Twelve, Joel appears

---

[26] For discussion of the reading and rereading of prophetic books, see the commentary on Micah by Ehud Ben Zvi, *Micah* (FOTL 21; Grand Rapids and Cambridge: William Eerdmans, 2000) 9–11; idem, *A Historical-Critical Study of the Book of Obadiah* (BZAW 242; Berlin and New York: Walter de Gruyter, 1996) 3–6.

before Obadiah so that in both cases, Joel presents the typology and Obadiah presents the realization of that typology. But Amos appears between Joel and Obadiah in the MT sequence, and this breaks the connection between the two books to a certain extent, i.e., the interrelationship between the two books is somewhat lost due to the appearance of the intervening book of Amos. This is addressed, in part, by the often noted reference to David's or Judah's possession of the remnant of Edom and all the nations in Amos 9:11–12. There are questions as to whether this reading is the result of redactional emendation, because the LXX reads Hebrew *'ĕdôm*, "Edom," as *'ādām* or Greek *tōn anthrōpōn*, "humanity," so that the passage reads as a reference to David's/Judah's possession of the remnant of humanity and all the nations.[27] It is not entirely certain, however, that the LXX reading is original as the recovery of Edom would have been a major issue in Israel and Judah throughout the late-ninth and eighth centuries B.C.E.[28] Apart from this issue, the LXX sequence, which places Joel immediately prior to Obadiah, makes a great deal of sense because the references to Obadiah in Joel are immediately clear to the reader, who encounters Obadiah after having just completed Joel. Edom then becomes the first of the nations mentioned in Joel's typological portrayal, and the other nations then follow as indicated earlier.

V

The preceding observations clearly indicate that Joel's place in the LXX sequence of the Book of the Twelve provides for a far more logically consistent progression among the individual books that holds out the experience of northern Israel in Hosea, Amos, and Micah as a model or paradigm for that of Jerusalem. In addition, it places books concerned with the nations together as a block in Obadiah (Edom), Jonah (mercy for Assyria), Nahum (fall of Assyria), and Habakkuk (Babylon), prior to returning to concern with Jerusalem's judgment in Zephaniah, its restoration at the center of the nations in Haggai and Zechariah, and the projection that the entire process is about to begin (Malachi). Thus, Joel, with its typological concern for the threat posed to Jerusalem by the nations and YHWH's pledge to deliver Jerusalem from that threat, provides an ideal transition between Hosea – Micah and Obadiah – Malachi. In the MT sequence, which focuses on Jerusalem throughout, tension appears among the various books as Joel provides a typological portrayal of Jerusalem's experience

---

[27] See the discussion in Nogalski, *Literary Precursors* 113–6.
[28] See 2 Kgs 8:20–22, which notes Edom's revolt against Judah during the reign of Jehoram/Joram. Cf. 2 Kgs 10:32–33, which notes the loss of the Trans-Jordan to Israel during the reign of Jehu. 2 Kings 14:25 refers to Jeroboam ben Joash's restoration of Israel and 2 Kgs 14:7 refers to Amaziah's defeat of the Edomites, but it is not clear that Edom was ever brought entirely under Israelite/Judean control during this period.

in relation to the nations, but the following sequence only highlights Jerusalem's idealization in the middle (Micah) prior to taking up the issue as to how that ideal will be realized in Zephaniah – Malachi.

This has some bearing on the historical setting in which the two forms of the Book of the Twelve were assembled insofar as they point to two very different concerns. The interest in comparing the experience of northern Israel, with its destruction and exile at the hands of the Assyrian empire in the late eighth century B.C.E., would have been of paramount concern in the late-monarchic period as well as during the exile and the early years of the Persian period. During these periods, Judean thinkers were attempting to come to terms with the destruction of the northern kingdom and its implications for Judah and Jerusalem. Such concern was inherent in the attempts by the southern kingdom of Judah to reestablish Davidic rule over the north, perhaps as early as the reigns of Ahaz or Hezekiah and as late as the reigns of Josiah and his successors. With the emergence of Babylon in the late seventh and early sixth centuries, concern would shift to understanding the implications of Israel's downfall in relation to the threat posed to Jerusalem and ultimately realized in the Babylonian exile. Certainly, the composition of the so-called Deuteronomistic History, with its posited Hezekian and Josian editions and its final exilic or early post-exilic edition,[29] demonstrates considerable interest in the fate of the northern kingdom of Israel and the implications this had for Judah. In the case of the earlier editions, the presentation of ideal Davidic monarchs would support a program of reunification of all Israel under Davidic rule. In the case of the final edition, it would look toward the restoration of Israel.

Such concerns are also inherent in the early edition of Jeremiah, which apparently is to be identified with the Hebrew *Vorlage* of the present form of LXXJeremiah.[30] The book begins in chapters 2–3 by articulating the prophet's concern for judgment against Israel and then it shifts to treatment of Judah and Jerusalem in chapters 3–25. Like the LXX form of the Book of the Twelve, LXXJeremiah places the oracles concerning the nations in the middle of the book (LXXJeremiah 25–32) prior to returning to its portrayal of Jerusalem's fall in LXXJeremiah 33–52. Similar patterns that point to a concern with understanding the fall of Israel in relation to Jerusalem's and Judah's experience appear in the book of Isaiah, in both its posited seventh and sixth century editions.[31] In the former instance, Isaiah 5–12 points to the fall of Israel as the impetus for a restored Davidic state prior to turning to the issue of judgment against the nations

---

[29] See my *King Josiah of Judah: The Lost Messiah of Israel* (New York and Oxford: Oxford University Press, 2001) for full discussion of the redaction of the Deuteronomistic History.

[30] See Jack R. Lundbom, "Jeremiah, Book of," *ABD* 3:706–21, esp. 707–8, for an overview of the issue.

[31] See my *Isaiah 1–39, with an Introduction to Prophetic Literature* (FOTL 16; Grand Rapids and Cambridge: William Eerdmans, 1996).

in Isaiah 13–23 and the judgment and restoration of Jerusalem in Isaiah 28–33. In the latter instance, the patterns of Isaiah 1–39 remain intact, and Isaiah 40–55 first treats the exile of Jacob in chapters 40–48 prior to the restoration of Zion in chapters 49–55. Indeed, the earliest edition of the Book of the Twelve posited by Nogalski and Schart, which includes early forms of Hosea, Amos, Micah, and Zephaniah, demonstrate a similar concern for the fate of Israel as a model for that of Jerusalem and Judah.[32] Although there are no early manuscripts of the Book of the Twelve that order the books according to their sequence in the LXX, concern with the judgment of Israel as a model for the experience of Jerusalem and Judah would not have been a major issue in the late-Persian, Hellenistic, Hasmonean or Roman periods when Judean attention focused especially on Jerusalem.

The MT sequence of the Book of the Twelve, which focuses especially on Jerusalem throughout, appears to be the product of the later Persian period when concern shifted away from the north to focus especially on Jerusalem. This concern is particularly noticeable in the period of Ezra and Nehemiah when Jerusalem was truly restored as the center of Persian-period Yehud, and various conflicts arose between the Jerusalem-based exiles who returned with these figures and the Persian-appointed authorities in Samaria. The specific concern with Jerusalem is evident in both the books of Ezra-Nehemiah and in the books of Chronicles, which apparently excises materials from the DtrH that are concerned with the north to focus almost entirely on Jerusalem and Judah. A similar agenda may be observed in the MT form of the book of Jeremiah, postulated by many to be an expanded and later edition of the book. Jeremiah 2:2, for example, expands this verse to indicate that Jeremiah's initial oracles concerning Israel are addressed to the people of Jerusalem (cf. LXXJer 2:2, which lacks reference to Jerusalem). Likewise, the oracles concerning the nations are placed at the end of the book in chapters 46–51 so that chapters 1–45 are ultimately concerned with Jerusalem and Judah throughout. Even the posited fifth century edition of the book of Isaiah begins and ends in chapters 1 and 56–66 with oracles that take up the fate of Jerusalem.[33] Indeed, the earliest manuscripts of the Book of the Twelve, i.e., the MurXII and 8ḤevXIIgr, reflect the MT order of the books, but these manuscripts are apparently the products of the Hasmonean period when concern with the restoration of Jerusalem from foreign/Seleucid rule was paramount.

In conclusion, it appears that the book of Joel does indeed play a key role in the Book of the Twelve. Although the book was likely composed in a relatively late period,[34] its typological character, its place, and its function in both the MT

---

[32] Nogalski, *Redactional Processes* 274–80; Schart, *Entstehung* 156–233.

[33] Sweeney, *Isaiah 1–39*.

[34] Wolff, for example, places the composition of the book in the early fourth century B.C.E. (*Joel and Amos* 5); cf. Mason, *Joel* 113–6, who points to the difficulties in dating the book. See also Sweeney, *Twelve Prophets* 1:149–50.

and LXX versions of the book apparently defines the overall outlook of each. Joel's typological character and the difficulties in establishing its historical setting make it an eminently mobile text within the sequence of the Twelve, and that mobility enables it to shape the sequence of the Twelve so that the Book of the Twelve as a whole might address two very different hermeneutical agendas that originated ultimately in different historical settings.

14. Micah's Debate with Isaiah

I

Scholars have long noted the appearance in both Micah 4:1–5 and Isaiah 2:2–4, 5 of the idyllic vision in which the nations stream to Zion, learn YHWH's Torah and ways, and beat their swords into plowshares and spears into pruning hooks to inaugurate an era of world peace. The extensive critical discussion concerning these texts has tended to focus on defining or reconstructing the supposed "original" form of the text on which Micah and Isaiah are based.[1] Although some argue that the text was originally composed by Isaiah ben Amoz in the late-eighth century B.C.E. and later adapted for use in Micah,[2] most scholars correctly maintain that it is an exilic or post-exilic composition that has been employed in both prophetic books.[3] But as scholars have assessed the differences between these two texts, they have begun to recognize that they cannot be treated simply as self-contained literary units in isolation from their respective literary contexts.

---

[1] For overviews and discussion concerning these passages, see B. Renaud, *La Formation du Livre de Michée. Tradition et Actualization* (EB; Paris: Gabalda, 1977) 150–81; idem, *Michée, Sophonie, Nahum* (SB; Paris: Gabalda, 1987) 72–81; Rudolph Kilian, *Jesaja 1–39* (Erträge der Forschung 200; Darmstadt: Wissenschaftliche Buchgesellschaft, 1983) 86–91; Jan A. Wagenaar, *Judgement and Salvation: The Composition and Redaction of Micah 2–5* (VTSup 85; Leiden: Brill, 2001) 2261–73; William McKane, *Micah: Introduction and Commentary* (Edinburgh: T & T Clark, 1998) 117–27; J. Vermeylen, *Du prophète à l'apocalyptique* (2 vols.; EB; Paris: Gabalda, 1977–78) 114–33; Hans Wildberger, *Isaiah 1–12: A Commentary* (ContCom; Minneapolis: Fortress, 1991) 81–97; Marvin A. Sweeney, *Isaiah 1–39, with an Introduction to Prophetic Literature* (FOTL 16; Grand Rapids and Cambridge: Eerdmans, 1996) 97–100.

[2] E. g., Henri Cazelles, "Qui aurait vise, à l'origine Isaïe ii 2–5?" *VT* 30 (1980) 409–20; Bertil Wiklander, *Prophecy as Literature: A Text-Linguistic and Rhetorical Approach to Isaiah 2–4* (ConBibOT 22; Lund: Gleerup, 1984); J. J. M. Roberts, "Isaiah 2 and the Prophet's Message to the North," *JQR* 75 (1985) 290–308; Wildberger, *Isaiah 1–12* 85–7; Wilhelm Rudolph, *Micha – Nahum – Habakuk – Zephanja* (KAT XIII/3; Gütersloh: Gerd Mohn, 1975) 77–81.

[3] E. g., James Luther Mays, *Micah: A Commentary* (OTL; Philadelphia: Westminster, 1976) 94–6; Renaud, *La Formation* 160–63; idem, *Michée* 72–3; Ronald E. Clements, *Isaiah 1–39* (NCenB; London: Marshall, Morgan, and Scott; Grand Rapids: William Eerdmans, 1980) 39–40; Wolfgang Werner, *Eschatologische Texte in Jesaja 1–39. Messias, Heiliger Rest, Völker* (Forschung zur Bibel 46; Würzburg: Echter, 1982) 151–63; Otto Kaiser, *Isaiah 1–12: A Commentary* (OTL; Philadelphia: Westminster, 1983) 49–52; Hans Walter Wolff, *Micah: A Commentary* (ContCom; Minneapolis: Augsburg, 1990) 116–18; Wagenaar, *Judgement and Salvation* 261–73; Sweeney, *Isaiah 1–39* 87–100; McKane, *Micah* 117–26. Vermeylen, *Du prophète* 114–33, dates the passage to the time of King Josiah's reform.

Instead, they have observed that each functions as an integral component of a larger literary unit, i.e., Micah 4:1–5 is a component of Micah 4–5 and Isaiah 2:2–4, 5 is a component of Isaiah 2–4, and that each of these larger textual blocks is uniquely formulated to convey its own specific perspectives, ideologies, and messages within the overall frameworks of the books of Micah and Isaiah. Furthermore, Micah 4:1–5 and Isaiah 2:2–4, 5 have each been adapted by the inclusion of unique material that ties each text into its respective literary context and enables it to function as part of the larger unit. The issue is further informed by the long-recognized lexical and thematic correspondences between two other texts that appear within Micah 4–5 and Isaiah 2–4, i.e., Micah 5:9–14, in which YHWH threatens to cut off horses, chariots, soothsayers, idols, etc., from the land, and Isaiah 2:6–8, in which YHWH makes similar threats as part of an overall "Day of YHWH" scenario.[4] Clearly, Micah 4–5 and Isaiah 2–4 are interrelated, although each constitutes a different literary context with its own distinctive perspectives and concerns.

The purpose of this paper, therefore, is to assess the interrelationship between Micah 4–5 and Isaiah 2–4 in an effort to determine how each employs the "common" textual materials in Micah 4:1–5 and Isaiah 2:2–4, 5 as part of a larger interest in depicting an emerging scenario of peace among the nations and between the nations and Israel. Based upon a comparative examination of the unique formulations and functions of Micah 4:1–5 and Isaiah 2:2–4, 5 within their respective contexts as well as a comparative examination of the overall literary structures and perspectives of Micah 4–5 and Isaiah 2–4, it attempts to demonstrate that there is a significant difference between the books of Micah and Isaiah regarding their portrayals of the future era of peace between the nations, Israel, and YHWH at Zion. Whereas the book of Isaiah presents a scenario of world-wide punishment of both the nations and Israel by YHWH that will result in peace and universal recognition of YHWH at Zion, Micah presents a scenario in which peace among the nations and universal recognition of YHWH will emerge following a period in which a new Davidic king will arise to punish the nations for their own prior abuse of Israel. These observations point to a debate concerning Judah's relationship to the nations in early Persian period Judaism[5]; whereas Isaiah's scenario supports submission to Persia as an expression of YHWH's will for the future of Zion, Micah's scenario supports the overthrow

---

[4] E.g., Renaud, *La Formation* 267; idem, *Michée* 112–3.

[5] Note A. S. Van der Woude's earlier contention that Micah debated false prophets who quoted Isaiah in support of their idea ("Micah in Dispute with the Pseudo-Prophets," *VT* 19 [1969] 244–60; "Micah IV 1–5: An Instance of the Pseudo-Prophets Quoting Isaiah," *Symbolae Biblicae et Mesopotamicae Francisco Mario Theodoro de Liagre Böhl Dedicatae* [ed. M. Beek et al.; Leiden: Brill, 1973] 396–402). Unfortunately, van der Woude assumes the model of debate between canonical and false prophets in his analysis of the Mican passages without critically demonstrating its validity.

of Persian rule and the reestablishment of the Davidic monarchy as part of its vision for the future of Zion.

II

The first task is an assessment of the formulations of Micah 4:1–5 and Isaiah 2:2–4, 5 within their respective literary contexts. Scholars have invested a great deal of effort in identifying and assessing the variations within the material shared by both of these texts in Micah 4:1–3 and Isaiah 2:2–4.[6] The variations include the placement of *nākôn*, "established," in the midst of the phrase, "the mountain of the house of YHWH shall be *established* at the head of the mountain," in Micah 4:1a instead of at the head of the phrase, "*established* shall be the mountain of the house of YHWH at the head of the mountains," in Isa 2:2a; the appearance of *hû*' in Micah 4:1a, "and *it* shall be raised up above the hills," which is lacking in Isa 2:2a; the appearance of the phrase *wěnaharû ʿālāyw ʿammîm* in Mic 4:1b, "and *peoples* shall flow *upon it*," versus *wěnāhărû ʾēlāyw kol-haggôyim* in Isa 2:2b, "and *all the nations* shall flow *unto it*"; the appearance of the phrase *wěhālěkû gôyim rabbîm* in Mic 4:2a, "and many *nations* shall go," versus *wěhālěkû ʿammîm rabbîm* in Isa 2:3a, "and many *peoples* shall go"; the appearance of *ʿammîm rabbîm* in Mic 4:3a. "and he shall judge between *many peoples*," versus *haggôyim* in Isa 2:4a, "and he shall judge between *nations*"; the appearance of *lěgôyim ʿăṣumîm* in Mic 4:3a, "and he shall arbitrate *for strong nations* far away," versus *lěʿammîm rabbîm* in Isa 2:4a, "and he shall arbitrate for many peoples"; the appearance of *ʿad rāḥôq*, "far away," in Mic 4:3a, which is lacking in Isa 2:4a; and the appearance of the plural verb *lōʾ yiśʾû*, "they shall not lift up," in Mic 4:3b versus the singular *lōʾ yiśśāʾ*, "it shall not lift up," in Isa 2:4b. In addition, there are several orthographic variants that need not be repeated here. Despite the many attempts by scholars to discern some significance in these variations for the problem of establishing the original form of the text, all that can be said with confidence is that they simply represent variant renderings of the same text.[7] Perhaps the variations result from the efforts of scribes to record an oral text heard during the course of some liturgical or other public performance,[8] but scholars have been unable to demonstrate convincingly any interpretative differences between them.

The statements that follow the common material in each oracle, however, prove to be much more interesting, both because they differ from each other

---

[6] For identification and discussion of these differences, see McKane, *Micah* 121–6.

[7] N.b., McKane's discussion of the textual differences between the two passages results only in the conclusion that neither Micah nor Isaiah could be the author of the text and that neither text can be explained as a derivation of the other (*Micah* 121–6).

[8] See Eduard Nielsen, *Oral Tradition: A Modern Problem in Old Testament Introduction* (SBT 11; London: SCM, 1954) 79–93.

and because they emphasize the verb *hlk*, "to walk," which suggests that they represent adaptations from a common source. Isaiah 2:5 reads, "O house of Jacob, come, and let us walk in the light of YHWH," whereas Micah 4:4–5 reads, "and each shall sit under his vine and under his fig tree, and no one shall frighten (them), for the mouth of YHWH Ṣebaoth has spoken, for all the peoples shall walk, each in the name of its (own) god, and we shall walk in the name of YHWH, our G-d, forever and ever."

Several conclusions can be drawn concerning the significance of each of these statements. First, there is no reason to argue that both statements presuppose a common *Urtext*, either from a liturgical composition or from an earlier form of a prophetic oracle. Indeed, the prominence of the verb *hlk* in both texts may be explained as the result of efforts to elaborate somehow on the significance of the verb in the preceding material that is common to both texts. Micah 4:2a and Isa 2:3a respectively portray "many nations" or "many peoples" walking and saying that they wish to go up to YHWH's mountain, "and many nations/peoples went/walked (*wĕhālĕkû*) and said, 'come, and let us go up to the mountain of YHWH …'" Likewise, the verb *hlk* plays a major role in the nations'/peoples' statement in Mic 4:2a/Isa 2:3a concerning the reason for their journey, "and he will teach us his ways that we may walk (*wĕnēlĕkâ*) in his paths." This would suggest that both statements in Isaiah 2:5 and Micah 4:4–5 represent attempts to expound upon the significance of the nations'/peoples' walking to YHWH's mountain and the results thereof as they walk in YHWH's ways. As I have noted before, the form of the verbs *lĕkû wĕnēlĕkâ*, "come, and let us walk (in the light of YHWH)," in Isaiah 2:5 is dependent upon the form of the people's proposal to go up to YHWH's mountain in Isaiah 2:3a, *lĕkû wĕnaʿăleh*, "come, and let us go up (unto the mountain of YHWH)."[9] Likewise, the form of the verb *nēlēk*, "and we shall walk (in the name of YHWH our G-d," in Micah 4:5b appears to presuppose *wĕnēlĕkâ*, "and we shall walk (in his paths)," in Micah 4:2a.

Second, the portrayal of walking in each text differs markedly from the other in terms of the results that may be expected of those who walk. Isaiah 2:5, "O house of Jacob, come, and let us walk in the light of YHWH," represents an invitation to the house of Jacob, or people of Israel in general, to join the nations or peoples in their pilgrimage to Mount Zion. Israel is not explicitly mentioned among the nations that would stream to Zion in Isaiah 2:2–4, but verse 5 defines a way in which Israel might be included together with the nations in this impending scenario of world peace. Indeed, the reference to Israel as "the house of Jacob" (*bêt yaʿăqōb*) appears to presuppose the reference to the Temple as "the house of the G-d of Jacob" (*bêt ʾĕlōqê yaʿăqōb*) in Isaiah 2:3a. Such a scenario

---

[9] Sweeney, *Isaiah 1–39* 90, 93–4; idem, *Isaiah 1–4 and the Post-Exilic Understanding of the Isaianic Tradition* (BZAW 171; Berlin and New York: Walter de Gruyter, 1988) 135–6, 138–9; see also R. B. Y. Scott, "Isaiah 1–39," *The Interpreter's Bible* (ed. G. A. Buttrick; Nashville: Abingdon, 1956) 5:182; Vermeylen, *Du Prophète* 131.

according to Isaiah 2:2–4, 5 would entail an era of world peace in which both the nations and Israel were included among those who came to Mt. Zion to learn YHWH's Torah, to submit to YHWH's authority as judge and ruler, and to enjoy the resulting era of peace.

Micah 4:4–5 presents a very different scenario in which the nations and Israel will enjoy an era of world peace under YHWH's world-wide sovereignty, but they will do so by going their separate ways religiously. Indeed, Micah 4:4 signals the overall concern with peace and YHWH's authority by including the statement, "and each shall sit under his vine and under his fig tree and no one shall frighten (him), because the mouth of YHWH Sebaoth has spoken." Such a portrayal appears to presuppose the idyllic picture of peace for Israel in Solomon's time as presented in 1 Kings 5:5, although the present text goes several steps further in emphasizing that no one will frighten anyone else, either among the nations or within Israel, because the nations themselves will voluntarily submit to YHWH's sovereignty. The key difference between Micah 4:4–5 and Isaiah 2:5, however, appears in Micah 4:5, which emphasizes the differences between the nations and Israel with regard to the gods that each will follow. Although the text clearly portrays YHWH as the world sovereign, accepted as such by the nations, verse 5a asserts that the nations will continue to follow their own gods despite the acceptance of YHWH's overall sovereignty, i.e., "for all the peoples shall walk, each in the name of its gods." In contrast, verse 5b employs an emphatic *wa'ănaḥnû*, "and we," to emphasize that Israel will continue to follow YHWH, "and we shall walk in the name of YHWH, our G-d, forever and ever." Although such an assertion presumes YHWH's sovereignty over both the nations and Israel, it identifies Israel much more closely with YHWH. Nevertheless, when read in isolation from its literary context, Micah 4:1–5 does not comment upon the significance of this differentiation.

This points to the third conclusion to be drawn from the statements in Isaiah 2:5 and Micah 4:4–5, i.e., they cannot be read solely in relation to the respective forms of their preceding oracles, but they must be read in relation to the larger literary contexts in which these oracles function, specifically in relation to Isaiah 2–4 and Micah 4–5 respectively, and ultimately, in relation to the books of Isaiah and Micah as a whole.

This is clearly the case in Isaiah 2:5. Although this verse may be read as the concluding invitation to Jacob to join the nations in their pilgrimage to Mount Zion in Isaiah 2:2–4, the presence of the particle *kî* at the beginning of Isaiah 2:6 must be noted. The functions of *kî* are not well understood, but it does function as a syntactical connector so that in the present instance it links verses 6ff to verse 5, i.e., "for you have rejected your people, the house of Jacob."[10] The

---

[10] For discussion of the syntactical functions of the particle, *kî*, see Bruce K. Waltke and M. O'Connor, *An Introduction to Biblical Hebrew Syntax* (Winona Lake: Eisenbrauns, 1990) secs. 38–39; James Muilenberg, "The Linguistic and Rhetorical Uses of the Partical כי in the

identification of the "house of Jacob" as the object of this statement reinforces this syntactical link. Although some interpreters understand the verse to be an address to the house of Jacob, the shift in address forms from second person masculine plural in verse 5 to second person masculine singular in verse 6 indicates that there is a shift in the addressee. Isaiah 2:6 ff is not addressed to the house of Jacob as is the case with Isaiah 2:5; instead, it is addressed to YHWH who is said to have rejected the people of Israel. This understanding is reinforced by the objective third person portrayal in the balance of verses 6–9 of the people's wrongdoing which constitutes the cause for YHWH's rejection of the people, i.e., they are filled with soothsayers, they clasp hands with foreigners, their land is filled with silver and gold, horses, and idols so that they are ultimately abased by their own idolatry. In short, the following material explains why the house of Jacob is unable to accept the invitation to join the nations in their pilgrimage to Mount Zion, i.e., they are abased by idolatry and are therefore unable to make the ascent to Zion. This stands in striking contrast to Micah 4:4–5 which asserts that the nations follow their own gods and that Israel follows YHWH.

The contrast with Micah is accentuated when one considers the overall structure and presentation of Isaiah 2–4, the larger literary context in which Isaiah 2:2–4, 5 functions. Indeed, Isaiah 2:10–22 must be read together with Isaiah 2:5, 6–9, as this passage portrays the "Day of YHWH" in which YHWH will take action to remove the idols and other symbols of pride and arrogance from the land in a process of purification that pertains to the entire earth. Furthermore, the introductory *kî* in Isaiah 3:1 indicates that the unit does not conclude with Isaiah 2:10–22, but continues with the portrayal of YHWH's judgment against both the men and the women of Jerusalem and Judah in Isaiah 3:1–4:1. The introductory *bayyôm hahû'* formula in Isaiah 4:2 indicates that the portrayal in Isaiah 4:2–6 of the restored remnant of Israel in a newly purified Jerusalem and Judah completes the presentation of the Day of YHWH as a process in which Jacob and the land will be cleansed of its idolatry and purified so that it might join the nations in their ascent or pilgrimage to Zion.

The details of this structural analysis are presented elsewhere,[11] but the structure of Isaiah 2–4 is designed to convey this process of purification so that Israel/Jacob may join in the ideal scenario of world peace. Following the superscription for the entire passage in Isaiah 2:1, Isaiah 2:2–4:6 constitutes a prophetic announcement concerning the cleansing of Zion for its role as the center for YHWH's world rule. Isaiah 2:2–4 announces the future establishment of Zion as the center for YHWH's world rule, and Isaiah 2:5–4:6 then lays out the process by which Zion will be cleansed and prepared for this role in a series of three addresses. The first address to YHWH in Isaiah 2:5–9 employs the

---

Old Testament," *HUCA* 32 (1961) 135–60; Anton Schoors, "The Particle כי," *OTS* 21 (1981) 240–76.

[11] Sweeney, *Isaiah 1–39* 87–96.

invitation to Jacob as a means to establish the need for such cleansing due to the idolatry in the land. The second address in Isaiah 2:10–21 is directed to the people and announces the process of cleansing the entire land that will take place on the Day of YHWH. The third address in Isaiah 2:22–4:6, again to the people, announces the process of cleansing Jerusalem and Judah to serve as the center of Israel and the world at large. The overall scenario is one in which the land or earth in general as well as Jerusalem and Judah are prepared for the idyllic picture of Isaiah 2:2–4 in which Jacob and the nations together will ultimately ascend to Mount Zion to inaugurate a period of world peace. In this scenario, both the nations and Israel suffer punishment from YHWH in preparation for the era of world peace.

A somewhat different scenario emerges when one considers the literary context of Micah 4:1–5. In contrast to the relationship of Isaiah 2:5 to Isaiah 2:2–4, Micah 4:4–5 does not open a new literary sub-unit within the overall structure of the text but instead constitutes a continuation of Micah 4:1–3. The introductory *waw*-consecutive formulation of verse 4a, "and each shall sit (*wĕyāšĕbû ʾîš*) under his vine ..." and the introductory *kî* in both verses 4b and 5 establishes a syntactical relationship between verses 4–5 and the preceding material in verses 1–3. In short, Micah 4:1–5 constitutes a single linguistic unit. As noted above, verse 4 builds upon the idyllic portrayal of peace in verses 1–3 by stating that each person will sit under his own vine and fig tree and by pointing to YHWH as the ultimate authority who authorizes such a future. Verse 5, however, introduces a somewhat new element in the reading of this oracle in that it points to a distinction between the nations and Israel based upon their adherence to different gods, i.e., the nations shall walk in the name of their own gods and Israel will walk in the name of YHWH.

The implications of such a distinction are not made clear within the bounds of Micah 4:1–5, but they are spelled out in the following material in Micah 4:6–5:14 which elaborates upon the meaning of the exaltation of Zion. This material is linked to Micah 4:1–5 by the introductory *bayyôm hahûʾ* formula in Micah 4:6 which presupposes the initial reference to the "later days" (*wĕhāyâ bĕʾaḥărît hayyāmîm*) in Micah 4:1 as its referent. The prophet announces in the initial statement of this section in Micah 4:6–7 YHWH's plans to restore the lame and outcast remnant of Jacob (cf. Mic 5:6, 7 below) as a strong nation over which YHWH will rule on Mount Zion. Two addresses to Zion and Bethlehem Ephrata respectively follow in Micah 4:8–14 and 5:1–14, each of which begins with the address form *wĕʾattâ*, "and you." The first (Micah 4:8–14), addressed explicitly to Migdal Eder, Ophel Bat Zion, promises the restoration of the dominion of the daughter of Zion over the nations that are assembled against her following a period of exile in Babylon where she will be redeemed. The reference to Zion as Ophel Bat Zion is particularly significant because Ophel (*ʿōpel*), "hill," designates the site of the Davidic palace from which the kings of Judah ruled over all Israel and the nations that at various times constituted the Davidic empire. The second (Micah 5:1–14), addressed explicitly to Beth Lehem, Ephrata, promises the establishment of a new Davidic monarch who will bring peace (verses 1–3, 4a), defeat the Assyrians if they threaten the land (verses 4b–5), and restore the remnant of Jacob as the dominant power in the midst of the nations (verses 6–8). Again, there will be a period of punishment for Jacob as his horses, chariots, cities, strongholds, sorceries, soothsayers, images, Masseboth, and Asherim are destroyed, but the period of punishment will culminate in YHWH's vengeance against the nations that did not obey (verses 9–14). The language employed in Micah 5:9–14 corresponds to that employed in Isaiah 2:6–8 to describe the unwanted elements in Israel that must be purged before restoration takes place.[12]

Altogether, Micah 4–5 presents a scenario of world peace in which Jacob or Israel will suffer punishment, including exile to Babylon, at the hands of the nations. Jacob will be redeemed as a result of that punishment to emerge as the dominant power at the center of the nations. It will serve as YHWH's agent to punish the nations and facilitate their submission to YHWH. A restored Davidic monarchy figures prominently in this scenario and presumably serves as the focal point for YHWH's rule over the nations in the envisioned era of peace. Indeed, the relationship of Micah 4–5 to Micah 2–3, and especially to Micah 3:9–12, makes it clear that a major goal of this process in the book of Micah is to reestablish righteous monarchic rule in Jerusalem. Micah 4–5 is tied syntactically to Micah 3:9–12, which announces Zion's destruction as a result of the corruption of the leaders of Jacob/Israel in Jerusalem, and the whole of Micah 3:9–5:14 functions within the context of Micah 2–5 to announce Micah's overall scenario of the punishment and restoration of Jerusalem and Judah at the center of the nations.[13]

Indeed, the scenario by which world peace is achieved in Micah 4–5 differs markedly from that portrayed in Isaiah 2–4. The book of Isaiah envisions a process in which both Israel and the nations suffer punishment from YHWH as part of the process by which the entire earth is prepared for the emergence of YHWH's sovereignty in Zion and the resulting era of world peace. The book of Micah, however, envisions a process in which the nations first punish Jacob

---

[12] For discussion of the interrelationship between Isaiah 2:6–8 and Micah 5:9–14, see Renaud, *La Formation* 267; idem, *Michée* 112–3; Ina Willi-Plein, *Vorformen der Schriftexegese innerhalb des Alten Testaments* (BZAW 123; Berlin and New York: Walter de Gruyter, 1971) 95–7.

[13] For a more detailed discussion of the structure of Micah 4–5 within the larger context of Micah 2–5, see now the relevant section of my monograph, *King Josiah of Judah: The Lost Messiah of Israel* (Oxford and New York, 2001), and my commentary, *The Twelve Prophets* (Berit Olam; Collegeville: Liturgical, 2000). See also Wagenaar, *Judgement and Salvation*, who likewise identifies Micah 2–5 as a major structural component of the book while identifying its constituent sub-units as independent oracles.

and Jerusalem for the corruption of its leaders, and then Jacob, led by a new and righteous Davidic monarch, plays the major role in punishing the nations so that they will submit to YHWH's sovereignty at Zion. Whereas Isaiah portrays the nations and Jacob as the victims of YHWH's purge, Micah portrays the newly purged Jacob and the Davidic monarchy first as YHWH's victims and then as YHWH's agents in bringing about the punishment of the nations and thereby inaugurating the envisioned era of world peace.

Interestingly, these different constructions of the interrelationship of Israel and the nations in the envisioned era of world peace reflect the respective religio-political perspectives articulated throughout the books of Isaiah and Micah.[14] Isaiah 2–4 posits neither a Davidic monarch nor a gentile monarch in its vision of the future, but points only to YHWH as the sovereign. This is particularly important when these chapters are read in relation to the rest of the book. Although early portions of Isaiah point to the emergence of a righteous Davidic monarch (i. e., Isa 8:23–9:6; 11:1–16; 32:1–20), the latter portions of the book identify Cyrus of Persia as YHWH's anointed monarch (Isa 44:24–28; 45:1–8) or YHWH as king (Isaiah 65–66). The identification of Cyrus is especially striking when one considers that the nations listed for punishment in Isaiah's oracles against the nations, including Babylon, Assyria, Philistia, Moab, Aram, northern Israel, Egypt, Midbar Yam, Dumah, Arabia, Jerusalem, Tyre, and later Edom (Isaiah 13–23; 34), are all nations that were incorporated into the Persian empire beginning in the late-sixth century B.C.E.[15] At no point is Persia ever singled out for punishment, and indeed the Elamites and Medes, both of whom supported Persia, are identified as nations that will assault Babylon in Isaiah 22:2. Essentially, the book of Isaiah identifies YHWH's actions and plans with those of the Persian empire. This holds true even in the final chapters of the book which envisions the punishment of the wicked under YHWH's sovereignty. Such punishment does not envision a fundamental dichotomy between Judah/Jerusalem and the nations with regard to punishment. Instead, the nations restore the exiled Jews to Jerusalem and join them there to worship YHWH; the wicked to be punished may be drawn from either the nations or Israel. The nations and Israel suffer and rejoice together under the sovereignty of YHWH. Although past nations have fallen, i. e., Assyria and Babylon, no downfall for Persia is envisioned. In sum, the book of Isaiah envisions a restored Israel as part of the larger Persian empire, which stands ultimately under the sovereignty of YHWH.

---

[14] See Benjamin Uffenheimer, "Isaiah's and Micah's Approaches to Policy and History," *Politics and Theopolitics in the Bible and Postbiblical Literature* (ed. h. Graf Reventlow et al.; JSOTSup 171; Sheffield: JSOT Press, 1994) 176–88, who argues that Isaiah calls for quiet resistance to the Assyrians and dependence on YHWH, whereas Micah calls for direct military confrontation.

[15] See Sweeney, *Isaiah 1–39* 212–7 for discussion of this point.

Micah, however, presents a very different scenario in which the dichotomy between the nations and Israel is recognized and fostered throughout the book. The nations play a role in punishing Israel and destroying Jerusalem, but once the punishment is over, a new Davidic monarch will arise to punish the nations in turn. At no point is YHWH identified with a specific empire in the manner by which Isaiah identifies YHWH with Persia, nor does Micah envision a future in which YHWH authorizes the rule of Israel/Jerusalem by a foreign monarch. For Micah, the issue is corrupt leadership within Jacob that must be corrected so that righteous Davidic leadership can emerge. In short, Micah does not envision Jacob's ultimate submission to the nations, but instead looks toward the restoration of an independent Israelite/Judean state ruled by a Davidic monarch.

III

Clearly, Isaiah and Micah look forward to an era of peace for Israel and the world at large, but they conceive that era differently. Such differences point to debate in Judah during the early Persian or post-exilic period concerning the future of the newly restored state centered at the Temple in Jerusalem. The book of Isaiah points to a future when Israel will be restored, but it will stand as part of the larger Persian empire with which YHWH identifies. Such a position corresponds to that represented in Ezra and Nehemiah, which project a future in which Judah continues to function as a province of the Persian empire and its major leaders are authorized by the Persian state.[16] Micah, however, points to the emergence of an independent state, ruled by a Davidic monarch that will bring YHWH's punishment to the nations and stand at their center. Such a position corresponds to that of Haggai and Zechariah, both of which point to the overthrow of the nations as part of their respective scenarios for the future of Jerusalem/Judah and the world at large.[17] Although past reconstructions of post-exilic Judean debates concerning the future of the nation have posited institutional conflict between priestly and visionary parties,[18] this analysis points to debate within post-exilic

---

[16] See Klaus Koch, "Ezra and the Origins of Judaism," *JSS* 19 (1974) 173–97, who argues that Ezra's return to Jerusalem is styled as a fulfillment of prophecies concerning the return to Jerusalem from Babylonian exile in the book of Isaiah. See also J. G. McConville, "Ezra-Nehemiah and the Fulfillment of Prophecy," *VT* 36 (1986) 205–24, who points to the interrelationship between Ezra-Nehemiah and prophetic texts in Isaiah and Jeremiah, but argues that Ezra-Nehemiah indicate dissatisfaction with Persian rule.

[17] See the relevant sections of my commentary, *The Book of the Twelve Prophets*, for discussion of Haggai and Zechariah.

[18] E. g., Paul Hanson, *The Dawn of Apocalyptic* (Philadelphia: Fortress, 1975). Cf. Stephen Cook, *Prophecy and Apocalypticism: The Postexilic Social Setting* (Minneapolis: Fortress, 1995), who argues that the apocalyptic literature presupposes the language and perspectives of the Zadokite priesthood that stood at the center of Judean society rather than the marginalized visionary groups postulated by Hanson.

prophetic circles concerning the future of Jerusalem/Judah either as part of the larger Persian empire or as a restored Davidic monarchy.[19]

Appendix 1

Structure Analysis: Isaiah 2–4

Prophetic Announcement Concerning the Cleansing of Zion for Its Role as the Center for YHWH's World Rule	Isaiah 2–4
I. Superscription	2:1
II. Announcement Proper	2:2–4.6
A. Announcement concerning the future establishment of Zion as center for YHWH's world rule	2:2–4
B. Address concerning the cleansing of Zion for this role	2:5–4:6
1. first address concerning the need for cleansing	2:5–9
a. invitation to house of Jacob to join with nations and YHWH at Zion	2:5
b. explanatory address to YHWH concerning Jacob's unfitness to assume this role	2:6–9
2. second address concerning process of cleansing: announcement of the Day of YHWH	2:10–21
3. third address concerning the process of cleansing: application to Judah and Jerusalem	2:22–4:6
a. introductory plea to desist from self-reliance	2:22
b. explication concerning Jerusalem and Judah	3:1–4:6
1) prophetic judgment speech against Jerusalem and Judah	3:1–4:1
2) prophetic announcement of salvation for cleansed remnant of Israel in Jerusalem	4:2–6

Reference:

Marvin A. Sweeney, *Isaiah 1–39, with an Introduction to Prophetic Literature* (FOTL 16; Grand Rapids and Cambridge: William Eerdmans, 1996) 87–96.

---

[19] This is a slightly revised version of a paper presented at the Society of Biblical Literature International Meeting, Lahti, Finland, July 19, 1999.

Appendix 2

Structure Analysis: Micah 2–5

Prophetic Announcement Concerning the Punishment and Restoration of Jerusalem and Judah	Micah 2–5
I. Woe speech against Israel culminating in Israel's exile	2:1–13
II. Prophet's response: announcement concerning YHWH's plan to exalt remnant of Israel/Jacob in Zion	3:1–5:14
A. speech formula	3:1aα^1
B. speech proper: prophetic announcement concerning YHWH's plan to exalt remnant of Israel/Jacob in Zion	3:1aα^2–5:14
1. concerning the failure of Israel's leaders	3:1aα^2–8
2. concerning the punishment and exaltation of Jerusalem/Judah	3:9–5:14
a. concerning the punishment of Zion	3:9–12
b. concerning the exaltation of Zion	4:1–5:14
1) exaltation of Zion at center of nations	4:1–5
2) exaltation of Zion defined	4:6–5:14
a) initial statement: YHWH/shepherd will gather lame/dispersed for eternal rule on Zion	4:6–7
b) addresses to Zion and Beth Lehem/Ephrata concerning YHWH's plans	4:8–5:14
i. to Zion: dominion will come after distress	4:8–14
ii. to Beth Lehem/Ephrata: Davidic king will come to restore security of Israel	5:1–14

References:

Marvin A. Sweeney, *King Josiah of Judah: The Lost Messiah of Israel* (Oxford and New York: Oxford University Press, 2001) 287–300;
idem, *The Book of the Twelve Prophets* (Berit Olam; Collegeville: Liturgical, 2000) 2:337–416.

15. Zechariah's Debate with Isaiah

I

The last several decades have seen tremendous methodological change in the modern critical study of the prophetic books.[1] For much of the late-nineteenth and twentieth centuries, scholars employed a variety of diachronic tools, such as form- and redaction-critical analysis, that frequently resulted in a fragmented reading of the prophetic books. Books such as Isaiah were divided into several parts that were considered as if they were independent prophetic books, based upon the view that the segments of the book presented the works of different prophets who lived in different historical periods. Likewise, individual oracles would be singled out as "authentic," resulting in the dismissal of much material as the theologically irrelevant works of later redactors or tradents who misunderstood the words of the prophets and corrupted their meaning. But scholars are increasingly turning to synchronic literary reading strategies that consider the literary form, perspectives, and intertextual relationships of an entire prophetic book. Frequently, the perspectives of traditional interpreters play an important role in such discussion. This, of course, does not entail a naive rejection of earlier diachronic methods, but it often provides an opportunity for both synchronic and diachronic perspectives to be employed together. The book of Isaiah, for

---

[1] For discussion of the contemporary study of the prophetic literature, see Joseph Blenkinsopp, *A History of Prophecy in Israel* (revised edition; Louisville: Westminster John Knox, 1996); Marvin A. Sweeney, "Formation and Form in Prophetic Literature," *Old Testament Interpretation: Past, Present, and Future: Essays in Honor of Gene M. Tucker* (ed. J. L. Mays et al.; Nashville: Abingdon, 1995) 113–26; idem, *Isaiah 1–39, with an Introduction to Prophetic Literature* (FOTL 16; Grand Rapids and Cambridge, 1996) 1–30; idem, "The Latter Prophets (Isaiah, Jeremiah, Ezekiel)," *The Hebrew Bible Today: An Introduction to Critical Issues* (ed. S. L. McKenzie and M. P. Graham; Louisville: Westminster John Knox, 1998) 69–94; David L. Petersen, "The Book of the Twelve/the Minor Prophets (Hosea, Joel, Amos, Obadiah, Jonah, Micah, Nahum, Habakkuk, Zephaniah, Haggai, Zechariah, Malachi)," *The Hebrew Bible Today* 95–126. For discussion of exegetical methodology in the broader filed of biblical studies, see Steven L. McKenzie and Stephen R. Haynes, eds., *To Each Its Own Meaning: An Introduction to Biblical Criticisms and their Application* (Louisville: Westminster John Knox, revised edition, 1999); John Barton, *Reading the Old Testament: Method in Biblical Study* (Louisville: Westminster John Knox, revised edition, 1996); Robert Morgan with John Barton, *Biblical Interpretation* (The Oxford Bible Series; Oxford: Oxford University Press, 1988); Douglas A. Knight and Gene M. Tucker, *The Hebrew Bible and its Modern Interpreters* (Philadelphia: Fortress, Chico: Scholars Press, 1985).

example, has benefited immensely from such study, resulting in a much richer interpretation that takes seriously both the form and formation of the entire Isaian corpus.[2]

It is with these considerations in mind that the present paper reexamines several aspects of the book of Zechariah. Three fundamental reasons underlie the choice of Zechariah. First, like Isaiah, Zechariah is generally divided into a First, Second, and Third Zechariah with little consideration as to how the component parts of the book relate to each other within the whole.[3] Second, traditional Jewish interpretation of Zechariah, including Targum Jonathan,[4] the Babylonian Talmud, and the commentaries of Rashi (R. Solomon ben Isaac, 1040–1105),[5] Abraham Ibn Ezra (1089–1164),[6] and Radak (R. David Kimḥi, 1160–1235),[7] indicate the identification of the prophet Zechariah ben Berechiah ben Iddo with one of the two men commissioned by the prophet Isaiah ben Amoz to witness the

---

[2] See Marvin A. Sweeney, "The Book of Isaiah in Recent Research," *CR:BS* 1 (1993) 141–62; idem, "Reevaluating Isaiah 1–39 in Recent Critical Research," *CR:BS* 4 (1996) 79–113; Uwe Becker, "Jesajaforschung (Jes. 1–39)," *Theologische Rundschau* 64 (1999) 1–37.

[3] For discussion of research on Zechariah, see Brevard S. Childs, *Introduction to the Old Testament as Scripture* (Philadelphia: Fortress, 1979) 472–87; Wilhelm Rudolph, *Haggai – Sacharja 1–8 – Sacharja 9–14 – Maleachi* (KAT XIII/4; Gütersloh: Gerd Mohn, 1976); David L. Petersen, *Haggai and Zechariah 1–8: A Commentary* (OTL; Philadelphia: Westminster, 1984); R. J. Coggins, *Haggai, Zechariah, Malachi* (OTG; Sheffield: Sheffield Academic Press, 1987); Carol L. Meyers and Eric M. Meyers, *Haggai and Zechariah 1–8* (AB 25B; New York: Doubleday, 1987); Samuel Amsler, André LaCocque, and René Vuilleumier, *Aggée, Zacharie, Malachie* (CAT XI/C; Geneva: Labor et Fides, 1988); Carol L. Meyers and Eric M. Meyers, *Zechariah 9–14* (AB 25C; New York: Doubleday, 1993); Henning Graf Reventlow, *Die Propheten Haggai, Sacharja und Maleachi* (ATD 25,2; Göttingen: Vandenhoeck & Ruprecht, 1993); Paul L. Redditt, *Haggai, Zechariah, Malachi* (NCeB; Grand Rapids: Eerdmans, 1993); David L. Petersen, *Zechariah 9–14 and Malachi: A Commentary* (OTL; Louisville: Westminster John Knox, 1995); Robert Hanhart, *Sacharja* (BKAT XIV/7:1–8; Neukirchen-Vluyn: Neukirchener, 1999); Edgar W. Conrad, *Zechariah* (Readings; Sheffield: Sheffield Academic Press, 1999); Michael H. Floyd, *The Minor Prophets, Part 2* (FOTL 22; Grand Rapids and Cambridge: Eerdmans, 2000) 301–58; Marvin A. Sweeney, *The Twelve Prophets* (Berit Olam; Collegeville: Liturgical, 2000) 2:559–709.

[4] For a critical edition of Targum Jonathan to the Prophets, see Alexander Sperber, *The Bible in Aramaic. Part III: The Latter Prophets according to Targum Jonathan* (Leiden: Brill, 1962).

[5] For the commentaries of Rashi on the Prophets, see standard editions of *Mikra'ot Gedolot* on the Prophets. Discussion of Rashi appears in "Rashi," *Encyclopaedia Judaica* 13:1558–65.

[6] For the commentary of Ibn Ezra on Isaiah, see many editions of *Mikra'ot Gedolot*, although it is frequently printed at the end of the book. A critical edition appears in M. Friedländer, *Commentary of Ibn Ezra on Isaiah* (2 vols.; New York: Philipp Feldheim, n.b., first edition, London, 1873). For discussion of Ibn Ezra, see "Ibn Ezra, Abraham," *Encyclopaedia Judaica* 8:1163–70.

[7] For the commentaries of Radak on the prophets, see standard editions of *Mikra'ot Gedolot*. A critical edition of Radak's commentary on Isaiah 1–39 appears in Louis Finkelstein, *The Commentary of David Kimḥi on Isaiah* (Columbia University Oriental Studies 19; New York: Columbia University, 1926). Discussion of Radak appears in "Kimḥi, David," *Encyclopaedia Judaica* 10:1001–04; Frank Talmadge, *David Kimḥi: The Man and His Commentaries* (Cambridge and London: Harvard University Press, 1975).

naming and significance of his son Maher-Shalal-Ḥash-Baz. Third, the extensive intertextual citations and allusions in Zechariah point to a special interest in the book of Isaiah on the part of Zechariah.

Consideration of each of these factors points to a concern within the book of Zechariah to present the prophet as an authentic witness to the prophecy of Isaiah. Specifically, it presents Zechariah's prophecy as a challenge to and ultimate fulfillment of the earlier work of Isaiah; whereas Isaiah viewed the rise of the Persian empire and Cyrus as an act of G-d that called upon Jews to cooperate with the Persian authorities, Zechariah maintains that the building of the Temple points to the overthrow of the Persian empire as divine sovereignty from Jerusalem is to be established over all the nations.

II

The current consensus in modern critical research holds that the book of Zechariah comprises two and possibly three major components, each of which constitutes the work of a different prophet.[8] Thus, Zechariah 1–8 is generally held to represent the work of the late-sixth century prophet, Zechariah, who prophesied in support of the building of the Second Temple. The primary basis for this conclusion is the appearance of the prophet's first person accounts of his eight visions in which he relates various images pertaining to the significance of the building of the Temple. Zechariah 9–11/12–14 is generally held to represent the work of a second, much later writer from the early Hellenistic period, who presented an apocalyptic vision of the return of the Messiah to Jerusalem and the overthrow of past leadership. The primary bases for this assertion are the formally distinct character of this material, which begins with the superscription *maśśā'*, its apocalyptic content, and the explicit mention of the Greeks as part of its portrayal of the king's return. Zechariah 12–14 is sometimes considered to be an even later work of a third Zechariah based upon its own *maśśā'* superscription and its overall portrayal of cosmic war against the nations that ultimately results in their worship of G-d at Zion during the festival of Sukkot.

Nevertheless, there is ample reason to contest the assertion that Zechariah 1–8; 9–14 or 9–11; 12–14 constitutes the literary structure of the book.[9] The fundamental reason for such a challenge is that the current consensus is based on redaction-critical considerations that are designed to identify and to isolate early or original literary units, but that do not address the question as to how those units might work together to create a rhetorically coherent text that is

---

[8] For bibliography, see the works cited in note 3 above.
[9] See now, Conrad, *Zechariah* 11–44; Sweeney, *The Twelve Prophets* esp. 561–67.

designed to communicate with its reading or listening audience.[10] Consideration of such features provides the basis for a very different view of the book's literary structure.

Indeed, the book begins, not with a superscription, but with a narrative statement that provides the chronological setting from which the entire book is to be read, "in the eighth month, in the second year of Darius, the word of YHWH was unto Zechariah ben Berechiah ben Iddo the prophet, saying ..." The following material in verses 2–6 then relates YHWH's words to the prophet in which YHWH expresses past anger at earlier generations and how those generations responded to the call to return to YHWH and follow YHWH's ways. This material therefore serves as a dated introduction to the book because it commissions the prophet to call upon the present generation to do the same thing, i. e., return to YHWH and carry out YHWH's purposes in relation to the construction of the new Temple.

Two additional narrative date formulas like that of Zechariah 1:1 appear respectively in Zechariah 1:7 and 7:1. Insofar as their dates proceed from the initial date of Zechariah 1:1 and provide the context for the material that follows in each instance, they appear to signal the beginnings of two further blocks of material that together constitute the body of the book of Zechariah.

The first appears in Zechariah 1:7, "On the twenty-fourth day of the eleventh month – it was the month of Shevat – of the second year of Darius, the word of YHWH was unto Zechariah ben Berechiah ben Iddo the prophet saying ..." The balance of the text in Zechariah 1:7–6:15 then presents the prophet's autobiographical account of the eight visions in which an angelic guide explains to him the significance of the various images that relate to the reconstruction of the Temple, including the divine horses (Zech 1:7–17); the four horns (Zech 2:1–4); the city with a wall of fire (Zech 2:5–17); the ordination of Joshua ben Jehozadak as high priest (Zech 3:1–10); the menorah and two olive shoots (Zech 4:1–14); the flying scroll (Zech 5:1–4); the woman in the ephah (Zech 5:5–11); and the four chariots proclaiming the "branch," Joshua ben Jehozadak (Zech 6:1–15).

The second appears in Zechariah 7:1, and it is syntactically related to the formula in Zechariah 1:7 by the initial, *wayĕhî*, "and it came to pass in the fourth year of Darius the king, that the word of YHWH was unto Zechariah on the fourth day of the ninth month, in Kislev ..." The narrative then relates a question posed to YHWH/Zechariah concerning the propriety of continued mourning for the loss of the Temple. Following the posing of the question in verses 1–3, the

---

[10] For discussion of rhetorical criticism and its role in assessing the interrelationship between text and audience, see Phyllis Trible, *Rhetorical Criticism: Context, Method, and the Book of Jonah* (Guides to Biblical Scholarship; Minneapolis: Fortress, 1994); Patricia K. Tull, "Rhetorical Criticism and Intertextuality," *To Each Its Own Meaning* 156–80. For discussion of the impact of such considerations on form-critical methodology, see Marvin A. Sweeney, "Form Criticism," *To Each Its Own Meaning* 58–89; Ehud Ben Zvi, *Micah* (FOTL 21B; Grand Rapids and Cambridge: Eerdmans, 2000).

prophet's answers to the question then appear in a series of sections beginning in Zechariah 7:4, each of which is introduced by a version of the formula, "and the word of YHWH was unto me/Zechariah, saying." The first in Zechariah 7:4–7 relates the prophet's contention that YHWH did not request the fast. The second in Zechariah 7:8–14 calls for righteous action on the part of the people. The third in Zechariah 8:1–17 conveys the message of past prophets who likewise called for righteous action. The fourth in Zechariah 8:18–23 portrays YHWH's call for rejoicing, not fasting, as the nations will come to Zion to join Jews now that the new Temple is about to be established.

Although most scholars consider Zechariah 7–8 to be a self-contained unit, one must ask about the function of the following material in Zechariah 9–11/12–14 insofar as it, too, is concerned with nations that will come to Zion. Although these chapters are formally distinct and may well have been composed at different times and for different purposes than Zechariah 7–8, they play an important role in the present form of the book by providing a detailed portrayal as to how the scenario of the nations' coming to Jerusalem to join Jews will take place. Thus, Zechariah 9–11 provides a detailed description of the righteous king's approach to Jerusalem and the overthrow of the worthless shepherds who have governed the people and prevented the full restoration of the nation from exile. Zechariah 12–14 then relates the warfare that will emanate from the holy center in Jerusalem as first Israel and then the nations are defeated and brought under YHWH's sovereignty, culminating in the worship of YHWH at Sukkot as all the nations join Israel in recognizing YHWH's sovereignty over all creation. It would seem then that the narrative statement in Zechariah 7:1 establishing the chronology of the question concerning fasting posed to Zechariah and the prophet's answer introduces not only Zechariah 7–8, but Zechariah 9–14, insofar as Zechariah 9–14 provides the bulk of the prophet's answer as to how YHWH's call for rejoicing at the establishment of the Temple will actually be realized throughout all of creation.

Thus, the overall structure of the book is designed to call upon the people to return to YHWH by relating the significance of the restoration of the Temple. The introductory instruction of the book in Zechariah 1:1–6 relates the basic theme that the people should adhere to YHWH's expectations. The balance of the book in Zechariah 1:7–14:21 then provides the rationale for why they should do so. Zechariah 1:7–6:15 relates the prophet's visions that point to the ultimate significance of the building of the Temple that will result in the crowning of Joshua ben Jehozadak as the "branch" or YHWH's righteous ruler. Zechariah 7–14 then relates YHWH's calls for rejoicing at the full completion of the Temple when the righteous king has been established, the worthless shepherds overthrown, and the nations join Israel at Jerusalem to acknowledge YHWH's world wide sovereignty at Sukkot.

III

Having established the literary and thematic coherence of the book on synchronic grounds, it is now necessary to consider the identity of the prophet to whom the book is attributed. The introductory chronological statements in Zechariah 1:1 and 1:7 identify the prophet as Zechariah ben Berechiah ben Iddo. This would not provide cause for special notice were it not for the fact that the narrative historical accounts of the restoration of the Temple in Ezra-Nehemiah identify the prophet not as Zechariah ben Berechiah ben Iddo, but simply as Zechariah bar Iddo (Ezra 5:1; 6:14).[11] The discrepancy in names is frequently noted, but rarely examined closely as most scholars are willing to accept the evidence of Nehemiah 12:16 that Zechariah is clearly a descendant of Iddo. Insofar as the designation "ben/bar Iddo" could indicate either that Zechariah is the son of Iddo or his grandson, the matter is not considered to be overly important to contemporary scholars.

Nevertheless, it is noteworthy that the first two elements of the name Zechariah ben Berechiah (ben Iddo) do correspond very closely to the name of one of the men chosen by the prophet Isaiah ben Amoz to witness to the birth of his son Maher-Shalal-Ḥash-Baz as a sign or symbol for the coming invasion of Israel by the Assyrian empire. According to Isaiah 8:1–4, Isaiah selected Uriah the priest and Zechariah ben Yeberechyahu to serve as "reliable witnesses" for the writing of the tablet on which the name Maher-Shalal-Ḥash-Baz was inscribed. Indeed, the name Yeberechyahu (*yĕberekyāhû*) in Isa 8:2 is a minor linguistic variant of the name Berechiah of Zech 1:1, 7 (*berekyâ*).

Although most modern scholars would correctly maintain that Isaiah and Zechariah refer to two entirely different figures who were separated historically by some three centuries, ancient and medieval sources and commentators have noted their correspondence and have drawn some conclusions as to the identity of the two figures. Thus, Targum Jonathan renders YHWH's statement to the prophet in Isaiah 8:2, "and call to witness before me as reliable witnesses the curses that I spoke for the future in the prophecy of Uriah the priest, and behold, they have come; also all the comfort that I spoke for the future in the prophecy of Zechariah bar Yeberechyah, I am about to bring it back." The reference to the curses in the prophecy of Uriah the priest refers to the prophet Uriah mentioned in Jeremiah 26:20–23, who was executed by King Jehoiakim for speaking against the city of Jerusalem in the late-sixth/early-fifth century B.C.E. The reference to the comfort of Zechariah bar Yeberechya refers to the scenario of restoration articulated by the prophet Zechariah ben Berechiah ben Iddo in the book of Zechariah.

---

[11] Cf. Nehemiah 12:16, which indicates that Zechariah is part of the Iddo clan or "house of the father."

The Babylonian Talmud likewise equates the two faithful witnesses mentioned in Isaiah 8:2 with the later prophets Uriah and Zechariah ben Berechiah ben Iddo. A baraita in bMakkot 24 relates that R. Gamaliel, R. Eleazar ben Azariah, R. Joshua, and R. Akiba went to Jerusalem. When they came to Zophim, the present-day site of Hebrew University which overlooks the old city of Jerusalem, they rent their garments and wept when they saw a fox emerge from the ruined site of the Holy of Holies following the Roman destruction of the Temple. R. Akiba, however, expressed joy. When asked to explain by his colleagues, Akiba cited Isaiah 8:2, in which G-d instructs Isaiah to summon two faithful witnesses, Uriah and Zechariah ben Yeberechyahu. Akiba states that there is no other connection between the two than to show that the words of Zechariah are conditioned by the words of Uriah, i.e., in order for Zechariah's scenario of restoration to take place, Uriah's scenario of destruction must first be realized. In the perspective of the Talmud, Isaiah's witness refers to the prophet Zechariah.

Rashi makes these identifications clear in his commentary on Isa 8:2 in which he points specifically to the identification of Isaiah's Uriah the priest with the prophet Uriah ben Shemaiah from Kiriath Yearim in Jeremiah 26 and to the identification of Isaiah's Zechariah ben Yeberechiah with the book of Zechariah's purported subject, Zechariah ben Berechiah ben Iddo from the second year of Darius. To support his claim for the latter, Rashi cites Zech 8:4, "again, old men and old women will sit in the streets of Jerusalem," as a representation of the comforts that Zechariah would speak concerning the future. Rashi further asserts that Uriah serves as a sign for Zechariah in so far as Zechariah's prophecies of comfort presuppose the judgments or curses previously spoken by Uriah and realized in the form of the Babylonian destruction of Jerusalem. In this respect, he draws upon the Talmud's statement that the fulfillment of the prophecy of restoration by Zechariah is conditioned upon the fulfillment of the prophecy of destruction by Uriah. Again, Rashi presupposes the equation of the Isaian Zechariah with the later prophet Zechariah.

R. Abraham Ibn Ezra also draws upon this understanding in his commentary on Isaiah 8:2. He does not relate the equation in detail, but simply states that Uriah was then the high priest, that Zechariah was a great human being, and that the statements of the sages concerning the prophecies of Uriah and Zechariah are well known. His statement that Uriah was then the high priest explains why the priest Uriah in Isaiah 8:2 and the prophet Uriah in Jeremiah 26:20–23 should be considered as the same man. His reference to the sages of course refers to the above-cited Talmudic tradition in bMakkot 24. His reference to Zechariah as a great human being is somewhat enigmatic with respect to chronology, but it does indicate that Ibn Ezra views Isaiah's Zechariah and the prophet of the book of Zechariah as one and the same person.

Radak builds upon Rashi's position with a much more extensive commentary on Isaiah 8:2. He likewise notes the identification of Isaiah's Uriah the Priest and

Zechariah ben Yeberechyahu with Jeremiah's Uriah ben Shemaiah and Zechariah ben Berechiah ben Iddo with much the same phraseology and citations as Rashi and Ibn Ezra, but he adds references to Isaiah's later commands to "bind up the testimony and seal the Torah among my teachings" in Isaiah 8:16 so that they might be read and realized in the future. He states that although Uriah and Zechariah were from the time of Isaiah, the Talmudic sages (i. e., bMakkot 24) certify that in fact they spoke at different times as indicated by the later witnesses to their prophecy in the books of Jeremiah and Zechariah. Indeed, it is striking that Radak wrestles with the chronological implications of this claim. He states in the introduction to his commentary on Isaiah that G-d sent other prophets in the days of Isaiah, including Amos, Zechariah, and Hosea. He also states in his commentary on Zechariah 1:1 that the prophet returned to Zechariah, apparently a reference to his earlier equation of the Isaian figure with the prophet Zechariah and to his view that Zechariah's (grand)father Iddo was the author of the words of Iddo mentioned in reference to the reign of Rehoboam in 2 Chr 12:15. Certainly, the figures of Rehoboam, Isaiah, and Zechariah span a period of some four hundred years, and scholars have long recognized Radak's tendency to compress time in his understanding of historical events–he was after all fundamentally a grammarian, philosopher, and exegete, not a historian.[12] Nevertheless, Radak's placement of the prophecy of Zechariah's (grand)father Iddo in the days of Rehoboam and the writing of Zechariah's prophecy in the days of Isaiah, allows him to construct a temporal sequence that reinforces the notion that Zechariah's (and Uriah's) prophecy is well-known prior to its realization in the Second Temple period. Again, the Isaian Zechariah ben Yeberechyahu and the prophet Zechariah ben Berechiah ben Iddo are one and the same person in Radak's view.

Although one can hardly conclude on historical grounds that Isaiah's Zechariah ben Yeberechyahu and the prophet Zechariah ben Berechiah ben Iddo were the same person, the recognition of some relationship between the two figures in Targum Jonathan, the Babylonian Talmud, and in the commentaries of Rashi, Ibn Ezra, and Radak is noteworthy. Given the extensive use of the book of Isaiah in Zechariah, it would appear that the rendering of the prophet's name as Zechariah ben Berechiah ben Iddo, in contrast to Zechariah ben/bar Iddo in Ezra 5:1; 6:14, may have been a deliberate attempt by the author of Zechariah to equate the prophet with the Isaian figure.[13]

---

[12] See, e. g., Talmage, *David Kimhi* 115, who points to Radak's understanding of chronology in Judges 18–21 which requires him to follow midrashic tradition in concluding that Phineas was three hundred years old.

[13] A similar conflation of figures from two very different historical periods appears in LXX 3 Kingdoms 12:24o, in which the prophet Shemaiah the Enlamite (*Samaian ton Enlami*) delivers the dynastic oracle to Jeroboam ben Nebat. Shemaiah thereby replaces Ahijah the Shilonite who delivers the oracles to Jeroboam in MT 1 Kings 11:29–39 and LXX 3 Kingdoms 11:29–39. Most interpreters assume that Shemaiah is the same prophet who tells Rehoboam not to go to

IV

Scholars have long noted that the book of Zechariah makes extensive use of earlier biblical tradition from both the Pentateuch and the Prophets. Indeed, the prophets are well represented in the introduction to the book which refers to the attempts by the former prophets to convince the people to return to YHWH. One might also note Zechariah's citation of Jeremiah's prophecies in Jer 25:11; 29:10 that the Babylonian exile would last for some seventy years and the references to Zerubbabel or Joshua ben Jehozadak as the "branch" (Zech 3:8; 6:12), reflecting earlier statements in Jer 23:5; 33:15 that refer to the future righteous Davidic monarch as the "branch." They are also well represented throughout Zechariah 7–14[14] and the prophet Isaiah is particularly well represented in these chapters to the extent that some early modern critics even argued that Zechariah 9–14 represented the earlier work of Isaiah or at least that of the Isaian figure Zechariah ben Yeberechyahu.[15] Although this hypothesis can hardly be accepted, it is apparent that Zechariah 7–14 indicates a major interest in the prophets and especially in the Isaian tradition.

Zechariah's interest in Isaiah appears in chapters 7–8, which relate the question concerning the need for continued mourning for the loss of the Temple now that it is to be rebuilt. After questioning whether the requirement for mourning was indeed authorized by YHWH, the narrative in Zechariah 7:4–7 reports Zechariah's initial answer that the time for rejoicing has come instead, and that such rejoicing was authorized by the former prophets. Zechariah 7:8–14 then reiterates the rationale for punishment as the people refused to listen to the former prophets. Zechariah 8:1–17 then relates a number of quotations from and allusions to the words of various prophets, including Jeremiah, Haggai, and especially Isaiah, who appears to be the source for the statements of YHWH's zeal for Zion (Zech 8:1–2; Isa 9:6); that Jerusalem will once again be called a

---

battle against Jeroboam in 1 Kings 12:22–24, but the name, *Samaian ton Enlami*, apparently transliterates, *šĕmayāyāhû hanneḥlāmî*, "Shemaiah the Nehelemite," the false prophet mentioned in Jeremiah's letter to the exiles in Jeremiah 29:24–29. The so-called LXXB account of 3 Kingdoms 12:24a–z thereby attributes Jeremiah's dynastic oracle to a false prophet, which undermines his claims to the throne of northern Israel (cf. Zipora Talshir, *The Alternative Story: 3 Kingdoms 12:24a–z* [Jerusalem Biblical Studies 6; Jerusalem: Simor, 1993] 105).

[14] In addition to the commentaries cited above, see also W. A. M. Beuken, *Haggai – Sacharja 1–8. Studien zur Überlieferungsgeschichte der frühnachexilischen Prophetie* (SSN 10; Assen: Van Gorcum, 1967); Albert Petitjean, *Les Oracles du Proto-Zacharie* (EB; Paris: J. Gabalda; Louvain: Éditions Imprimerie Orientaliste, 1969); R. A. Mason, "The Use of Earlier Biblical Material in Zech 9–14 (A Study in Inner-biblical Exegesis)" (Ph.D. dissertation; University of London, 1973); K. Larkin, *The Eschatology of Second Zechariah. A Study of the Formation of Mantological Wisdom Anthology* (CBET 6; Kampen: Kok Pharos, 1994); Nicholas Ho Fai Tai, *Prophetie als Schriftauslegung in Sacharja 9–14. Traditions- und kompositionsgeschichtliche Studien* (Calwer Theologische Mongraphien 17; Stuttgart: Calwer, 1996).

[15] See "Zechariah," *Encyclopaedia Judaica* 16:953–8, 958, which ascribes this conjecture to Berthold as early as 1814.

righteous city (Zech 8:3; Isa 1:21–26); that old men and old women will once again sit in the streets of Jerusalem (Zech 8:4–5; cf. Isa 65:20); the references to the remnant of the people (of Israel) who will witness restoration (Zech 8:6; cf. 8:11–12); the bringing of a deliverer from the east (Zech 8:7–8; Isa 41:2; 41:25); the references to new growth in the land (Zech 8:12; Isa 1:29–31; 6:11–13; 11:1–16; 37:30–32; 40:1–11; 41:17–20; etc.); etc.

The culmination of this interest in the early words of comfort by the prophets – and especially by Isaiah – appears in Zechariah 8:19–23, which relates the interest of the nations in coming to Zion to seek YHWH and to join with Jews because they have heard that YHWH is with you (cf. Isa 7:14). The language and imagery of this passage draw heavily on the idyllic image of the nations streaming to Jerusalem to seek YHWH with the result that they will turn their swords into plowshares and their spears into pruning hooks so that they will learn war no more. This vision has a prominent place at the outset of the book of Isaiah in Isaiah 2:2–4, but it is noteworthy that the Zecharian citations of the passage do not correspond to those of the Isaian version, but to the version in Micah 4:1–5. This is particularly noteworthy in that the Mican version of this passage introduces a sequence in Micah 4–5 in which the nations will first oppress and exile Israel, and then Israel under the leadership of its new righteous Davidic monarch will attack, defeat, and subjugate the nations, resulting in the idyllic scenario articulated in Micah 4:1–5. This stands in striking contrast to the Isaian version of the passage, which presupposes that Israel will join the nations in seeking YHWH and that both the nations and Israel will share in punishment from YHWH as they are purified and prepared for the idyllic vision of Isaiah 2:2–4.[16]

It is also striking that the scenario by which this idyllic situation is achieved in Zechariah 9–14 draws heavily on Isaian texts and imagery. Ultimately, its portrayal of Jerusalem's and Israel's combat against the nations prior to their submission to YHWH corresponds to the Mican scenario by which world peace is achieved, not to the Isaian version which posits mutual punishment from YHWH for both Israel and the nations. This suggests that the Zecharian scenario by which YHWH's world wide sovereignty is recognized is deliberately intended to differ from that articulated by Isaiah. In effect, Zechariah engages in debate with Isaiah and differs concerning the means by which YHWH's sovereignty is established and recognized throughout the world. Instead of positing the scenario of mutual punishment from YHWH for both Israel and the nations as articulated in Isaiah, Zechariah follows Micah's scenario of combat between Israel and the nations that results ultimately in world peace.

---

[16] For discussion of these perspectives, see Marvin A. Sweeney, "Micah's Debate with Isaiah," *JSOT* 93 (2001) 111–24. See also Sweeney, *Isaiah 1–39*; idem, *The Twelve Prophets* ad loc.

The use of Isaian imagery appears already in the portrayal of the righteous king's approach to Jerusalem in Zechariah 9. Although many maintain that the reference to Greece in Zech 9:13 indicates that the chapter depicts Alexander the Great's approach to Jerusalem, the itinerary varies from that of Alexander and corresponds much more closely to the itinerary of the Assyrian kings mentioned in Isaiah 10:5–34 and Isaiah 36.[17] Indeed, this itinerary provides an important part of the basis for those who would claim that elements of Zechariah 9–14 are to be dated to the time of Isaiah. It is noteworthy that in the Isaian itineraries, the route from Aram through Phoenicia and Philistia was a route by which Israel was conquered and subjugated to the Assyrians, the route in Zechariah becomes the route by which the righteous king approaches Jerusalem to redeem it from the oppression of enemy nations.

Isaian imagery continues to play a major role in Zechariah 10–11, which relates YHWH's calls for the removal of the shepherds who rule the people. After stating that the people wander like sheep for lack of a shepherd, Zechariah states the intention to punish the leaders so that the people of Judah and Joseph will be strengthened. The scenario continues with YHWH's signaling for the restoration of the exiles of the people from Assyria and Egypt; this of course employs the imagery of Isaiah 11, which envisions the restoration of Israel's and Judah's exiles at the time when a righteous Davidic monarch will ascend to the throne. It concludes with a symbolic act by the prophet, who dismisses three shepherds in the Temple and dons the implements of a worthless shepherd to symbolize the incompetent leadership of the people. Most scholars presuppose that this material criticizes the Jewish leadership of the people in the post-exilic period, but several observations are in order: 1) the use of Isaiah 11 in this passage points to the restoration of righteous Davidic rule; 2) the term shepherd in Isaiah never denotes a Jewish monarch, but it is employed in reference to the Persian king Cyrus, i.e., "my shepherd" (Isa 44:28), who is also designated as YHWH's messiah and Temple builder in Isaiah 44:28; 45:1; and 3) the symbolic dismissal of three shepherds likely refers to the failure of the first three Persian monarchs, Cyrus, Cambyses, and Darius, to bring about YHWH's plans for world peace as articulated in Isaiah. The concluding curse against the worthless

---

[17] Alexander marched along the southern coast of Asia Minor, and defeated the Persians at Issue, located at the point where the eastern Mediterranean coast turns to the south. He reportedly sent an expedition to Damascus, but led the bulk of his army south along the Mediterranean coast into Phoenicia (See Martin Hengel, "The Political and Social History of Palestine from Alexander to Antiochus III [333–187 B.C.E.] in *The Cambridge History of Judaism. Volume 2: The Hellenistic Age* [ed. W. D. Davies and L. Finkelstein; Cambridge: Cambridge University Press, 1989] 35–78, esp. 35–45). By contrast, Zechariah 9 indicates an itinerary that begins in northern Syria, i.e., Hadrach, Damascus, and Hamath, which corresponds generally to the Isaian depiction of the routes taken by the Assyrian kings in their invasions of the land of Israel (see Isaiah 10:5–34; 36:13–31). When read in relation to the return of the righteous kin in Zech 9:9–10, the itinerary suggests the routes by which the new Davidic king would return to Jerusalem from exile in Mesopotamia.

shepherd in Zechariah 11:17, that a sword may strike his arm and that his right eye may become dim, apparently takes up Isaian references to YHWH's grasping the right hand of the "shepherd" Cyrus in Isaiah 45:1 and statements that YHWH's servant is a dim wick that will not be quenched (Isa 42:3–4). It would appear that Zechariah 10–11 disputes Isaiah's contention that YHWH's messiah Cyrus, and indeed the Persian kings at large, would bring about the restoration of the people and the city of Jerusalem as the center for YHWH's world-wide sovereignty.

Finally, Zechariah 12–14 lays out the scenario of combat against the nations that will take place on the Day of YHWH. Indeed, the Day of YHWH is one of the most prominent motifs of the book of Isaiah; following the idyllic picture in which Israel is invited to join the nations who seek YHWH at Zion in Isa 2:2–5, Isaiah 2:6–21 describes a scenario of world wide judgment in which YHWH will punish all who are arrogant on the Day of YHWH. The motif appears at several key points afterwards, i.e., Isaiah 13; 34; etc. and the constant references to "that day" in the first part of the book demonstrate its pervasive role. But whereas Isaiah envisions a cooperative effort in which YHWH's Torah and justice will go out to the nations who will then return the exiles of Israel and Judah to Jerusalem, Zechariah 12–14 envisions a scenario in which Judah and Jerusalem will engage in combat against the nations of the world that threaten them, most notably against the shepherd associated with YHWH, until Judah and the house of David are purified and the nations acknowledge YHWH's sovereignty by worshipping at the Temple at Sukkot. At that point, the book of Zechariah closes with the assertion that Jerusalem and Judah will then constitute the holy center of the world.

Again, Zechariah challenges Isaiah's assertion that YHWH's purposes are to be accomplished through the rule of the Persian monarchs. Instead, it envisions a scenario in which foreign rule is overthrown, and Judah and Jerusalem are purified to serve as the holy center for YHWH's world-wide sovereignty.

V

In conclusion, it appears that a synchronic reading of the book coupled with the observation made by the Targum, Talmud, Rashi, Ibn Ezra, and Radak, that Zechariah ben Berechiah ben Iddo is to be associated with the Isaian figure Zechariah ben Yeberechyahu, points to a deliberate attempt by the author of the book of Zechariah to challenge or debate key elements of Isaiah's vision for the establishment of YHWH's sovereignty throughout the world. Whereas Isaiah envisions a cooperative effort between the nations and Israel in which the Persian king, Cyrus, will act as YHWH's messiah and temple builder, the book of Zechariah envisions the overthrow of foreign rule and the reinstitution of a purified Judah and house of David as a result of the reestablishment of the Temple in Jerusalem. This of course points to debate within Judaism, particularly within the prophetic tradition, during the early Persian period concerning the significance of the restoration of the Temple and the continuity of foreign rule. Whereas parties centered around the Isaian tradition, such as Ezra and Nehemiah, would have advocated submission to and cooperation with the ruling Persian authorities as the appropriate means to realize YHWH's sovereignty in the world, other parties centered around the Mican and Zecharian traditions, such as Haggai and perhaps Zerubbabel, would have looked forward to the overthrow of Persian rule as the final step prior to the establishment of YHWH's sovereignty on earth.[18]

Appendix

The Book of Zechariah: Structure Analysis

I. Introduction to the Book of Zechariah: Narrator's Presentation of YHWH's initial word to Zechariah, 1(?) Heshvan/8th month, 520 B.C.E./year2Darius=Y2D	1:1–6
II. Narrator's Presentation of Y's later words to Z: visions & pronouncements	1:7–14:21
A. Narrator's Presentation of Visions, 24 Shebat/11th month, 519 B.C.E./Y2D	1:7–6:15
1. 1st vision: divine horses: Y's anger against nations and plan to restore Temple and Jerusalem	1:7–17
2. 2nd vision: 4 horns: restoration of altar symbolizing scattering of Israel and punishment of nations	2:1–4
3. 3rd vision: city with wall of fire: restoration of J-m and joining of nations	2:5–17
4. 4th vision: ordination of Joshua ben Jehozadak as high priest: Branch and stone	3:1–10
5. 5th vision: menorah and 2 olive shoots: Zerubbabel and foundation stone	4:1–14
6. 6th vision: the flying scroll: justice for land from Temple	5:1–4
7. 7th vision: woman in ephah: iniquity of land sent to Shinar/Babylon	5:5–11
8. 8th vision: 4 chariots proclaim crowning of Branch/ Joshua ben Jehozadak	6:1–15

---

[18] Earlier versions of this paper were presented at the Annual Meeting of the Association for Jewish Studies, Chicago, IL, December 19–21, 1999, the Claremont Bible Lectures, Claremont School of Theology, Claremont, CA, March 27–28, 2000, the Methodist Theological Seminary, Seoul, May 17, 2000, and the University of Pretoria, July 20, 2000. I would like to thank Prof. Marc Brettler, Association for Jewish Studies Program Chair in Bible, Associate Dean Karen Dalton, Claremont School of Theology, Prof. Tai-il Wang, Methodist Theological Seminary, Seoul, and Prof. Jan G. Van der Watt, University of Pretoria, for their efforts in making these presentations possible.

15. Zechariah's Debate with Isaiah 235

B. Narrator's Presentation of Pronouncements, 4 Kislev/9th month, 518 B.C.E./Y4D	7:1–14:21
1. question posed to YHWH/Zechariah concerning continued mourning for loss of Temple: Torah question/Priestly Torah	7:1–7
a. report of question posed	7:1–3
b. Zechariah's report of his initial response: YHWH did not request fast	7:4–7
1) Zechariah's introduction to YHWH's speech: prophetic word transmission formula	7:4
2) YHWH's speech: instruction to speak; assertion of what YHWH wants	7:5–7
2. YHWH's/Zechariah's answer: YHWH wants rejoicing and righteous action, not fasting: Torah answer/ Priestly Torah	7:8–14:21
a. first part: call for righteous action and explanation of punishment	7:8–14
b. second part: summation of former prophets: call for righteous action	8:1–17
c. third part: Zechariah's report of YHWH's oracles and pronouncements concerning restoration of Zion/ Temple as holy center of world	8:18–14:21
1) introduction: prophetic word transmission formula	8:18
2) oracles and pronouncements proper	8:19–14:21
a) oracles	8:19–23
(1) time for rejoicing, not fasting	8:19
(2) nations come to Zion to seek YHWH	8:20–22
(3) nations join Jews	8:23
b) pronouncements	9:1–14:21
(1) removal of worthless shepherds	9:1–11:17
(2) nations' recognition of YHWH's sovereignty at Zion/Sukkot	12:1–14:21

Part 5: Apocalyptic and Proto-Apocalyptic Texts

16. The Priesthood and the Proto-Apocalyptic Reading of Prophetic and Pentateuchal Texts

I

Scholarly consensus correctly holds that apocalyptic literature developed initially from prophetic literature.[1] Many scholars also follow the lead of Otto Plöger, Paul Hanson, and others in maintaining that apocalyptic literature reflects the frustrations and dissatisfaction of visionary or prophetic elements in exilic and early-Persian period Judean society that were opposed and suppressed by the emerging power of the Zadokite priesthood in Jerusalem.[2] Such elements attempted to express their visions of an ideal eschatological era in which the deity would act to restore the peace and stability of the created world by destroying the wicked. Of course, such visions of the future were rejected by Zadokite priestly circles that viewed the restoration of the Jerusalem Temple as the signal that such divine action was already underway.

A recent study by Stephen Cook challenges this polarized view of the emergence of apocalyptic by demonstrating that proto-apocalyptic literature in Ezekiel 38–39; Zechariah 1–8; and Joel reflects the language and perspectives of the central Zadokite priesthood rather than that of marginalized or disenfranchised groups.[3] This, of course, makes a great deal of sense when one considers the role of the priesthood in the development of later prophetic literature, i. e., Jeremiah, Ezekiel, Zechariah, who themselves are Levitical or Zadokite priests, or the role

---

[1] Such a conclusion is supported especially by the appearance of a number of proto-apocalyptic texts within the context of larger prophetic books, i. e., Isaiah 24–27; 34–35; 56–66; Ezekiel 38–39, or proto-apocalyptic prophetic books that appear within the larger corpus of prophetic literature, i. e., Zechariah and Joel. Although some have argued that wisdom literature also provides an essential source for apocalyptic, it should be noted that wisdom perspectives, particularly the analytical evaluation of elements in the world of creation, play a foundational role in ancient Near Easter and Israelite/Judean oracular divination and prophecy. For overviews of this discussion, see esp. A. Kirk Grayson and John J. Collins, "Apocalypses and Apocalypticism," *ABD* 1:279–88; Paul Hanson, "Apocalypticism," *IDB[S]* 28–34.

[2] Otto Plöger, *Theocracy and Eschatology* (trans. S. Rudman; Oxford: Basil Blackwell, 1968); Paul Hanson, *The Dawn of Apocalyptic* (Philadelphia: Fortress, 1975). See also Robert P. Carroll, *When Prophecy Failed: Cognitive Dissonance in the Prophetic Traditions of the Old Testament* (New York: Seabury, 1979).

[3] Stephen L. Cook, *Prophecy and Apocalypticism: The Postexilic Social Setting* (Minneapolis: Fortress, 1995).

of the Levitical singers in Chronicles where they are identified as prophets.[4] Cook does not, however, consider the role that intertextual citation of or allusion to earlier prophetic and pentateuchal texts and traditions plays in each of these proto-apocalyptic texts.[5]

Inner-biblical citations and allusions, especially from the Pentateuch and the Prophets, do indeed play a key role in every proto-apocalyptic text of the Hebrew Bible. This calls for consideration of the role that such citations and allusions play in defining the Zadokite character of each work. This paper therefore reexamines key proto-apocalyptic texts, including Joel; Zechariah; Ezekiel 38–39; and Isaiah 24–27; 56–66, in an effort to demonstrate their use of earlier prophetic and pentateuchal texts and traditions to define their central Zadokite perspectives. On this basis, it maintains that the Jerusalemite priesthood provided the social matrix for the reading and reinterpretation of earlier prophetic and pentateuchal texts and traditions that was intended to point to the restoration of the Temple at the center of creation as the goal for the scenarios of punishment and restoration laid out in earlier prophetic and pentateuchal works. It therefore represents the sympathetic appropriation of such literature by the priesthood that is concerned with carrying out its essential function to teach the people YHWH's Torah.

II

We begin with Joel, whose inner-biblical citations and allusions are among the best documented of the proto-apocalyptic texts.[6] Cook's analysis of Joel is based

---

[4] Of course, such priestly prophets recall earlier figures, such as Moses and Samuel, who likewise combined priestly and prophetic roles. For discussion of the role of priestly identity in relation to Jeremiah, Ezekiel, and Zechariah, see Marvin A. Sweeney, "The Latter Prophets (Isaiah, Jeremiah, Ezekiel)," *The Hebrew Bible Today: An Introduction to Critical Issues* (ed. S. L. McKenzie and M. P. Graham; Louisville: Westminster John Knox, 1998) 69–94; idem, *The Twelve Prophets* (Berit Olam; Collegeville: Liturgical, 2000) 2:559–709; idem, "Ezekiel: Zadokite Priest and Visionary Prophet of the Exile," *OPIAC* 41 (2001). For discussion of the Levitical singers or prophets in Chronicles, see David L. Petersen, *Late Israelite Prophecy: Studies in Deutero-Prophetic Literature and in Chronicles* (SBLMS 23; Missoula: Scholars Press, 1977).

[5] For discussion of intertextual citation and allusion in biblical literature, see esp. Michael Fishbane, *Biblical Interpretation in Ancient Israel* (Oxford: Clarendon Press, 1985); Patricia Tull Willey, *Remember the Former Things: The Recollection of Previous Texts in Second Isaiah* (SBLDS 161; Atlanta: Scholars Press, 1997); Benjamin D. Sommer, *A Prophet Reads Scripture: Allusion in Isaiah 40–66* (Stnaford: Stanford University Press, 1998) esp. 6–31; and Patricia Tull, "Rhetorical Criticism and Intertexutality," *To Each its Own Meaning: Biblical Criticisms and their Application* (Louisville: Westminster John Knox, 1999) 105–21.

[6] For discussion of the inner-biblical citations and allusions in Joel, see esp. Siegfried Bergler, *Joel als Schriftinterpret* (BEATAJ 16; Frankfurt: Peter Lang, 1988) and Marvin A. Sweeney, *The Twelve Prophets* 1:145–87; idem, "The Place and Function of Joel in the Book

in part upon an integrated reading of the book in which he argues that Joel 1–2 expresses the fear of apocalyptic desolation and Joel 3–4 expresses the hope for apocalyptic salvation.[7] Although the structure of the book may be configured differently, he demonstrates the interrelationship between the so-called historical and apocalyptic sections of the book insofar as it expresses Joel's eschatological scenario concerning the Day of YHWH in which apocalyptic judgment is redirected so that Judah's elect will survive the judgment. The Zadokite character of the book appears in its use of cultic terminology and especially in its use of Zion theology to depict YHWH's defense of the Jerusalem Temple.

It is in relation to Joel's use of Temple-centered Zion theology that the inner-biblical citations and allusions must be considered. Cook notes Joel's dependence on Ezekiel 38–39, which depicts YHWH's defense of Zion from attack by the nations, but he does not discuss Joel's use of the Exodus tradition, nor does his discussion of the Day of YHWH motif in Joel indicate Joel's dependence on earlier prophetic texts. Both are essential to defining the Zadokite character of the work because they point to the use of natural elements from the world of creation to express YHWH's actions in the world. They thereby express the Zadokite notion that the Jerusalem Temple constitutes the holy center of all creation that ensures the stability and proper functioning of the created world order.[8] Bergler in particular notes Joel's use of the Exodus locust plague tradition (see esp. Exod 10:1–20) to depict YHWH's defense of Jerusalem and the Temple against an unspecified or typological threat. The reference to YHWH's wind that will be poured out over all flesh is also noteworthy insofar as it is based upon the dry "east wind," i. e., the Ḥamsin or Sharav that brings about both the locust plague and the plague of darkness in Exod 10:1–20, 21–29.[9] The Sharav is a natural feature of the climate of the land of Israel, and indeed it darkens the sun and prompts the moon to appear blood-red as portrayed in Joel 3:1–5.

The depiction of YHWH's wind in Joel 3 is also noteworthy insofar as it expresses the manifestation of the Day of YHWH motif that permeates Joel's apocalyptic scenario. The motif is well-known in prophetic tradition, but it appears especially through Joel's extensive citations of the book of Obadiah throughout Joel 3–4. Obadiah employs the Day of YHWH motif to depict divine judgment against Edom, and Joel's use of the Obadian texts likewise represents a typologization of the Day of YHWH motif to express YHWH's capacities to judge and defend the Jerusalem Temple. The use of other biblical traditions, including Jehoshaphat's defeat of Edom and other nations in the

---

of the Twelve," *Society of Biblical Literature 1999 Seminar Papers* (Atlanta: Society of Biblical Literature, 1999).

[7] For his discussion of Joel, see Cook *Prophecy and Apocalypticism* 167–209.

[8] See also Jon D. Levenson, *Sinai and Zion: An Entry into the Jewish Bible* (Minneapolis: Winston, 1985); idem, *Creation and the Persistence of Evil: The Jewish Drama of Divine Omnipotence* (New York: Harper and Row, 1988).

[9] Bergler, *Joel als Schriftinterpret*; Sweeney, *Twelve Prophets* 1:173–6.

"Valley of Blessing" (2 Chronicles 20), the reversal of the famous "swords into plowshares" oracle from Mic 4:1–5/Isa 2:2–4, and Amos' depiction of mountains dripping wine and hills flowing with milk, likewise contribute to Joel's depiction of YHWH's deliverance of Jerusalem and the Temple.

In all cases, Joel's use of the Exodus and prophetic material demonstrates a capacity to eliminate the specific referents of these texts, i.e., Egypt and Edom in particular, so that they might be employed typologically to depict YHWH's actions in relation to any enemy that might threaten Jerusalem. In this manner, Joel demonstrates a capacity to extract earlier texts and traditions from their original contexts so that they might be applied to later contexts. The identity of the enemy that threatens Jerusalem might change, but the results are the same.

Similar observations may be made in relation to Gog and Magog text in Ezekiel 38–39. Cook correctly maintains that these chapters must be read as part of the Ezekiel tradition, rather than as a later insertion, and that they express Zadokite language and perspectives.[10] Especially noteworthy are his observations of links to the language of the Holiness Code and the extensive influence of the Zion tradition concerning YHWH's defense of Jerusalem and the Temple.

Ezekiel is elsewhere heavily dependent upon earlier biblical (and non-biblical) tradition, and Ezekiel 38–39 is no exception. One may note the reference in Ezek 38:17 to past prophecy in YHWH's statement to Gog, "Thus says my L-rd YHWH, 'Are you he of whom I spoke in the earlier days by the hands of my servants the prophets of Israel, who prophesied in those days for years that (I would) bring you upon them?'" No specific identity for the earlier prophets is given, but subsequent allusions indicate Isaiah and possibly Jeremiah. There is also a concern to draw upon texts from Genesis that are concerned both with creation and its reversal. Thus, the announcement of YHWH's judgment against Gog in Ezek 38:18–23 includes a catalog of creatures in the created world that are drawn from Genesis 1, "and the fish of the sea and the birds of the heavens and the beasts of the field and all the creeping things that crawl upon the earth and every human being that is upon the face of the earth shall shake before me," which relates once again the Zadokite view of the Temple as the center of the created world order. The references to plague, bloodshed, torrential rain, hailstones, fire, and sulfur likewise recall the reversal of creation in the flood traditions, the destruction of Sodom and Gomorrah, and the curses of Deuteronomy. Allusions to the prophetic traditions of Isaiah appear in Ezek 39:4–5 in the images of Gog and his warriors fallen upon the mountains and the open fields so that they will become the prey of birds and wild animals. Such an image is particularly well known in Isa 14:3–23, which describes the downfall of the oppressor who would shake the earth and its kingdoms only to be killed and left unburied on the battlefield to be trampled like a cast off branch, and Isa 14:24–27, which describes

---

[10] Cook, *Prophecy and Apocalyptic* 85–121.

YHWH's slaying of the Assyrian tyrant on the mountains of Israel. The images of the fires that burn for seven years to cleanse the land draw upon the seven year sabbatical cycle of Lev 25:1–7; Exod 23:10–11; Deut 15:1–18 that is necessary to maintain the purity of the land in Zadokite thought. The burial of Gog and his warriors in the "Valley of Hamon-Gog" is a deliberate pun on the "Valley of Hinnom," mentioned in 2 Kgs 23:10; Jer 7:30–34 as a place of idolatry where children and dead bodies were burned. The depiction of the sacrificial feast at which the birds and wild animals will eat constitutes a play on Isaiah's image of a banquet of the nations on Zion (Isa 25:6–10) and recalls the curses of Lev 26:22 and Deut 28:26. It also aids in completing the process of the cleansing of the land so that YHWH's "glory" might be manifested in it once again. The reference to YHWH's hiding the divine face so that Israel would go into exile likewise recalls the Isaian expression of this theme (Isa 8:16–18).

Ezekiel 38–39 appears to draw upon earlier tradition, particularly from Genesis, Leviticus, and Isaiah, to depict the defeat of Gog as a fulfillment of past prophecy. Insofar as Gog represents the nations that exiled Israel and defiled the land, it would appear that he represents Babylon and its allies, which is also the target of the prophecies in Isaiah 14. This is particularly striking when one considers that Isaiah 14 originally depicted YHWH's judgment against an Assyrian monarch, but it was later applied to Babylon.[11]

The book of Zechariah is quite clearly the product of Zadokite priestly circles insofar as Zechariah himself is identified as a priest. Although Cook takes up the entire book, he focuses his discussion on Zechariah 1–8, primarily because earlier scholars argue that such priestly literature could not be classified as apocalyptic.[12] In arguing for the proto-apocalyptic character of the book, Cook notes its radical eschatology, dualism, visionary patterning, superhuman figures, and messianic concerns. Messianic concerns in Zechariah 9–14 indicate a continuing phase of the same tradition history.

Scholars have long recognized the use of earlier pentateuchal and prophetic tradition in both the first and second parts of Zechariah.[13] The visions in particular draw upon pentateuchal traditions concerned with the construction of the tabernacle and the ordination of the priesthood.[14]

---

[11] Marvin A. Sweeney, *Isaiah 1–39, with an Introduction to Prophetic Literature* (FOTL 16; Grand Rapids and Cambridge, 1996) 218–39.

[12] Cook, *Prophecy and Apocalyptic* 123–65.

[13] For discussion of the inner-biblical citations and allusions in Zechariah as a whole, see esp. Sweeney, *Twelve Prophets* 559–709; Rex Mason, "The Use of Earlier Biblical Material in Zech 9–14. A Study in Inner-biblical Exegesis" (Ph.D. dissertation; University of London, 1973; Katrina J. Larkin, *The Eschatology of Second Zechariah: A Study of the Formation of a Mantological Wisdom Anthology* (CBET 6; Kampen: Kok Pharos, 1994); and Nicholas Ho Fai Tai, *Prophetie als Schriftauslegung. Traditions- und kompositionsgeschichtliche Studien* (CTM 17; Stuttgart: Calwer, 1996).

[14] Thus, the vision of the four horns and artisans presupposes the construction of the altar in Exod 27:1–8; 38:1–8. The vision of the ordination of Joshua ben Jehozadak presupposes the

The prophetic citations and allusions are much more pronounced, especially since the vision reports employ the standard formulas of prophetic visionary experience and oracles. Indeed, the introduction to the book calls for the people's return to YHWH, citing the past experience of the nation's ancestors who failed to heed the former prophets. It also portrays Zechariah as a witness to the Isaian tradition, insofar as it identifies the prophet known simply as Zechariah bar Iddo in Ezra 5:1; 6:14 as Zechariah ben Berechiah ben Iddo, in keeping with the reference to Zechariah ben Yeberechiah in Isa 8:1–4, who served as a witness to the birth of Isaiah's son and the oracles associated with that event. I have attempted to demonstrate elsewhere that the book of Zechariah is especially concerned with the book of Isaiah insofar as it presents Zechariah as a witness to the Isaiah tradition.[15] Indeed, the book of Zechariah employs this device to debate the program laid out in the book of Isaiah insofar as it understands the construction of the Temple to be a signal for the overthrow of the power of the nations rather than as a signal for Israel's submission to and cooperation with the nations. Thus, Zechariah 7–8 employs Isaian and other prophetic texts or traditions to indicate that the time of rejoicing proclaimed by the former prophets has now arrived with the construction of the Temple. Especially notable is the citation in Zech 8:9–23 of the famous "swords into plowshares" passage from Isa 2:2–4/Mic 4:1–5, which portrays the nations coming to Zion to learn YHWH's Torah. Interestingly, this passage introduces the apocalyptic scenario in Zechariah 9–14, which portrays YHWH's wars against Israel followed by the nations in order to bring about that scenario of world peace around the Temple at Sukkot. These chapters draw upon Isaiah's depiction of the approach of the Assyrian monarch in Isa 10:5–34 to portray the approach of the righteous king in Zechariah 9. Zechariah 10–11 employ the imagery of the righteous Davidic king from Isaiah 11 to depict YHWH's rejection of the three shepherds, apparently the Persian monarchs, Cyrus, Cambyses, and Darius, in an effort to oppose the Isaian calls for acceptance of the Persian monarch Cyrus as YHWH's messiah and Temple builder. Lacking a Davidic king in this period, it is perhaps no accident that Zechariah 6 considers the high priest Joshua ben Jehozadak to be YHWH's righteous monarch. Finally, the scenario of combat against the nations in Zechariah 12–14 draws heavily upon the Isaian tradition of world-wide combat on the

---

ordination of the priests in Exodus 29; Leviticus 8–9. The vision of the menorah presupposes the construction of the tabernacle *měnōrôt* in Exod 25:31–40; 37:17–24 and the eternal lights mentioned in Exod 27:20–21; Lev 24:1–4. The vision of the flying scroll presupposes the tradition of reading the Torah before the Temple in Deut 31:9–14 and the dimensions of the Temple Ulam from which it was read (see 1 Kings 6:3; cf. 6:23–28).

[15] In addition to my commentary on Zechariah noted above (Sweeney, *Twelve Prophets* 559–709), see Marvin A. Sweeney, "Zechariah's Debate with Isaiah," *The Changing Face of Form Criticism for the Twenty-First Century* (ed., M. A. Sweeney and E. Ben Zvi; Grand Rapids and Eerdmans, 2003) 335–50.

day of YHWH against all the arrogant of the earth, both in Israel and among the nations (Isaiah 2:6–21; 13–27).

Again, the use of earlier pentateuchal and prophetic tradition is designed to demonstrate the fulfillment of that tradition in the building of the Temple and the ordination of Joshua ben Jehozadak. Ironically, however, earlier material is employed to argue against the Isaian program of acceptance of Persian rule to call for YHWH's combat against the wicked of Israel and the nations so that all might acknowledge YHWH at the Jerusalem Temple on the festival of Sukkot.

The last set of texts to be considered is Isaiah 24–27; 56–66. Cook does not treat these texts, but Plöger and Hanson consider them as expressions of proto-Hasidean or visionary groups that are opposed to the priestly establishment of their day.[16] Both scholars base their arguments in distinctions made between the righteous and the wicked in these texts. Plöger argues that the eschatological outlook of the righteous distinguishes them from the non-eschatological outlook of the Chronicler and the priests. Hanson likewise employs eschatological criteria and adds to it the reinterpretation of myth to posit a visionary group that opposed the Zadokite priesthood of the Jerusalem Temple.

Nevertheless, both scholars overlook some important considerations that point to eschatological thinking among Zadokite priestly circles. One is the fundamental distinction that priestly literature makes between the righteous and the wicked, both on moral and ritual grounds.[17] Another is the view that the Jerusalem Temple is the holy center of creation, in which the Temple provides the focal point for the revelation of YHWH's Torah to human beings by which they will sanctify and thus complete creation. Third, is the role that mythology plays in defining that role, i. e., there is an interrelationship between elements of the Pentateuchal narrative and the structure of the Temple, such as the depiction of Eden imagery in the Temple itself, that symbolizes the challenges posed to human beings in relating to YHWH.[18] In this respect, the Zadokite priesthood followed by the chosen people of Israel serve as the representatives of all humankind before YHWH at the Temple. Their task is to sanctify creation by implementing YHWH's Torah within it. Fourth, is the depiction in Ezra-Nehemiah of Ezra's return to Jerusalem as a fulfillment of (Deutero-)Isaiah's prophecy of a new exodus.[19] It must be kept in mind, however, that Ezra-Nehemiah does not portray the full realization of the Isaian program, only its beginning.

Both Isaiah 24–27 and 56–66 posit a fundamental transformation of the world of creation as the Temple is reestablished at its center. Isaiah 24–27 posits a world that lies wasted and desolate as a result of its inhabitants having violated

---

[16] See Hanson, *Dawn* 32–208; Plöger, *Theocracy* 53–78.
[17] See, for example, texts such as Leviticus 19 and the Temple entrance liturgies of Psalms 15; 24.
[18] See the discussion by Levenson, *Sinai and Zion* 137–42. See also Ezekiel 47.
[19] See esp. Klaus Koch, "Ezra and the Origins of Judaism," *JSS* 19 (1974) 173–97.

the *běrît ʿôlām*, "eternal/world covenant," a fundamental concept in priestly theology.[20] In such a scenario, the punishment of the wicked signals the return of YHWH, celebrated in liturgical song, that leads to a banquet or feast upon YHWH's holy mountain for all peoples. This in turn signals the restoration of holy sacrifice at the center of creation in the Jerusalem Temple. Among the results are the restoration of all creation, the removal of death, and the downfall of the city of chaos as the world is cleansed of the iniquity of the evil. It must be kept in mind that death appears within the overall framework of the priestly creation epic as a result of human wrongdoing in the Garden of Eden, and that it is the priesthood that stands between the people and the impurity of death (see Num 16:1–17:15). The use of the term "city of chaos" (Hebrew, *qiryat tôhû*) is likewise telling insofar as the priestly account of creation posits that creation proceeds out of chaos, and that human wrongdoing has the capacity to return the world to chaos. I have discussed the use of earlier prophetic tradition, both from Isaiah and from other prophetic traditions including Jeremiah, Hosea, Amos, and Micah, and note that these citations both facilitate the integration of Isaiah 24–27 into the book as a whole and point to the reestablishment of YHWH's sovereignty over all creation (and humankind) at Zion.[21] Such concerns of course recall the initial image in Isa 2:2–4 of the procession of the nations to Zion so that they might learn YHWH's Torah.

Similar observations may be made concerning Isaiah 56–66. Overall, these chapters portray the restoration of Israel, the Temple, and YHWH's sovereignty at Zion and the significance of this restoration for creation and humankind at large. The depiction of YHWH's throne in heaven and footstool on earth hardly represents a rejection of the Temple; instead it portrays the fundamental role of the Temple as the symbol of the interrelationship between heaven and earth in priestly thought. Many note the inclusion of foreigners and eunuchs in the worship of the Temple, but such inclusion calls for observance of justice, the Shabbat, and YHWH's covenant, all of which entail observance of the tradition as conceived by the Zadokite tradition. It thereby also entails an early form of conversion to Judaism. In this respect, it is noteworthy that Ezra holds to Deuteronomic Torah, which calls for the acceptance of *gērîm*, "resident aliens," who accept Israel's G-d and laws, and he never expels foreign men, presumably because they would constitute such *gērîm*. Furthermore, the portrayal of the

---

[20] For general discussion of Isaiah 24–27, see Sweeney, *Isaiah 1–39* 311–53.

[21] In addition to my commentary cited above (Sweeney, *Isaiah 1–39*), see Sweeney, "New Gleanings from an Old Vineyard: Isaiah 27 Reconsidered," *Early Jewish and Christian Exegesis* (ed., C. A. Evans and W. F. Stinespring; Atlanta: Scholars Press, 1987) 51–66; idem, "Textual Citations in Isaiah 24–27," *JBL* 107 (1988) 39–52; John Day, "A Case of Inner-Scriptural Interpretation: The Dependence of Isaiah xxvi.13–xxvii 11 on Hosea xiii 4–xiv 10 (Eng. 9) and its Relevance to Some Theories of the Redaction of the Isaian Apocalypse," *JTS* 31 (1980) 309–19; Donald C. Polaski, *Authorizing an End: The Isaiah Apocalypse and Intertextuality* (BibInt 50; Leiden: Brill, 2001).

nations returning the exiles to Jerusalem and offering sacrifices at the Temple is consistent with the priestly view that the Temple stands at the holy center of all creation and humankind. Although some have read Isa 66:23 as an indication that YHWH will select priests and Levites from among the nations, the recent study by Schramm indicates that this is a misunderstanding and that YHWH will chose priests and Levites from among the returned exiles.[22] Again, I have traced the intertextual references within this material to other texts throughout the book of Isaiah, which both points to an effort to integrate these chapters into the book as a whole and to redefine the concept of the Davidic covenant so that it calls for the acceptance of the reestablished Temple and priesthood under Persian rule.[23] Such a conceptualization is in keeping with priestly thought, which posits that YHWH is the sovereign of the world.

III

In conclusion then, it would appear that the use of earlier pentateuchal and prophetic texts and traditions play a constitutive role in defining the Zadokite perspective concerning the role of the Temple at the center of creation in proto-apocalyptic texts. It is especially noteworthy that such use demonstrates a capacity to extract fundamental principles or models from one historical context so that they might be applied to the very different circumstances of a later apocalyptic scenario. Such use points to an interest in the sympathetic reading and interpretation of earlier texts and traditions that support the Zadokite view concerning the restoration of creation. In this respect, such reading and interpretation presupposes one of the essential roles of the priesthood to teach the people the Torah of YHWH so that they might understand and fulfill the expectations of YHWH (see Lev 10:10–11).

---

[22] Brooks Schramm, *The Opponents of Third Isaiah: Reconstructing the Cultic History of the Restoration* (JSOTSup 193; Sheffield: Sheffield Academic Press, 1995) 171–73.

[23] For studies of intertextual citation and allusion in Isaiah 56–66, see Marvin A. Sweeney, "Prophetic Exegesis in Isaiah 65–66," *Writing and Reading the Scroll of Isaiah: Studies of an Interpretative Tradition* (ed. C. C. Broyles and C. A. Evans; VTSup 70.1; Leiden: Brill, 1997) 455–74; idem, "The Reconceptualization of the Davidic Covenant in Isaiah," *Studies in the Book of Isaiah. Festschrift W. A. M. Beuken* (BETL 132; Leuven: Peeters and Leuven University Press, 1997) 41–61; see also Sweeney, "Isaiah and Theodicy after the Shoah," *Strange Fire: Reading the Bible after the Holocaust* (BibSem 71; ed. T. Linafelt; Sheffield: Sheffield Academic Press, 2000) 208–19.

17. The End of Eschatology in Daniel?
Theological and Socio-Political Ramifications of the Changing Contexts of Interpretation[1]

I

The book of Daniel is well recognized as the only full example of an apocalyptic book in the Hebrew Bible.[2] Within a narrative context that presents a series of visions revealed to the Jewish sage Daniel and interpreted to him by angelic figures, it projects the course of human history through four major world empires. The sequence begins with Babylonia and culminates in the establishment of the kingdom of "the holy ones of the Most High" following the downfall of the unnamed fourth empire and its arrogant boasting monarch. Insofar as this kingdom will arise "at the time of the end" (Dan 9:17; 10:40; 12:4) through the action of hands that are not human (cf. Dan 2:34; 8:25), Daniel also emerges as the quintessential eschatological book of the Hebrew Bible. Both Rabbinic Judaism and early Christianity tend to view the book as a prediction of the last things following the downfall of the Roman empire according to their respective understandings of the manifestation of G-d's rule or the messianic age.[3] Later interpreters within both traditions would shift the identity of the last empire–medieval Jewish interpreters would generally view the fourth empire as Islam or later oppressors, and medieval Christian interpreters would tend to focus on the Antichrist – but the projected scenario of an eschatological end of human history remained intact. In contrast to the majority of their ancient and

---

[1] This is a revised version of a paper originally read at a conference entitled, "From Alexander to Machiavelli: Heritage and New Age," Institute for Antiquity and Christianity, Claremont Graduate University, February 27, 1998. I would like to thank the conference organizers, Nancy van Deusen and Jon Ma. Asgeirsson, for their invitation to participate in the conference.

[2] For discussion of the characteristics of apocalyptic literature, see John J. Collins, *Daniel, with an Introduction to Apocalyptic Literature* (FOTL 20; Grand Rapids: Eerdmans, 1984) 1–24; John J. Collins, ed., "Apocalypse: The Morphology of a Genre," *Semeia* 14 (1979). For surveys of research on Daniel, see Klaus Koch et al., *Das Buch Daniel* (Erträge der Forschung, 144; Darmstadt: Wissenschaftliche Buchgesellschaft, 1980); P. R. Davies, *Daniel* (OTG; Sheffield: JSOT Press, 1985).

[3] For discussion of the history of interpretation on Daniel in Jewish and Christian traditions, see John J. Collins, with Adela Yarbro Collins, *Daniel* (Hermeneia; Minneapolis: Fortress, 1993) 72–123.

medieval predecessors, modern historical-critical scholars are nearly unanimous in arguing that the present form of Daniel was composed between the years 167 and 164 B.C.E. to support the Judean revolt against the Seleucid Syrian monarch Antiochus IV Epiphanes (r. 175 to 164 B.C.E.).[4]

Many details remain to be settled, but it is quite clear that the book of Daniel has a blatantly political and nationalistic agenda which it conveys with religious language concerning divine action on behalf of the righteous at the end of time. Nevertheless, theological interpretation of Daniel has yet to come fully to grips with this perspective. Most modern theological interpreters attempt to differentiate by one means or another between the political goals of the Hasmonean revolt and the theological goals of the book as suggested by its religious language. Many simply ignore the political dimensions of Daniel or judge them to be irrelevant in assessing its theological message, and focus exclusively on its eschatological elements in order to project an ahistorical and apolitical kingdom of G-d as the culmination of human history.[5] Others point to the long history of composition, and argue that the political agenda stems from a relatively late redaction that influenced only limited portions of the book.[6] The earliest levels of composition, such as the court tales in chapters 1–6, indeed were composed to demonstrate how Jews might accommodate themselves to the realities of Gentile rule and have nothing to do with the Hasmonean revolt.[7] Some even suggest that the Jewish revolt against the Hellenistic Seleucid empire is sinful or contrary to the will of G-d.[8] Such sentiments are no doubt influenced by the failure of the Hasmonean dynasty to maintain Judean independence; the ultimate destruction of Jerusalem, the Temple, and Judea in the failed revolts against Rome in the

---

[4] For discussion of the rise of the Seleucid and Ptolemaic empires and their impact upon Judea, see Victor Tcherikover, *Hellenistic Civilization and the Jews* (New York: Atheneum, 1982); W. D. Davies and Louis Finkelstein, eds., *The Cambridge History of Judaism. Volume Two: The Hellenistic Age* (Cambridge: Cambridge University Press, 1989); Elias Bickerman, *The Jews in the Greek Age* (Cambridge: Harvard University Press, 1988); idem, *From Ezra to the Last of the Maccabees: Foundations of Postbiblical Judaism* (New York: Schocken, 1962); Martin Hengel, *Judaism and Hellenism* (Philadelphia: Fortress, 1974); Emil Schürer, revised and edited by Geza Vermes et al., *The History of the Jewish People in the Age of Jesus Christ* (Edinburgh: T&T Clark, 1973) 1:125–99.

[5] Davies, *Daniel* 81–8; Aage Bentzen, *Daniel* (HAT 19; Tübingen: J. C. B. Mohr [Paul Siebeck], 1952) 7–10; Otto Plöger, *Das Buch Daniel* (KAT 18; Gütersloh: Gerd Mohn, 1965) 174–9; W. Sibley Towner, *Daniel* (Interpretation; Atlanta: John Knox, 1984) 1–15; Gerhard von Rad, *Old Testament Theology* (New York: Harper & Row, 1965) 2:308–15.

[6] Collins, *Daniel*, 1993, 37–8; André LaCocque, *Le Livre de Daniel* (CAT 15b; Neuchâtel and Paris: Delachaux et Niestlé, 1976) 19–20.

[7] W. Lee Humphreys, "A Life Style for Diaspora: A Study of the Tales of Esther and Daniel," *JBL* 92 (1973) 211–23.

[8] Norman Porteous, *Daniel: A Commentary* (OTL; Philadelphia: Westminster, 1965) 21, for example, states, "The narrowness of the reaction to hellenism with its failure to recognize the great contribution that Hellenism had to make to the world doubtless in the event condemned Israel to the ghetto, but there were those who did not lose heart because the end did not come as the author of this book expected it would."

first and second centuries C.E.; and the subsequent ascendancy of Christianity with its own eschatology developed around the figure of Jesus. They are also influenced by the perspectives of Christian theology, which views the destruction of the Jewish state and the Jerusalem Temple as a confirmation of Jesus' messiahship and a justification for the spread of Christianity throughout the world.[9]

Indeed, subsequent theological interpretation reflects the failure of Daniel's political aims as Judea was destroyed by Rome, and Jews were forced into exile from their own land and persecution at the hands of foreigners over the course of some eighteen hundred years. Daniel therefore represents not the hope for Jewish national independence – after all, that hope had failed, at least until 1948 – but the hope of all humankind for redemption. To a certain extent, such interpretation of Daniel presupposes an Enlightenment hermeneutical perspective, derived ultimately from the universal worldview of Hellenism, that values the needs and perspectives of the many over those of the few in that it fundamentally calls for the assimilation of the particular into the universal as an expression of the will of G-d.[10] Such a perspective may represent a sincere attempt to promote the good of humankind at large by attempting to apply the book to as much of humanity as possible, but equally well meaning critics point out that such a perspective suppresses and destroys the rights and perspectives of the few who differ from those of the many.

As we enter a new hermeneutical age of postmodernism that values the needs and perspectives of the few as autonomous and potentially interrelated or interactive components of the many,[11] the time has come to reassess the importance of the political agenda of the book of Daniel in theological interpretation. Two major aspects of the book will be treated, including the interpretation of the so-called court tales in Daniel 1–6 within the context of the book as a whole and the function of mythology and earlier biblical tradition in the visions of Daniel 7–12. Overall, the balance of this paper attempts to demonstrate three major points. The first is that the political and religious aims of the Hasmonean revolt

---

[9] See Mark 13, especially vv. 24–27, which is dependent upon the book of Daniel.

[10] For perspectives on the treatment of Jews during the period of the Enlightenment, particularly the expectation that they should assimilate into the larger gentile culture, see Arthur Hertzberg, *The French Enlightenment and the Jews: The Origins of Modern Anti-Semitism* (New York: Columbia University Press, 1968); Paul Lawrence Rose, *Revolutionary Antisemitism in Germany from Kant to Wagner* (Princeton: Princeton University Press, 1990).

[11] For discussion of postmodern biblical study, see Marvin A. Sweeney, "Reconceiving the Paradigms of Old Testament Theology in the Post-*Shoah* Period," *Biblical Interpretation* 6 (1998) 140–61; Leo Perdue, *The Collapse of History: Reconstructing Old Testament Theology* (OBT; Minneapolis: Fortress, 1994); A. K. M. Adam, *What is Postmodern Biblical Criticism?* (Guides to Biblical Scholarship; Minneapolis: Fortress, 1995). Cf. John Barton, *Reading the Old Testament: Method in Biblical Study* (revised edition; Louisville: Westminster John Knox, 1996); Steven L. McKenzie and Stephen R. Haynes, eds., *To Each Its Own Meaning: An Introduction to Biblical Criticisms and Their Application* (Louisville: Westminster John Knox, 1993); Robert Morgan with John Barton, *Biblical Interpretation* (The Oxford Bible Series; Oxford: Oxford University Press, 1988).

permeate the entire book, not only the visions of Daniel 7–12, and that they must be taken seriously in theological interpretation. The book of Daniel does not seek to escape this world; it is actively engaged in it.[12] The second is that the use of mythological and symbolic language in the vision accounts reflects the language and perspectives of the priesthood and priestly interest in freeing the Jerusalem Temple from foreign control. The third is that the book of Daniel is designed as a response to prophetic books, such as Isaiah, Jeremiah, and Ezekiel, that identify G-d's will with the efforts of foreign nations to conquer, absorb, and thereby to punish or purify Israel and Judah. In contrast, Daniel maintains that the time of punishment has come to an end and that G-d now identifies with the overthrow of foreign oppressors and the establishment of an autonomous Jewish state. Such a perspective has theological ramifications concerning the need to establish and maintain autonomous identity in a pluralistic world.

II

Modern critical scholars generally agree that the book of Daniel is a composite work in that the vision reports of chapters 7–12 and the court tales of chapters 1–6 appear to have very different compositional histories.[13] Whereas the vision reports presuppose the period of Antiochus' attempts to suppress Judea and the beginnings of the Hasmonean-led revolt against the Seleucid empire, chapters 1–6 reflect a very different socio-historical milieu and perspective in that they focus on the experiences of Jews who attempt to maintain their Jewish identities while serving in the court of a foreign king. There is little indication that the Jewish protagonists in the court tales, Daniel and his three companions, have any interest in challenging or overthrowing the gentile monarchs that they serve. They are loyal courtiers who have good relations with their gentile overlords and provide them with their talents and skills. At the same time, they maintain their adherence to G-d and their observance of Jewish practice, and continue to demonstrate their loyalty to the monarch even at times when their adherence to Judaism prompts charges of disloyalty. There are formal differences between chapters 1–6 and 7–12 as well. Chapters 1–6 are formulated as third person narratives about Daniel and his companions, whereas chapters 7–12 are formulated as first person accounts by Daniel of his visionary experiences. Furthermore, the events reported in chapters 1–6 are set in the royal courts of Babylon, whereas

---

[12] Several recent studies and commentaries share this contention, e. g., L. F. Hartman and A. A. Di Lella, *Daniel* (AB 23; Garden City: Doubleday, 1978) 103–10; Daniel L. Smith-Christopher, "The Book of Daniel: Introduction, Commentary, and Reflections," *The New Interpreter's Bible* (ed. L. E. Keck et al.; Nashville: Abingdon, 1996) 7:17–152. Cf. Brevard Childs, *Introduction to the Old Testament as Scripture* (Philadelphia: Fortress, 1979) 608–23.

[13] See John J. Collins, *The Apocalyptic Vision of the Book of Daniel* (HSM 16; Missoula: Scholars Press, 1977) 8–11.

the events related in the visions of chapters 7–12 are concerned with the land of Israel. As a result of these differences, critics maintain that chapters 1–6 were composed in a much earlier period of good relations between Jews and gentile monarchs, perhaps during the fourth or third centuries B.C.E., and were only later placed into their present literary context with the anti-Seleucid visions of chapters 7–12.

Nevertheless, there are various indications that the present form of the court tales in Daniel 1–6 have been redactionally reworked and reread for placement within their present context in order to support Jewish efforts to oppose the anti-Jewish policies of Antiochus IV and to overthrow the Seleucid monarchy.[14] Although the court tales of Daniel 1–6 are formulated in third person narrative style in contrast to the first person perspectives of the vision reports, the two segments are linked together in a consistent narrative framework by introductory third person notices in Dan 7:1 and 10:1, which provide a transition from the earlier narratives about Daniel to his vision reports. Whatever their compositional prehistory might be, the redactional combination of these two portions indicates that they are meant to be read together in the present form of the book. H. H. Rowley has already made a number of observations concerning the interest in Daniel 1–6 in supporting the Maccabean revolt,[15] but his conclusions have not been widely accepted. He was unable to account adequately for the role of the Jerusalem Temple as the holy center of Judaism on the one hand and of the cosmos on the other. He likewise did not account for the satirical aspects of these narratives in which Nebuchadnezzar, the Babylonian monarch who destroyed the Temple of Solomon in 587 B.C.E., is presented as a positive role model for a Gentile monarch who acknowledges the power and sovereignty of G-d. The following considerations indicate that, like the vision reports in Daniel 7–12, the present forms of the court tales in Daniel 1–6 are indeed redactionally reformulated to support the Maccabean revolt.

The first involves the narrative of chapter 1, in which Daniel and his three companions, Hananiah, Mishael, and Azariah, are brought to Babylon to be trained for service in the court of King Nebuchadnezzar. Nebuchadnezzar is well-

---

[14] See recent studies on the court tales which maintain that they are designed to take up issues of political power (John Goldingay, "The Stories in Daniel: A Narrative Politics," *JSOT* 37 [1987] 99–116), identity (Lawrence M. Wills, *The Jew in the Court of the Foreign King: Ancient Jewish Court Legends* [Minneapolis: Fortress, 1990], or sovereignty (Danna Nolan Fewell, *Circle of Sovereignty: Plotting Politics in the Book of Daniel* [2nd edition; Nashville: Abingdon, 1991]). For recent discussion of the issues of rewriting and rereading text in redaction critical theory, see Rolf Knierim, "Criticism of Literary Features, Form, Tradition, and Redaction," *The Hebrew Bible and Its Modern Interpreters* (eds. D. A. Knight and G. M. Tucker; Chico: Scholars Press, 1985) 123–65; Marvin A. Sweeney, "Formation and Form in Prophetic Literature," *Old Testament Interpretation: Past, Present, and Future* (Fest. G. M. Tucker; ed., J. L. Mays et al.; Nashville: Abingdon, 1995) 113–26.

[15] "The Unity of the Book of Daniel," *The Servant of the L-rd and Other Essays on the Old Testament* (2nd edition; Oxford: Blackwell, 1965) 247–80.

known as the monarch who destroyed Jerusalem and the Temple of Solomon, and carried the Jewish people into Babylonian exile. This point is emphasized at the outset of the narrative which rehearses this role and highlights his carrying off to Babylon the holy vessels of the Temple as spoil. It is also of relevance to the Maccabean revolt, which was prompted in part by Antiochus' profaning the Jerusalem Temple, interfering with the succession of the high priests, setting up an image of Zeus (and later himself) for worship, requiring the sacrifice of swine's flesh, and other measures.[16] All of these actions render the Temple unfit for its role as the sacred center of Judaism.[17] Against this background, Daniel and his companions are given gentile names, trained in Babylonian language and literature, and assigned portions of food from the king's table. Such measures, of course, undermine Jewish identity and facilitate the assimilation of the four young Jews into Babylonian culture. The issue of food is particularly important in that kosher meat was produced in ancient Judaism from animals that were slaughtered at the Temple altar. The request to eat only vegetables emphasizes this concern. The narrative is thereby designed to focus the reader's attention on the absence of the Temple as holy center and the efforts of Daniel and his companions to function despite its absence. They demonstrate their willingness to cooperate with Nebuchadnezzar, but they maintain their loyalty to Judaism and they are rewarded by G-d for doing so. The figure of Nebuchadnezzar constitutes a foil for Antiochus IV in that he does not continue to act against Jews once they have submitted to him. Antiochus, however, continues to attack Jews and Judaism even after Judea has submitted to the Seleucid empire.

The second court tale in chapter 2 presents Daniel's interpretation of Nebuchadnezzar's dream. The Babylonian monarch had seen a great statue whose head was made of gold, its chest and arms of silver, its middle and thighs of bronze, its legs of iron, and its feet of iron and clay. A nonhuman hand struck the feet of the statue with a stone, causing it to collapse. Daniel's interpretation of the dream identifies the various body parts with a succession of kingdoms in which the gold head is identified with Nebuchadnezzar's Babylon and the mixed iron and clay feet with the Ptolemaic and Seleucid dynasties, both of which were of mixed Greek and indigenous descent. The destruction of the two feet of course symbolizes the destruction of the Ptolemaic and Seleucid dynasties by G-d, which will result in the establishment of an everlasting kingdom. The statue calls to mind the common ancient Near Eastern and Greek practice of erecting large statues of gods or monarchs, i.e., colossi, for worship or veneration. Some have attempted to associate Nebuchadnezzar's statue with that erected

---

[16] See 1 Macc 1:41–61; 2 Macc 3:1–6:11.

[17] On the role of the Temple as sacred center of Judaism and the cosmos, see Jon D. Levenson, "The Temple and the World," *Journal of Religion* 64 (1984) 275–98; idem, *Sinai and Zion: An Entry into the Jewish Bible* (Minneapolis: Winston, 1985).

by Antiochus in the Jerusalem Temple.[18] Such identification is inconclusive, of course, but the emphasis on G-d's role in establishing and deposing kings is noteworthy with respect to the Maccabean period. There were no major attempts on the part of Jews to revolt against a Hellenistic monarch until the time of Antiochus IV. Indeed, Alexander was warmly welcomed into Jerusalem, and the period of Ptolemaic rule was relatively peaceful and stable.[19] Sentiments for the overthrow of the Hellenistic monarchies emerge only in relation to Seleucid rule. Some suggest that the favorable attitude displayed to Nebuchadnezzar in Daniel 2 renders him an inappropriate model for Antiochus IV, but this misses the point.[20] Nebuchadnezzar is not a model for Antiochus in the present context, even though he destroyed the Temple and carried Jews into Babylonian exile. Nebuchadnezzar appears at the beginning of the historical process in Daniel 2, and the Seleucid and Ptolemaic dynasties appear only at the end of the process. It was only in the Hellenistic period that the exile or the period of foreign rule initiated by the Babylonians would come to an end.

Daniel 3 relates directly to the Maccabean period in that it presents Nebuchadnezzar's decree that all in his empire would have to worship a golden statue that he had built, or suffer death by burning in a fiery furnace. Various officers of the king charged that Jews were disloyal in that they did not worship the statue, and Daniel's companions were thrown into a fiery furnace as punishment. The three Jews were protected by G-d, and when Nebuchadnezzar saw that they were unharmed, he acknowledged the power of G-d and freed them. This narrative relates easily to the accounts of Antiochus's attempts to establish pagan cults in the Jerusalem Temple, where he erected an idol of Zeus Olympus or Baal Shamem for worship, forbade the practice of Judaism, and decreed death for those who did not obey. Again, objections are raised to a correlation between the portrayal of Nebuchadnezzar and Antiochus.[21] Nebuchadnezzar repents, but Antiochus does not. But the presentation of Nebuchadnezzar here represents the ideal model of action that Antiochus should follow according to the author of Daniel 3. Even Nebuchadnezzar, who destroyed the Temple in Jerusalem, repents before the power of G-d.

Daniel 4 relates the narrative concerning Nebuchadnezzar's madness and his acknowledgement once again of the power of G-d. According to the narrative, the king has a dream in which he is portrayed as a great tree that is cut down, and his mind is changed from that of a human to that of an animal as he lives with the animals in the wild. This portrayal draws heavily on Isaiah 10–11 and Ezekiel 31, both of which employ the image of a great tree chopped down to symbolize the downfall of an oppressive monarch. Daniel interprets the dream

---

[18] For discussion, see Collins, *Daniel*, 1993, 162–5.
[19] Tcherikover, *Hellenistic Civilization* 39–49, 59–73.
[20] E.g., Collins, *Apocalyptic Vision* 10.
[21] Collins, *Apocalyptic Vision* 10.

as a decree by G-d that is designed to teach Nebuchadnezzar that heaven is sovereign. Some argue that the narrative relates to the Babylonian monarch Nabonidus, who left Babylon to live in the wilderness for a lengthy period of time while his son Belshazzar served as regent. This may have played a role in the composition of an earlier version of the story, but the present form and context of the narrative establishes a very clear association with Antiochus IV, who had a reputation for madness and erratic behavior. A primary example is his claim to be a manifestation of Zeus, which prompted him to adopt the name Epiphanes (manifest god). Polybius, Livy, and Diodorus, however, refer to Antiochus as Epimanes (mad) instead.[22] Once again, Nebuchadnezzar's acknowledgement of G-d's sovereignty is intended as a model for Antiochus.

Daniel 5 relates the narrative concerning Belshazzar's banquet in which the young king, erroneously presented here as the son of Nebuchadnezzar, sees the writing on the wall that points to the overthrow of his kingdom. Once again, the issue of the profaned Temple comes to the forefront as Belshazzar and his companions drink from the vessels taken by his father from the Jerusalem Temple and praise their various gods. Many argue that the story presupposes the fall of Nabonidus and his son Belshazzar to the Persian empire,[23] but the present form and context of the narrative points once again to Antiochus, who removed the holy vessels from the Jerusalem Temple as part of his efforts to finance his Egyptian campaign and to convert the Temple into a pagan shrine. During the course of his interpretation of the writing on the wall, Daniel reiterates Nebuchadnezzar's fall from greatness and his acknowledgement of the power of G-d. Because Belshazzar does not likewise acknowledge G-d, he dies at the end of the chapter, perhaps as a projection of Antiochus's fate.

Finally, Daniel 6 relates a plot against Daniel in which the sage violates a decree by Darius the Mede, a fictitious figure presented here as the new king after Belshazzar, that forbade praying to anyone but the king for thirty days. As an observant Jew, Daniel of course continues to pray to G-d at the prescribed times. When the plotters point this out to Darius, who knew nothing of the plot against Daniel, the unwitting king reluctantly condemns Daniel to be thrown into a lion's den. When Daniel is saved by G-d, Darius acknowledges G-d as the true power in the universe. The narrative relates once again to Antiochus, who demanded worship of himself as a god and forbade the practice of Judaism on pain of death. The presentation of Darius the Mede in this story is again to be read as a foil for Antiochus. Like Nebuchadnezzar, Darius submits to G-d, but Antiochus does not.

Although earlier versions of the court tales of Daniel 1–6 may well have been composed at a different time and for a different purpose, their present form and

---

[22] Polybius 26.10; 31.3–4; Livy 41.19–20; Diodorus 29.32; 31.16.1–2. For discussion, see Tcherikover, *Hellenistic Civilization* 175–6.

[23] See Collins, *Daniel* 243–4, for discussion.

context within the book of Daniel certainly indicate that they are meant to be read in relation to the Maccabean revolt against Antiochus IV. They call for the downfall of the Hellenistic Ptolemaic and Seleucid empires; they call for the establishment of an eternal kingdom of G-d; they satirically present Nebuchadnezzar and Darius the Mede as ideal models for the behavior of a gentile king in marked contrast to Antiochus IV; and they highlight the desecration of the Jerusalem Temple. They do not call for Jews to accommodate themselves to pagan rule. Rather, they present Jews as loyal subjects who do not deserve the enmity of foreign kings, and they call upon foreign monarchs to acknowledge the power and sovereignty of G-d. Ultimately, they call upon Jews to maintain their Jewish identity and practice like Daniel and his friends, by arguing that G-d will redeem the righteous and bring down those who would force them to renounce their heritage and their G-d.

III

It is already well known that the vision reports of Daniel 7–12 are designed to predict the downfall of Antiochus IV and the establishment of a kingdom of the holy ones of the Most High in the aftermath of his demise. It is also well known that these chapters draw upon mythological themes from both pagan and biblical tradition and that they presuppose earlier prophetic tradition, particularly the books of Ezekiel, Jeremiah, and Isaiah. In assessing the use of these traditions in Daniel, however, most interpreters presuppose Gunkel's principle, *Endzeit gleich Urzeit*, "the time of the end is like the time of the beginning," i.e., the world will return to a state of being like that preceding creation and all earthly history.[24] Thus, the visions of Daniel point to the end of human history in which the heavenly realm will replace earthly reality.

This principle has had immense influence on our understanding of apocalyptic literature in general as scholars have developed constructs of apocalyptic circles that essentially give up hope for success or fulfillment in earthly reality and begin to look beyond this world for deliverance or understanding. Such a view presupposes that the apocalypticists have given up on trying to change this world or to bring about righteousness, and simply wait for G-d to punish the wicked. Thus, Carroll argues that the origins of apocalyptic literature and thinking reflect a deep sense of cognitive dissonance in late prophetic circles, which were unable to reconcile the divine promises of protection and security for the people of Israel and Judah with the experiences of Assyrian, Babylonian, and Persian exile and subjugation.[25] Hanson posits the origins of apocalyptic

---

[24] See David L. Petersen, "Eschatology (OT)," *ABD* 2:575–9, esp. 578.

[25] Robert P. Carroll, *When Prophecy Failed: Cognitive Dissonance in the Prophetic Traditions of the Old Testament* (New York: Seabury, 1979).

in a fundamental conflict between visionary circles and priestly circles as the visionaries began to reject the postexilic priestly establishment and to look to the end of human history for the ultimate realization of G-d's promises.[26] Although both of these scholars deal primarily with earlier prophetic traditions, their views reflect discussion of Daniel in that Daniel's visions must reflect an outgrowth of prophetic visionary experience or wisdom speculation that looks beyond a world in which the Temple and priesthood have failed to provide an adequate ground for existence and understanding of reality for the Jewish people.

But scholars are coming to recognize that these models of a prophetic or wisdom-oriented visionary tradition that stands in opposition to priestly circles derive from much later Wellhausenian models that are based ultimately in Protestant Christianity's attempts to identify with its own understanding of prophetic perspective and its rejection of Roman Catholic and Jewish models of priestly hierarchy and legal authority. In essence, the vision of a new heavenly world order in apocalyptic literature was read as an expression of Protestant Christianity's theological perspectives and world view, i. e., as a reenactment of Martin Luther's challenge to the Roman Catholic Church or Jesus' rejection of the Temple and Pharisaic law. More recent advances in the study of the social functions and symbolic character of myth points to the fact that although myth employs the symbols, images, and language of a world beyond earthly reality, it attempts to express current earthly reality and to influence its course.[27] Thus, the Babylonian creation epic *Enuma Elish* not only explains the origins of the universe, it also portrays Babylonian political hegemony as a reality that is rooted and legitimized in the creation of the universe. Likewise, the Psalms' portrayal of YHWH's defense of Zion from the nations expresses the belief that YHWH (and Judean soldiers) will defend Jerusalem from very real historical enemies. When these models are applied to the study of apocalyptic literature, they point to attempts to influence action and perspectives in this world.

Furthermore, recent study of the symbolism, images, and basic world view of apocalyptic literature stresses that it does not come from marginalized groups that are opposed to the Temple establishment; rather, it derives from central priestly circles themselves who employ mythology to express their views concerning events that take place in the world.[28] It must be kept in mind that the Temple in Jerusalem was conceived in priestly circles to be the holy center of all creation, not simply the holy center of the people of Israel or Judah.[29] Mythological symbolism permeates the Temple structure, its furnishings, and its observances: the

---

[26] Paul D. Hanson, *The Dawn of Apocalyptic: The Historical and Sociological Root of Jewish* Eschatology (Philadelphia: Fortress, 1975).

[27] See the articles on "Myth and Mythology" by Robert A. Oden Jr. and Fritz Graf, *ABD* 4:946–65.

[28] See Stephen L. Cook, *Prophecy and Apocalypticism: The Postexilic Social Setting* (Minneapolis: Fortress, 1995).

[29] Levenson, "The Temple and the World"; idem, "The Jerusalem Temple in Devotional and

lamp stand or menorah represents the trees of the garden of Eden,[30] the molten sea represents the Red Sea of the Exodus tradition, the holy of holies and the ark symbolize YHWH's identification with the royal house of David,[31] the major festivals, Passover, Shavuot, and Sukkot, represent the change in seasons and the agricultural cycle, etc. Heavenly and earthly reality coexist in the Jerusalem Temple, and it is expressed symbolically in the Bible's mythology.

Indeed, the forms in which Daniel's visions are expressed and their use of symbolic imagery is deeply indebted to priestly tradition and the Jerusalem Temple, even when they employ motifs derived from pagan mythology. The throne vision of Daniel 7 is a case in point. Daniel sees the four winds stirring up the sea so that four beasts emerge, a lion with eagle's wings, a bear with three tusks in its mouth, a leopard with four wings and heads, and a beast with iron teeth, ten horns, and a small horn with human eyes and a mouth speaking arrogantly. These, of course, symbolize the succession of nations that ruled Judea: Babylon, Media, Persia, and Greece, including the Ptolemaic and Seleucid rulers culminating in Antiochus IV. Daniel then sees a figure described as "One Ancient of Days," dressed in white with hair like wool, take his place on a fiery throne with wheels of burning fire. A river of fire streams forth and myriads serve and attend him as he opens the books for judgment. As Daniel watches, a human being (son of Man) comes to the Ancient One who gives him kingship. He sees the war of the arrogant small horn against the Holy Ones, and hears the judgment uttered against him for speaking against the Most High and attempting to change the seasons and the law.

Many scholars correctly note the correspondence of images in this vision with pagan themes: Daniel himself is drawn from the Ugaritic Aqhat myth; motifs from Babylonian and Ugaritic versions of the combat myth in which Marduk or Baal subdues the sea; the succession of beasts (or metals) to portray the course of world history in ancient Persian literature; the portrayal of the Ancient One in imagery much like the Canaanite El; etc.[32] Nevertheless, many of these themes are also Israelite or Judean: the combat myth is well known in biblical literature as YHWH defeats the Egyptian Pharaoh with the Red Sea; YHWH defeats mythological sea monsters such as Leviathan, Rahab, and Behemeth[33]; YHWH sits in judgment over the people Israel/Judah and the nations and their

---

Visionary Experience," *Jewish Spirituality: From the Bible to the Middle Ages* (ed. A. Green; New York: Crossroad, 1988) 32–61.

[30] Cf. Joan E. Taylor, "The Asherah, the Menorah and the Sacred Tree," *JSOT* 66 (1995) 29–54.

[31] See Baruch Halpern, *The First Historians: The Hebrew Bible and History* (San Francisco: Harper & Row, 1988) 46–54, who points to the similarity in structure between royal palaces, particularly the Davidic palace, built around an elevated throne room and the Jerusalem Temple built around the Holy of Holies.

[32] Collins, *Daniel*, 1993, 280–94.

[33] See Psalms 74; 104; Isaiah 11:11–16; 27:1; 51:9–11; Job 38:8–11.

gods (e.g., Psalms 2; 82). The use of potentially foreign motifs should not be surprising; the priest and prophet Ezekiel knows something of the Canaanite Dan El figure who brings his son back to life (Ezekiel 14:14, 20); the priestly account of the flood in Genesis 6–9 seems to be influenced by Babylonian versions of the story; the priest and prophet Zechariah is well familiar with the notion of the four winds that appears in both Babylonian and Israelite literature (Zechariah 2:10); the Psalms and Habakkuk portray YHWH's chariot racing through the heavens much like Baal who was also known as "Rider of the Clouds" (Psalm 68; Habakkuk 3).

The use of the throne vision motif, however, appears to be especially rooted in priestly traditions associated with the Jerusalem Temple or other Israelite shrines. Ezekiel 1 is the primary example of this motif, in which the priest Ezekiel sees a vision of the throne chariot of G-d while standing on the banks of Chebar canal in Babylonia. The image of YHWH and a throne chariot owes much to the imagery of the holy of holies of the Jerusalem Temple in which the ark of the covenant was kept.[34] As a priest, Ezekiel would have been quite familiar with this imagery, and it expresses his understanding of the presence of G-d. Isaiah likewise sees a vision of YHWH with the seraphim flying about singing YHWH's praises. This, too, presupposes the imagery of the Holy of Holies. Although Isaiah is no priest, his view of the divine throne presupposes his placement by the pillar of the Temple where the king stands, which allows him a view into the Holy of Holies. It is hardly surprising that a prophet like Isaiah might have a vision that is informed by Temple imagery. Prophets in Israel and the ancient Near East often appear to be Temple-based oracle diviners,[35] such as Samuel (1 Samuel 3), who experiences a revelation from G-d while sleeping by the ark in the Shiloh sanctuary. Indeed, other elements of Daniel's vision correspond well to Temple or priestly imagery: the four winds correspond to the four horns of the Temple altar in Zechariah's visions; the throne with wheels and fire of the One Ancient of Days corresponds well to the image of the ark and to Ezekiel's visions; the white garments of the One Ancient of Days call to mind the white linen garments worn by priests who serve on the altar; the opening of the books for judgment is a motif of the Temple-based Yom Kippur observance; the designation "Son of Man" is derived from Ezekiel; and the charge that the little horn (Antiochus) sought to change the seasons and the law speaks to the role of Temple as the center of the cosmos in which the times of the seasons (the holidays) and the laws that govern the universe are set.

---

[34] For discussion, see Marvin A. Sweeney, "The Latter Prophets: Isaiah, Jeremiah, Ezekiel," *The Hebrew Bible Today* (ed. S. L. McKenzie and M. P. Graham; Louisville: Westminster John Knox, 1998) 69–94.

[35] Frederick H. Cryer, *Divination in Ancient Israel and Its Near Eastern Environment: A Socio-Historical Investigation* (JSOTSup 142; Sheffield: JSOT Press, 1994). See also the portrayal of the prophet Isaiah in Isa 37:14–35/2 Kgs 19:14–34.

Indeed, the throne vision of Daniel 7 provides the context by which the other visions might be understood. The vision of the ram and the goat presents a symbolic portrayal of the conflict between Persia and Greece. Once the goat (Greece) emerges victorious, a little horn grows out of it toward the south and east and toward the "beautiful land" (Israel). The horn then throws down some of the hosts (priests of the Temple), takes away the regular burnt offering, and overthrows the place of the sanctuary, all of which express Antiochus's actions against the Jerusalem Temple. By the end of the vision, the small horn is condemned to judgment for these actions. Daniel 9 employs Jeremiah's principle of a seventy-year exile to calculate the time of the end of the punishment by Antiochus, but it combines this figure with the priestly principle of a seven/forty-nine-year Jubilee or sabbatical system, in which the land is allowed to lie fallow and all debts are forgiven, to produce a calculation of seventy weeks of years (i.e., 490 years) as the period when the persecution will end.[36] The final vision in Daniel 10–12, of course, attempts to project the events that will lead to the downfall of Antiochus and the emergence of the new kingdom. It is noteworthy that Daniel stands on the bank of the River Tigris, much like Ezekiel stands on the bank of the Chebar Canal, in preparation for the vision. Like Ezekiel and Zechariah, he sees a gleaming man dressed in white linen, the characteristic dress of a priest, who raises him through a touch of the hand and guides him through the process. Like Ezekiel (and Isaiah before him), he employs the imagery of resurrection as a means to symbolize the ultimate victory of the Hasmoneans against their persecutors.[37]

Altogether, the visions of Daniel 7–12 are permeated with priestly imagery, symbolism, and concepts. The use of such priestly motifs to project the downfall of Antiochus and the rise of a new kingdom of the Holy Ones of the Most High indicates that Daniel presupposes the role of the Jerusalem Temple as the holy center of creation where both heaven and earth meet and exist simultaneously. The establishment of an eternal divine kingdom represents the heavenly counterpart of an earthly autonomous Jewish kingdom.

IV

As the preceding comments demonstrate, the book of Daniel is an apocalyptic book, but it does not abandon concern for this world in an attempt to achieve

---

[36] Jer 25:11, 12; 29:10; Lev 26:34–35; cf. 2 Chr 36:21. Note also that the portrayal of the Temple menorah in Zechariah 4 allows for a total of forty-nine lights, which apparently symbolizes the sacred reckoning of time for the forty-nine-year Jubilee system. See my commentary on this chapter in Marvin A. Sweeney, *The Twelve* Prophets (2 vols.; Berit Olam: Studies in Hebrew Narrative and Poetry; Collegeville: Liturgical Press, 2000).

[37] For discussion of the motif of resurrection in Daniel and its antecedents in biblical, pseudepigraphical, and pagan literature, see Collins, *Daniel*, 1993, 390–8.

redemption in a heavenly realm beyond the bounds of human history. It is indeed concerned with the heavenly realm, but its mythological or symbolical portrayal of the heavenly realm presupposes the role of the Jerusalem Temple as sacred center of both the cosmos in general and Judaism and the land of Judea in particular. The portrayal of heavenly reality provides a perspective by which to view the human world that both reflects actual events and attempts to influence the future course of action in this world, in this case, to bring an end to Antiochus IV's attempts to suppress Judaism and the Jerusalem Temple and to exercise hegemony over Judea. The book of Daniel does not seek to escape this world, it attempts to engage it and change it for the better.

Although Daniel is often considered as an outgrowth of prophecy or wisdom, it is indeed a priestly work that is concerned with the sanctity of the Jerusalem Temple, the assertion of Jewish identity, and the maintenance of Judean independence in the face of a foreign threat. It provides a striking contrast in perspective to prophetic books, such as Ezekiel, Jeremiah, and Isaiah, that call upon Israelites and Judeans to recognize foreign conquest and oppression as an act of YHWH designed to punish and purify the nation for YHWH's divine purposes.[38] Daniel takes a very different position. It takes seriously the promises made by YHWH in the prophetic books to bring about a new age when the oppressors would be vanquished and Israel and Judah would be restored to their former splendor. Rather than identify YHWH with the foreign oppressor, Daniel identifies G-d with those opposed to foreign oppression who believed the divine promises of security for Israel and Judaism.

---

[38] See my discussion of the oracles against the nations, Marvin A. Sweeney, *Isaiah 1–39, with an Introduction to Prophetic Literature* (FOTL 16; Grand Rapids and Cambridge: Eerdmans, 1996) 212–7, esp. 216–7, which points to the identification of the oracles against the nations in the prophetic books with the political agendas of major world empires.

18. Davidic Typology in the Forty Year War Between the Sons of Light and the Sons of Darkness

In the years since the publication of the War Scroll from Qumran (1QM), scholars have attempted a number of explanations for the origin of the War Scroll's unprecedented forty year war pattern. The most cogent is that of Yadin, who maintains a specific analogy between the forty year war of 1QM and the forty year period of wilderness wandering by the Israelite tribes following the Exodus from Egypt. Yadin argues that the military structure of the army of the Sons of Light is based on the structure of the Israelite tribes during the wilderness period as portrayed in Numbers 1–10, and it reflects the organizational structure of the sect in the wilderness of Qumran.[1] He therefore asserts that the number forty derives from "two conceptions which are in fact one."[2] The first is the forty year sojourn of the Israelites in the wilderness prior to their return and reentry into the land of Israel. The second relates to Rabbinic comments that the time of the Messiah would last forty years. Yadin is followed by Davies, who likewise points to similarities between the organization of the tribes in Numbers 1–10 and that of the tribes in 1QM 2–4. Davies maintains that 1QM 2–9 portrays "a new 'entry into a promised land' which, like the original entry, involves a period of forty years."[3]

The position adopted by Yadin and Davies has much to commend it. Not only does the War Scroll portray a holy war for possession of the land such as that anticipated by the Wilderness traditions, it also describes the army of the Sons of Light with wilderness terminology, viz., *gōlat hammidbār*, "the exile of the wilderness," in 1QM 1:2 and *běnê ʾôr mimmidbār haʿammîm*, "when the exile of the Sons of Light returns from the wilderness of the peoples" in 1QM 1:3. Furthermore, the decision to prevent the Mosaic slave generation from entering the promised land due to its lack of faith in G-d's promise of possession of the land in Numbers 14 may well have contributed to the dualism of the War Scroll, especially since the army of the Sons of Darkness includes *maršîʿê běrît*, "the betrayers of the covenant." In contrast, the army of the Sons of Light which

---

[1] Yigael Yadin, *The Scroll of the War of the Sons of Light against the Sons of Darkness* (London: Oxford University Press, 1962) 38.
[2] Yadin, *Scroll* 37.
[3] Philip R. Davies, *1QM, the War Scroll from Qumran: Its Structure and History* (Rome: Biblical Institute Press, 1977) 28.

returned from the wilderness of the peoples includes those who maintained the covenant. It therefore corresponds to the generation that was born in the wilderness and conquered the promised land.

Such considerations lend support to the view that the Wilderness traditions influenced the War Scroll's concept of the forty year war. Nevertheless, there are a number of problems with this hypothesis that indicate that it does not fully explain the origin of the concept of the forty year war in 1QM.

First, although the wilderness traditions of the Pentateuch anticipate a holy war campaign for possession of the land of Israel, they do not report the details of the campaign itself which do not appear until the book of Joshua. The War Scroll explicitly reports the components of both armies, the duration of the war, military organization, weapons and equipment, and the plan of battle. The Pentateuchal Wilderness traditions, on the other hand, do report an unsuccessful attempt to enter the land as well as many details of community organization, holy war practices, etc. Nevertheless, the wilderness traditions are not directly concerned with the campaign, but with the reasons why Israel was not yet ready to carry out the conquest. They focus on overcoming the obstacles that are impeding the campaign.

Second, whereas the Pentateuchal Wilderness traditions anticipate the campaign for conquest of the land of Israel, the War Scroll takes up a campaign for lands well beyond Israel's borders. Although possession of the land of Israel, or at least of the city of Jerusalem, does appear to be a goal of the army of the Sons of Light, other lands are involved as well. Column 1 lists Edom, Ammon, Philistia, the Kittim of Assur, and possibly the Kittim of Egypt and the Kings of the North as components of the army of the Sons of Darkness. Likewise, column 2 envisions an offensive campaign against the remaining nations that comprise the sons of Shem, as well as the sons of Ham and apparently the sons of Japhet.[4] As Shem, Ham, and Japhet constitute the basic divisions of all the peoples of the world, 1QM anticipates the conquest of all lands, not just the land of Israel.

Third, the Pentateuchal Wilderness traditions anticipate a campaign of conquest that will involve all the tribes of Israel. The situation of the War Scroll, however, is much more complex. Column 1 speaks of a campaign that involves only the tribes of Levi, Judah, and Benjamin. It is only in column 2 that all tribes are included in the campaign. A number of scholars have taken this discrepancy as one indication that the War Scroll is a composite literary work. Whether or not this is the case, the present form of the War Scroll indicates that there will be stages in the campaign. Only three tribes will be involved in the initial stage of the campaign whose goal appears to include the conquest of Jerusalem and the land of Israel, followed by stages in which all the tribes are included in a

---

[4] The "Sons of Japhet" should be read in 1QM 2:14 (cf. J. Van der Ploeg, *Le rouleau de la Guerre* [Leiden: Brill, 1959] 76).

campaign against the other nations of the world. This certainly differs from the Wilderness traditions where even those tribes that settled east of the Jordan River are included in the campaign for the rest of the land of Israel.

Finally, there is a major concern in the Pentateuchal Wilderness traditions to eliminate the Mosaic slave generation as unworthy to possess the land. The War Scroll, on the other hand, shows no interest in eliminating the unworthies from the army of the Sons of Light. In fact, the army appears to be augmented when the transition from an army consisting of the tribes of Levi, Judah, and Benjamin to one consisting of all the tribes is made. In the War Scroll, the unfit who need to be eliminated are the army of the Sons of Darkness.

These considerations indicate that the Pentateuchal Wilderness tradition of forty years of wandering by the tribes prior to their conquest of the land of Israel does not fully explain the origin of the forty year war in 1QM. It is therefore necessary to look elsewhere for an explanation for an origin of the concept. Several characteristics of the war are relevant in addition to those listed above.

First, 1QM portrays a war that is conducted according to a seven year Sabbatical scheme. According to this scheme, the war proceeds by stages in which six years are devoted to the actual combat followed by a year of release during the seventh year in which no hostilities are conducted. Obviously, this is derived from the regulations concerning an agricultural Sabbatical year in Leviticus 25 and those concerning the release of debts every seven years in Deuteronomy 15. Again, the issue is somewhat confused due to discrepancies between the first and second columns of the scroll. In column 1, the war proceeds in seven "lots," here understood as periods of time or stages in the war whereby the Sons of Light prevail for three lots (1QM 1:13), the army of Belial strengthens itself for three lots (1QM 1:13), and finally in the seventh lot, the hand of G-d intervenes to defeat the forces of Belial (1QM 1:14–15). Column 2:7–9 simply states that the war will be conducted according to the seven year Sabbatical pattern whereby every seventh year will be a year of release in which the army will not go out to war. Although the discrepancies between columns 1 and 2 may be due to the composite nature of the scroll, the seven lots mentioned in column 1 have been incorporated into the Sabbatical system of column 2 in its final form. The six lots of combat mentioned in column 1 are understood as the first six years in which war is waged by the entire community in 1QM 2:9. The seventh lot would then correspond to the first year of release in the war.

Second, this seven year Sabbatical pattern takes on additional significance in relation to the goal of the war in the first seven year period. 1QM 1:3 describes the army of the Sons of Light returning from the "wilderness of the peoples" to encamp in the "wilderness of Jerusalem." Although the issue is complicated due to the loss of text at the bottom of column 1, it appears that Jerusalem was the goal of the Sons of Light in the first seven year period. Column 2 begins with a description of the priests and the leaders of the community arrayed according to their stations "before G-d" (1QM 2:2) and "at the gates of the Sanctuary" (1QM 2:3). It appears that the "Sanctuary," i.e., the Temple in Jerusalem, serves as the center for conducting the balance of the war against the nations. Consequently, the first seven years focus on securing Jerusalem, including six years of combat and one year of release (1QM 2:6), and the remaining thirty-three years focus on combat against the nations (cf. 1QM 2:6), including twenty-nine years of combat and four years of release (cf. 1QM 2:10).

Third, Yadin and others have shown that the structure of David's army as portrayed in 1 Chronicles 27 is very influential in determining the structure of the army of the Sons of Light. In addition to similarities in the designations of officers, the primary feature of the army's organization in 1QM 2 is directly attributed to 1 Chronicles 27. This concerns the organization of David's army into twelve divisions (*hammaḥlĕqôt*) of twenty-four thousand men each. According to 1 Chronicles 27, the divisions rotated their service throughout the year so that each of them served active duty for one month of each year. This method of military organization apparently was employed in 1QM 2:10 ff to describe the "war of the divisions" (*milḥămôt hammaḥlĕqôt*) for the twenty-nine years of warfare against the remaining sons of Shem, the sons of Ham, and the sons of Japhet.

This last point is particularly important because it suggests a link to traditions concerning David. According to 1 Chr 29:26–30, David ruled over Israel for years. While this in itself does not constitute sufficient grounds for concluding that the author of the scroll employed a Davidic model in formulating the forty year war scheme, a number of additional considerations, particularly from the Chronicler's history of David's reign and the revolt of the northern tribes against the house of David, indicate the influence of Davidic typology on the author's formulation of a forty year eschatological war in 1QM.

Prior to his forty year reign over Israel, David is forced into exile in the wilderness as a result of Saul's jealousy. According to traditions preserved in 1 Samuel, David spent much of his time in the wilderness of Ziph (1 Sam 23:14) and the wilderness of Ein Gedi (1 Sam 24:1) before moving to Ziklag as a Philistine vassal. His move to Ziklag is particularly important because at this point, David was forced into exile among the nations insofar as Philistia is a gentile nation. According to 1 Chr 12:9, Ziklag is described as David's "fortress in the wilderness" (*mĕṣad midbārāh*). This of course calls to mind the War Scroll's description of the sons of Levi, Judah, and Benjamin as the "exile of the Wilderness" (1QM 1:2). Unlike the traditions in 1 Samuel which do not specify the tribes of David's warriors during this period, 1 Chr 12:17–19 reports that men from Benjamin and Judah joined David in the wilderness. According to 1 Sam 22:20–23, the Levitical priest Abiathar also joined David during his wilderness period. In this respect, the return of the army of the Sons of Light from the "exile of the people to the wilderness of Jerusalem" in 1QM 1:3 would correspond to David's return from the wilderness to become king of Judah at Hebron.

David was not able to make Jerusalem his capital until his seventh year. According to 1 Chr 29:26–30, David ruled in Hebron for seven years and Jerusalem for thirty-three years. This of course has obvious parallels with the pattern of conflict in the War Scroll where the first seven years of conflict for control of Jerusalem are followed by thirty-three years of conflict against nations outside the land of Israel. Furthermore, the pattern of David's conflict during his reign also corresponds to that of the War Scroll. Prior to taking Jerusalem, David was at intermittent war with the northern tribes of Israel. Following the deaths of Esh-Baal/Ish-Bosheth and Abner, all Israel capitulated and, as reported in 1 Chr 12:24–41, joined David at Hebron. This enabled David to establish Jerusalem as his capital and cultic center for a united Israel. His remaining thirty-three years were spent in conflict with nations outside the land of Israel, which were conquered and incorporated into David's empire.

This pattern of David's career corresponds to the War Scroll's description of a seven year campaign to secure Jerusalem and its subsequent description of a united Israel, with its cultic center at the Jerusalem sanctuary, in a campaign of divisions against the nations of the world for thirty-three years. It also appears to clarify the "betrayers of the covenant" mentioned in 1QM 1:2. Since the army of the Sons of Light comprised Levi, Judah, and Benjamin, it seems likely that, in the view of the author of the War Scroll, the "betrayers of the covenant" are the other Israelite tribes. In this respect, it is important to note that according to 2 Chr 11:1–4, 13–17, the tribes of Judah, Benjamin, and Levi continued to follow the Davidic monarch Rehoboam following the revolt of the northern tribes of Israel. According to 2 Chr 13:7, the men who followed Jeroboam were referred to as "the sons of Belial." These citations then explain the designations of the Sons of Light as Levi, Judah, and Benjamin, and the Sons of Darkness as the Army of Belial in column 1. The situation is resolved by column 2 when all the tribes of Israel take part in the war. A unified Israel, at war with the nations and centered around the sanctuary at Jerusalem in David's remaining thirty-three years, corresponds to the remaining thirty-three years of conflict portrayed in the War Scroll.

These considerations demonstrate quite clearly that the forty year war scheme of 1QM is heavily influenced by Davidic typology, especially as portrayed in Chronicles. This has several implications for clarifying the author's overall understanding of the forty year war between the Sons of Light and the Sons of Darkness.

The first concerns the composition of the army of the Sons of Darkness. According to 1QM 1:1–2, it includes "the band of Edom and Moab and the Sons of Ammon and (the Amalekites and the people of)[5] Philistia and the Kittim of Assur and in assistance with them the betrayers of the covenant." Carmingnac's

---

[5] Cf. J. Carmignac, *La Règle de la Guerre* (Paris: Letouzey et Ane, 1958) 3–4.

argument that this list of nations is merely a general designation for the enemies of Israel that is dependent on the list given in Ps 83:7–9 must be rejected.[6] Psalm 83:7–9 lists a number of enemies not included in the War Scroll, such as Ishmael, Harim, Gebal, and Tyre. If the author of the War Scroll was dependent on this list, surely these nations would have been included. Other texts cited to support the contention that these are the traditional enemies of Israel do not present the same combination of nations. The list does correspond to the lands incorporated into David's empire, however. 1 Chronicles 18:11 lists Edom, Moab, the Sons of Ammon, the Philistines, and Amalek as nations paying tribute to David. Furthermore, given Yadin's argument that the Kittim of Assur must be located to the north of Israel, between the Euphrates and the land of Israel, their territory would correspond to that of Aram, which was also brought into the Davidic empire in 1 Chr 18:3–10. Finally, if the "betrayers of the covenant" are identified as the remaining tribes of Israel apart from Levi, Judah, and Benjamin, as argued above, the result is a portrayal of the Sons of Darkness in 1QM 1:1–2 as those peoples who were incorporated into the Davidic empire following his period of rule in Hebron.

The second concerns the extent of the remaining thirty-three years of war against the rest of the nations of the world. The first nine years of war will include the remaining sons of Shem, specified as Aram Naharaim; the Sons of Lud; the remnant of the Sons of Aram in Uz, Hul, Togar, and Mesha across the Euphrates; Arpachshad; the Sons of Assur and Persia and the Kadmonites; Elam; Ishmael; and Keturah. The second and third decades of war will be fought against the Sons of Ham and the Sons of Japhet respectively. This list is clearly derived from the list of nations in Genesis 10, and it is intended to encompass the entire world.[7] Apart from the thirty-three years of war based from Jerusalem, it is clear that the author of the War Scroll has gone well beyond the Davidic analogy. The lands conquered by David were taken up in the first seven years of war. This stage includes the nations that were not a part of David's empire.

The third implication concerns the fact that despite the emphasis on Davidic typology, no clear Davidic Messiah appears in the War Scroll. The Scroll frequently mentions priestly leaders and 1QM 5:1 refers to the "Prince of the entire congregation" (*nĕśî' kol hā'ēdâ*) but there is no indication that either of these figures has any clearly Messianic role. In fact, the only Messiah figures mentioned in the War Scroll are the prophets (1QM 11:7–8). This appears to be deliberate. An altered version of Num 24:17–19 is quoted in the same context (1QM 11:6–7). Although this text is frequently understood in reference to a royal Messiah figure, the context indicates that here it refers not to a royal messiah figure, but to G-d. This is supported by 1QM 11:1 ff which refers to David's vic-

---

[6] J. Carmignac, "Les Citations de l'ancien Testament dans la Guerre des fils de lumière contre les fils de ténèbres," *RB* 63 (1956) 239–40; *La Règle de la Guerre* 9.

[7] Carmignac, *La Règle de la Guerre* 9.

tory over Goliath as a victory of G-d, not of David. Here, the Davidic typology is present, but a Davidic messiah is not. The author of the War Scroll sees G-d as the leader of the Sons of Light, not a Davidic figure.

In conclusion, it is quite apparent that the author of the War Scroll employed Davidic typology in constructing the scheme of a forty year war of the Sons of Light against the Sons of Darkness. Clearly, the author of the Scroll was dependent on past tradition, but the variations from the Davidic pattern indicate that the author did not expect a mere duplication of the past. Our author's pattern was much more grandiose. Instead, our author saw in the forty year war a repeated pattern in Israel's history that would lead to the achievement of G-d's intentions for establishing holiness in the world. David had established the people of Israel as a small empire centered in the Jerusalem Temple with himself as king. Due to the revolt by the northern tribes, however, David's empire failed. In its place, the author of the War Scroll envisioned the establishment of a world-wide holy empire of the Sons of Light centered in Jerusalem with G-d as king that would be free of the evil that caused the collapse of the original Davidic empire.

19. Pardes Revisited Once Again: A Reassessment of the Rabbinic Legend concerning the Four Who Entered Pardes[1]

I

The Rabbinic legend concerning the four who entered Pardes plays a particularly important role in scholarly discussion concerning the character of Jewish mysticism and its assessment in the Talmudic period. The legend appears in various forms throughout the ancient Rabbinic literature in the Tosephta (tHagigah 2:3–4), the Jerusalem Talmud (yHagigah 2:1, 77b), the Babylonian Talmud (bHagigah 14b, 15a,b), the Midrash on the Song of Songs (SongR 1:4), and in a paraphrased version in the mystical treatise Hekhalot Zutarti (Schäfer, *Synopse* §§ 344–345).[2] It expresses the experiences of four Tannaim who attempted "to enter Pardes": Simeon ben Azzai cast a look and died, Simeon ben Zoma looked and was smitten (i. e., with insanity), Aḥer (Elisha ben Abuyah) cut the shoots (i. e., became a heretic), and R. Akiba entered safely and went out safely.

---

[1] This is a revised version of a paper presented under the title, "Paradise Revisited: The Talmud and Jewish Mysticism," as the Eighteenth Annual Stone Lectureship in Judaism at Augustana College, Rock Island, Illinois, March 21, 2002). I would like to thank Professors Robert D. Haak and Eleanor Ferris Beach for their invitation to present this lecture and for their kind hospitality during my stay at Augustana. Earlier versions of this paper have been presented at the American Academy of Religion Southeastern Regional Meeting (Gainesville, Florida, March 1995) and the University of Miami Religious Studies Colloquium (Coral Gables, Florida, March, 1995). I would like to thank the members of the Religious Studies Department of the University of Miami for their invitation to lecture in my former department. I would also like to thanks Prof. David S. Williams, University of Georgia, and Prof. Lewis M. Barth, Hebrew Union College–Jewish Institute of Religion, Los Angeles, for their comments on earlier drafts of this paper. Of course, they are not to be held responsible for the views put forth here. This paper is dedicated to the memory of Dr. Morton M. Axler, a retired pediatrician and enthusiastic student, who contributed considerable insight while auditing my classes at the University of Miami. Special thanks go an anonymous reader of this paper who turned out to be a patient of Dr. Axler in the 1950's!

[2] For the texts of Hekhalot Zutarti, see Peter Schäfer, ed., *Synopse zur Hekhalot-Literatur* (TSAJ 2; Tübingen: Mohr Siebeck, 1981) §§ 335–374, 407–426, 496–497. For current discussions of the sources for this narrative, surveys of scholarship and detailed treatments of its problems, see Alon Goshen Gottstein, "Four Entered Paradise Revisited," *HTR* 88 (1995) 69–133; David Halpern, *The Merkabah in Rabbinic Literature* (AOS 62; New Haven: American Oriental Society, 1980) 86–92; and Ithamar Gruenwald, *Apocalyptic and Merkavah Mysticism* (AGAJU 14; Leiden: Brill, 1980) 82–92.

Although the version of the Babylonian Talmud is generally considered to be the normative form of this legend, most scholars maintain that the Tosephta's version is the earliest from which the others are derived.[3] They likewise generally agree that all of the various versions of the tradition express a warning that attempts to dissuade those who might attempt to "enter pardes," i. e., to engage in the study of Jewish mysticism in keeping with Mishnah Hagigah 2:1. Interpreters therefore understand the legend to express Rabbinic Judaism's opposition to mystical speculation, interpretation, or practice.[4] The full version of the Tosephta reads as follows:

Four entered Pardes: ben Azzai, ben Zoma, Aḥer (i. e., Elisha ben Abuyah), and Rabbi Akiba. Ben Azzai looked and died. About him it is written, saying, "Precious in the eyes of the L-rd is the death of his saints" (Ps 116:15). Ben Zoma looked and was smitten (i. e., became demented). About him it is written, saying, "Have you found honey? Eat (only) what is sufficient for you, (lest you be filled with it and vomit it)" (Prov 25:16). Aḥer looked and cut the shoots (i. e., of plants; became a heretic). About him it is written, saying, "Do not allow your mouth to cause your flesh to sin" (Qoh 5:5). Rabbi Akiba entered in peace, and he went out in peace. About him it is written, saying, "Draw me after you, let us run, (the king has brought me into his chambers)" (Song 1:4).[5]

Serious disagreements appear, however, in relation to the interpretation of the expression "to enter Pardes." The Hebrew term *pardēs* is a Persian or Greek loan word that means literally "garden," "park," or "enclosure," and frequently refers to "paradise" in Rabbinic literature.[6] Early critical scholars, beginning with Graetz, and more recently Maier, Fischel, and Segal, understand the expression allegorically as a reference to the study or practice of Gnosticism.[7] A second group of interpreters, including Bousset, Scholem, Neher, Goldberg, and

---

[3] Joseph Dan, "The Religious Experience of the Merkavah," *Jewish Spirituality: From the Bible through the Middle Ages* (ed. A. Green; New York: Crossroad, 1988) 289–307, esp. 293. For critical editions of the Tosephta text, see Saul Lieberman, ed., *The* Tosephta (4 vols.; New York: Jewish Theological Seminary, 1955–88); M. S. Zuckermandel, ed., *Tosephta, based on the Erfurt and Vienna Codices* (Jerusalem: Wahrmann, 1970) 234.

[4] In addition to the works cited above, see Joseph Dan, *The Ancient Jewish Mysticism* (Tel Aviv: MOD Books, 1993) 93.

[5] Translation mine from the above-cited Zuckermandel edition of the Tosephta (see note 2 above).

[6] Marcus Jastrow, *A Dictionary of the Targumim, the Talmud Babli and Yerushalmi, and the Midtrashic Literature* (Brooklyn: P. Shalom, 1967) 1216; Francis Brown, Samuel Rolles Driver, and Charles A. Briggs, ed., *A Hebrew and Aramaic Lexicon of the Old Testament* (Oxford: Clarendeon, 1907) 825.

[7] Heinrich Graetz, *Gnosticismus und Judenthum* (Krotoschin: Monasd & Gohn, 1846) 59 (see also his *History of the Jews. Volume 3: From the Revolt against the Zendik [511 C.E.] to the Capture of St. Jean d'Acreby by the Mahometans [1291 C.E.]* [Philadelphia: Jewish Publication Society, 1894] 549); Johann Maier, "Das Gefährdungsmotiv bei der Himmelsreise in der jüdische Apokalyptik and 'Gnosis'," *Kairos* 5 (1963) 18–40; Henry A. Fischel, *Rabbinic Judaism and Greco-Roman Philosophy: A Study of Epicurea and Rhetorica in Early Midrashic Writings* (SPB 21; Leiden: Brill, 1973); Alan F. Segal, *Two Powers in Heaven: Early Rabbinic Reportsabout Christianity and* Gnosticism (SJLA 25; Leiden: Brill, 1977) 60–73.

Gruenwald, interpret it as a reference to the very real psychological dangers of engaging in ecstatic mystical experience.[8] A third group of scholars, including Goshen-Gottstein, Urbach, Halperin, and Dan, on the other hand, understand it as a reference to the proper exposition of Biblical literature, particularly the interpretation of the Creation narrative in Genesis 1 (Ma'aseh Bereshit; the "Work of Creation") and Ezekiel's account of his vision of G-d's throne chariot in Ezekiel 1 (Ma'aseh Merkavah; the "Work of the Chariot").[9]

Unfortunately, most scholarly discussion of this legend has focused primarily on attempts to identify the earliest version of the narrative. Efforts to interpret the narrative are therefore concerned with reconstructing the history of its literary development. Consequently, there has been relatively little effort to interpret the narrative features of the legend. Three major features of the narrative that remain relatively constant throughout its various forms require our attention. The first and most important is R. Akiba's successful entry into and exit from Pardes, in contrast to the experiences of his three predecessors. Akiba's successful completion of his journey suggests that the purpose of the story might not be limited to warning those who would "enter Pardes" of the dangers of such an enterprise; instead, it might provide a model or criteria for its realization.[10] The second pertains to the identity of the Rabbis who appear in the legend. The rationale for the inclusion of R. Akiba and Elisha ben Abuyah (Aḥer) seems clear, in that they are antitypes in Rabbinical literature; Akiba is the quintessential sage of Talmudic tradition whereas Elisha ben Abuyah is the quintessential heretic who abandoned Judaism to pursue Greek philosophy later in life. The roles of Simeon ben Azzai and Simeon ben Zoma are less clear, however, in that they are evaluated positively elsewhere in Rabbinical literature, which describes them as the most "diligent student" and the greatest "expounder" of Torah respectively

---

[8] W. Bousset, "Die Himmelsreise der Seele," *Archiv für Religionswissenschaft* 4 (1901) 145–57; Gershom Scholem, *Major Trends in Jewish Mysticism* (New York: Schocken, 1961) 52–3; idem, *Jewish Gnosticism, Merkabah Mysticism, and Talmudic Tradition* (New York: Jewish Theological Seminary, 1965) 14–19; André Neher, "Le voyage mystique des quatre," *RevHistRel* 140 (1951) 59–82; Arnold Goldberg, "Der verkannte G-tt. Prüfung und Scheitern der Adepten in der Merkawamystik," *ZRGG* 26 (1974) 17–29; Gruenwald, *Apocalyptic* 86.

[9] Goshen Gottstein, "Four Entered Paradise Revisted"; idem, *The Sinner and the Amnesiac: The Rabbinic Intervention of Elisha ben Abuya and Eleazar ben Arach* (Contraversions; Stanford: Stanford University Press, 2000) esp. 47–61; Ephraim E. Urbach, "The Tradition concerning the Mystical Torah in the Age of the Tannaim," *Studies in Mysticism and Religion* (Fest. G. Scholem; Jerusalem: Magnes, 1967) 1–28 (in Hebrew; see also his *The Sages: Their Concepts and Beliefs* [Jerusalem: Magnes, 1979] 1:193, 417); Halperin, *The Merkabah* 92, 167, 175, 180–1; idem, *The Faces of the Chariot: Early Jewish Responses to Ezekiel's Vision* (TSAJ 16; Tübingen: Mohr Siebeck, 1988) 23–37; Dan, "Religious Experience," 296.

[10] Cf. Ithamar Gruenwald, "Two Types of Jewish Esoteric Literature in the Time of the Mishnah and Talmud," *From Apocalypticism to Gnosticism: Studies in Apocalypticism, Merkavah Mysticism and Gnosticism* (BEATAJ 14; Frankfurt am Main: Peter Lang, 1988) 53–64, esp. 62, who maintains that the warning is directed to those who are not "qualified or fit" to engage in the subject. See also Gruenwald, *Apocalyptic and Merkavah Mysticism* 88.

(mSotah 9:15). Nevertheless, their failure to enter Pardes indicates that like Aḥer, they function as foils in relation to the successful R. Akiba. Indeed, neither is ordained, which suggests that like Elisha ben Abuyah, they too embody some shortcoming in relation to R. Akiba, and thereby contribute to his idealization in this legend.

Finally, each Rabbi is associated with a specific verse from Scripture which relates to some especially pertinent action or characteristic.[11] The function of the verses associated with Akiba and Aḥer is clear in that they point to the contrasting role of each Rabbi in the narrative, but the issue is less clear in the cases of Simeon ben Azzai and Simeon ben Zoma. In both cases, it is evident that the scriptural verses point to some characteristic feature of each, but it is not entirely clear how these characteristics function in relation to the presentation of R. Akiba. In any case, clarification of the role and function of Simeon ben Azzai and Simeon ben Zoma in the narrative would certainly contribute to its overall interpretation.

These considerations demonstrate the need to reassess the narrative concerning the four who entered Pardes, especially with regard to the inclusion of Simeon ben Azzai and Simeon ben Zoma and their respective functions within the narrative. Based upon an examination of the contrasting experiences of Akiba and the other three Rabbis, the roles and functions of Simeon ben Azzai and Simeon ben Zoma in the narrative, and the biblical quotations associated with each, I propose a revised understanding of the narrative. Indeed, the narrative warns those who would attempt to "enter pardes" or engage in the study of Jewish mysticism, but it defines the qualities necessary for a successful entry. R. Akiba is presented as the exemplar of one who would successfully enter Pardes, in that he embodies specific qualities that each of the others lacks. Furthermore, clarification of the roles played by each of the Rabbis in this narrative, and the function of the biblical quotations associated with them, demonstrates that the expression "to enter Pardes" refers to proper biblical interpretation in the Rabbinic tradition. Overall, the narrative speaks to the concern of the Mishnah (mHagigah 2:1) that one who would expound the "work of the chariot" (i.e., Ezekiel 1) be "a sage who understands his own knowledge," like R. Akiba.[12]

---

[11] Akiba is associated with Song 1:4; Aḥer with Qoh 5:5; ben Azzai with Ps 116:15; and ben Zoma with Prov 25:16. The Talmud Yerushalmi and various manuscripts of the Tosephta associate Ps 116:15 with ben Zoma and Prov 25:16 with ben Azzai (Halperin, *The Merkabah* 86–7). For treatment of these verses in relation to the respective Tannaim, see below.

[12] This would account for the literary context of the Tosephta, Babylonian Talmud, and Talmud Yerushalmi, all of which build upon mHagigah 2:1. Note also that each includes the tradition concerning R. Eleazar ben Arakh's exposition of Maaseh Merkavah before R. Yohanan ben Zakkai. In each case, R. Yohanan approves of Eleazar's exposition and kisses him on the head. Cf. SongR 1:4, which likewise presents the narrative in relation to the proper interpretation of scripture in that it relates the narrative as part of its exposition of Song 1:4.

II

One of the fundamental elements of the legend concerning the four who attempted to enter Pardes is R. Akiva's successful completion of the journey. It is expressed differently among the various traditions. According to the version of the Babylonian Talmud, Akiba "went out in peace" (bḤag 14b) or "ascended in peace and descended in peace" (bḤag 15b); Talmud Yerushalmi states that Akiba "entered in peace and went out in peace" (yḤag 2:1, 77b); and the Tosephta states that Akiba "ascended in peace and descended in peace" (tḤag 2:3–4).[13]

Although the meaning of the Pardes experience is understood and expressed differently in the various versions of the tradition, the traditions consistently present R. Akiba as the only one of the four who successfully experiences Pardes, whatever that experience may be. This is significant in that R. Akiba is one of the most celebrated and idealized figures in all of Talmudic tradition.[14] Although he was originally an illiterate shepherd, an ʿam hāʾāreṣ, who boasted that he would "maul (a scholar) like an ass" (bPesaḥim 49b), his love for Rachel, the daughter of his employer, prompted him to learn to read and to become a scholar. When she gave up the inheritance of her wealthy father to marry Akiba, she did so on the condition that he would devote himself to the study of Torah so that he might teach their children (bNedarim 50a; bKetubot 62b). Although Akiba apparently faltered in his initial attempts, the need to educate their son prompted him to pursue his studies so that he might teach him as well (Abot de Rabbi Nathan 2:6).

As a result, Akiba became one of the greatest sages of Talmudic tradition. The Jerusalem Talmud describes him as "one of the fathers of the world" (ySheqalim 3:1, 47b), and credits him with systematizing the principles upon which the

---

[13] Note that the Erfurt manuscript of the Tosephta states that he "entered in peace and went out in peace." Halperin argues that the statement concerning Akiba's successful "ascent" and "descent" constitutes partial evidence that the Babylonian Talmud is the latest tradition and that it attempts to portray the entry into pardes as an actual mystic ascent rather than as the correct exposition of scripture (*The Merkabah* 92). Several features of the Babylonian Talmud tradition, however, undermine this interpretation: the literary context indicates that the story is meant to explain the Mishnah's statement that one who "expounds" upon Maaseh Merkavah must be "a sage who understands his own knowledge"; the Babylonian Talmud also includes a tradition that explains Akiba's safe ascent to Pardes as the result of his correct exposition of scripture (bḤag 15b–16a); the Babylonian Talmud includes the readings of both the Tosephta and the Talmud Yerushalmi. These factors indicate that indeed the Babylonian Talmud contains the latest version of the tradition, but it appears to be a harmonization of the older traditions that include both extant versions. The Babylonian Talmud thereby includes both understandings of the experience, i.e., as an actual mystic ascent and as the exposition of scripture.

[14] For a detailed survey of the traditions concerning R. Akiba, see Wilhelm Bacher, *Die Agada der Tannaiten. Erster Band. Von Hillel bis Akiba* (2nd edition; Strassburg: Karl J. Trübner, 1903) 263–342. See also Louis Finkelstein, *Akiba: Scholar, Saint and Martyr* (New York: Atheneum, 1981), which presents a critically constructed account of R. Akiba's life in narrative form.

tradition of Rabbinic biblical interpretation, the Midrash halakhot and aggadot, are built (ySheq 3:1, 48a). Akiba laid the foundations for much of Rabbinic midrashic biblical exegesis by maintaining that all features of the text of the Torah have meaning, no matter how insignificant they may seem.[15] The Tosephta describes him as one who "arranges halakhot," i.e., as one who organizes, clarifies, and explains the reasons for Rabbinic laws (tZabim 1:5). The Rabbinic commentaries on the biblical books of the Song of Songs (Song Rabbah 8:2) and Ecclesiastes (Qohelet Rabbah 6:2) describe several early collections of Mishnah teachings, including those of R. Hiyya the Elder, Hoshaia, Bar Qappara, and R. Akiba, which apparently provided the basis for the compilation of the Mishnah by Judah the Prince. The Babylonian Talmud likewise acknowledges Akiba's role in defining the legal interpretations or halakhic midrashim: "The author of an anonymous Mishnah is R. Meir; an anonymous Tosephta, R. Nehemiah; an anonymous Sifra, R. Judah; in the Sifrei, R. Simeon; and all are taught according to the views of Akiba" (bSanhedrin 86a). Essentially, Rabbinic tradition regards Akiba as one of the leading figures in the foundation and teaching of Rabbinic biblical interpretation (Midrash) and Rabbinic law (Halakhah). The regard in which he was held is illustrated by the tradition that G-d brought Moses into Akiba's classroom to show him the results of his teachings. When Moses complained that he was unable to understand Akiba's teachings, his mind was set at ease when Akiba explained a teaching as a halakhah given to Moses at Sinai (bMenahot 29b).

The idealization of R. Akiba likewise appears in relation to his death as a martyr at the hands of the Romans during the Bar Kochba revolt of 132–135 C.E., in which the Roman army, led by the emperor Hadrian, slaughtered approximately half a million people and forbade the practice of Judaism in the land of Israel. Indeed, Hadrian's persecution brought an end to Jewish life in the land of Israel, which he renamed Palestine to eradicate any memory that Jews had once lived there until the reestablishment of the modern state of Israel in 1948. Rabbi Akiba is consistently listed among the martyrs of Hadrian's persecution.[16] Following his arrest and imprisonment for violating Hadrian's decree forbidding the teaching and practice of Judaism, the ninety-eight-year-old Akiba was tortured by the Romans, who tore his flesh from his body with iron combs. Despite the pain and suffering, Akiba maintained his adherence to Torah by stating that his suffering finally enabled him to understand the command expressed in Deut 6:5, "and you shall love the L-rd your G-d with all your heart and with all your might ... even

---

[15] Consequently, the accusative particle 'et in Gen 1:1, which can also mean "with" in other contexts, indicates that "heaven and earth" are not names of G-d, but refer to the actual heaven and the actual earth, i.e., Heaven and Earth are not the subjects of creation, but the objects (bHag 12a–b). Likewise, the appearance of 'et in Deut 6:13 indicates that scholars are to be respected together with G-d (bPes 22b).

[16] See now Gottfried Reeg, *Die Geschichte von den Zehn Märtyren* (TSAJ 10; Tübingen: Mohr Siebeck, 1985).

if you must pay for it with your life" (bBerakot 61b). He therefore died with the words of the Shema from Deut 6:4 ff, "Hear O Israel, the L-rd our G-d, the L-rd is one ...," on his lips.

Given the great regard with which Akiba is held in Rabbinic tradition, it seems unlikely that the tradition of the four who entered Pardes is intended only as a warning for those who would attempt a similar experience. Rabbi Akiba is one of the greatest and most admired of the Talmudic Rabbis. His successful experience of Pardes in this legend thereby indicates that such experience, however it is defined, is possible. R. Akiba therefore serves as the exemplar of one who is able and qualified to experience Pardes.[17]

III

The other constant elements in the story are the inclusion of the three Rabbis who failed to experience Pardes successfully and the biblical citations associated with them. The three include Simeon ben Azzai, who is associated with Ps 116:15, "Precious in the sight of the L-rd is the death of His saints"; Simeon ben Zoma, who is associated with Prov 25:16, "Have you found honey? Eat so much as is sufficient for you, lest you be filled and vomit it"; and Aḥer or Elisha ben Abuyah, who is associated with Eccl/Qoh 5:5, "Do not allow your mouth to cause your flesh to sin."

Relatively little attention has been given to the reasons for the inclusion of these particular individuals or for the citations of these particular verses. Scholars have generally recognized that the verses express some aspect of the character of each figure, but they have not analyzed the biblical citations as a significant element in the interpretation of the narrative. Otherwise, they have assumed that the three were included because they were engaged somehow in mystical study or practice, but this is hardly an adequate explanation. Rabbinic tradition associates three of our figures with various forms of mystical practice, i.e., Akiba engages in theurgic or magical practice (bSan 68a),[18] Simeon ben Zoma engages in speculation concerning the creation of the cosmos (bHag 15a; Genesis Rabbah 2:4), and Aḥer or Elisha ben Abuyah engages in the study of forbidden books (bHag 15b), but Simeon ben Azzai's association with such

---

[17] Such concern with the qualifications of one who would experience Pardes likewise calls to mind the eight qualities necessary for successful descent on the Merkavah as defined in the Hekhalot Rabbati, including adherence to all the positive and negative commands of Rabbinic tradition (15:2).

[18] Apparently, this tradition plays a role in the identification of Akiba as the author of various theurgic works, such as the Shiʿur Qomah or the Sefer Yetzirah. See Martin Cohen, *The Shiʿur Qomah: Liturgy and Theurgy in Pre-Kabbalistic Jewish Mysticism* (Lanham, New York, and London: University Press, of America, 1983) 84–5.

practices is questionable (SongR 1:10).[19] Furthermore, other prominent figures who were well-known for their engagement with mysticism, such as R. Yohanan ben Zakkai (bḤag 14b)[20] or R. Simeon bar Yohai (bShabbat 33b),[21] were not included in our story.

In keeping with the overall interest in the narrative to present a contrast between the experiences of R. Akiba and the other three, it seems appropriate to consider the possibility that Simeon ben Azzai, Simeon ben Zoma, and Elisha ben Abuyah are included in order to serve as antitypes to the figure of R. Akiba. This certainly seems to be the case with Elisha ben Abuyah. As noted above, Akiba is idealized in Rabbinic literature as the epitome of the Talmudic sage who lays the foundations for Rabbinic law and biblical interpretation or halakhah and midrash. Elisha ben Abuyah, on the other hand, is presented in Rabbinic literature as the epitome of the heretic, whose apostasy is so great that he will never be able to repent of his sins and thereby gain a share of the world to come.[22] The traditions of the Babylonian Talmud are adamant on this point. At three different points, the mystical collection in the Babylonian Talmud (bḤag 15a) relates the call to repentance from Jeremiah 3:22, but denies the possibility of repentance to Aḥer: "Return you backsliding children–except Aḥer." It likewise presents Elisha ben Abuyah as violating the observance of Shabbat by tearing a radish out of the ground while negotiating with a prostitute and by riding a horse; thirteen different schoolboys recite biblical verses to his face that condemn his evil; and it raises questions as to whether Elisha ben Abuyah's daughter should claim him as her father. The Talmudic tradition does relent to some extent in that it acknowl-

---

[19] In SongR 1:10, fire surrounds ben Azzai when he expounds upon scripture, but he denies that he is engaged in the mysteries of the merkavah. Cf. Fischel, *Rabbinic Literature* 8–9, who denies any association of ben Azzai with mysticism, and contends that he was included in the tradition of the four who attempted to enter Pardes because of his celibacy. On ben Azzai's celibacy, see below.

[20] On the Merkabah traditions associated with R. Yohanan ben Zakkai, see Jacob Neusner, *Development of a Legend: Studies on the Traditions concerning Yohanan ben Zakkai* (SPB 16; Leiden: Brill, 1970) 247–52, 265–301. Neusner notes that the Babylonian Talmud's version of the tradition associating Yohanan ben Zakkai with Merkabah mysticism is the most highly developed and therefore the latest version. He also notes that although there is an attempt to employ the Merkabah theme to shape the image of Yohanan in relation to that of the mystic Elazar ben Arakh (p. 276–7), the preservation of the Merkabah theme in Akiban circles indicates that it was probably related to Yohanan's life and thought (p. 299).

[21] Simeon bar Yohai survived the war by hiding in a cave with his son for thirteen years. According to bShabbat 33b, they studied Torah while sitting naked up to their necks in sand throughout this period, and when they emerged, fire from their eyes consumed whatever they saw. The tradition later became the basis for identifying Simeon bar Yohai as the author of the Zohar (see Scholem, *Major Trends* 156–204). For discussion of the Talmudic narratives concerning Simeon bar Yohai, see Jeffrey L. Rubenstein, *Talmudic Stories: Narrative Art, Composition, and Culture* (Baltimore and London: Johns Hopkins University Press, 1999) 105–38.

[22] For discussion of the traditions concerning Elisha ben Abuyah, see Bacher, *Die Aggada der Tannaiten* 430–4; Rubenstein, *Talmudic Stories* 64–104; Goshen Gottstein, *The Sinner and the Amnesiac* 21–229.

edges Elisha ben Abuyah's teaching of Torah before his apostasy, and maintains that one can learn from his earlier teachings even though he later proved to be a heretic. In the end, R Meir and R. Yohanan are said to have interceded with G-d on Aḥer's behalf, resulting in his eventual forgiveness.

In searching for the cause of Aḥer's actions, the Babylonian Talmud points to his study of Greek literature or forbidden books: "But what of Aḥer?–Greek song did not cease from his mouth. It is told of Aḥer that when he used to rise [to go] from the schoolhouse, many heretical books used to fall from his lap" (bḤag 15b). The Jerusalem Talmud relates three reasons, including his observation of arbitrary reward or punishment for two men who took eggs from a mother bird's nest in violation of Deut 22:6–7; his witness of the execution of R. Judah Naḥtum by the Romans in which the dead Rabbi's tongue, which had uttered so many beautiful teachings, was carried off in the mouth of dog; and his mother's smelling of pagan incense (yḤag 2:1). In each case, the tradition points to reasons for Elisha ben Abuyah's lack of faith in Jewish tradition. This stands behind the narrative in the Jerusalem Talmud which relates Elisha ben Abuyah's apostasy when he succeeded in entering Pardes or the throne room of G-d. Upon seeing G-d's chief angel, Metatron, seated on the divine throne, Elisha ben Abuyah declared "there are two powers (in heaven)!" i.e., there is not one, but two gods. He therefore abandoned the most fundamental teaching of Jewish tradition, i.e., belief in one and only one G-d. When Metatron was punished for his actions, he was also given permission to strike out the merits of Aḥer. In this regard, the citation of Eccl/Qoh 5:5, "Do not allow your mouth to cause your flesh to sin," expresses Elisha ben Abuyah's shortcomings in this narrative. He studied and expressed the ideas of forbidden literature, which led him to question Jewish tradition and eventually to become a heretic by his statements.

In view of the attention given to Aḥer's apostasy, it seems clear that he is intended to function as an antitype to the ideal figure of Akiba in the narrative. Akiba is the ideal Rabbinic sage, who not only defines Rabbinic law or halakhah and biblical interpretation or midrash but maintains his adherence to Judaism by dying as a martyr with the words of the Shema on his lips. Elisha ben Abuyah, although he was a Rabbinic sage in his own right, abandoned the most fundamental principle of Judaism, belief in one G-d, as a result of his interest in Greek literature. Consequently, Aḥer's lack of faith in Rabbinic tradition leads him to outside sources and results in his apostasy. Akiba's adherence to Rabbinic tradition throughout his life and death, on the other hand, demonstrates his faith and qualifies him to experience Pardes. Furthermore, Akiba's dying statement of the Shema expresses his adherence to Judaism, whereas Aḥer's last statement results in his condemnation.[23]

---

[23] Note also Akiba's statement in time of adversity, "Whatever G-d does is for the best" (bBer 60b).

The situation with Simeon ben Azzai and Simeon ben Zoma is not so clear, however, in that each is honored in Rabbinic tradition. According to the Mishnah, "all the diligent students ceased" when Simeon ben Azzai died, and "there were no more expounders (of the Torah)" when Simeon ben Zoma died (mSotah 9:15). Both are quoted in mAboth 4:1–3, which indicates their status among the most respected of the early Tannaim.[24]

Despite ben Azzai's stellar reputation as a pious sage,[25] however, Rabbinic tradition indicates that he had one major shortcoming, i.e., he never married and he never produced children. The Babylonian Talmud (bYebamot 63b; cf. tYeb 8:7) relates a discussion in which R. Eliezer asserts that failure to produce children is like shedding blood, and R. Jacob asserts that it diminishes the Divine image. When ben Azzai combines the opinions of these two Rabbis, stating that the failure to produce children constitutes both the shedding of blood and the diminution of the Divine image, his colleagues object that he preaches well but he does not act well in that he has neither married nor produced children. Ben Azzai's response, "What shall I do, seeing that my soul is in love with the Torah; the world can be carried on by others," is scandalous in that it demonstrates his failure to observe the first and most fundamental halakhah or law in Jewish tradition: "be fruitful and multiply" (Gen 9:16). Not only does ben Azzai himself equate such action with the shedding of blood and diminishing the Divine image, but Abba Hanan in the name of R. Eliezer states in the same context that one who fails to produce children deserves the penalty of death.[26]

There is some indication that R. Akiba's daughter may have followed her mother's example in marrying and supporting ben Azzai (bKet 63a), but the tradition is not entirely clear. In any case, it is clear that ben Azzai never had children. Consequently, he never reproduced physically and therefore did not have children to whom he could pass on his knowledge of Torah. This is in striking contrast to Akiba, whose marriage to Rachel and the birth of his children not only fulfilled the most fundamental command of Jewish tradition, but led him to become one of the greatest sages of Talmudic tradition precisely so he could teach his son. Ben Azzai's failure to reproduce physically corresponds to his punishment upon attempting to enter Pardes, i.e., he dies and suffers physical punishment of the body precisely because he failed to fulfill his duty to produce children and to teach them Torah.[27] Furthermore, it explains the citation of Psalm

---

[24] N.b., Ben Azzai is also known for advocating the teaching of Torah to one's daughter so that she might know her merits in case of trial (mSotah 3:4).

[25] For a survey of traditions concerning Simeon ben Azzai, see Bacher, *Die Aggada der Tannaiten* 406–22; Fischel, *Rabbinic Literature* 90–97.

[26] Elsewhere, R. Huna maintains that a man who is not married by the age of twenty spends his days in sin, or at least sinful thoughts (bQiddushin 29b). Ben Azzai's failure to observe the first commandment is in striking contrast to his insistence that even minor commandments be observed (Abot R. Nat. 1:25).

[27] Note that the New York manuscript of Hekhalot Zutarti (JTS 8128) emphasizes that

116:15 in relation to ben Azzai, "Precious in the sight of the L-rd is the death of His saints." The term "precious," *yāqār*, is best translated as "costly," and indicates that ben Azzai's lack of children at his death cost the world dearly in lost potential.

Simeon ben Zoma enjoyed a distinguished reputation as one of the foremost aggadic expounders of Torah,[28] but like his colleague ben Azzai, he was never ordained as a Rabbi. This means that despite his reputation as an aggadic preacher, he never completed his full education in halakhah or Jewish law. This is important in the present context in that the mystical collection in the Babylonian Talmud (bHagigah) contains various references to ben Zoma's interpretation of scripture, but they demonstrate that he was frequently in error and therefore not a scholar in his own right. For example, ben Zoma holds that the high priest may marry a pregnant maiden, citing R. Samuel who held that the maiden may have become pregnant in a bath without sexual intercourse (bHag 14b–15a). But the text continues with a statement from R. Samuel that contradicts this ruling; only a spermatic emission that "shoots forth like an arrow" can cause pregnancy, i.e., only sexual relations can cause pregnancy. A second tradition relates that ben Zoma failed to stand before his teacher R. Joshua ben Hanania because he was so lost in thought, and thereby failed to show proper respect. When asked what he was thinking, ben Zoma replied that he was considering the division between Heaven and Earth in relation to Gen 1:2, "and the wind of G-d hovered over the face of the waters." He concluded on the basis of this verse, therefore, that there must be only be three fingers breadth between them. R. Joshua then pointed out to his disciples the fallacy in ben Zoma's thinking; the wind of G-d hovers on the first day, but the division between heaven and earth did not take place until the second day. His statement that ben Zoma is "still outside," may mean either that he has lost his mind or that he has stepped outside the bounds of proper interpretation.[29] In either case the tradition points to the deficiency in his reasoning while interpreting scriptural texts. Again, this presents ben Zoma in striking contrast to R. Akiba. Whereas ben Zoma never completed his ordination and errs repeatedly in biblical interpretation, Akiba defined the very bases of Rabbinic halakhah. It is therefore no accident that ben Zoma goes insane upon his attempt to experience Pardes. For lack of a completed education, his

---

ben Azzai's body was not able to endure the experience of the sixth palace (Schäfer, *Synopse* § 345).

[28] For discussion of the traditions concerning Simeon ben Zoma, see Bacher, *Die Aggada der Tannaiten* 422–30; Fischel, *Rabbinic Literature* 51–89; Samson H. Levey, "The Best Kept Secret of the Rabbinic Tradition," *Judaism* 21 (1972) 454–69.

[29] Note that the versions of this story recorded in tHag 2:6; yHag 2:1; and GenR 2:4 on Gen 1:7 do not include R. Joshua's reference to ben Zoma's fallacy. Furthermore, they tie the story to ben Zoma's death. Cf. Levey, "The Best Kept Secret," who argues that ben Zoma may have been an early convert to Christianity.

mind was not prepared,[30] and he cannot be considered a scholar in his own right. Furthermore, the citation of Prov 25:16 in relation to ben Zoma, "Have you found honey? Eat so much as is sufficient for you, lest you be filled and vomit it," is significant here. The throne chariot text in Ezek 3:1–3 portrays the prophet Ezekiel's reception of G-d's words with the imagery of his eating a scroll that tasted like honey. Whereas Ezekiel was capable of understanding properly the message that he ingested, ben Zoma was not.

IV

Clearly, Simeon ben Azzai, Simeon ben Zoma, and Aḥer or Elisha ben Abuyah each lacks a quality that prevents him from successfully experiencing pardes. Furthermore, the scripture citations associated with each somehow expresses his shortcomings. When viewed in relation to R. Akiba, the shortcomings of the three emphasize Akiba's ability to engage in the experience of Pardes in that he possesses each of the qualities that the other three lack. Unlike Simeon ben Azzai who had no children, Akiba's wife and children prompted him to learn to read and eventually to become a sage. Unlike Simeon ben Zoma who failed to master Rabbinic learning in its entirety, Akiba laid the foundation for Jewish law or halakhah and biblical interpretation or midrash. Unlike Aḥer who failed to adhere to Rabbinic tradition and eventually uttered the heretical words that led to his condemnation, Akiba held firm to Judaism up to the moment of his martyrdom, and died with the words of the Shema on his lips. Clearly, the Rabbinic legend of the four who entered Pardes defines the qualities of one would enter Pardes. He should be an ideal Rabbinic figure, like R. Akiba.

The biblical verse associated with Akiba in the tradition, "Draw me after you, let us make haste, (the king has brought me into his chambers)" (Song 1:4) metaphorically expresses Akiba's success at entering Pardes. The citation of this verse and those associated with the other three Rabbis have important implications for understanding meaning of the expression, "to enter Pardes," in that they point to the character of the experience as the proper interpretation of scripture rather than as an actual mystical ascent. The Mishnah elsewhere (mYadayim 2:5) reports that R. Akiba considered the Song of Songs to be the most important biblical book revealed to Israel. He refers to it as the "Holy of Holies," employing the same language used for the innermost chamber of the Temple where the Ark of the Covenant was kept in First Temple times. The context indicates that Akiba's statement is made in relation to a discussion concerning whether or not Song of Songs should be considered Holy Scripture. Song of Songs portrays the

---

[30] The New York manuscript of Hekhalot Zutarti (JTS 8128) emphasizes that although ben Zoma's body endured the experience of the sixth palace (in contrast to ben Azzai), his knowledge was not able to endure (Schäfer, *Synopse* § 345).

relationship of two lovers, which would raise questions concerning its character. But because it is understood in Rabbinic tradition as a metaphorical portrayal of the relationship between G-d and Israel, it is accepted as Holy Scripture. This indicates Akiba's concern with the proper interpretation of Song of Songs. The citation of Song 1:4 likewise indicates a concern with scriptural interpretation in that the verse is interpreted allegorically to express Akiba's qualifications to enter Pardes. Because he is a father who teaches his son, the founder of Rabbinic law or halakhah and biblical interpretation or midrash, and a faithful adherent to Rabbinic tradition even to his death, he understands Jewish tradition properly, and therefore he enters pardes safely.

In contrast, Simeon ben Azzai, Simeon ben Zoma, and Aḥer or Elisha ben Abuyah all violate Jewish tradition in way or another, and therefore do not understand it or apply it properly. In each case, a verse of scripture, properly interpreted, is applied to express their respective shortcomings. The association of scriptural verses with each Rabbi to express an outstanding characteristic that disqualifies him from entering Pardes, therefore highlights the issue of scriptural interpretation, and suggests that the original meaning of the expression, "to enter Pardes," relates to the proper exposition of scripture.[31] Given the potentially heretical character of much of the mystical, theurgic, and hekhalot literature of the early Talmudic period,[32] this suggests that the purpose of the legend concerning the four who entered Pardes is to attempt to gain some control over the proper exposition of the mystical texts, the account of creation in Genesis 1 (Maʿaseh Bereshit) and the account of Ezekiel's vision of G-d in Ezekiel 1 (Maʿaseh Merkavah).[33] By defining R. Akiba as the epitome of one qualified to expound

---

[31] Akiba's initial statement in the version of the Babylonian Talmud, "When you arrive at the stones of pure marble, do not say, 'Water, water!' For it is said, 'He that speaks falsehood shall not be established before my eyes' (Ps 101:7)," is also relevant to the issue of scriptural interpretation. Not only does the tradition associate this statement with Psalm 101:7, but Neher, "Le voyage mystique," 64–8, ties it to the image of the restored Temple in Ezek 47:1–12, from which water gushes out to create a new garden throughout the world. As in Ezekiel 1, the Temple symbolism dominates the surface images of this text, but its true significance lies in interpreting the meaning of the text that is conveyed by its surface symbolism. Here, water serves as an image in the text that points to the new creation symbolized by the erection of the new Temple. The interpreter must penetrate this image to understand the significance of the text and avoid speaking falsehood.

[32] So Halperin, *The Faces of the Chariot* passim, who maintains that much of the mystical literature from this period expresses interpretation of Ezekiel's vision that was in opposition to Rabbinic tradition in the early Talmudic period.

[33] Cf. Ira Chernus, "Revelation and Merkabah Mysticism in Tannaitic Midrash," *Mysticism in Rabbinic Judaism: Studies in the History of Midrash* (SJ 11; Berlin and New York: Walter de Gruyter, 1982) 1–16, who notes the similarities between language pertaining to the revelation of Torah and that pertaining to Merkabah mysticism in Tannaitic midrash. After surveying the relevant texts, he concludes that this represents "the ability and desire of the rabbis to incorporate esotericism into their religious community without changing the community's basic principles" (p. 16). Chernus also notes that the Israelites respond to the revelation of Torah on Sinai by singing the Song of Songs as a hymn to G-d, "so that they might learn the divine teachings which

upon these texts, the legend attempts to insure that they will be interpreted in accordance with Rabbinic tradition. When considered in relation to the Mishnah's statement that one who would expound the mystical texts be "a sage that understands his own knowledge," i.e., a Rabbi fully versed in Jewish tradition, the story of the four who attempted to enter Pardes indicates that R. Akiba is the example of the person who is qualified to undertake such an exposition.

---

have hitherto been unknown to human beings" (p. 11). Note in SongR 1:12, R. Akiba interprets the statement, "while the king was still at his table" (Song 1:12) in reference to the statement in Exodus 24:16, "And the glory of the L-rd dwelt upon Mount Sinai."

Source Index

[includes passages with discussion and/or translation]

Hebrew Bible

Genesis

1	242, 271, 281
1:2	279
1:7	279
6–9	259
9:16	278
12:1–9	169
15	169
17	169

Exodus

10:1–20	198, 199, 241
10:21–29	198, 200, 241
14–15	200
24:16	282
25:31–40	244
27:1–8	243
27:20–21	244
29	244
32–34	151
37:17–24	244
38:1–8	243

Leviticus

4:1–5:26	135
6:17–7:10	135
8–9	128, 244
10:10–11	150, 247
16	152, 169
17–18	169
21:1–12	139
24:1–4	244
26	169, 170

Numbers

1–10	262
14	151, 262
16:1–17:15	246
24:17–19	267

Deuteronomy

6:4	275
6:5	274
22:6–7	277
31:9–14	244

Joshua

7	151

1 Samuel

23:14	265
24:1	265

1 Kings

6–7	141
6:3	244
6:23–28	244
18	151

2 Kings

18:1–8	135, 151
23:1–25	135, 151

Isaiah

–, Book of	1, 13–27, 28, 2105–221, 222–235
1–39	1, 14, 15
1–33	16–18
2–33	18
1	17, 18, 54–55
1:1	15
1:10	21–22, 25
1:27–28	19
2–4	18, 217–218
2:1	18
2:2–4	13–15, 22, 25, 34, 203, 210–221, 231, 244, 246
2:3	22, 25
2:5	210–221
2:6–21	201, 245
4:2–6	26
5–12	18
5:1–30	87
5:24	22, 25
5:26–29	91–92
6:1–9:6	16
6	16, 26, 55–56
6:5	26
6:13	31
8:1–4	44, 227–229, 244
8:6–8	42–45
8:6	36–45
8:16	22–23, 25
8:20	22–23, 25
9:1–6	17, 28–35
9:7–10:4	89
10:5–34	17, 244
11	244
11:1–16	17, 56
11:11–16	17, 200
12	20
13–27	18, 245
13–23	19
13:1–14:23	17
13	201
14	243
14:24–27	17
24–27	245–247
24:5	23, 25
27:12–13	17, 21, 26
30:9	23
32	34
32:1–20	17
34–66	16, 17–18
34–54	18
34–35	17, 18
34	17
35:1–10	26
35:8–10	21
36–39	16–17
37:30–32	58
40–55	14
40	1
40:1–11	16, 21, 26
42:4	23, 25
42:21	24, 25
42:24	24, 25
43:14–21	26
44:24–45:7	19
44:24–28	18
44:28	34
45:1–7	18
45:1	34
48:20–21	26
51:4	24, 25
51:7	24, 25
51:10–11	26
55	15
55:3	34
56–66	14, 18, 245–247
56–59	19
56	19
56:1–8	20
60–62	18, 19, 34
62:10–12	21, 26
63–66	19
65–66	18, 19, 46–62
66:5–24	60–61
66:7–9	58
66:8–24	20
66:10–14	36, 43–45, 58–59
66:23	247

Jeremiah

–, Book of	1, 65–77, 78–93
1–25	1
1–7	101

1:1–3	100–101	31:21–22	110
2–6	94–108	31:23–34	116
2:1–2	96, 105–107	31:23–25	117–119
2:1	101–102	31:27–30	110
2:1–3:5	102–103	31:27–28	117
2:1–4:4	97	31:31–34	110, 117
2:1–4:2	98, 99–100, 101	31:35–36	117, 119
2:28	96	31:37–40	110, 117
3:6–11	96, 102, 104–107	31:27	117
3:22	276	32–45	1
4:3–6:30	96, 101	33:14–26	109
4:3–4	105–107	36–44	1
5:12–13	90	46–51	1, 2
5:15–17	91–92	52	1, 2
7	84–86		
7:1	101	*Ezekiel*	
19–20	1	–, Book of	2, 125–143
23:1–8	89–90	1–7	129–134
23:9–40	88–90	1:1–3:15	128–129
24	87	1	271, 272, 281
26–29	1	3:1–3	280
26	1, 85–86	3:16–5:17	128
26:20–23	228	8–19	134–137
27–28	86–88	8–11	144–155
28–29	1	8:1–2	147
29	87	8:3–6	147
28:1	80	8:7–13	148
30–33	109	8:14–15	148
30–31	1, 2, 109–122	8:16–10:22	148–149
30:1–4	119	11:1–23	149
30:1	112	11:24–25	149
30:2–31:40	112	14:14	259
30:2–3	112–113, 117	14:20	259
30:2–17	113	20:1–23:49	137–140
30:4	110, 117	24:1–25:17	137–140
30:5–11	110, 117	26:1–28:36	137–140
30:12–17	117	29:1–16	137–140
30:12–15	110	29:17–30:19	137–140
30:18–31:22	117	30	201
30:18–31:1	110, 113, 117	30:20–26	137–140
30:18–21	110	31:1–18	137–140
31:2–14	114–115, 117	32:1–16	137–140
31:2–6	110	32:17–33:20	137–140
31:7–14	110	33–39	159, 172
31:15–17	110	33:1–20	158
31:15	115, 117	33:21–39:29	137–140, 156–172
31:16–22	110, 115, 117	33:21–22	159–160, 171
31:18–20	110		

33:23–39:29	160	9:11–12	206
33:23–33	160–161, 169	9:13	203, 205
34:1–31	161, 169–170		
35:1–36:15	161, 170	*Obadiah*	
36:16–37:14	161–162, 170	–, Book of	182–183
37:15–28	162, 170	11	202
37	129–140	17	202
38–39	140, 162–163, 241, 243	18	202
38:18–23	242	*Jonah*	
40–48	140–142	–, Book of	183

Twelve Prophets

–, Book of	2, 176–188, 189–209	*Micah*	
		–, Book of	184–185, 210–221
Hosea		4–5	210–221
–, Book of	181	4:1–5	203, 204–205, 231, 242, 244

Joel

–, Book of	183, 189–208, 240–242	*Nahum*	
1–2	192	–, Book of	185
1:1	193	*Habakkuk*	
1:2–4:21	194	–, Book of	185
1:2–20	194	3	259
1:2–2:17	192		
1:2–4	194	*Zephaniah*	
1:2	194	–, Book of	185
1:5–7	194	1:7–9	201
1:8–10	194	1:14–16	201
2:1–14	195		
2:15–4:21	195–197	*Haggai*	
2:15–17	195–196	–, Book of	185
2:1	193, 195		
2:15	193, 195	*Zechariah*	
2:18–4:21	192		
2:18	193, 195	–, Book of	185, 222–235, 243
2:27	193	1–8	243–245
3–4	192, 202, 241–242	1:1–6	226
3:1–5	199, 241	1:1	227, 229
4:9–21	201	1:7–14:21	226
		1:7–6:15	226
Amos		1:7	225, 227
–, Book of	181–182	2:10	259
1:2	203, 205	7–14	226
5:18–20	198, 201	7–8	226

7:1	225–226	4	254–255
8:9–23	244	5	255
8:19–23	231	6	255
9–14	243	7–12	250–251, 256–260
9–11	226	7	258, 260
9	232, 244	7:1	252
10–11	232, 244	9	260
12–14	226, 233, 244	10–12	260
		10:1	252

Malachi

–, Book of	185–186

Ezra

5:1	244
6:14	244
7–10	19
9:2	31

Psalms

2	259
68	259
82	259
83:7–9	267
101:7	281
116:15	272, 275, 278–279

Nehemiah

3–7	19
8–10	19, 20
11–13	19

Proverbs

25:16	272, 275, 280

1 Chronicles

12:9	265
12:17–19	265
12:24–41	266
18:3–10	267
18:11	267
27	265
29:26–30	265, 266

Song of Songs

1:4	272, 281
8:6	78

Qohelet/Ecclesiastes

5:5	272, 275, 280

2 Chronicles

11:1–4	266
11:13–17	266
13:7	266
20	201
29–31	135, 151

Daniel

–, Book of	248–261
1–6	251–256
1	252–253
2	253–254
3	254

Apocrypha

1 Maccabees

4:36–51	135, 151

4 Ezra

1:39–40	189

Sirach

49:10	177, 189

Pseudepigrapha

Lives of the Prophets

–, Book of   189

Martyrdom and Ascension of Isaiah

4:22   189

Qumran Scrolls

1QIsaa

8:6   40

2QJer

42:7–49:10*   66

4QJera

7:1–26:10*   66

4QJerbde

9:22–50:6*   66

4QJerc

4:5–33:20*   66

4QXIIa-g

–, Book of   177, 189, 190–191

MurXII

–, Book of   177, 189, 208

8ḤevXIIgr

–, Book of   177, 189, 208

1QM (War Scroll)

–, Book of	262–268
1	264–266
1:1–2	266, 267
1:2	262, 266
1:3	262, 266
1:13	264
1:14–15	264
2–9	262
2–4	262
2	264–266
2:2	265
2:3	265
2:6	265
2:7–9	264
2:9	264
2:10	265
5:1	267
11:1	267
11:6–7	267
11:7–8	267

Targum Jonathan

Isaiah

8:2   227
8:6   40

Septuagint

Isaiah

8:6   40–41

Jeremiah

–, Book of   65–77, 207–208
35:1   80

Twelve Prophets
–, Book of   175–188, 189–209

Vulgate

Isaiah
8:6   41

Peshitta

Isaiah
8:6   41

New Testament

Mark
13   250
13:24–27   250

Rabbinic Literature

Mishnah

mHagigah
2:1   270, 272

mSotah
9:15   272, 278

mTamid
1:2   136
3:1–9   136

mAbot
4:1–3   278

Tosephta

tHagigah
2:3–4   270–272, 273
2:6   279

tYebamot
8:7   278

tZabim
1:5   274

Babylonian Talmud

bBerakot
61b   275

bShabbat
13b   82, 129
33b   276

bPesahim
49b   273

bYoma

71b	129

bTaʿanit

17a	134

bMoʾed Qatan

5a	129
27b	129

bḤagigah

13a	129, 141
13b	129
14b	269, 273, 276
14b–15a	279
15a	269, 275
15b	269, 273, 275, 277

bYebamot

63b	278

bKetubot

50a	273
63a	278

bNedarim

62b	273

bSanhedrin

68a	275
81a	129

81b	129
86a	274

bMakkot

24	229

bMenaḥot

13a	141
45a	82, 129

Jerusalem Talmud (Yerushalmi)

ySheqalim

3:1/47b	273
3:1/48a	274

yḤagigah

2:1/77b	269, 273, 277, 279

Genesis Rabbah

2:4	275, 279

Song of Songs Rabbah

1:4	269
1:10	276
8:2	274

Qohelet Rabbah

6:2	274

Abot de R. Nathan

2:6	273

Medieval Rabbinic Literature

Guide for the Perplexed

2:36	79

Author Index

Ackroyd, P. R. 16, 47
Adam, A. K. M. 250
Albertz, R. 97, 98
Allen, L. 144
Althann, R. 106, 119
Amsler, S. 223
Anderson, B. W. 5, 26, 119
Anderson, G. 136

Bacher, W. 273, 276, 278, 279
Baillet, M. 66
Bakan, D. 79
Barth, H. 3, 32
Barthélemy, D. 37, 40, 114
Barton, J. 95, 175, 222, 250
Becker, J. 4, 144
Becker, U. 223
Becking, B. 113
Begrich, J. 150
Ben Zvi, E. 176, 177, 205, 225
Bentzen, A. 249
Bergler, S. 6, 183, 199, 202, 240
Beuken, W. A. M. 43, 47, 230
Bickerman, E. 249
Biddle, M. E. 95, 96, 98, 99, 109
Blenkinsopp, J. 1, 61, 222
Boadt, L. 126
Böhmer, S. 109
Bogaert, P.-M. 65
Bonnard, P.-E. 47, 48, 61
Bosshard-Nepustil, E. 6, 68, 175, 189
Bousset, W. 271
Bozak, B. 109, 111
Bredenkamp, C. J. 38
Briant, P. 61
Briggs, C. A. 270
Brock, S. 41
Brooke, G. J. 66
Brown, F. 270

Brownlee, W. H. 17, 40, 125
Brueggemann, W. 43
Buber, M. 80, 84
Budde, K. 39, 175, 189
Burrows, M. 40
Buss, M. J. 29–30

Carmingac, J. 266, 267
Carr, D. M. 46
Carroll, R. P. 4, 65, 95, 97, 110, 239, 256
Cathcart, K. J. 201
Cazelles, H. 210
Chernus, I. 281
Childs, B. 43, 156, 223, 251
Christensen, D. L. 106
Claburn, W. E. 106
Clements, R. E. 3, 4, 5, 17, 38, 39, 43, 74, 210
Coggins, R. J. 175, 180, 189, 223
Cohen, M. 275
Collins, A. Y. 248
Collins, J. J. 6, 239, 248, 249, 251, 254, 255, 258, 260
Collins, T. 175, 185, 189
Conrad, E. W. 4, 223, 224
Cook, S. L. 7, 162, 171, 193, 239–246, 257
Cooke, G. A. 161
Crenshaw, J. L. 6, 80, 195
Cryer, F. H. 61, 127, 259

Dan, J. 270, 271
Darr, K. P. 5, 57, 126, 142, 144
Davies, P. R. 248, 249, 262
Davies, W. D. 249
Day, J. 246
Di Lella, A. A. 251
Diodorus 255

Driver, S. R. 192, 270
Duhm, B. 1, 38, 39, 104, 192

Eaton, J. H. 20
Eissfeldt, O. 16
Eliade, M. 30
Ellermeier, F. 127
Elliger, K. 4, 47
Evans, C. A. 17

Fensham, F. C. 21
Fewell, D. N. 252
Finkelstein, L. 37, 249, 273
Fischel, H. 270, 276, 278, 279
Fischer, G. 110
Fishbane, M. 62, 240
Floyd, M. H. 223
Fohrer, G. 16, 46, 73, 109, 144, 145, 161, 162
Friedländer, M. 79, 223
Fuller, R. E. 177, 188
Fullerton, K. 38, 39

Galumbush, J. 139
Gerstenberger, E. S. 133
Gese, H. 140
Gesenius, W. 37
Giesebrecht, F. 38, 39
Goldberg, A. 271
Goldingay, J. 252
Goldman, Y. 4, 65, 66, 72, 109
Goshen Gottstein, A. 269, 271, 276
Grätz, H. 270
Graf, F. 267
Graffy, A. 160, 166
Grayson, A. K. 239
Greenberg, M. 5, 130, 136, 144, 157, 161, 162
Gruenwald, I. 269, 271

Halperin, D. J. 82, 126, 139, 269, 271, 272, 273, 281
Halpern, B. 258
Hals, R. M. 130, 144, 161, 162, 165
Hanhart, R. 223
Hanson, P. 7, 219, 239, 245, 257
Hardmeier, C. 96
Hartman, L. F. 251

Hayes, J. H. 125
Haynes, S. R. 222, 250
Hayward, C. T. 141
Hengel, M. 232, 249
Herrmann, S. 68, 95, 109
Hertzberg, A. 250
Hiebert, T. 192
Hill, J. 72
Hitzig, F. 38
Holladay, W. L. Jr. 4, 37, 65, 68, 84, 88, 91, 97, 110, 115, 116, 122
Hölscher, G. 2
Horst, F. 144, 150
Hossfeld, F. L. 80, 144, 145
House, P. R. 175, 189
Humphreys, W. L. 249

Ibn Ezra, A. 228
Irvine, S. A. 33, 36, 44
Isbell, C. 98

Janzen, J. G. 65, 66
Jastrow, M. 42, 270
Jellicoe, S. 188
Jensen, J. 21
Jeremias, J. 181
Jones, B. A. 175, 187, 189, 190
Jones, D. R. 47, 84, 90, 91

Kaiser, O. 38, 68, 73, 156, 210
Kapelrud, A. S. 192
Kiesow, K. 5, 26
Kilian, R. 210
Kilpp, N. 109, 118, 121
Kimḥi, D. (Radak) 37, 141, 228–229
Klein, H. 39
Knierim, R. P. 3, 30, 73, 95, 98, 111, 176, 193, 252
Knight, D. A. 222
Knohl, I. 133, 137
Koch, K. 15, 20, 31, 219, 245, 248
Kratz, R. G. 5, 18, 34, 72, 175, 189
Kutsch, E. 130
Kutsko, J. F. 167

Lack, R. 43, 46
LaCocque, A. 223, 249
Lang, B. 126

Lange, A. 80, 88, 90
Larkin, K. J. A. 6, 230, 243
Lau, W. 47, 61
Leene, H. 110, 114
Levenson, J. D. 25, 125, 135, 140, 141, 142, 241, 245, 253, 257
Levey, S. H. 279
L'Hereux, C. 33
Lieberman, S. 270
Liebreich, L. J. 46
Lindblom, J. 38
Livy 255
Liwack, R. 97, 99
Lohfink, N. 109, 110
Long, B. O. 150–151
Lord, A. B. 30
Luker, L. 115, 120
Lundbom, J. 4, 64, 68, 95, 109, 207
Lust, J. 121

Maier, J. 270
Maimon, Moses ben 79
Maimonides, 79
Marti, K. 2, 38
Mason, R. 6, 192, 230, 243
Matthies, G. H. 137
Mays, J. L. 210
McConville, J. G. 20, 219
McKane, W. 65, 104, 210, 212
McKenzie, S. L. 222, 250
McKeating, H. 126, 156, 158, 162
Meier, S. M. 146, 160, 164, 165
Meyer, I. 80, 84
Meyers, C. L. 137, 223
Meyers, E. M. 223
Milgrom, J. 135, 136
Milik, J. T. 66
Miller, J. E. 131
Morgan, R. 95, 222
Mowinckel, S. 1, 2, 4, 47, 104
Muilenberg, J. 214–215
Murphy, R. E. 78
Murray, D. F. 166

Neher, A. 271, 281
Neusner, J. 276
Nicholson, E. W. 3
Nielsen, E. 212

Nissinen, M. 127
Nogalski, J. D. 5, 175, 177, 178, 184, 189, 190, 191, 201, 202, 206, 208
Noth, M. 2

O'Connor, M. 214
Odashima, T. 97
Odeberg, H. 43
Odell, M. S. 127, 131, 134
Oden, R. A. Jr. 257
Ogden, G. S. 196
Osswald, E. 80
Overholt, T. W. 80, 84

Parpola, S. 127
Perdue, L. 250
Peters, M. K. 188
Petersen, D. L. 1, 222, 223, 240, 256
Petitjean, A. 230
Plöger, O. 239, 245, 249
Pohlmann, K.-F. 144, 145, 161
Polaski, D. C. 246
Polybius 255
Porteus, N. 249
Procksch, O. 38, 39

Quell G. 80

Raabe, P. R. 178
Rad, G. von 2, 3, 81, 249
Radak (David Kimḥi) 141, 228–229
Rashi (Solomon ben Isaac) 141, 228
Redditt, P. 178, 223
Reeg, G. 274
Renaud, B. 210, 211, 217
Rendtorff, R. 14, 28, 43, 47, 156
Reventlow, H. Graf 223
Richter, W. 30
Rignell, L. C. 44
Roberts, J. J. M. 210
Rose, P. L. 250
Ross, J. F. 50
Rothstein, J. W. 192
Rowley, H. H. 252
Rubenstein, J. L. 276
Rudolph, W. 37, 192, 210, 223
Ruiten, G. M. van 47

Sanders, J. A. 6, 31, 80, 84
Schäfer, P. 269, 279, 280
Schart, A. 190
Scholem, G. 271, 276
Schoors, A. 215
Schramm, B. 49, 59, 247
Schroeder, O. 39
Schröter, U. 110
Schürer, E. 249
Scott, R. B. Y. 213
Seidl, T. 100
Segal, A. F. 270
Seitz, C. R. 4, 16, 28, 35, 122
Seybold, K. 95
Shead, A. G. 65, 66
Sheppard, G. T. 24
Sister, M. 151
Smith-Christopher, D. L. 251
Solomon Ben Isaac (Rashi) 141, 228
Sommer, B. D. 5, 168, 240
Sperber, A. 40, 223
Steck, O. H. 4, 6, 17, 30, 33, 43, 47, 48–49, 175, 189, 190
Steinberg, N. 106, 119–120
Stipp, H.-J. 4, 65, 66
Stuhlman, L. 4, 69
Sweeney, D. 150
Sweeney, M. A. 1, 4, 5, 7–10, 14, 15, 16, 28, 31, 32, 33, 43, 46, 47, 48, 60, 61, 67, 68, 72, 74, 76, 81, 82, 83, 91, 92, 95, 98, 106, 112, 120, 126, 129, 132- 133, 145, 146, 150, 156, 157, 159, 165, 171, 176, 179, 182, 185, 190, 191, 193, 204, 207, 208, 210, 213, 215, 217, 218, 219, 220, 221, 222, 223, 224, 225, 231, 240–241, 243, 244, 246, 247, 250, 252, 259, 260, 261
Swete, H. B. 188

Tai, N. H. F. 6, 230, 243
Talmadge, F. 223, 229
Talshir, Z. 230
Taylor, J. E. 258
Tcherikover, V. 249, 254, 255
Thiel, W. 3, 90, 104
Tomasino, A. J. 46
Torrey, C. C. 48

Tov, E. 4, 65, 66, 188
Towner, W. S. 249
Trevor, J. 40
Trible, P. 119, 164, 225
Tucker, G. M. 112, 193, 222
Tuell, S. S. 140, 141
Tull (Willey), P. 5, 164, 225, 240

Uffenheimer, B. 218
Ulrich, E. 66
Urbach, E. E. 271

Van der Ploeg, J. 263
Van Hoonacker, A. 2
Vaux, R. de 66
Vermes, G. 249
Vermeylen, J. 3, 5, 43, 46, 47, 74, 210, 213
Volz, P. 110
Vuilleumier, R. 223

Wagenaar, J. A. 210, 217
Waltke, B. K. 214
Watts, J. W. 175, 189
Weber, R. 41
Weimer, P. 175, 189
Weinfeld, M. 167
Weippert, H. 3, 84
Wellhausen, J. 125
Wendel, U. 5, 74, 88
Werner, W. 210
Westermann, C. 20, 165
Wijesinghe, S. L. 65
Wilcoxen, J. 86, 106
Wildberger, H. 13, 14, 17, 38, 39, 210
Willey, P. Tull 5, 240
Williamson, H. G. M. 4, 61
Willi-Plein, I. 6, 217
Wills, L. M. 252
Wolfe, R. E. 175, 189
Wolff, H. W. 3, 6, 192, 203, 210,
Wong, K. L. 144, 168, 170
Woude, A. S. van der 82, 211
Wright, J. E. 76

Yadin, Y. 262

Zapff, B. M. 189–190

Ziegler, J. 41
Zimmerli, W. 3, 130, 136, 138, 139, 140, 144, 145, 161, 162, 165
Zlotowitz, B. N. 65
Zuckermandel, M. S. 270

www.ingramcontent.com/pod-product-compliance
Lightning Source LLC
Chambersburg PA
CBHW071234230426
43668CB00011B/1438